Social Class and Educational Inequ

Social class is often seen as an intractable barrier to success, yet a number of children from disadvantaged backgrounds still manage to show resilience and succeed against the odds. This book presents the findings from fifty Child and Family Case Studies (CFCS) conducted with 13–16 year olds. The authors look specifically at the roles that people and experiences – at home, in schools and in the wider community – have played in the learning life-courses of these children; how these factors have affected their achievement; and explanations and meanings given by respondents to the unique characteristics, experiences and events in their lives. Featuring the voices of real parents and children, and backed up by a decade of quantitative data, this is a compelling record that will help readers to understand the complex nature of social disadvantage and the interplay between risk and protective factors in homes and schools that can make for a transformational educational experience.

IRAM SIRAJ is Professor of Education in the Department of Early Years and Primary Education in the Institute of Education, University of London. She is also Visiting Professor at the Universities of Melbourne and Waikato, with some part-time secondment to the University of Wollongong, Australia.

AZIZA MAYO completed a doctorate at the Department for Social and Behavioural Sciences at the University of Amsterdam, and is currently Professor of Education at the University of Applied Sciences Leiden, Netherlands.

'This book is a stupendous achievement and deserves to be very widely read. The authors' large-scale longitudinal research into why some children succeed "against the odds" and others do worse than expected given their relatively privileged start in life is already widely known. This book puts "flesh" onto the bones of the data, providing case studies of fifty children (those who succeed and those who don't from both working-class and middle-class backgrounds) that exemplify their findings in a truly marvellous way. Equally impressive, Siraj and Mayo illustrate the power and importance of a solid theoretical foundation. They draw on scholars such as Urie Bronfenbrenner to show that the everyday activities and interactions that occur between children and their parents, their teachers, and people in the wider community have profound effects on academic performance from early childhood through adolescence. The authors also do a wonderful job revealing the way that these interactions also influence, and are influenced by, personal characteristics of the children themselves and of the various people with whom the children interact. The book's combination of intellectual rigour and ease of reading makes it a resource that will serve equally for undergraduates interested in understanding development and scholars working in the area of risk, resilience, parenting practices, and school achievement.'

Professor Jonathan Tudge
Human Development and Family Studies,
the University of North Carolina at Greensboro

'The child and family case studies presented in this important book add considerable value to the large-scale longitudinal study from which they are drawn. In studying children who succeeded against the odds or did not fulfil expectations, the authors lay bare the human stories that, in particular cases, confirm or interrupt the prevailing link between social background and educational achievement. By identifying what – in the home, the school and the community – can make a difference one way or the other, the message is ultimately an optimistic, though realistic, one.'

Professor Geoff Whitty
Director Emeritus, Institute of Education,
University of London and Research Professor in Education,
Bath Spa University

Social Class and Educational Inequality: The Impact of Parents and Schools

Iram Siraj
Aziza Mayo

 CAMBRIDGE
UNIVERSITY PRESS

CAMBRIDGE
UNIVERSITY PRESS

University Printing House, Cambridge CB2 8BS, United Kingdom

Cambridge University Press is part of the University of Cambridge.

It furthers the University's mission by disseminating knowledge in the pursuit of education, learning and research at the highest international levels of excellence.

www.cambridge.org
Information on this title: www.cambridge.org/9781107562301

First published 2014
First paperback edition 2015

A catalogue record for this publication is available from the British Library

Library of Congress Cataloguing in Publication data
Siraj, Iram.
Social class and educational inequality : the impact of parents and schools /
authors, Iram Siraj, Aziza Mayo.
    pages cm
ISBN 978-1-107-01805-1 (Hardback)
1. Education–Social aspects.   2. Social classes.   3. Educational
equalization.   4. Children with social disabilities–Education–Case studies.
5. Youth with social disabilities–Education–Case studies.
6. Education–Parent participation.   I. Mayo, Aziza.   II. Title.
LC191.S525 2014
306.43–dc23   2013049911

ISBN 978-1-107-01805-1 Hardback
ISBN 978-1-107-56230-1 Paperback

Contents

Figures

Tables

Acknowledgements

The Effective Pre-School, Primary and Secondary Education (EPPSE) project is a major longitudinal study funded by the UK Department for Education (1997–2014); we are grateful for the funding of this and for the funding of the sub-study Child and Family Case Studies (CFCS) upon which this book is based. The contents of this book are the sole responsibility of the authors and should not be taken to represent the views of the Department or of the other EPPSE investigators.

The research would not be possible without the support and co-operation of the six local authorities (LAs) and the many pre-school centres, primary schools, children and parents participating in the research. We would like to give special thanks to the children, parents and teachers who met with us to discuss their experiences and thoughts on school and learning. Their welcoming enthusiasm to meet with us face to face and their ongoing loyalty to EPPSE were heartwarming and extremely valuable. We are particularly grateful for the support and guidance we have had from John Blatchford in the early stages of this sub-study and for the training and expertise he provided in the NVivo software, and thanks to Edward Melhuish who helped us with the attainment models to extract our sample. We would also like to thank Kit Endean and Rachel Whitehead for their diligent transcribing and Wesley Welcomme for his contribution in preparing this book.

The biggest thanks go to our colleagues the Principal Investigators (PIs) of the EPPSE project. Iram Siraj, one of the authors of this book, is a PI, and the other four are Brenda Taggart and Professors Edward Melhuish, Pam Sammons and Kathy Sylva. The study rests on their collaboration and fifteen years of sustained data collection and intellectual rigour in the interpretation of results. We draw heavily on all these data to make sense of our fifty sub-study, in-depth Case Studies. We would like to thank all the researchers on the EPPSE project over the years and our fifty families in particular.

Abbreviations

BAS II	British Ability Scales, Second Edition (Elliot et al., 1996)
CFCS	Child and Family Case Studies (also referred to as 'Case Studies')
DCSF	Department for Children, Schools and Families (now Department for Education)
ECERS-E	Early Childhood Environment Rating Scales – Extension (Sylva et al., 2003, 2006)
ECERS-R	Early Childhood Environment Rating Scales – Revised (Harms et al., 1998)
EPPE	Effective Provision of Pre-School Education project
EPPE 3–11	Effective Pre-School and Primary Education project (1997–2008)
EPPSE 3–14; 3–16	Effective Pre-School, Primary and Secondary Education project (1997–2014)
EPPSEM	Effective Primary Pedagogical Strategies in English and Maths study
EYTSEN	Early Years Transition and Special Educational Needs project
FSM	free school meals
HLE	home learning environment
LA	local authority
PI	Principal Investigator (EPPSE project)
sd	standard deviation
SEN	special educational needs
SES	socio-economic status

1 Child and Family Case Studies in the context of the EPPSE study

In this first chapter we introduce the Case Studies in the context of the Effective Pre-School, Primary and Secondary Education (EPPSE 3–16) research study from which our fifty in-depth Case Studies originated. It also describes the aims of the study and the research questions that will be addressed.

Introduction

Our research, and much other educational research, is driven by one deceptively simple research question: why do some children succeed academically while others fail? For decades this particular question has been the focus of political, social and scientific debates and has led to an ongoing stream of reforms in the educational system since the last century. The political and social debates about educational inequalities and ways to improve children's chances of academic success that were prevalent in the 1990s in the United Kingdom and many other European countries made it possible for rigorous, longitudinal scientific studies to be conducted. These studies provided an empirical and scientific basis for educational reforms and aimed to improve in particular the chances of children who were found to be most vulnerable in the educational system. Although some reforms, such as the nationwide availability of pre-school education, have gone some way towards helping reduce educational inequality, other measures, such as the Key Stage 3 national assessments (at age 14) have been abandoned due to lack of visible effect.

In part this ongoing and widespread concern with educational inequality reflects the beliefs of society about fairness and equality: all children deserve good education and academic success. Therefore, as long as educational inequality continues to exist we need to aim our efforts towards improving the educational system. But the strong appeal that comes from the question of why we find such marked differences in academic success also has a personal side to it. After all, all of us are field-experts when it comes to education. At some stage in our lives we have participated in the great educational experiment. For some of us this experiment has been successful and for some of us not so much, and once we left the experiment, each one of us has experienced at first hand the significant and continuing impact of academic success or failure on our life-course. But perhaps the urgency of the question becomes even greater when it is no longer we who are part of the experiment, but when it concerns 'our' children.

Through our personal roles and positions in society, irrespective of whether we are educators, parents, family members, friends, neighbours, researchers, politicians, policymakers, etc., or a number of these personas at the same time, we feel a responsibility towards our children and their academic successes or failures. So we keep attempting to answer the question as well as a question that almost automatically follows: how can we help more children to become academically successful and fulfil their potential in life? This introductory chapter provides a description of the context of our book which is based on fifty in-depth case studies of children from a much bigger study. It provides a summary of key findings from this bigger study, the Effective Pre-School, Primary and Secondary Education (EPPSE 3–16) study (itself a series of sub-studies following the same children) and describes our understanding of concepts of 'risk' and 'resilience' in the learning life-course for our fifty children.

Background to the Child and Family Case Studies

The EPPSE 3–16 research project is a large-scale, longitudinal, mixed-methods research study (see Sammons et al., 2005; Siraj-Blatchford et al., 2006) that since 1997 has been following the progress of over 3,000 children aged 3–16 (Sylva et al., 2010). It started out as the Effective Provision of Pre-School Education study (EPPE) following our children from age 3 to age 7, and was further funded to become the Effective Pre-School and Primary Education (EPPE 3–11) study, following our children from ages 7–11. EPPSE was the continuation of the project through to the end of secondary schooling.

A continuing question for EPPSE was whether pre-school, primary and secondary schools and children's home learning or other experiences could help either to promote or to reduce inequality. As with other studies, the EPPSE study found that parents' socio-economic status (SES) and levels of education were significantly related to child outcomes. However, it also found that the child's early home learning environment (HLE) was important and showed that school influences (pre-school and primary school quality and effectiveness) shaped children's educational outcomes as well. What is more, the EPPE 3–11 research project (1997–2008) found that what parents did with their children was important in terms of the children's outcomes, rather than simply who they were (Melhuish et al., 2001, 2008; Sammons et al., 2002a).

In 2008 an extension, funded by the Cabinet Office for the Equalities Review, provided a pilot study for the Child and Family Case Studies presented in this book (Siraj-Blatchford et al., 2007; Siraj-Blatchford, 2010a). The pilot focused on the performance of disadvantaged children from white and minority ethnic groups. It found that disadvantaged families often had high aspirations for their children and provided significant educational support in a form similar to that described by Lareau (2003) as 'concerted cultivation' (Siraj-Blatchford, 2010a). In 2009, the Department for Children, Schools and Families (DCSF; now the Department for Education) funded a further extension of the mixed methodology EPPSE research to follow the students to the end of their compulsory schooling.

This book is largely about one aspect of the study, which has been to conduct fifty in-depth, mixed-methods Child and Family Case Studies (CFCS, further referred to as Case Studies; Siraj-Blatchford et al., 2011a). The Case Studies have been carefully sampled to show different learner trajectories in an attempt to probe further and understand why these trajectories differ and what influences a learner's learning life-course. In conducting the Case Studies we aimed to provide further information and explanations which might help us understand more fully the statistical patterns that have been found through quantitative analyses of the EPPSE sample, for instance on the effects of early HLEs and why some parents provide these while others do not. These Case Studies are the main topic of this book. Further details of the methods of our Case Studies and the wider EPPSE study are given in Chapter 3 of the book.

The aim of the Case Studies is to extend our understanding of how child, family, community, pre-school and school factors and experiences interact and contribute to the achievement or underachievement of children in school. Given the presence or absence of particular risk factors associated both with the child and the family (such as low birth weight, the occurrence of early developmental problems, limited educational experience of parents or low family income), predictions were made for children's attainment levels in English and Maths at the end of Primary School (i.e., Key stage 2 at age 11). Over time, the majority of the 3,000 plus EPPSE children have developed their academic skills according to the predictions that were made for each of them at the age of 3. Unfortunately this meant that for most children who were identified as being at risk, these predictions of low achievement proved to be correct.

Thus, many of the children identified as being 'at risk' actually turned out to have poor educational trajectories and to be 'vulnerable' with respect to their academic attainment in English and Maths. On the other hand, the children who were predicted to do well in fact generally did so. But there have been exceptions among both groups, and these children have developed academic trajectories that diverged significantly from their predicted pathways. Some of the children identified as 'at-risk' have excelled unexpectedly. They obtained results for English and Maths that were substantially higher than predicted. These children's developmental trajectories display what we will refer to as 'resilience'. On the other hand, some of children who were not considered at-risk have unexpectedly struggled and failed to meet their predicted attainment, despite favourable and promising characteristics and circumstances at a young age. So what sets apart these unexpected high or low achievers from each other, and from their peers who are performing according to prediction?

Quantitative analyses have already identified a range of factors that affect 'risk' and 'resilience' for children in the EPPSE sample, for instance low social class, poor maternal education, a low HLE in the first five years of life, developmental problems or poor quality pre-school (see Sammons et al., 2003; Anders et al., 2010; Hall et al., 2009; Taggart et al., 2006). However, such quantitative research cannot provide the explanations, illumination and insights that rigorous in-depth Case Studies can, through their focus on the authentic voices of individual children, families and teachers. By combining the results of quantitative and qualitative components in the EPPSE Case Studies research, new contributions to theoretical understanding and information of value to practitioners and policymakers can be generated. Each voice of a child, parent or teacher has something important to tell us about a learning life-course. Some are happy stories that tell us about successful academic careers, others are stories of struggles and worries and academic difficulties. But either way they contain information about perceptions, experiences, contexts, beliefs and values in the lives of children that might help us understand why their learning life-courses have proceeded in a particular way. Each child in our study is unique, but in many ways they are just ordinary children. If you saw one of our fifty young people on the street, you would probably not find them particularly remarkable. In many ways they are just regular adolescents, ages 13–16. But if you did notice them, what would you think? You might be able to identify their family background through the way they dress, the way they talk, the way they carry themselves. But would one be able to tell which of them are academically successful and which are not?

What might someone think of Charley, one of our Case Studies girls, and her friends, if one saw them hanging about in the town square after school? They all wear their hair straight, long and blond. Their earrings are big, their jeans are tight and their t-shirts are tiny. They are ostentatiously ignoring the pack of boys that is circling them. The girls talk about the baby doll each of them will be bringing home from school for the weekend. These are 'practice babies' that will need nappies and feeds and midnight soothing. The girls giggle when they talk about cuddling and bottle-feeding the baby. But they all complain at the top of their voices at the prospect of being woken by the baby's cries during the night and at having to change a diaper. Charley confidently says her boyfriend will definitely help out with the baby and if it keeps crying she will just hand it over to her mum.

What if you came across Shaquille rushing home after school? Despite his 15 years you might take this boy for a grown man. 'Tall, dark and handsome', is how his mother describes him. But this 'tall, dark and handsome' young man often stoops a bit and casts his eyes downwards. Shaquille says people often cross the street and clutch their bags when they see him walking home from school by himself, so he can imagine what they are thinking. The last thing he wants to do is to scare someone, because he knows too well what fear feels like. All he wants is to get home as soon as he can without running into the gang of boys and young men that rule the streets of the inner-city estate he lives on.

What might you think if you met Fareeda walking the short route to school surrounded by half a dozen of her closest girl friends? An endless stream of words passes between them. These days they only ever talk about GCSEs. Unless of course they are talking about clothes or handbags, or about the cute singers and actors they saw on the television the night before. You might notice Fareeda's beautiful dark eyes that sparkle with enjoyment or her warm laughter that follows every other sentence she speaks or hears. But you would not be able to see her smile or her fashionable clothes because they are discreetly covered by a shoulder-length black veil.

What about if you overheard a conversation between Steven and his best friend Ethan walking to school in the morning? Steven is skinny and tall with long limbs that move in every direction. As he talks he illustrates his words with elaborate hand-gestures. Steven enthusiastically explains in minute detail how he nearly managed to get his home-made rocket to fly. He readjusted the weight of this model by adding some additional fuel. He proudly says that this time he actually managed lift-off. Then he sheepishly admits that he also almost burned down the back yard in the process, as the rocket crashed into a heap of dry leaves which he was supposed to have cleared away as part of his chores.

Would you be surprised to learn that Charley, Shaquille, Fareeda and Steven are all at the top of their class? If you went only by their family backgrounds and the circumstances in which they live, they would typically be perceived as disadvantaged. Most of their parents left school at a young age with no formal qualifications to speak of; some have little command of the English language; if they have a job it often involves unskilled or semi-skilled labour; and family income leaves little room for luxuries after the necessary bills are paid at the end of each month. Sometimes their parents are still together, but often they live in single parent households; they share bedrooms with siblings in small flats in large council estates or in monotone streets with small, run-down terraced houses; a dozen different languages can be heard on their neighbourhood streets and in the local shops. In their school playgrounds, students from different ethnic-cultural backgrounds huddle together in separate groups; and while options to take vocational classes are often plentiful, chances of finding a way to take triple science are slim at their schools. But there is something about these children, about their homes, their parents, their friends, teachers and their support network that makes them defy these disadvantages and gears them on to exceed predictions and expectations. There is something that helps them become academically resilient.

'Working definitions' of resilience and vulnerability

To date, a broad literature on resilience exists, with many different perceptions and definitions of resilience, referring, for instance, to either an individual trait or a process (Luthar et al., 2000). Following Rutter (1987, 2007), we take 'resilience' to refer to outcomes of dynamic developmental processes rather than to an observable personality trait of an individual. Resilience is not something a child has or does not have. Rather it is the outcome of a continuing process of adaptation to adversity. As such, resilience is the capacity to cope with life's setbacks and challenges (Moen & Erickson, 1995). Resilience follows when the cumulative effects of 'protective' factors in the child, and in the life and environment in which the child develops, outweigh the negative effects of 'risk' factors in that child or in their socio-cultural context. The outcome of this process is expressed in the adaptive behaviour a person shows when dealing with the demands of his or her life. What these demands are and what qualifies as adaptive behaviour will unavoidably vary between cultures and contexts (Rogoff, 2003).

To take into account the cultural and contextual differences in how people express resilience, Ungar (2004) proposes a constructionist interpretation and refers to resilience as the outcome from negotiations with environment for resources to define oneself as successful amidst adversity. According to this approach risk factors are contextually specific, constructed and indefinite across populations. The impact of negative experiences also varies according to the individual child's perception of their experience, their social support networks and the cognitive and affective resources that they draw upon in facing these experiences (cf. Rutter, 2007). Risk factors can function on any level of a developing person's life. They can for instance be part of personal characteristics of a developing person, such as the presence of socio-emotional or behavioural problems; they can be psychological characteristics of the social environment in which the child develops, such as maternal depression; they can be negative life-events that affect the well-being of the developing person, such as the loss of a parent; they can be structural characteristics of the environment in which the child develops, such as poverty. Following this approach, protective factors are also multidimensional. They are unique to each developmental context and predict the successful outcomes as defined by individuals or their social reference group.

Protective factors are *psychosocial resources*, in the sense that they include both social and personal resources that help promote resilience in the face of adversity (Rutter, 1987; cf. Moen & Erickson, 1995). Social resources refer to a person's connectedness to the broader community in which he or she lives and develops; this connectedness enables individuals to withstand adversity. Social resources are ties that bind a person to his or her social environment. These ties are reflected in the many roles a person occupies in society, for instance their role as parent, child, employee, student, churchgoer or volunteer. They are reflected in the presence of close and confiding relationships with, for instance, spouses, friends or relatives; in the quality of their relationships with families and friends. But they are also reflected in a person's access to support networks in their immediate environment as well as in the wider community or at the level of society. Personal resources reflect a person's sense of competency and effectiveness. They include perceptions of subjective characteristics such as self-reliance, self-understanding, empathy, altruism, maturity, and a person's basic values and priorities.

In this book 'resilience' for us refers to 'achievement beyond expectation'. It is shown by those children in the EPPSE sample who managed to reach high attainment levels at age 11, despite the presence of numerous 'risk' factors early on in their learning life-courses. These children, as well as some children with few early risk factors from high-SES backgrounds who achieve high attainment levels at age 11, are regarded as the 'academically successful' children in our Case Studies. The 'vulnerable' children in this study are those children who reach attainment levels that are either below prediction or as low as predicted by disadvantageous personal or family characteristics. As Willis (1977) showed in his classic study of adolescent boys, throughout their learning life-course children adapt, either positively or negatively, to the physical and social environmental influences that they experience. He focused on the experiences of the sub-group of 'lads' who rejected education but he did not consider the lives of working-class boys who succeeded in education.

In this study we aim to increase our understanding and to explore, and explain, the pathways that lead to resilience or vulnerability. Every child's learning life-course is determined by a unique combination of experiences and events. Some of these experiences and events have the potential of leading to underachievement (risk factors), while others provide resources and contribute to resilience (protective factors). Various risk and protective factors interact in complex ways so that very different life-courses may therefore lead to similar outcomes, yet life-courses that appear very similar may lead to different learning outcomes for different individuals (Cicchetti & Rogosch, 1996). Life-experiences are interpreted according to, and in turn they contribute towards, the construction and reconstruction of the child's personality traits and characteristics. Parents can also pass 'risks' and 'resilience' on to their children, creating inter-generational social and economic immobility or mobility (Feinstein et al., 2008; Schoon, 2006). Positive or negative adaptations that people make during their learning life-course affect their future learning, and the resulting learning outcomes in turn shape the future environments that they offer to their children. That is, the children's own agency matters and interacts with others and their environment to shape them and their identities and futures.

We have key, targeted questions that will be addressed for the 'resilient' and 'vulnerable' children in our study. The general question addressed in this book is *when and why* do some 'at-risk' children 'succeed against the odds' while others make little progress or fall further behind? To answer this we will specifically look at the following research questions:

- What factors act as 'protective' influences in combating poor outcomes and what factors increase the 'risk' of poor outcomes? What are 'positive' or 'negative' influences for certain groups of children?

- What are the key factors within families that shape the educational and developmental outcomes of 'resilient' and 'vulnerable' children? How does this vary with ethnicity or gender differences?
- What is the role of pre-school, school and teachers in enhancing or constraining a child's academic and social potential at different ages, i.e., leading to 'resilience' or 'vulnerability'?
- What factors, external to school and family, influence children's views of themselves as successful learners (e.g., community, computer use, extra-curricular activities, pursuit of hobbies/interests, family learning or similar activities)?
- What are the views of 'vulnerable' and 'resilient' children and their parents of the children's educational experiences? How do they perceive the events and people that have shaped them and what explanations do they provide?

Outline of the book

The first four chapters of this book describe the background of the fifty Child and Family Case Studies and the ideas and constructs upon which this book is based. In this first chapter we have introduced the Case Studies in the context of the EPPSE 3–16 research project from which our fifty in-depth Case Studies originated. It also describes the aims of the study and the research questions that will be addressed. The second chapter provides an overview of the theoretical framework of the study based on some of the literature from the fields of (developmental) psychology, sociology and education. It proposes Bronfenbrenner's 'bioecological model of development' (see for instance Bronfenbrenner & Ceci, 1994; Bronfenbrenner & Morris, 2006) as an overall framework for the Case Studies. It specifically discusses mechanisms of development at work on the different levels of this framework and describes our understanding of concepts relevant to developmental processes. Chapter 3 describes the mixed-methods approach as applied in the Case Studies, and provides arguments regarding the added value of the approach. The chapter also offers extensive descriptions of the way the sample of participants for the Case Studies was constructed, the way the Case Studies interviews were developed and analysed and a description of the trajectory analyses that were part of the Case Studies. Finally it is argued that the design and analyses of the Case Studies fit within the boundaries set for research in the tradition of the bioecological model of human development. Chapter 4 describes cultural repertoires and experiences that are typical in the learning life-courses of the four sub-groups of participants we identified in the Case Studies. Through use of extensive, in-depth case studies we describe the full, detailed, learning trajectories of two children from disadvantaged SES backgrounds and of two children from middle-class families. Steven Peterson and Tom White are both growing up in working-class families, but while Tom is doing fairly poorly in school, i.e., achieving academically as had been predicted, Steven is academically succeeding against the odds of disadvantage. Marcy Stewart and Imogene Woods are both growing up in middle-class homes, but while Imogene is among the top students of her school and of the EPPSE sample, Marcy is struggling academically, against the odds of advantage.

The following chapters share a focus on proximal process experiences that are related to children's expected or unexpected academic achievements. Throughout these chapters we integrate findings from the Case Studies interviews that were obtained through two procedures of data analysis. Participants' perceptions of reasons for academic success and failure were extracted from the child, parent and teacher interview data by applying bottom-up analysis. For this analysis, coding categories were created according to themes that emerged from the analysis of perceptions of the participants as expressed in the interviews. For the second set of analyses, a 'top down' approach was used to develop categories of 'protective' and 'risk' factors. Coding categories were created based on evidence from the quantitative and qualitative EPPSE project data and the literature review.

Chapter 5 of the book looks at the 'person' characteristics that might help explain expected and unexpected academic trajectories. This chapter describes findings on how children become, or fail to become, active agents of their academic success. It relates protective and risk factors based on the literature review to factors explicitly identified as having contributed to academic success or difficulties by the children that were identified for the sample and their parents and teachers.

Chapters 6 and 7 discuss aspects of the family microsystem, of parenting and family histories in their relation to children's academic achievements. Chapter 6 describes the parenting practices in our four samples and includes sections on the HLE through the early, primary and secondary years. Chapter 7 continues by describing practices of 'family involvement with school and learning'. It relates these practices to empirical evidence for educational success as well as to their educational effect as perceived by children and parents and parents' reasons for providing these parenting repertoires.

In Chapter 8 learning processes in the classroom microsystem and the school context are discussed. This chapter relates examples of how the school environment has contributed to the academic success of the

Case Studies children to the broader literature. It examines factors at the school level, factors related to teachers and factors related to peers and friends in combination with perceptions of children, parents and their secondary school teachers of how schools, teachers and friends have contributed to academic achievement.

The last chapter on our findings, Chapter 9, examines learning experiences through additional microsystems in the child's developmental system. It provides descriptions from the Case Studies on how educational success was supported through children's engagement with the wider community, for instance by participating in extra-curricular activities, through hobbies, religious activities or involvement with support networks of extended family and friends of the family. Again, the findings are related to the literature as well as to the perceptions of our participants.

Finally, Chapter 10 summarizes and synthesizes our findings on what we have termed 'active cultivation' as a cultural practice of childrearing with our findings on effective support from significant others in schools, classrooms and the wider community in the form of cultural, social and emotional capital. It discusses how unexpected educational success requires agency in the form of effort and determination from the children themselves as well as from the people and institutions immediately accessible to them. Together these factors inspire children to become active agents in their learning life-courses. Possible implications of the study for practitioners and policymakers are discussed in the conclusions of some of the chapters and in the final chapter.

2   Studying learning life-courses

This chapter provides an overview of the theoretical framework of the study based on some of the literature from the fields of (developmental) psychology, sociology and education. It proposes Bronfenbrenner's 'bioecological model of development' as an overall framework for the Case Studies. It specifically discusses mechanisms of development at work on the different levels of this framework and describes our understanding of concepts relevant to developmental processes.

Introduction

The aim of this book is to identify, describe and discuss the processes throughout the learning life-courses of the fifty children in our study that, at least partly, explain their often unexpected academic achievements. In this chapter our approach to this task has been to bring together a range of theoretical, empirical and methodological literature from the fields of sociology, psychology and education. The choice to include multiple disciplines from the social sciences partly follows from our personal scientific backgrounds. The authors' experiences are rooted in different scientific traditions which have inevitably shaped our understanding of methodology, research practices, theoretical concepts and our inter-pretation of data. But we also felt that the process of unravelling the mechanism of development in the lives of these children might benefit from diverse perspectives. Once started, we found that combining the theoretical concepts and knowledge about research from our respective fields and traditions, expanded our understanding of the literature and findings and resulted in a shared frame. According to Sheldon Stryker:

A frame specifies a manageable set of general assumptions and concepts assumed important in investigating particular social behaviours. It tells researchers what concepts (or in operational terms, what variables) are likely important in studying what may be of interest to them, but it does not specify the connections between or among the concepts/variables. It is, in short, the basis on which theorists justify their confidence that the relationships among the frame's concepts will be a significant part of the explanation(s) for investigated behaviours. In contrast, a theory provides a testable explanation of empirical observations, making use of relationships among the concepts provided by the frame. (Stryker, 2008, p. 16)

Both frame and theory require researchers to explicate their assumptions. As a result we had to voice and discuss the particular concepts we felt needed to be incorporated in our study, our understanding of these concepts and of possible relations between them, and our understanding about mechanisms of development. It also meant that any differences of interpretation needed to be resolved in order for a shared understanding of frame and theory to emerge. As we examined our assumptions and concepts we found that we were often referring to the same or similar processes, approaches and concepts even though we frequently used different terminology. What gave us confidence to proceed to mix and match theoretical, empirical and methodological concepts from the different fields is that, in our understanding, works from different research traditions had key assumptions about developmental processes in common. We felt that, taken together, these concepts and assumptions provided us with a frame that indeed focused our research.

A primary assumption is that *children develop through their participation in day-to-day activities with people and objects* (see for instance Bernstein, 1975; Bourdieu, 1987; Bronfenbrenner & Ceci, 1994; Gauvain, 2001; Gottlieb, 2001, 2002; Greenfield, 2002; Rogoff, 2003; Rogoff & Toma, 1997; Tomasello, 1999; Tudge, 2008). By becoming engaged in activities in the home, the family, in childcare facilities, the neighbourhood, the playground, the classroom, the village, the workplace or whatever environment is available to the developing child, children develop knowledge and skills that allow them to successfully function in these contexts. Children observe, practise, listen and question these activities, and through these processes they gradually learn which behaviours, attitudes and skills are considered appropriate or inappropriate, valuable or worthless, necessary or unimportant. These activities are not necessarily instigated to provide a child with learning opportunities. Rather, they are a natural part of the habits and daily grinds of the child's life and of the different contexts in which this life is situated. Young children share meals with their parents and siblings, they help out when a parent is taking care of chores in and around the house, they participate in circle time at pre-school, resolve disputes over tricycles in playgrounds, take baths, build block towers, actively listen to picture books being read, watch television, talk and listen to others talking all day long. Through their participation in day-to-day activities and habitual routines children gradually come to grasp the intentional significance of a tool, action or symbol for its user and socially learn the conventional use and meaning (Bourdieu & Passeron, 1977; Gauvain, 1998; Rogoff, 1998, 2003; Rogoff et al., 2003; Tomasello, 1999).

A second assumption is that *children are active participants* in the developmental process (see for instance Rogoff, 1993, 2003; Bronfenbrenner & Morris, 2006). Children contribute their biological characteristics, their cognitive and socio-emotional abilities and behaviours, to their interactions and to the environments in which they interact. Well before their first birthday children come to understand other persons as intentional agents, just like they are themselves. This ability allows them to create and establish shared understanding with people in their environment about actions, symbols or objects by mentally placing themselves in the place of the other and by detecting and changing each others' minds by communicating to them how they feel, what they like, want or need (Tomasello, 1999; Trevarthen & Aitken, 2001). They engage in activities not simply because they are available to them or because other people ask, demand and encourage them to participate, but because they are internally motivated: they enjoy participating with others because they want to learn, because they want to do well in the eyes of others, because they want to be like others or because they want to play a part of the world in which they live. As children develop over the course of their lives the nature of their participation changes towards greater responsibility and independence (Rogoff, 2003). Hohmann and Weikart (1995) call this '*active learning*', and define this as 'learning in which the child, by acting on objects and interacting with people, ideas and events, constructs new understandings' (p. 17). This means that young children require direct and immediate experiences that will enable them to derive meaning from these experiences based on their previous ones. The learning environment must, therefore, provide children with opportunities to be active and take the initiative to learn. The role of the adult is to provide these opportunities and experiences through setting the environment and through consistent planning and rigorous assessment so that appropriate opportunities may be given. Adult support is also important to encourage children to learn in an active and participatory way (Siraj-Blatchford & Mayo, 2012).

A third assumption is that, together, the child, the people and objects with whom the child interacts and the environmental contexts in which they come together are interrelated and form *a unique developmental system*. Different authors from different disciplines have used different names for the unique constellation of child, people, objects and environment in which development is situated. Sociologists such as Pierre Bourdieu and Annette Lareau use the term *habitus* to describe differences in socialization contexts (Bodovsky, 2011; Bourdieu, 1986;

Lareau, 2003); anthropologists like Sarah Harkness and Charles Super (1992, 1999) talk about the *developmental niche*; developmental psychologists in the tradition of Urie Bronfenbrenner talk about the *bioecological system* (Bronfenbrenner & Ceci, 1994; Bronfenbrenner & Morris, 2006; Tudge, 2008). But regardless of the label given to the constellation, they all perceive this system as a dynamic one that is constantly reconstructed (partly reproduced) through the process of interaction (Bronfenbrenner & Ceci, 1994; Bronfenbrenner & Morris, 2006; Harkness & Super, 1992; Gauvain, 1998; Greenfield et al., 2003; Laland et al., 2000; Tomasello, 2001; Tudge, 2008). Because each child, each person, object and environmental context in this system brings into the system's dynamics its own set of biological, social, cultural, economic and/or historical characteristics, it is unlikely that any two systems will be exactly the same. Sometimes children share system components, or characteristics of components or experiences. Around the world many children for instance share the experience of being a girl, of being the eldest child in a family, of being the child of working-class parents. For many young children in the United Kingdom, as in many other Western countries around the world, formal childcare settings are an inherent part of life these days in addition to the care they receive at home. Within families, siblings share the same parents and in schools classmates share experiences of particular teachers and classrooms. But having components or characteristics of components in common does not mean that systems are identical, nor that the life-experiences within these systems will be comparable. Being the eldest child in a family of four will offer a different experience from being the eldest child in a family of eight. Having the same parents does not automatically mean that the interactions two siblings experience with or through their parents are the same. And although attending primary school is an experience children in the United Kingdom share with many generations before them, classroom experiences of children in the first decennium of the twenty-first century differ substantially in terms of such experiences as discipline, didactics and classroom demographics from the experiences of, for instance, their parents and grandparents.

Contextualist approaches to development

Our general assumptions fit within the tradition of contextualist developmental perspectives found in the work of scholars such as Lev Vygotsky, Barbara Rogoff, Urie Bronfenbrenner or Jonathan Tudge. These approaches share the understanding that the cultural environment, the developing person and the developmental processes are unavoidably interconnected, and that culture and development are not universal, but rather that forces that contribute to development are specific to historical time and social place. In his book *The everyday lives of young children* Tudge (2008) states that contextualist theories

have at their heart the 'stuff' of everyday life, the everyday dramas, events, and activities in which individuals participate, by themselves and with others. Necessarily, these dramas, events, and activities are intertwined within the contexts in which they take place, but that does not mean that development is a simple function of context, any more than that development is the result of individual competences, innate characteristics, and the like, important though these competences and characteristics are. Theories that fit within a contextualist paradigm are those that take seriously the complex interconnections among individual, interpersonal, and contextual aspects of development. (Tudge, 2008, p. 73)

The implication of these contextualist assumptions is that if you want to understand differences in developmental trajectories you need to take into account not just *how* the developmental processes of individual children differ (or for that matter, how developmental processes of children from different socio-economic, ethnic-cultural or gender groups differ), but also *why* they differ (Tudge, 2008).

The bioecological model of human development

The bioecological model of human development, developed by Urie Bronfenbrenner and colleagues (see for instance Bronfenbrenner & Ceci, 1994; Bronfenbrenner & Morris, 2006), in particular has played a pivotal role in shaping our understanding of children's developmental processes.

In the bioecological model, development is defined as the phenomenon of continuity and change in the biopsychological characteristics of human beings, both as individuals and as groups. The phenomenon extends over the life course, across successive generations, and through historical time, both past and future. (Bronfenbrenner & Morris, 2006, p. 793)

We feel that the work of Bronfenbrenner bridges the social and psychological aspects of human development and as such it seems the logical model for us, as two researchers from different disciplines, to synthesize our specific perspectives. We feel that this model of human development provides us with a theoretical framework that ties our assumptions together, but perhaps even more importantly, offers us a way to scrutinize possible mechanisms and pathways of development that follow from these assumptions.

The model is the accumulation of more than five decades of critical assessment, reassessment, revisions and extensions of Bronfenbrenner's theory of human development (Tudge et al., 2009). Throughout this time a basic premise of the theory has been that all levels of organization involved in human life are connected with each other as they constitute the course of an individual's life (Bronfenbrenner, 1979; Bronfenbrenner & Ceci, 1994; Bronfenbrenner & Morris, 2006). However, Bronfenbrenner's thinking and writings about this connectivity of the organization of life can be divided into two distinct periods (Bronfenbrenner, 1999). The first period ended with the publication of the *Ecology of Human Development* in 1979. The second period has resulted in the formulation of the *bioecological model of human development* by Bronfenbrenner and colleagues (Bronfenbrenner & Ceci, 1994; Bronfenbrenner & Morris, 2006).

In the first period the social context of human development, constituted by the interrelated microsystems, mesosystems, exosystems and macrosystems, formed the core of the theory (Bronfenbrenner, 1979). This social context shapes both what is regarded as successful socialization for a child as well as the experiences through which the child achieves or perhaps fails to achieve these socialization goals (cf. Tudge et al., 2009). Although person–context interrelatedness was always recognized in the earlier work (Tudge et al., 1997), Bronfenbrenner critically addressed his initial focus on context and instead emphasized the role an *individual* plays in his or her own development during the second period in his thinking (Tudge et al., 2009). According to Tudge and colleagues, the single most important difference from Bronfenbrenner's early writings is his later concern with *processes* of human development, accumulating in the identification of proximal processes as the key factor in development (Bronfenbrenner, 1995; Bronfenbrenner & Ceci, 1994; Bronfenbrenner & Morris, 2006). This is what has interested us too in the way these proximal experiences interact to shape our children's lives and their learning.

Defining properties of the bioecological model

The bioecological model in its mature form has four interrelated defining properties that together set the stage for human development: (1) Process, (2) Person, (3) Context and (4) Time (Bronfenbrenner, 2005; Bronfenbrenner & Evans, 2000; Bronfenbrenner & Morris, 2006). Although we will reflect on the separate roles that these defining properties play in the process of human development, this separation is only artificial. Jonathan Tudge described the interrelated nature of the properties of developmental systems as follows:

Activities only are possible within contexts, and the contexts themselves are transformed in the course of those activities. Activities are only possible with individuals to do them, and the activities are necessarily transformed depending on the characteristics of the individuals who are engaged in them. Age, gender, temperament, motivation, experience with the activity – all are implicated in the process by which any activity is altered by the characteristics of the individuals involved. At the same time, as I have illustrated, individuals themselves are transformed in the course of engaging repeatedly in activities. (Tudge, 2008, p. 75)

Process The first defining property, process, constitutes the core of the bioecological model. Proximal processes are particular forms of interaction between the child and environment that provide the child with culturally regulated experiences through which children's genetic potential for effective psychological functioning are actualized (Bronfenbrenner & Ceci, 1994). For genetic predispositions to become actualized children need to be able to engage in relevant experiences through opportunity structures in the immediate settings of their lives (Bronfenbrenner & Ceci, 1994). Learning to play the violin, for instance, at least requires access to such an instrument, and in nearly all cases access to a music instructor as well.

According to the bioecological model, developmental outcomes are the result of progressively more complex interactional processes, in which children actively engage with other people (especially at a younger age with those close to them such as parents, siblings, teachers or peers) or with cultural artefacts (such as books, computers, toys, television programmes) (Bronfenbrenner & Ceci, 1994). The content, instructions and support children encounter during proximal processes should ideally stimulate them to think and act *beyond* the comfort of the skills and knowledge they have already mastered; i.e., interaction in what Vygotsky termed their *zone of proximal development* rather than in their zone of functional development (Fischer & Bidell, 1998; Kumpulainen & Kaartinen, 2003; Rogoff, 1998). As children develop and mature, the complexity of these processes needs to increase to continue to stimulate them to expand existing knowledge and skills. A prerequisite condition in order for proximal processes to become more complex is that they need to last long enough to do so and that they need to reoccur frequently (Bronfenbrenner & Ceci, 1994; Bronfenbrenner & Morris, 2006; see further for instance Chen & Siegler, 2000; Gunnar & Cheatham, 2003; Landry et al., 2003; Leseman & van den Boom, 1999). If the content of proximal processes is not just developmentally appropriate but culturally appropriate as well (Bernstein, 1971), the processes offer learning experiences that will help the child to develop the necessary and appropriate skills and knowledge to cope with demands and opportunities of their social environment (Gauvain, 2001; Hatano &

Wertsch, 2001; Rogoff, 1998). What proximal processes look like in everyday life, with whom or what they occur, how effective they are for development and whether this development is positive or negative varies according to the specific combination of characteristics of the developing person, of the direct and remote environments in which the processes are set, the nature of the developmental outcome that is considered and the characteristics of social life in the time the development takes place (Bronfenbrenner & Morris, 2006; cf. Moriarty & Siraj-Blatchford, 1998).

Person The second defining property of the bioecological model refers to the developing person in question. According to Bronfenbrenner and Morris (2006) cognitive and socio-emotional characteristics of the person function as precursors and producers of later development. Their effectiveness follows from their capacity to influence the emergence and operation of proximal processes. The bioecological model distinguishes between three types of person characteristics that individuals bring into social interactions and which function as shapers of development: *demand*, *resource* and *force* characteristics.

Demand or 'personal stimulus' characteristics such as gender, age, skin colour and physical appearance trigger instantaneous expectations about a child and as a result can influence initial interaction between the developing child and the social partner. *Resource* characteristics are not immediately apparent but are induced from the observed demand characteristics. The resource characteristics relate to mental (e.g., language skills or intelligence), emotional (e.g., positive experiences with previous teachers), social (e.g., a support network of friends and family) and material resources (e.g., a safe home to live in) that are appropriate to the needs of the particular society in which the child is developing (Tudge et al., 2009). Finally, *force* characteristics are active behavioural dispositions, such as temperament, motivation and persistence, that can have positive or negative effects on proximal processes.

Developmentally generative characteristics are force characteristics that can set proximal processes in motion or sustain their operation, for instance active orientations of the developing person such as curiosity, tendency to initiate and engage in activity alone or with others, responsiveness to initiatives by others, and readiness to defer immediate gratification to pursue long-term goals. *Developmentally disruptive* force characteristics, on the other hand, may actively interfere with, constrain, hold back, or even prevent the occurrence of proximal processes. Disruptive force characteristics can indicate a person's difficulties in maintaining control over emotions and behaviour, such as impulsiveness, explosiveness, distractibility, inability to defer gratification, or aggression and even violence. Equally disruptive to proximal processes, but completely different in nature, are personal attributes such as apathy, inattentiveness, unresponsiveness, lack of interest in surroundings, feelings of insecurity, shyness or a general tendency to withdraw from activity (Bronfenbrenner & Morris, 2006). Through all the person characteristics that children bring into any proximal process, they actively or passively shape the nature of these processes. By changing the nature of the proximal processes they engage in, children will eventually alter the characteristics of the social context in which these processes are situated.

Context The third defining property refers to the social context in which the developmental processes of an individual are situated. The ecology or social context of human development consists of four interrelated systems: *micro-*, *meso-*, *exo-* and *macrosystems* (see for instance Bronfenbrenner, 1979; Bronfenbrenner, 1994; Bronfenbrenner & Morris, 2006). These environmental contexts influence proximal processes and development through the resources they make available as well as through the degree of stability and consistency they are able to provide over time, which are necessary conditions for proximal processes to become effective for development (Bronfenbrenner & Ceci, 1994). The settings in which children spend a great deal of time directly engaging in interaction with other people, objects or symbols, i.e., engaging in proximal processes, are referred to as microsystems. Microsystems include for instance the child's family, peer groups, classrooms and religious groups. The interrelations among two or more microsystems in a child's life are referred to as the mesosystem, for instance involvement of parents in the child's schooling through their participation in parent–teacher conferences, by going along on school trips or helping out with special class projects. When different settings are linked and processes take place between two or more settings without the child being involved in at least one of these settings, the environmental setting is referred to as an exosystem. Events that occur in the exosystem affect the developing child indirectly, through the influence they have on the proximal processes within the immediate settings of the developing child's life. For example when a father loses his job and as a consequence spends more time at home interacting with the child. Finally, the macrosystem consists of the overarching pattern of micro-, meso- and exosystem characteristics of the culture or general society in which the child develops, such as cultural values, parental belief systems, political ideologies, economic patterns, social conditions and life-course options that are embedded in each of these broader systems. For any particular value system to exert influence on a developing child it needs to be experienced within one or more of the microsystems that form the immediate setting of the child's proximal process experiences (Bronfenbrenner, 1993).

Time The final defining property of the bioecological model refers to the dimension of time. Bronfenbrenner and Morris (2006) describe three successive levels for this dimension: *micro-, meso-* and *macrotime*. Microtime refers to the extent to which activities and interactions occur with some consistency in the developing person's environment. Mesotime is the regular reoccurrence of these episodes across greater intervals, such as days or weeks. Macrotime focuses on the changing expectations and events in the larger society, both within and across generations. The changes in society of historical time influence, and are influenced by, processes and outcomes of human development over the life-course. The importance of micro- and mesotime and timing relates for human development to the effectiveness of proximal processes. Activities that occur regularly and for extended periods of time create the necessary conditions for these activities to become increasingly complex and thus for children to develop new knowledge and skills or extend existing ones (Bronfenbrenner & Ceci, 1994). When a parent for instance for the first time sits down to read a picture book with a young child, chances are that the child will be more interested in flipping the pages than in listening to the actual story. However, if they allow a child time to get used to the activity of joint reading, for instance by making it part of the child's bedtime routine, reading sessions can soon include not just the reading of the story, but opportunities for parent and child to identify objects, figures and activities depicted on the pages, to comment on events in the story, to anticipate what will come next or even to create alternative endings or plots. The importance of macrotime for a child's development relates to the fact that the actual proximal processes a child experiences are likely to vary according to the specific historical events that are occurring and according to the specific age of the child (Bronfenbrenner, 1999; Tudge et al., 2009). Life-course research such as the study of Glenn Elder on children of the Great Depression (1974) clearly demonstrates the significance of macrotime for developmental trajectories. According to Elder (1998a, 1998b), the life-course comprises multiple social trajectories of education, work and family which individuals or groups follow through society as well as the developmental implications of these trajectories. Bronfenbrenner (1999) explicitly cites the four basic principles of Elders' theory of life-course development as complementing the notion of [*macro*]*time* and *timing* as put forward in the bioecological model. The first principle, that of *historical time* and *place*, states that 'the life-course of individuals is embedded in and shaped by the historical times and places they experience over their lifetime' (Elder, 1998a, p. 3). Historical forces shape social trajectories, but these trajectories in turn shape the behaviour and specific lines of development of an individual. For instance the fifty children in our study are growing up in a historically well-established social democracy that aims not just to provide access to education for all children but also to keep children in the educational system as long as possible. As a result, the majority of these children, like the majority of their age peers, effectively started their educational trajectories around the age of 3 or 4 when they enrolled in free pre-school programs, instead of at the age of 5 when education became compulsory. And although education at the time was compulsory only up to the age of 16, the majority of students will continue in some form of education, academic or vocational, up to the age of 18. This education is free, unless children and parents choose otherwise, and bursaries are available sometimes for students facing financial difficulties and who nonetheless choose to remain in full-time education up to the age of 19. However, with the recent economic downturn, continuation into higher education may be less of a given for our children and their generation than it has been for several generations before them. With university tuitions being raised and chances of finding a paying job once a bachelor degree is earned decreasing, a division in university enrolment is once again likely to occur between children from lower income families, who do not have the means to financially support their children well into their twenties, and children from more affluent homes who can afford to do so.

The second principle, *timing in lives*, puts forward that 'the developmental impact of a succession of life transitions or events is contingent on when they occur in a person's life' (Elder, 1998a, p. 3). The timing of biological and social transitions relates to the culturally defined age and role expectations and opportunities throughout the life-course (Bronfenbrenner, 1999). Life transitions – such as starting pre-school, moving from primary school to secondary school, getting married, becoming a parent – are an inherent part of social trajectories and shape the course of and give meaning to the individual's developmental trajectory (Elder, 1998a, 1998b). Entry into the reception class of primary school forms an important life transition for young children. In the United Kingdom the culturally defined age for this transition is between 4 and 5. Most children start reception with their year group in September. However, children born in August will be up to eleven months younger than their oldest classmates. This difference can typically translate to a prominent negative achievement gap for these summer-born children. Research, including that of the Effective Pre-School and Primary Education (EPPE 3–11) project, generally shows that the younger students in an academic year tend to have poorer academic attainment compared to their older peers (Mortimore et al., 1988; Sharp et al., 2009; Sylva et al., 2008). Children who were autumn-born (September, October, November and December) more often attained the highest levels in their Key Stage 2 assessments (33.9 per cent compared to 23.3 per cent) than the considerably younger summer-born children (May, June, July and August). EPPE 3–11 further found indications that a possible consequence of this difference in cognitive performance was that younger children had a greater chance of being identified as having special education needs (SEN) (Anders et al., 2010; Sammons et al., 2002b; Sharp et al., 2009; Taggart et al., 2006). Although the gap usually narrows over the course of their primary and secondary education, it can still be substantial for some children by the end of secondary education and particularly August-born children are slightly less likely to attend university (see for instance Crawford et al., 2007).

The third principle refers to *linked lives*, stating that 'lives are lived interdependently, and social and historical influences are expressed through this network of shared relations' (Elder, 1998a, p. 4). According to Bronfenbrenner (1999), the developmental course of family members within and across generations is affected by how each family member reacts to the historical events or role transitions in their lives. Finally, the principle of *human agency* states that 'individuals construct their own life course through the choices and actions they take within the opportunities and constraints of history and social circumstances' (Elder, 1998a, p. 4).

Shaping development through the family microsystem

In this book we take the bioecological model of human development as a framework to examine how the learning life-courses of children who start from more or less similar circumstances and environments result in academic achievements that differ substantially. The model offers us a way to look at the parts that are played in these trajectories by the children, by the key, close people in their lives and by their environments, through the way they contribute to or impede the child's experiences and opportunities to engage in proximal processes of learning.

The second part of this book examines the experiences of children and their families that have contributed to or interfered with the learning life-courses of the children and tries to determine why children have particular experiences. In other words, it deals with the findings from our study about the *how* and the *why* of these proximal processes and the microsystems in which these processes are situated. The remaining paragraphs of this chapter are used to discuss findings from the literature about the more 'distal' aspects in the bioecological model; about processes on the levels of meso-, exo- and macrosystems; and about influences from the historical time and place in which the children's developmental experiences are situated. Specifically, we focus on characteristics of systems and mechanisms that influence the actual proximal process that children experience with the family microsystem. These paragraphs illustrate our understanding of how the bioecological model 'functions' to produce expected or unexpected academic success.

We strongly believe that family and parents in particular play an essential role in child development; both directly through what they offer in terms of immediate resources and experiences and indirectly through choices regarding opportunities and experiences for the child outside of the home. By no means do we wish to imply that, for instance, the role of the child, or of other microsystems such as the classroom, are less important than the role of the parent, but we do believe that particularly in the foundational and early years of children's learning life-course family and parents are the key in the child's expanding web of knowledge, relationships and experiences. Children shape their environment and learning experiences right from the moment they are born, but initially their influence is restricted to the effect their emotional states and dispositional tendencies have on their parents or carers. As children gradually develop their physical, cognitive, social and emotional skills and knowledge and gain autonomy, their range of influence on their learning experiences and environments expands (Bronfenbrenner & Ceci, 1994; Rogoff, 2003). Classroom environments, and the proximal processes they offer, generally become of importance only after the foundations of children's learning and development have been established through, for instance, initial interactions with parents. For parents, on the other hand, possibilities to shape the learning experiences of their child are manifold, right from the moment the child is born, or even conceived. They shape the learning environment of their infant through their direct responses to the child's needs and wants, through their personal interactions with the child and through the opportunities they create for the child to interact, or not to interact, with other people, objects, toys or symbols with or without the presence and participation of the parent (Bronfenbrenner & Ceci, 1994). As children develop and venture out into the world, parents not only continue to provide a substantial amount of the actual proximal processes, they also influence children's proximal processes outside the family context by managing and regulating their access to other contexts (Parke, 2004).

In their book *Education and the family: passing success across the generations*, Feinstein et al. (2008) provide an extensive overview of how proximal processes that take place at the microsystem level function as a mechanism through which educational success is transmitted from one generation to the next, and so play a fundamental role in the persistence of social inequalities. Their model of inter-generational transmission proposes that each microsystem has characteristics on a distal, internal and proximal level. On a distal level characteristics are of a structural nature and provide an index of a system's demographic or socio-economic situation. These distal factors can function as 'protective' influences in combating poor child outcomes or as 'risk' factors that increase the risk of poor child outcomes (Feinstein et al., 2008). Distal family factors (for instance family structure and size, income and poverty or maternal employment) influence internal family characteristics (such as parental cognitions, their mental health and well-being, their resources, or physical health) which then influence proximal family processes (i.e., parenting style and educational behaviours) and through those impact child developmental outcomes. But family systems do not stand by themselves and parents do not raise their children in a vacuum of family life. As the family microsystem is inherently part of the larger developmental system, these distal, internal and proximal characteristics of the family will be influenced by, and in turn will exert their influence on, processes and characteristics of the meso-, exo- and macrolevels of the system. If we want to understand why proximal processes in the family context, or in any other microsystem for that matter, differ in their effectiveness for academic development, we need to understand how these processes take shape under influence of the surrounding system.

Cultural values and beliefs in macrosystems

Culture reflects the shared understanding of a community of individuals about values and beliefs at a particular point in time expressed through their practices and their use of cultural tools. Culture continues to evolve as community members engage in an ongoing process of renegotiating their values, beliefs, practices and cultural tools (Mayo & Leseman, 2004). In the bioecological model, macrosystems refer to any cultural group that shares values and belief systems, regardless of whether this group consists of millions of people or just a handful (Bronfenbrenner & Morris, 2006). On the one hand a macrosystem might consist of the overarching pattern of micro-, meso- and exosystem characteristics of the national culture in which the child develops. These are the patterns we refer to when we, for instance, talk about 'the English' or 'the English culture'. But at the same time the macrosystem consists of many, many subcultures and sub-groups. These subcultures for instance are defined by socio-economic family characteristics (e.g., middle class vs working class), by the ethnic-cultural heritage of the parents (for instance white UK majority vs ethnic-cultural minority; or Western vs non-Western cultural background; or English, Pakistani, Indian, Black African, Black Caribbean, etc.) or by the religious denomination and traditions of their family (for example Anglicanism, Roman Catholicism, Islam, Hinduism, Sikhism, etc.). Often, cultural 'membership' is not a person's by choice. Our fifty children, for instance, were all born and are being raised within the overarching pattern of the English culture. For these children and for many of their parents, being part of the English culture and society is simply a given; this is the culture they were born to, so this is the culture they become part of and make do with. On the other hand, for some of our children's parents, membership of the English culture has been a (more or less) conscious choice. They left their culture and country of origin behind to build a new life for themselves and their families in England because they believed the English culture would allow them to do so. As children mature, develop and venture out into the world, they are likely to find their way into new cultural environments, for instance those of their peer groups. Sometimes they will even shed, or at least attempt to shed, some of the cultural groups they were brought into through their parents.

Each culture or cultural sub-group has its own beliefs and values which are reflected in differences between the practices that are used to socialize new members, such as children, into that particular group culture (Rogoff, 2003). In different cultures and in different cultural groups, different experiences will be used and emphasized to help children develop those skills and that knowledge considered (most) valuable to achieve success within their society (Rogoff, 2003; Tudge, 2008). What constitutes appropriate and valued development at any point in a person's life, and which developmental outcomes are regarded as successful, will therefore depend on the specific cultural context in which this development is situated. Jonathan Tudge argues that

Because culture influences the types of activities that occur and the manner of interactions, we cannot think that engagement in more of any type of activity (or greater interaction of a certain type) by members of one cultural group than another indicates that the members of the first group are in any way better or worse than members in the second. Rather, we need to think about the reason for variation between the groups. (Tudge, 2008, p. 265)

Here, cultural influences are not just related to ethnic background but to gender, social class and other differences.

A national culture of academic learning

For our children, growing up in England around the turn of the millennium, acquiring extensive academic skills and knowledge, reflected in (advanced) academic qualifications, is among the most highly valued developmental outcomes, at least from the perspective of the national culture. Children's academic success, or lack thereof, is likely to have lifelong consequences, as it will influence their future positions on the labour market, their future earnings, and even the educational future of their own children (Kohn, 1995; Schoon, 2001). The educational system in England is structured according to 'Key Stages' at the end of each of which children are usually assessed to determine if they have achieved the attainment targets set for these age groups. Any parent raising a child in England will to some extent be aware of the importance of education for their child's future in society. One of the overarching cultural patterns in England regarding parenting almost seems to dictate that parents should start preparing their children for participation in the educational system well before children actually start their formal, primary school education. Through publications in the media, national government's educational policies, local infrastructures for parents and children and word of mouth from friends and relatives, parents are encouraged to find ways to stimulate their children's early language skills, early Literacy skills and early Numeracy skills well before children start school. Parents for instance are strongly encouraged to enrol their child in a pre-school setting and over 98 per cent do! During the last decades, free pre-school education has become available to any child of age 3–4, because participation in pre-school is found to have a positive effect on academic achievement later on in school – as the Effective Pre-School, Primary and Secondary Education (EPPSE) research showed (Sylva et al., 2008; cf. Sammons et al., 2008a, 2008b). As a result, the number of children who will not have had any pre-school experiences by the time their compulsory education starts after their fifth birthday has become a small minority.

Parents are also encouraged and expected to provide their children with a stimulating home learning environment (HLE). Longitudinal research such as the EPPE/EPPSE project has provided evidence for the strong and lasting effect of this early HLE, and of (high quality) pre-school, on both cognitive and social/behavioural development of children in England (Sylva et al., 2008; cf. Sammons et al., 2008a, 2008b).

The term '(early) HLE' (Sylva et al., 2008) refers to a range of experiences for children within or through the family microsystem that are positively associated with children's (emerging) academic skills and knowledge. At the pre-school age, home learning activities such as joint storybook reading, oral storytelling, mealtime conversations, painting and drawing, and also frequent visits to the library or teaching and playing with children with letters and numbers are of particular importance (Melhuish et al., 2008; cf. Bradley, 2002; Bus et al., 1995; Duursma et al., 2007; Leseman et al., 2007; Weizman & Snow, 2001). One of the reasons these activities seem to make an important contribution to the development of children's early academic skills is that they incorporate features of the academic language register that children will encounter and will need to master as they embark on their academic learning courses (Bernstein, 1975; Brooks-Gunn & Markman, 2005; Hoff, 2003). More than other activities, such as television watching or conversations in general, these particular activities provide young children with large quantities of speech that is lexically rich, includes syntactically complex utterances, frequently includes wh- questions and metalinguistic references (Hart & Risley, 1995; cf. Aarts et al., 2011; Henrichs, 2010). Once children start pre-school or reception, their command of early academic skills and knowledge positively influences their learning experiences in these settings. Tudge and his colleagues, for instance, found that children who were more familiar with decontextualized conversations because of their earlier family experiences more often initiated and engaged in conversations in class, and were subsequently perceived by their teachers as more competent (Tudge et al., 2003). In terms of the bioecological model, the HLE and pre-school participation provide young children with opportunities to participate in proximal processes that generate culturally valued knowledge and skills (Bronfenbrenner & Ceci, 1994).

Historical time and place

From the macro-level perspective of time and place, this overarching cultural pattern of emphasizing academic skills and knowledge within the national macrosystem level is made possible by a long period of relative economic, political and social stability in England. The children of our study were born and are growing up in a country is generally considered safe, prosperous and stable. According to the United Nations Development Programme (UNDP) the United Kingdom ranks at 26 out of 169 countries on the Human Development Index (HDI) of 2010. On average, people in the United Kingdom have a very high level of human development (0.849 on a scale from 0.0 to 1.0) compared to people in other countries around the world. They are expected to live a long and healthy life (79.8 years on average), they have good access to knowledge (mean years of schooling 9.5; expected years of schooling for children entering the educational system 15.9) and a decent standard of living (the gross national income per capita is a little over $35,000, or almost £22,000 per year (UNDP 2010)). One might argue that over the last few years major political changes have occurred that are changing the social climate of the country as the Conservatives and Liberal Democrats took over government from New Labour; that the world-wide recession, sparked by the banking crisis, has resulted in drastic cuts in government spending, affecting the lives of many people on a daily basis; that the country has been actively involved in the ongoing conflicts in Iraq and Afghanistan and that the detrimental consequences of these conflicts have been brought home to everyone in the country through the 7/7 bombings in London and the daily confrontation with the faces and names in the media of the young men and women who have lost their lives in the conflicts; that all is apparently not well because recently thousands of young people around the country felt they needed to, and could, go out into the streets to loot and burn shops, houses and cars. Despite all this, the fact remains that England is still a country in which children's chances to reach adulthood, to participate in education and to eventually find a job that pays enough to support a family, are well above those of most children around the world. With free health care through the National Health System, with an extensive system of social benefits in place and with free education from pre-school to pre-university, worries about 'academic survival' have gradually replaced worries about 'daily survival' for many parents and children in the country.

However, global rankings of fortuity and national value and belief systems remain relatively remote factors of influence on children's development. They exert their influence as they allow for and put in place institutions and infrastructures on the exosystem level that in turn support microsystems to provide culturally appropriate proximal processes. What they cannot do is ensure that every child will be able to benefit from these institutions and infrastructure in the same way. The extent to which a child gets to participate and benefit from these experiences will much depend on the cultural beliefs and values their parents prioritize within the family microsystem. It will also depend on the culturally relevant resources and experiences parents provide for the child, through access to participation in additional microsystems. And these, in turn, will much depend on the membership and participation of parents in sub-cultures within the national English culture and society.

The macrosystem of socio-economic status

When it comes to children's development in general and their academic achievement in particular, one of the most influential subcultures within the macrosystem seems to be that of socio-economic status (SES). The macrosystem of socio-economic class refers to overarching patterns of micro-, meso- and exosystem characteristics and practices that vary between particular socio-economic sub-groups. SES is used both as an indicator for class (i.e., economic position) and for social status (i.e., prestige, social and cultural capital). Either way, SES refers to the standing of a group or individual within a particular culture or society and the social structure of the English society in which our children and families live is still very much influenced by concepts of social class and status (Savage, 2007; cf. Bernstein, 1975; Bourdieu, 1987). Although definitions and measurements of SES are subject to ongoing debate, they typically include (one or more) distal characteristics of the family microsystem: family wealth or income, parental occupation or parental education. Individually, as well as combined, these indicators have been related to the academic success of children, typically showing that children from families with fewer socio-economic resources are less successful academically than their peers from families with more resources (for overviews see Bradley & Corwyn, 2002; cf. Bennett et al., 2002; Bornstein et al., 1998; Burchinal et al., 2002; Foster et al., 2005; Hoff, 2006; Raviv et al., 2004; Sonnenschein & Munstermann, 2002), although the strength of these relationships often differs substantially between cultures.

So why does SES matter for children's academic achievement? What are the mechanisms through which SES exerts its influence on children's development? When we consider these questions from the perspective of the bioecological model, the answers seem clear: SES matters because differences in socio-economic status reflect differences in the developmental context of children and subsequently in the proximal processes children experience during their learning life-courses. In terms of sociological understanding, differences between socio-economic sub-groups are reproduced from one generation to the next through a system of family-based resources and practices (Bourdieu, 1986; cf. Bodovski, 2011). These resources and practices are related to the capital people accumulate throughout their life-course. Pierre Bourdieu (1986) differentiated between three forms of capital: *economic capital*, expressed through the financial resources people have available to them; *cultural capital* that follows from their educational qualifications and experiences with education; *social capital* comprising the network of people they know. As people become parents these forms of capital shape the developmental system of the learning experiences of the child. In Bourdieu's view, parents can, and usually will, use all three forms of capital in their possession to ensure the best possible future for their child, but possibilities to exceed limits of available capital and to facilitate upward social mobility are limited.

Social class and differentiating proximal processes

Overall, empirical findings seem to indicate that the impact of social class on academic achievement follows from the effect that aspects of social class, such as parental education, income, poverty and employment, have on the way proximal processes take shape in the family microsystem (Bradley & Corwyn, 2002; Feinstein et al., 2008; Hoff, 2006; Parke, 2004). Although high quality early HLEs are found among all socioeconomic strata (Siraj-Blatchford, 2010), research shows that these early learning activities are more commonly part of childrearing practices in the home environment of middle-class families (Sylva et al., 2004, 2008; cf. Arnold & Doctoroff, 2003; Bradley & Corwyn, 2002; Brooks-Gunn & Duncan, 1997; Hoff, 2003). Studies focusing on early language development, for instance, show that effective early home learning activities such as storybook reading activities, storytelling, conversations and access to printed materials in the home not only occur more frequently in higher SES families (Hart & Risley, 1995; Hoff, 2003; Mayo & Leseman, 2008; Molfese et al., 2003; Tudge et al., 2003) but that the overall quality of these interactions was less effective for children's language development in lower SES and poor families as these mothers generally (but not always) talked less, used a smaller range of words, used more directives and asked fewer questions than higher SES mothers (Bernstein, 1971; Hart & Risley, 1995; Hoff et al., 2002). These differences in early HLE result in substantial differences in language abilities at the start of school, and these persistently affect children's further achievement in school, with the growing early Maths literature mirroring the Literacy field (Sylva et al., 2004, 2008; cf. Brooks-Gunn & Markman, 2005; Hoff et al., 2002; Hoff & Tian, 2005; Stipek, 2001; Tudge et al., 2006). In his book *The everyday lives of young children*, Tudge found that in all but one of the seven included cities he studied from around the world

children from middle-class families were more likely than those from working-class families to play with objects designed with school in mind and to engage more in academic lessons. It's difficult to avoid the view that these middle-class families were more likely than working-class families to provide their children with more opportunities to engage in these activities because they viewed them as more important. The implication again seems to be clear, that parents from each group are preparing their children for success in different domains by giving them different experiences. In turn, these types of differences support the position that social class is akin to culture – defined as a group whose values, beliefs, and practices distinguish them from other groups and which tries to pass on those values, beliefs, and practices to the next generation. (Tudge, 2008, p. 267)

Differences between SES groups seen in the early HLE persist as children get older and the characteristics of the HLE shift to include more school-related activities, such as parental involvement with school and learning (see for instance Bradley, 2002; Bradley et al., 2000; Feinstein et al., 2008; Parke, 2004). Parents who have experienced fewer years of education, for instance, tend to be less involved with their child's school work (Desforges & Abouchaar, 2003; Fantuzzo et al., 2000; Wa Wong & Hughes, 2006). This is even more relevant as findings from empirical studies and reviews show that parental involvement is particularly effective for children 'at risk', such as children from families with limited years of parental education and disadvantaged socio-economic backgrounds (Dearing et al., 2004, 2006; Epstein, 1992; Fantuzzo et al., 2004; Jeynes, 2005). So why are some parents more involved with school and learning than others and how does this relate to differences in SES?

Parenting cognitions

A study with primary school parents in the USA that was designed to empirically test constructs for parent involvement (Green et al., 2007) showed that the association between family SES and parental involvement is influenced by the internal features of the family, in particular parental beliefs or cognitions. Internal features that are typically associated with more academically effective experiences, and with higher academic achievement for children, are more often found to be part of the middle-class family context than of the family microsystems of working-class or poor families (Bradley & Corwyn, 2002; Feinstein et al., 2008; Parke, 2004). But when differences in SES are controlled for, internal features, such as parents' perception of self-efficacy, remain strong predictors for home-based involvement such as providing help with homework (Green et al., 2007; see further Hoover-Dempsey & Sandler, 1995, 1997). This suggests that certain types of parental beliefs or cognitions might function as a buffer against negative effects of distal family factors such as low SES.

Parental beliefs or cognitions refer to parents' understandings concerning child development and parenting. They include the developmental goals parents aspire to for their child, behaviours they consider appropriate for their children, parenting strategies they believe effective and appropriate, their perception of their ability to influence children's development, cultural tools they believe will contribute to children's development, or developmental timetables for children's social, emotional, physical and cognitive development (Sigel, 1992; cf. Harkness & Super, 1999; Harkness et al., 2000). Quantitative studies into the role of parental involvement with school and learning show that parents' beliefs about the role they should play in their child's academic development, their perceived self-efficacy in fulfilling this role, the parenting style they use in their dealings with their child and their academic expectations for their child, influence not just how parents shape the out-of-school learning contexts for their children at home and in other microsystems, but also how academically effective these experiences and activities will be (Eccles & Harold, 1996; Fan & Chen, 2001; Jeynes, 2005). The HLE, for instance, appears to be particularly effective if the parenting style is characterized by responsiveness and warmth towards the child (Bradley, 2002). These characteristics are part of what has been referred to as an authoritative parenting style, following Baumrind's typology of authoritative, authoritarian and permissive styles (1978, quoted in Steinberg & Morris, 2001). The literature on parenting styles and adolescents' school achievement indicates that adolescents' actual school performance, adjustment to school and psychosocial maturity benefit from having parents who are authoritative: warm, firm and accepting of their needs for psychological autonomy but demanding in their expectations (Steinberg, 2001). A large-scale study among a socio-economically and ethnically diverse sample of adolescents in the USA revealed that the positive association between authoritative parenting and educational achievement transcends distal family charac-teristics such as ethnicity, SES and family structure. Adolescents whose parents were accepting, firm and democratic earned higher grades in school, were more self-reliant, reported less anxiety and depression and were less likely to engage in delinquent behaviour (Steinberg et al., 1991).

In a way, parental cognitions are to a family what culture is to society. They present an amalgam of values and beliefs at a particular point in time and are expressed through the parenting practices in the family microsystem and through the way parents function in their role of gate-keepers with regard to children's access and participation in other micro-sytems. Like culture, parental cognitions have developed over the course of history. They have been shaped by their experiences of growing up in particular families, in particular places and cultures, at particular times in history. By their personal experiences with education, with work, with media, with their friends. And they will be renegotiated and changed as time passes by and the parents move into different spheres of influence in the micro-, meso-, exo- or macrosystems in their lives. They change as they suffer losses and gain experiences that alter their perceptions of who they are, who they want to be and of who they want their children to become. Their children will mature and gradually move towards partici-pation in microsystems that are less easily influenced by their parents. And as they do, their needs and abilities change as do the parts their parents have to play in their lives.

A clear example of how parental cognitions are shaped by their per-sonal histories, by their position in macrosystems and by their participa-tion in exosystems, comes from the work of Melvin Kohn. Kohn (1995) describes how, after twenty-five years of research into the relationship between social class and personality, he and Carmi Schooler could describe the processes through which macrosystem characteristics influ-enced personal characteristics of individuals. Based on their research, they concluded that a person's position in the larger social structure (macrosystem) profoundly affects the conditions of his or her life experi-ences, particularly workplace conditions (exosystem), and that these conditions, in turn, affect a person's personality as expressed through his or her values, orientations and cognitive functioning. Their research showed that for people who occupied higher positions in society's class or prestige orders, their chances increased to experience self-direction in the workplace. Compared to their peers from less prestigious or working-class backgrounds, their jobs included more complex and less routine tasks and they were less often closely supervised when performing their tasks. As a result of these occupational experiences these people placed greater value on opportunities and abilities to exercise self-direction and intellectual flexibility in life, both for themselves and their children (Kohn & Schooler, 1983).

The cultural logic of childrearing

The ethnographic research of Annette Lareau further illustrates how profoundly the macrosystem of social class affects the beliefs of parents and the everyday learning experiences of children. In her book *Unequal childhoods: class, race, and family life*, Lareau (2003) describes the findings from an extensive qualitative study investigating the parenting practices in twelve high- and low-SES families from White and African-American heritage in the United States. In line with the inter-generational transmission models of authors such as Kohn or Feinstein, Lareau proposes that the transfer of advantages from parents to children differs between social classes as a consequence of differences in contexts of childrearing. She found that differences in educational experiences, income levels and occupation of parents resulted in differences in parenting beliefs which in turn resulted in two different socialization strategies, i.e., different parenting practices: 'concerted cultivation' for middle-class families and 'accomplishment of natural growth' for poor and working-class families (see also Rogoff et al., 2003). As found by Kohn, these patterns of socialization of middle-class and working-class parents aimed to instil very distinctive orientations about self and society in their children: self-direction for children from middle-class families and conformity for children from working-class families. Although the orientations and social competences that were transmitted in each child-rearing context in themselves were valuable, they also differed by social class and in the case of children from low-SES or poor families were less effective for particular purposes such as educational achievement in the USA (see also Bodovski & Farkas, 2008; McNeal, 2001; Parke, 2004; Sampson, 2007).

The cultural logic of childrearing adopted by the middle-class parents in Lareau's study stressed the 'concerted cultivation' of children. Middle-class families engaged in a process of actively, even assertively, cultivating their child's talents by making sure their children participated in organized activities, established and controlled by parents. These children had little say over their leisure activities. Peer interactions took place during organized activities or play dates, rather than leaving their occurrence to chance or choice. In their dealings with institutions middle-class parents did not hesitate to openly criticize authority figures or to intervene on behalf of their child, when they felt the child's needs and talents were not optimally met. In their communications with the child these parents elicited the child's opinions, feelings and thoughts. In these families children readily contested adult statements and parents and children engaged in extended negotiation. In their communications with other adults such as teachers or doctors, middle-class children were stimulated to question adults and address them as relative equals. From this a robust sense of entitlement took root in the child which played an especially important role in the child's dealing with institutional settings such as schools. Children learned that they had a right to be, in fact that they needed to be, assertive consumers of what settings such as class-rooms, sport classes or Brownies had to offer them, in order for them to benefit most from the learning processes these settings offered.

In contrast, the working-class and poor parents in the study tended to undertake what Lareau termed the 'accomplishment of natural growth', a pattern of childrearing in which concerted cultivation is not considered an essential aspect of good parenting. Children experienced long stretches of leisure time, more child-initiated play, and daily interaction with extended family; and as there were clear boundaries between adults and children, children had substantial control over their leisure activities. Communications in working-class and poor families showed an emphasis on the use of directives and children rarely questioned or challenged adults. Parents in working-class and poor families displayed a sense of dependency towards institutions such as school that did not allow them to object or intervene on behalf of the child and as a result left them feeling powerless and frustrated.

According to Lareau the context of 'accomplishment of natural growth' was less adapted to the demands of institutions such as schools than the context of 'concerted cultivation', which socializes children to benefit optimally from educational systems and prepares them well for future dealings with society's institutions. For middle-class children their childrearing experiences seemed to lead to an emergent sense of entitlement that allowed them to make the rules work in their favour, and as a result, to augment their social and cultural capital. For working-class and poor children, the mismatch between their family's practices of childrearing and the practices valued and administered by institutions and professionals resulted in an emergent sense of constraint, and in the development of skills that were often less suitable when dealing with society's institutions (Lareau, 2003).

Implications for the Child and Family Case Studies

From the perspective of the bioecological model for development, differences in developmental outcomes follow from differences between the defining properties of the child-specific developmental system. So, if we want to understand differences in outcomes, we need to understand the differences between developmental systems, and how differences in system-characteristics result in differences in the learning experiences they provide. We are aware that we will be treading on thin ice by comparing children and experiences from working-class and middle-class families. The literature review in the foregoing paragraphs has shown that the particular set of beliefs, values and practices of the culture in which our children participate in the educational system are often much more in line with those cultivated in the homes of middle-class families than with those in working-class families. When we compare working-class and middle-class practices and beliefs towards learning and education it could easily seem as though we are making a value judgement about how well or poorly these families raise their children. That is by no means our intention. We do not wish to make a judgement about the different traditions of childrearing as such. But if we want to understand how it is that some children can succeed against the odds (or fail against the odds, for that matter), we need to look at and learn from their specific experiences and how these are shaped by their personal circumstances and daily lives, because the discrepancies we find between the cultural logics of different socio-economic groups in society are part of the reality of the culture these children live in, and the implications of these differences will mark their futures. It affects children's academic success throughout their learning life-course, their future job prospects and earnings and their future position in society. If we want to help more children do well in society, to help them overcome their disadvantages, we need to explicitly identify difference in experiences and traditions that lead to successful or unsuccessful adaptation to society's academic standards. We need to gain a better understanding of how experiences and traditions differ and why they differ. And we need to do this in great detail and not just between socio-cultural groups but within these groups as well. If we want to understand how children come to succeed against the odds (or fail against the odds), we need to look at and learn from their specific experiences and how these are shaped by their personal developmental system, because, for these particular children and their families, who they are appears to be less important than what they do in breaking cycles of disadvantage. We are therefore more concerned to understand processes and the role of parents and schools than the role of society.

Our perception of development and educational success as an outcome of reciprocal proximal processes between a child and the people, events and objects that operate within, and are influenced by the processes and characteristics of the wider developmental context, has several implications for research that tries to answer the question of why particular children 'succeed against the odds' of disadvantage and others do not. Firstly, it makes it necessary to identify personal characteristics that facilitate 'resilience' ('protective' factors) or 'risk' with regard to achievement. We need to understand which 'protective' and 'risk' factors or behaviours and beliefs develop for children who manage to overcome disadvantages, and how they differ from those of children who do not. Secondly, we need to understand how children develop these behaviours and beliefs. This calls for identification and investigation of possible 'risk' and 'protective' characteristics in the child's microsystems; perhaps even in the meso-, exo- and macrosystems or on the macrotime level. It also calls for investigation of the proximal processes between the child and other people in these contexts to determine how these system character-istics come to facilitate 'risk' or 'resilience' in children. For instance, what brings parents to shape their child's learning experiences and environments in a particular way? Finally, it calls for investigation of how these contexts interact with each other in order to understand how they influence each others' characteristics that are relevant to the child's developmental processes.

3   Methods and sample of the Child and Family Case Studies

This chapter describes the mixed-methods methodology as applied in the Case Studies, including a description of the sampling procedures; it provides arguments regarding the added value of the approach. It begins with a discussion and rationale for the value of mixed-method designs in studies such as this one. The chapter goes into some detail on the construction of the sample, the design of the research and the strategies of analysis applied in the Case Studies, and discusses how the Case Studies fit in with research in the tradition of the bioecological theory of human development.

Rationale for the mixed-method design

There is nothing new about mixed-methods research (e.g., Niglas, 2001a, 2001b). It has only become controversial in recent years because of the paradigm wars between quantitative and qualitative research communities. Oakley (2004) has argued that the 'paradigm divide' continues to constitute a major problem in educational research. We argue that this persists in being the case in educational research when other fields have moved beyond this false dichotomy. Oakley refers to a number of critiques of alleged 'misplaced positivism' in educational research. Research in education has not been immune to these criticisms and specific concerns have been expressed regarding alleged technicism and the reification of dominant conceptions of educational quality (Siraj-Blatchford, 2010b).

A good place to start in understanding the controversy regarding mixed-methods research is to consider – **How do we understand the difference between quantitative and qualitative research?**

Gray and Densten (1998) suggest considering the two approaches of qualitative and quantitative as being on a continuum rather than in the form of a dichotomy that researchers have to select between. 'Qualitative and quantitative evidence', therefore, refers to a false dualism (Frazer 1995), and one that we are probably better off without. (Gorard & Taylor, 2004, p. 6)

Clearly to measure the quality of something you must first apply theory to define the quality that is to be measured. Many (so-called) quantitative studies begin with a qualitative literature review (i.e., they are mixed). Other studies considered to be 'qualitative' often include some degree of quantification (e.g., of observations or narrative content). In fact, as Gorard and Taylor argue, 'patterns' are, by definition, numbers – and the things that are numbered are qualities. Mixed-method approaches and perspectives therefore also provide a means of rising above the false dualities (of qualitative versus quantitative) and essentializations characteristic of the 'paradigm wars'.

Stephen Fuchs' (2001) sociology of cultural networks 'dissolves' (as opposed to solves) the problems of such paradigmatic incommensurability (along with insider and outsider perspectives) by showing that essentialization may itself be seen as the response of tightly connected social networks (e.g., educational or social science research communities) to any competition or threat to their foundations, where they act to 'isolate and shelter [their] basic certainties' (pp. 16–17). In these circumstances

Each network will observe the other's core as a contingent construct, not as a basic natural necessity. They will behave as constructivists about the other's core practices, and as realists about their own. They will debunk each others' core as being composed of 'ideologies' – beliefs and ideas suspiciously unaware or deceitful of their 'true' motives and interests – while asserting that their own ideas and beliefs are just right and righteous, and that they capture the empirical and moral order of the world as it really is, without any construction going on at all. (Fuchs, 2001, p. 34)

The lesson to be learnt from considering these 'paradigm' struggles in this way is, as Fuchs suggests, to recognize that ' ... the truth of a science is its truth, not the truth of science as such. A science has only the foundations it builds for itself, and it has those until further notice, until it changes these foundations' (p. 74). Fuchs' overall argument is therefore that we should respond to the challenges of anti-foundationalism and scepticism with a sociology (or presumably any other social science) of *foundations* that *explains* them (or their absence):

In this approach antifoundationalism and skepticism signal a local fragmentation in social solidarity within 'weak' cultures, not a global and philosophical crisis of representation. (p. 74)

As Fuchs convincingly continues to point out, 'paradigm incommensurability' is more the result than any cause of a breakdown in communication. Also, the good news is that

incommensurability is not opposed to communication, but actually encourages and energizes it, by irritating the background certainties and institutional invisibilities taken for granted in each of the interacting cultures. (Fuchs, 2001, p. 93)

From our perspective, efforts should therefore be made to reduce fragmentation through improved communication and collaboration. As Tashakkori and Teddlie (2003) argue, in the USA it has been, in part, the success of mixed-method research that has caused the 'paradigm wars' to be 'largely discredited'. In the United Kingdom, Furlong (2003) and others have also been suggesting for some years that we should now 'rise above such divisions'. The research carried out by the Effective Provision of Pre-School Education (EPPE) team since 1997 provides a notable example of a recent, and extremely influential, mixed-method study, that has combined both sophisticated statistical and constructivist analysis, while making no foundationalist claims or assumptions (Siraj-Blatchford et al., 2006).

The dialectical nature of the EPPE and Case Studies

For the majority of social researchers, and for the EPPE research team (to learn more about the EPPE research see www.ioe.ac.uk/research/153. html), post-positivist approaches provide a means of rejecting naive positivist excesses without rejecting what they consider to be the underlying discipline of social science. Taking a scientific-realist stance, the EPPE team has explicitly rejected naive empiricism and argued that knowledge can be both fallible, partial and approximate, yet still remain 'objective' (Bunge, 1993; Siraj-Blatchford et al., 2006).

The longitudinal, mixed-method design of the EPPE project brought together a large-scale quantitative survey approach that involved the psychometric and standardized assessment of child development and the standardized assessment of centre and school quality, along with both structured and non-structured interviews and observations of practitioners and children. As Green (2005) has argued, a mixed-method approach to educational enquiry engages directly with difference, and is thus able to address what she refers to as 'inherent tensions' in our work.

The tensions she refers to are concerned with the multiple audiences our research inevitably has to address, including the multiple focuses upon teaching and learning programme design, implementation and outcomes, and the inevitable effects of working in complex real-world contexts that have some characteristics that are unique and others that are shared across contexts. In this book we are trying to cross boundaries across education, psychology and sociology. Green's (2005) argument is that in all of these respects mixed-method approaches provide a means by which differences of needs and perspectives are both respected and engaged (p. 210).

The EPPE mixed-method analysis was iterative in nature, as the different phases of the research and the analysis periods overlapped and facilitated in-depth discussion of emerging issues and findings from 1997 to 2014. But the combination of qualitative and quantitative methods has at times itself been seen as a problem, according to some, due to the inherent incompatibility or incommensurability of their underlying paradigms (Smith & Heshusius, 1986). Yet Tashakkori and Teddlie (2003) outline contenders for a distinct paradigm of its own for mixed-methods research:

1. Pragmatism (Tashakkori & Teddlie, 2003);
2. The transformative-emancipatory paradigm (Mertens, 1999);
3. Dialectical thesis (Green & Caracelli, 1997);
4. The multiple paradigm thesis (Creswell, 2003).

Scott (2007) has also made a strong argument for *critical realism* towards a resolution of the quantitative/qualitative divide, and in combining methodologies. Perhaps most significantly, critical realism has sometimes been considered to offer the possibility of identifying the contributions of both the social structures and the agencies that characterize all aspects of social life.

It is interesting to note that the EPPE team never sought to achieve any kind of epistemological consensus. The multi-disciplinary team shared different areas of research expertise and approach. The Principal Investigators of the team met one day a week for over a decade to complete their work, and the dialogue this engendered proved fruitful in allowing emerging findings and interim analyses from the different approaches to inform and stimulate each other. The EPPE/EPPSE project, on which the Case Studies is a sub-study, might therefore be best considered to have operated more closely to the way described by Greene and Caracelli (1997) as 'dialectical'. We continued this work and methodology in the Case Studies. 'Dialectical' is a term that they attribute to Geertz (1979),

who argued for a continuous 'dialogical tacking' between experience-near (particular, context specific, ideographic) and experience-distant (general, universal, nomothetic) concepts, because both types of concepts are needed for comprehensiveness and meaningful understanding. (Greene and Caracelli, 1997, p. 10)

But EPPE would have to be considered a dialectical project by default rather than by prior design. It is only in retrospect that we could identify with Greene and Caracelli's (2003) description of an approach that involved a 'mixed-method way of thinking' (p. 93). In retrospect it is clear that we were habitually inviting each other openly to express ourselves through our own disciplines and terms, to contribute to an ongoing dialogue about structures and behaviours, the particular and the general, the emic and the etic, and about our value commitments and the need for neutrality. These conversations were not (in the main) philosophical ones; as Greene and Caracelli (2003) note, such conversations are related closely to the phenomenon being studied: 'But the contradictions, tensions, and oppositions are rooted in, and thereby reflect, different ways of knowing and valuing' (p. 97).

The result of these conversations was a practical, paradigmatic integration of methods through sustained and respectful interaction. One of the major advantages of adopting a mixed-method research approach in EPPE and later in the Case Studies was that the studies could combine explanatory theory generating research questions (e.g., what is effective pedagogic practice in schools and early childhood) with confirmatory questions (e.g., was there really a pre-school effect). The use of mixed methods provided a study of pre-school, home and school influence that was more meaningful, and provided a wider evidence base for both policymakers and practitioners than reliance on any one form of data gathering and approach to analysis would have achieved. Complex and pluralistic approaches to our Case Studies continued, as social contexts that are formed by multiple and diverse perspectives demand analysis, and this is more fruitful than reliance on only one philosophical position or methodological approach (or indeed, belief). The EPPE and Case Studies conclusions, we consider, are stronger for having applied a mixed-method approach within an ongoing dialogic engagement.

The mixed-methods nature of the Case Studies

In developing the Case Studies we applied an adaptation of grounded theory using a mixed-methods framework. For the Case Studies we combined quantitative data from the Effective Pre-School, Primary and Secondary Education (EPPSE) project, a review of the international literature on aspects of 'risk' and 'resilience' for academic success, learning life-course trajectory analyses and qualitative interview data designed and collected specifically for the Case Studies and an earlier pilot study (see Siraj-Blatchford, 2010a). Although these different quantitative and qualitative data sets could easily stand by themselves we used them in a way that we felt they would complement and extend each other.

For instance, the quantitative data from EPPSE gathered on each child for over a decade has been extensively interrogated by the EPPSE team and has provided firm confirmation of the importance of, for instance, certain child, family, school and neighbourhood factors for educational success. It has also shown broad patterns of relationships between more distal and proximal contexts of development for different groups of children. Throughout the book reference is made to the many existing publications and Technical Papers produced during the life of the EPPSE study (1997–2014). However, although the quantitative data showed which factors in the lives of children impacted on their educational success, by its nature it did not necessarily allow questions addressing why these factors mattered. By adding data from our fifty in-depth, qualitative, Case Studies to the overall quantitative data we were able to 'drill-down' and answer the 'why' questions and provide the meanings families and children gave for their educational outcomes and experiences. As such, the Case Studies have explored the explanations and meanings respondents gave to their unique characteristics, experiences and events, providing information that might go some way to explaining the statistical patterns that have been found through quantitative analyses of the EPPSE sample. But then again, without the quantitative EPPSE data we would not have been able to create the purposeful sample for the Case Studies that yielded this information.

The adaptation of grounded theory using mixed methods also shows in the way we made use of the review of international literature from a range of social science disciplines. Firstly, and in contrast with grounded theory, the review served to create the initial theoretical framework for the Case Studies and to identify processes that function as mechanisms of development as discussed in Chapter 2. After identifying and clarifying our assumptions about how children learn and develop, we found that the bioecological model of development as proposed by Uri Bronfenbrenner (Bronfenbrenner & Ceci, 1994; Bronfenbrenner & Morris, 2006) would provide a workable and constructive overall framework. We then turned to a wider range of literature from the field of sociology, touching on such works as the different forms of capital as proposed by Pierre Bourdieu (1986) and the concepts of 'concerted cultivation' and 'accomplishment of natural growth' as put forward by Annette Lareau (2003), and from the field of developmental psychology, such as the concept of proximal processes (Bronfenbrenner & Ceci, 1994), to identify processes that function as possible mechanisms of development within these contexts. While the theoretical frame of the Case Studies was constructed we also used the literature to identify general themes and focus areas for the in-depth qualitative interviews with parents, children and teachers which would form the core of the Case Studies.

The grounded theory and mixed-method approach are perhaps most clearly visible in the way the Case Studies' in-depth interviews were constructed and analysed. In addition to general questions based on findings from the EPPSE project and from the international literature review, 'case specific' questions and retrographs were generated for each of the fifty children. A first set of case-specific questions and the retrographs were based on the survey and questionnaire data available through EPPSE for each individual child.

We pulled the data collected over the course of the EPPSE study to create detailed background profiles for each of the fifty children in our final Case Studies sample. These files included both raw data and composite measures created for and used in analyses conducted with the full EPPSE sample. This meant that we could use a measure such as the family's early HLE index to provide an overall qualification of proximal processes in the family microsystem during the early years, but that we could also go back to the original data to investigate specifically how often that child at that time had for instance been engaged in reading activities. The data had been collected through the use of questionnaires for children, parents and teachers; through use of observations in pre-schools and classrooms; and through standardized psychometric testing of cognitive abilities and social skills.

The data we pulled included demographic information about the child, the family, the neighbourhood and (pre-)school, such as age, term of birth, gender, ethnic heritage, parents' educational qualifications, parents' employment, family social class, level of deprivation in the neighbourhood or percentage of free school meals (FSM) provided by the school. The data further included information about children's duration in (pre-)school settings, information about problems with any aspects of their development and possible Special Education Needs (SEN), information about the languages spoken in the home and if English was used as primary or additional language, as well as information about children's ability to 'socialize' with other adults and children and their general behaviour to others measured by teachers'/pre-school staff's ratings. It also included information about children's attitudes towards school subjects and teachers, about how they felt in class and school, about time spent on homework and study. We included the (early) HLE indices, measures of pre-school effectiveness and quality and academic effectiveness of the primary schools our children attended. More detailed information about how these measures were constructed will be provided as part of the discussions about their influence on children's academic trajectories in later chapters of this book.

The retrographs of the child's life-course included information such as the names of (pre-)schools attended by the child, information about changes in the family constellation (e.g., birth of siblings, divorce), and information about children's extra-curricular activities. These retrographs were used as memory aids and prompts during these interviews (see Appendix 4 for an example).

A second set of case-specific questions was based on learning lifecourse trajectory analyses for each of our fifty children. Using the data obtained through standardized psychometric testing of cognitive abilities available from the EPPSE project for each individual child, we created trajectories for the fifty children in our Case Studies. These trajectories allowed us to distinguish for each individual between academically more and less successful periods in the learning life-course and to identify transitional periods which could be explored during the interviews. They also allowed us to compare patterns of learning life-courses within and between the four groups in our Case Studies.

Once the interview data were collected and prepared using NVivo software, the interviews were coded and analysed in two ways: 'bottomup' and 'top-down'. Through the 'bottom-up' analysis of these interviews we investigated the perceptions of our participants, taking into account the people, events and circumstances these children, parents and teachers themselves identified as having had a positive or negative influence on their child's academic achievement over the years. A subsample of children with 'ideal types' of trajectories was used to generate initial coding categories; these were subsequently reassessed using the full Case Studies sample. For the 'top-down' analysis, coding categories were created, based on existing evidence from the EPPSE project and the literature review. These codes allowed us to analyse the occurrence of well-established 'risk' and 'protective' factors and the specific interplay and constellation of these factors in the learning life-courses of the children. Codes continued to be readjusted as we moved back and forth iteratively between the different data sources.

To our knowledge, this particular kind of mixed-methods research, that not only combines extensive qualitative and quantitative data sets, but creates an iterative dialogue between the two types of methods, data and analysis to this extent, is rare, if not unique. The following paragraphs of this chapter describe in greater detail the procedures followed during the construction of the Case Studies sample, the development and analyses of the Case Study interviews and the construction and analyses of the learning life-course trajectories.

Constructing a purposeful sample for the Case Studies

The quantitative data from the EPPSE study was used to obtain a systematic, purposeful sample of participants for the Case Studies.

Table 3.1 *Overview of the number of families and teachers from the EPPSE project participating in the CFCS, grouped by SES and attainment; drawn from three cohorts of the longitudinal EPPSE study*

	Group 1 Low SES & high attainment	Group 2 Low SES & predicted attainment	Group 3 High SES & low attainment	Group 4 High SES & predicted attainment	Total
	n	n	n	n	N
CFCS family participants	20	15	9	6	50
Boys	8	10	3	3	24
Girls	12	5	6	3	26
CFCS teacher participants	11	8	6	4	29
Boys	6	4	2	2	14
Girls	5	4	4	2	15

The Case Studies sample comprised fifty children, their parents and one of their secondary school teachers, from four groups (see Table 3.1 below). The families came from five different regions in England, from which the EPPSE sample was originally recruited. These five regions were randomly selected but were representative of urban, rural and inner-city areas around the country.

Each of the four groups has a distinctive combination of family background characteristics and academic trajectories. The first and largest group includes twenty children from working-class families who were 'succeeding against the odds' at the end of their time in primary school. Their academic attainment at age 11 was significantly higher than that predicted for them at age 3, given their personal and family characteristics. As it were, at the end of primary school these children had successfully managed to narrow the achievement gap with their peers from more advantaged and affluent homes. In the Case Studies the learning life-courses of these twenty unexpectedly educationally successful children are compared to the learning life-courses of three additional groups of children. The second group, fifteen children from working-class families who were performing as poorly as had been predicted, were included to show what the experiences in the learning life-course of children from disadvantaged backgrounds can 'typically' look like.

We also included two smaller samples of children from middle-class families. Six of these children were doing well, as had been predicted

(Group 4). Their experiences in many ways represent the 'dominant set of cultural repertoires' (Lareau, 2003) that are (implicitly) expected from families in order for their children to gain the greatest advantages from education. However, nine children from similar middle-class families who were doing less well than predicted by their background (Group 3) were also included to show that vulnerability (risk factors) in education can be all too real even when overall conditions in the developmental system appear to be in favour of educational success at an early age.

The Case Studies sample of fifty children was selected using the quantitative data collected as part of the EPPSE project following a four-step process:

> *Step 1:* Achievement in English and Maths was assessed through the nationally standardized, teacher-conducted, national assessment of achievement in English and Maths at age 11 (i.e., at the end of Key Stage 2). Then, achievement in English and Maths at age 11 was predicted for the full sample of EPPE 3–11 children (N=2900) using multilevel modelling (see Melhuish et al., 2006, for a full description of the procedure). Children's attainment in Literacy and Numeracy will be affected by demographic characteristics such as gender, socio-economic status (SES) and parent education. The impact of child, family and neighbourhood characteristics upon child cognitive and social development has been described by Melhuish (2010). For example, low-SES children will, on average, have lower attainment than high-SES children; as a result, a high-attaining but low-SES child might only be in the average band (or above) for the whole population. Therefore, in defining level of attainment it is proposed to produce a statistical model of attainment as a function of a specified child (e.g., birth weight, gender), family (e.g., mother's education, SES) and neighbourhood (e.g., level of deprivation) factors. On the basis of this model it will be possible to identify those individuals who are attaining higher than expected, as expected, or lower than expected, after allowing for the effects of the specified child, family and neighbourhood background factors. Through the use of multilevel model analysis, residual scores were obtained for each child in the EPPSE sample. These residual scores indicate differences in predicted and obtained academic achievement for English and Maths at age 11, while controlling for key characteristics including age, gender, birth weight, early

developmental problems, parent education, SES and family income (Melhuish et al., 2008).

Step 2: These individual-level residuals were used to form three performance groups. The first group, the unexpected overachievers, included the children whose residuals for both English and Maths fell within the highest 20 per cent of residual scores (n=333). The second group consisted of children who attained as predicted (i.e., residuals between 40 per cent and 60 per cent, n=189). The third group, the unexpected underachievers, contrasted the first group and included those children whose residuals fell within the bottom 20 per cent of scores (n=367).

Step 3: To refine the sample for the four groups of children in the Case Studies we included family SES as a further selection criterion. Parental occupation information had been collected by means of a parental interview when children were recruited to the EPPE project. The Office of Population Census and Surveys (OPCS) 1995 Classification of Occupations was used to classify mothers' and fathers' current employment into one of eight groups: professional I, other professional non-manual II, skilled non-manual III, skilled manual IV, semi-skilled manual V, unskilled manual VI, never worked VII and no response VIII. Family SES was obtained by assigning the SES classification based on the parent with the higher occupational status. This left us with sixty-four children from families with a lower SES (i.e., the highest job level held in the family was manual, semi-skilled or unskilled, or the parents had never worked) who attained better than predicted, one hundred and twenty-three children from high-SES families (i.e., parents worked in professional jobs) who did worse than expected, and forty-two children from low-SES families and fifty-two children from high-SES families whose achievement at age 11 was according to prediction.

Step 4: Before we contacted families about possibly participating in the Case Studies, each group was split by gender as we aimed to include equal numbers of boys and girls. Within each gender we randomly selected children to be approached, but checked to make sure that some of the larger minority-ethnic groups within England could be included.

The initial aim for the Case Studies was to include at least thirty families, although we hoped we might manage to include more. Given the detailed and in-depth nature of the interviews we expected attrition rates to be relatively high particularly in the low-SES and underachieving groups. We therefore oversampled these groups and selected seventy families to be approached by telephone. Eight families could not be contacted even after several attempts. The positive response rate of the families we spoke to on the telephone was very high – we believe this might be because the families and children have been with us for over a decade and received our newsletters and birthday cards, as well as constant tracking through assessments and questionnaires. There is a good relationship with the full sample where we have only had modest attrition rates. Four families declined to participate, but the remaining fifty-eight families said they would be happy to be interviewed and looked forward to meeting some-one from the EPPSE project in person.

Before we set up the interview appointments families received a letter explaining the aims of the interviews and were asked to return a signed consent form. Five families with boys did not return their consent forms and one girl and one boy said they no longer wanted to be interviewed once we visited them. Data from one family with a girl was lost due to malfunctioning equipment. This brought overall attrition to an accept-able 14 per cent, although it was rather skewed if considered by gender. The six boys who dropped out were all doing poorly in school; three came from middle-class families and three had working-class back-grounds. The two girls each came from working-class families and were performing as predicted (i.e., poorly). Although we nearly managed to balance gender for the sample as a whole (twenty-four boys and twenty-six girls), the boy–girl ratio unfortunately differs between the four groups. Almost half of the children we have in our sample are from minority ethnic backgrounds. At the end of the interview each child gave us the name of one of their current teachers whom they felt knew them best. With the permission of the children these teachers were contacted by letter and telephone and asked to participate in a short telephone interview about the child. The response rate within each of the four attainment groups was over 50 per cent for the teachers, and included interviews with teachers of both boys and girls within each group (for an overview see Table 3.2). All names have been changed to protect anonymity.

The Case Studies interviews

As mentioned, the schedules for the semi-structured interviews with parents and children were carefully constructed using the literature review described in the previous chapter, using findings from the EPPSE

Table 3.2 *Overview of the participants in the CFCS, by attainment group and gender*

Group	Gender	Name	Age	Ethnic heritage	Parent	Teacher
Group 1: **Low SES** **high** **attainment**	**Girls**	Charley	15	White UK	Mother	
		Natalie	15	White UK	Both	
		Tanya	14	Black Caribbean	Both	
		Sharlene	15	Black Caribbean	Mother	✓
		Reanna	15	Black Caribbean	Mother	✓
		Anjali	16	Indian (Sikh)	Father	✓
		Ife	14	Black African	Mother	
		Leanna	16	Black Caribbean	Mother	✓
		Brenda	14	White UK	Mother	
		Shelly	15	White UK	Mother	
		Martha	14	White UK	Mother	✓
		Asya	14	Pakistani	Mother	
	Boys	Jarell	14	Mixed heritage	Mother	
		Rajnish	14	Indian (Hindu)	Mother	
		Steven	14	White UK	Mother	✓
		Abdi	14	Black African	Both	✓
		Mark	15	White UK	Father	✓
		Shaquille	15	Black Caribbean	Mother	✓
		Peter	14	White UK	Mother	✓
		Robert	16	White UK	Mother	✓
Group 2: **Low SES** **predicted** **attainment**	**Girls**	Amina	16	Black African	Mother	✓
		Fareeda	16	Pakistani	Mother	
		Bunmi	14	Black African	Mother	✓
		Ebun	14	Black African	Mother	✓
		Susan	14	White UK	Mother	✓
	Boys	John	16	White UK	Mother	✓
		Christopher	14	White European	Mother	
		Patrick	14	White UK	Mother	✓
		Ted	15	White UK	Mother	

Table 3.2 (*cont.*)

Group	Gender	Name	Age	Ethnic heritage	Parent	Teacher
		Harry	15	White UK	Both	
		Hamid	15	Pakistani	Mother	✓
		Jamal	15	Black Caribbean	Mother	
		Tremaine	16	Black Caribbean	Mother	✓
		Tom	15	White UK	Both	
		Richard	14	White UK	Mother	
Group 3:	**Girls**	Anna	16	White UK	Mother	
High SES		Gimbya	15	Black African	Mother	✓
low						
attainment		Ella	14	Mixed heritage	Mother	
		Helena	14	White UK	Both	✓
		Laurie	16	White UK	Mother	✓
		Marcy	14	White UK	Mother	
	Boys	Sean	14	White UK	Both	✓
		Subash	14	Indian (Hindu)	Father	✓
		Alex	15	White UK	Mother	
Group 4:	**Girls**	Breona	15	Black Caribbean	Mother	
High SES						
predicted		Abby	15	White UK	Mother	✓
attainment		Imogene	15	White UK	Mother	✓
	Boys	Lucas	14	White UK	Mother	✓
		Benjamin	15	White UK	Mother	✓
		Jason	14	White UK	Mother	

project, using the detailed background profiles that we created from the rich and extensive quantitative data derived from assessments and questionnaires collected in the course of thirteen years of EPPSE research and using the trajectory analysis of the learning life-course of each child. We also drew on the experience of the twenty-four child case studies selected from the EPPSE sample undertaken for the Equalities Review in 2007 (see Siraj-Blatchford, 2010a). A pilot study was conducted with six children and five parents in order to assess the practical aspects of the interview process and to determine whether the interview schedules were appropriate to answer the research questions described in Chapter 1 of this book.

Each of the final interview schedules was extensively personalized but they all included questions at three levels. Samples of the interview schedules can be found in Appendices 1, 2 and 3. First-level questions were similar for all respondents. They were included to provide data on the level of support and the role of the family, peers and community in the students learning and on any 'concerted cultivation' (Lareau, 2003). Respondents were asked about their personal perceptions and opinions regarding the cause of the child's particular learning trajectory. Questions were included to identify the level of information and understanding that the families had regarding the formal and informal educational resources and provisions available, and regarding their understanding of the potential benefits of each. Additionally, questions were included to identify 'significant others' (including grandparents and peers) that might or might not have influenced the families' understandings and engagement with education. Finally, questions were included to collect more descriptive data about the practical and process aspects of the HLE, parents' formal educational experiences and the families' involvement in their children's schooling.

Second-level questions were developed in the initial stages of the Case Studies using the EPPSE qualitative and quantitative data that had been collected on each individual child up to that point in time. These case-specific questions were included to identify the most probable (and likely multiple) explanatory hypotheses explaining each child's particular learning trajectory. These questions were thus posed to investigate the probable causes and motivations in greater depth. These hypotheses investigated, for instance, positive or negative effects of the home learning environment (HLE) in early childhood and during the school years and the processes affecting this; or the positive or negative effects of quality and effectiveness of the children's pre-school, primary and/or secondary school experiences and the processes affecting this.

At the third level additional individual (inductive) questions were determined in the process of the field work. Throughout the three levels of the interview questions, quantitative EPPSE data were used to create child- and parent-specific prompts (e.g., 'What language did you use when you were reading a story to Hamid?') or follow-up questions (e.g., 'How did the primary school deal with the concerns you raised about Alex's reading difficulties?') and to add child- and parent-specific questions (e.g., 'How do you think the loss of her father might have affected how Breona was doing in school towards the end of primary school?').

For the teacher interviews we again used the quantitative EPPSE data to provide child-specific prompts and follow-up questions as well as information from the answers given during the student and parent interviews about, for instance, children's learning styles and the perceived influence of friends on their school attainment. Although we could only interview children's current secondary school teachers and the sample was relatively small (29 out of 50), the data still provided a good way to triangulate the information gathered through the child and parent interviews about the secondary school years.

Interview data collection procedures

The actual face-to-face child and parent data were collected over a three-month period in early 2009. The families were visited after school on weekdays, during weekends and during half-term and Easter holidays. The visits were scheduled to take about three hours, but were often extended as the researcher (the second author of this book) was invited to stay for a meal or to meet other members of the family. On the whole the visits were a very positive experience for all concerned. Families were often delighted to welcome the researcher into their homes and had set aside plenty of time for the interviews; they enjoyed talking about their child.

For the interviews we asked the families to choose a place in the home where we would be able to talk without being disturbed. They usually opted for the living room or kitchen. Children and parents were free to decide whether they wanted the other to be present during their interview. In less than half of the interviews children stayed when parents were interviewed, or vice versa. Interestingly, the children and parents were never in disagreement about staying or going. In those families where children and parents stayed on, the family members seemed used to talking in front of each other and answered freely, even when personal topics were raised. In only one case a mother and daughter argued. Most parents and children appeared to be very interested in what the other had to say. They were often visibly touched by what was said and seemed to feel supported by each others' presence. The pilot study had shown that parents often offered information during their interviews that could be used to prompt their child's memory, and therefore parents were generally interviewed first. The majority of the interviews were held with the mother of the child (forty-one). For one mother a single interview was used to obtain information about her twin daughters, who were both part of the group with working-class children achieving as predicted (Group 2). In five of the remaining families we spoke with both parents and in three families interviews were conducted with the father of the child. In three cases the children translated for their mothers, from and to Somali, Panjabi or Urdu. The Urdu and Panjabi interviews have been checked by native speakers of these languages.

Parents seemed to enjoy this opportunity to talk about their child and their lives with somebody who showed a sincere interest. Most of them were able to recall with great detail the activities they had undertaken with their children when they were little. At the same time it seemed that for many they had not previously given much thought to why they had chosen these activities in particular. As a general observation, it appeared that parents who had stayed in education longer found it easier to talk, and more often offered explanations of why they had made certain choices or had done certain things with their child. Parents with little education themselves often started their answers with 'I don't know ...' However, when given some time, or a memory prompt, they usually managed to answer very well. This observation by no means implies that higher educated parents were always more eloquent than less educated parents or that less educated parents had less clear ideas about childrearing and child development. Rather, it seemed that some parents, particularly those with more education and professional jobs, were used to expressing their thoughts and providing explanations and reasons for actions, while other parents, often those with less educational experience, seemed to feel that their reasons for behaving in a certain way might be so apparent or obvious that there was no need to make this explicit. Mostly, parents' descriptions of their child's progress and abilities matched the child's learning trajectories based on the EPPSE data.

The children were aged between 14 and 16 at the time of the interviews. Some children came across as quite young given their age, both in appearance and in conduct, while others already seemed rather mature. The difference was particularly noticeable among boys. This is not surprising given that adolescence is a transitional stage of development and that the age of onset of puberty can vary by several years. Although the girls typically seemed to be used to voicing explanations about their actions and expressing their feelings and thoughts, they often seemed self-conscious and at times were reluctant to talk about topics such as their friends. It was interesting to find that during the interviews, boys generally appeared more at ease than girls, even though many of these boys appeared to have little experience at sitting down with an adult to talk about themselves in such an in-depth way. Although some of them evidently found it difficult to answer the questions, they nonetheless clearly tried their best. The boys also generally needed more prompts than girls to answer questions and to move beyond single-sentence answers. It was a pleasure to observe that after the first few interview questions most boys started to really enjoy talking and thinking of explanations and examples. Generally speaking, those children who were doing particularly well in school (both from lower- and higher-SES families) found it easier to put their thoughts into words. While most children from professional families were very much at ease during the interview, children from the lower-SES families were often more nervous about talking to an unfamiliar adult (see Lareau, 2003, for similar observations). Nonetheless, the interviews yielded good, sufficient data for coding and analysis and because more talkative boys and girls were found in each of the four groups there were sufficient sources for explanations and perceptions across the sample.

On average the parent interviews took about one hour and fifteen minutes, but the range was substantial (between forty-five minutes and two and a half hours). In the few cases where parent interviews were particularly long, mothers had recently been through stressful life events such as divorce or loss of a person close to them. The interviews with the children took between thirty-five minutes and one and a half hours. The families had been informed in advance that the interviews would be sound recorded. At the end of the interviews parents and children were each given a sheet on which they could write any additional thoughts or comments. Several parents and children returned these, often adding how much they enjoyed being part of the EPPSE project. To add a 'personal' touch the researcher took biscuits or flowers on the visit, and a few days after the visit families received a hand-written 'thank you' note.

The teacher interviews took place by telephone and were sound recorded. As could be expected given their profession, teachers had few problems talking about the student in question in terms of school attainment, behaviour in class and peer relationships. However, the majority of teachers indicated they had never met the student's parents, or felt they did not know the parents well enough to discuss the parents' role in their child's school attainment.

Interview coding procedures

We used the voice recordings of the interviews to create verbatim transcripts of our conversations with children, parents and teachers. The majority of the interviews were transcribed by two trained research assistants following a considered and strict protocol. On average it took about one hour to transcribe six minutes of interview. Each completed transcript was checked by a researcher and anonymized. All names of children, parents, teachers and learning institutions attended by children that are used throughout this book are fictional. We carefully picked first names and family names to resemble the original name, for instance by using a name with a similar meaning or making sure the cultural heritage was reflected in the fictitious name. After being checked all interview transcripts were imported to NVivo 8.0 for coding and analysis.

The NVivo software provided flexibility and allowed us to code the transcripts on different levels and adjust/redefine the coding throughout the process.

During coding, the analysis involved constantly moving back and forth between the qualitative interview data, the quantitative EPPSE data and the relevant national and international literature. On several occasions, data were coded independently by two researchers. Inter-coder reliability was established by visual comparison and found to be good. Any differences in coding were resolved through discussion and applied in subsequent coding. For the purpose of analysing the interview data, each of the interview transcripts was coded in four separate steps:

> *Step 1:* Coded on an initial general level organizing the data into relevant time periods following the structure of the interviews: early family life, pre-school years, primary school years, secondary school years, future years and parental history.
>
> *Step 2:* The events, activities and expressions of belief that the participants mention during the interviews have been coded according to the person(s) that the statements refer to (e.g., the child, parental figures, siblings, relatives, teachers, out-of-school teachers, significant other adults, peers and a 'miscellaneous' category).
>
> *Step 3:* 'Protective' and 'risk' factors, identified through a synthetic review of the relevant sociological, psychological and socio-cultural literatures associated with 'resilience' and 'vulnerability', self-efficacy, self-identity, locus of control, self-regulation, motivation, friendships, socio-cultural context and cultural/social capital, were coded.
>
> *Step 4:* Perceptions of 'vulnerable' students, their parents and teachers, about why and when these students succeeded (Group 1) or did not succeed (Groups 2 & 3) were identified and coded. Additionally, perceptions of the small group of children, parents and teachers who were not 'vulnerable' and succeeded as expected were identified and coded to serve as a reference (Group 4).

Learning life-course trajectories

As described, we sampled four groups of children whose actual attainment in English and Maths at age 11 was below prediction, as predicted, or above prediction, when controlling for demographic variables. As a result we knew how the attainment of each child compared to that of their peers with similar demographic backgrounds. This way we could determine how their attainment compared to that of children with different SES backgrounds. So while the children whom we identified as 'succeeding against the odds' might have had Key Stage 2 test results that were comparable to those of their higher achieving middle-class peers, their result could also have been similar to the *average* attainment of the children with more favourable demographic characteristics or even below this attainment level.

In order to understand how children's attainment compared across our SES groups we needed trajectories that allowed us to compare learning life-courses within and between SES groups. We created these trajectories with data available through the EPPSE project for the whole 3,000-plus sample of children, concerning children's cognitive abilities and academic attainment for English and Maths from age 3 to age 14. For their attainment during the Foundation Stage (ages 3–5) of their trajectories we used the children's scores on the British Ability Scales Second Edition (BAS II) (Elliot et al., 1996). For 'English' we used the composite measure of children's verbal scores; for 'Maths' we used the non-verbal composite (Sammons et al., 2002a). The battery of assessments was specially developed by NFER-Nelson to assess very young children's abilities. We used the results of the assessments at entry to the Effective Provision of Pre-School Education (EPPE) study (age 3 or 4), entry to Reception (age 5) and end of Year 1 (age 6). For the measures of children's attainment for English and Maths during their primary and secondary school years we used the national formal performance assessments administered by teachers, that are conducted at the end of each Key Stage, ages 7, 11, 14 and 16.

The national assessments are intended to show if children are working at, above, or below the target level for their age. At the end of the first Key Stage these assessments take account of how children performed in Key Stage 1 tasks and tests for 7 year olds. The tasks and tests cover speaking and listening, reading, writing (including handwriting and spelling) and Maths. At the end of primary school, children complete the second Key Stage, through the nationally standardized, teacher-conducted, national assessment of achievement in English and Maths at age 11. The assessments and tests for Maths include mental arithmetic, and for English they include reading, writing (including handwriting) and spelling. The Key Stage 3 teacher assessment for 14 year olds covers a wide range of subjects but we used only those for English and Maths. Recently, Key Stage 3 assessments have been discarded.

We applied fractional percentage rankings to indicate the relative position of each child's assessments at each of the six measurement

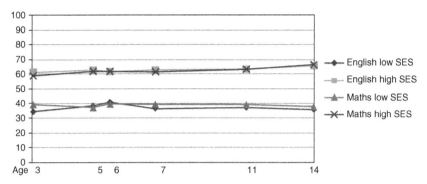

Figure 3.1 Average rankings for Literacy/English and Numeracy/Maths for the low- and high-SES sub-samples from the full EPPSE sample

points. As a result children received rankings between 0 and 100 for each assessment. A child with a ranking of 81 for English at Key Stage 2, for instance, achieved a test score that was better than the achieved test scores of 80 per cent of the children in the full EPPSE sample. Additionally, we determined the mean rankings for all children from socio-economically disadvantaged families (i.e., low SES, which included our children from Groups 1 and 2) and from socio-economically privileged backgrounds (i.e., high SES, which included our children from Groups 3 and 4) to provide points of reference for children's rankings.

Figure 3.1 provides an overview of the average rankings for the low- and high-SES samples in EPPSE. This shows that within the full EPPSE sample average scores for both the low- and high-SES samples are fairly similar over time for both domains and fairly stable over time: around rank 40 for the low-SES sample and slightly above 60 for the high-SES sample.

The figure also shows that, on average, the difference between children from low- and high-SES backgrounds is considerable: children from more privileged backgrounds on average out-rank their working-class peers by about twenty points. The attainment gap exists, and for most children in these groups persists, over the learning life-course. This is of great concern to those interested in social mobility, social justice and the role of education in transforming lives and not just reproducing inequalities.

Given the relatively small size of the Case Studies sample (given that the full EPPSE sample consists of over 3,000 children) and the four analytical groups within the sample, we can only provide descriptions of the trajectory data. However, by any standards related to existing research, a sample of fifty cases is quite large for case-study research.

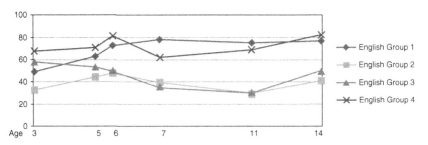

Figure 3.2 Average trajectories for Literacy/English for each of the four groups in the CFCS

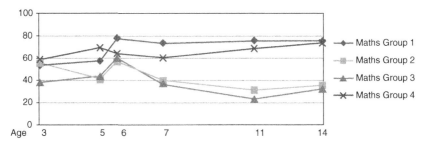

Figure 3.3 Average trajectories for Numeracy/Maths for each of the four groups in the CFCS

Any statements about differences between the four groups are based on visual observations and are not to be interpreted as statistical differences (for statistical analyses of the trajectories of the full EPPSE sample please refer to Melhuish et al., 2011). Nonetheless, visual inspection of the academic trajectories of each of the four groups in the Case Studies makes it clear that differences between the children from disadvantaged backgrounds who 'succeeded against the odds' (Group 1: Low SES, higher attainment) and their socio-economic peers who attained as predicted (Group 2: Low SES, predicted attainment) were visible from the outset for Literacy/English. Over time, the gap between their attainments increased substantially. Figures 3.2 and 3.3 provide a visual overview of the average trajectories for each of the four groups. Although these graphs give us an idea of how attainment levels in the four different groups relate to each other, it should be noted that differences within each of the four groups are substantial (standard deviations range between 10 and 30) and therefore individual trajectories will differ substantially from these group trajectories. Visual presentations of the individual trajectories are provided in Appendix 7.

While rankings at all measurement times of the children from Group 2 approached the average of the low-SES sample in EPPSE, their unexpectedly successful peers (Group 1) started somewhat above this average. By entry into Reception (first pre-primary class in primary school) these particular children from disadvantaged backgrounds were performing at the high-SES sample's average, only to continue their climb in rankings once in primary education. Their average academic achievement level was at a par with, or above, those of their academically successful, high-SES peers (i.e., Group 4).

Differences in Literacy/English between the two high-SES groups were small at the start of their trajectories, with average rankings for both groups closely reflecting the high-SES sample average at 60. However, the groups' trajectories diverged more and more once children started their schooling. By the time of the Key Stage 2 national assessments at the end of primary school, the average rankings of the high-SES children who were doing more poorly than predicted (Group 3) were similar to those of the low-SES children who were doing (poorly) as predicted (Group 2).

Initially there were no visible differences in Numeracy skills between the two groups of low socio-economic status children. In fact, both sets of children from low-SES backgrounds appeared to rank well above the EPPSE's low-SES sample average of around 40. However, once children started their education in Reception, the trajectories of the children in the two groups started to move apart. On average the children 'succeeding against the odds' (Group 1) again ranked among the highest-achieving children in the EPPSE sample; indeed even slightly above their high-SES peers who were doing well as predicted (Group 4).

For the two groups of high-SES children differences were more prominent right from the outset. The unexpected underachievers from Group 3 showed initial Numeracy skills that ranked substantially below the high-SES sample average of 60. Their average ranking was similar to the average found for the full low-SES sample in EPPSE. Although these children's rankings had improved to the average level of their peers from similarly advantaged backgrounds by the end of Reception, their rankings again decreased substantially once in primary school and were at a similar low level to the rankings of the low-SES children who achieved as predicted (Group 2).

Research in the tradition of the bioecological theory of human development

In Chapter 2 we described the theoretical background of the Case Studies. In their critical assessment of research based on Urie Bronfenbrenner's theory of human development, Tudge and colleagues (2009) conclude that any such research should incorporate at least some aspects of each of the four defining properties. In their view, it is essential that such studies focus on proximal processes: for instance, by assessing how activities and interactions that are believed to be relevant for the developmental outcomes under study are part of children's everyday lives. To understand the role of the developing child within these proximal processes, they deem it necessary at least to assess the ways in which *demand* characteristics (for instance age) influenced their experiences, but preferably to examine the ways in which relevant *resource* characteristics (for instance language abilities) or *force* characteristics (for instance motivation) influenced the ways in which the children acted and interacted. Because proximal processes are influenced by the contexts in which they are situated, studies should at least evaluate the differential influence of two microsystems (for instance the home and classroom environments) or two macrosystems (working class vs middle class) on activities and interactions. As for the property of *time*, the study should be longitudinal in order to determine the effects of proximal processes on development over time and should take into account what is occurring at the current historical time in relation to these children. Although the Case studies of the EPPSE project were not necessarily set up as a study based on the bioecological model we do feel that the overall approach in research design, methods, instruments and analyses warrants regarding it as such.

As for the property of *time*, the requirement that the study should be longitudinal was easily met. We were very fortunate to have a wide range of high-quality longitudinal data available because the Case Studies are part of the longitudinal EPPSE study. As a result we were able to ground the partly retrospective qualitative interview data, with children, parents and in some cases teachers, in existing qualitative and quantitative EPPSE data about their lives, experiences and development from the age of 3 onwards. In fact, the first parent interviews when the children were 3 years of age asked questions about the children from their birth. At the time of the interviews the children were between the ages of 14 and 16 and attending secondary school.

The existing EPPSE data played a crucial role in the procedures we followed to obtain a systematic, purposeful sample of fifty children, their parents (and their teachers) from *two macrosystems*: working-class families and middle-class families. As the primary aim of our study was to understand the learning life-courses of children 'succeeding against the odds', we chose to include four different groups of learner life-course trajectories. These groups were selected on the basis of whether their educational attainment was as expected or not, given their socio-economic backgrounds.

Through qualitative interview data and through quantitative questionnaire data we were able to collect extensive information about *proximal processes* in the family microsystem, the classroom microsystem and peer groups; data was also collected about additional supportive microsystems, such as those providing religious, cultural, sports, music or drama classes, or social networks of significant others that contributed to children's learning and education. For instance, we assessed the presence of proximal processes in the family microsystem through the use of quantitative data about the (early) HLE. These data were collected through parent questionnaires when children were about 3, 6, 11 and 14 years of age.

In the questionnaires, parents indicated how often the child engaged in a wide range of activities, providing us with indications of micro- and mesotime. Over the years, the EPPSE project has developed HLE indexes for different age groups. Although the activities included in each of these indexes change as children mature, the indexes have in common that they provide a quantified measure of the amount of time children spend participating in activities that positively influence the development of their academic skills. Through the use of qualitative interviews with children and parents (and, in some cases, teachers) when children were between 14 and 16 years old, we were then able to investigate how these activities shaped everyday learning experiences, why parents facilitated these experiences and how children and parents thought these activities had influenced the child's learning over the years. Through the perceptions of the children and parents we were able to give meaning to their learning trajectories.

We also used these interviews to learn more about how *children's characteristics and behaviours* had influenced or were perceived to have influenced these experiences. During the interviews we tried, for instance, to find out about children's motivation for learning and about their perceptions of themselves as learners. These qualitative data about the person were substantiated by longitudinal quantitative data about, for instance, children's socio-emotional/behavioural development as assessed by teachers.

We will now proceed to describe four full cases, to exemplify the depth of the information from the Case Studies data and to provide the reader with a flavour of what our fifty children experienced during their learning life-course in one of the four trajectory groups we studied.

4   Cultural repertoires of childrearing across and within social classes

This chapter describes the four groups of participants. For each group we will use an extensive case-study example to describe the cultural repertoires and experiences that are typical in their learning life-courses.

Introduction

When we first met our fifty children and their families the children were between 3 and 4 years old. Many had just started attending a pre-school but some still spent their days at home, in the company of their mothers and sometimes their siblings. At this young age most of the children loved participating in the game-like (standardized) assessments we presented, to determine the levels of their early language and Numeracy skills. Some were talkative, others were shy, and several had a different home language and had not yet learned any English language skills. Over the years we have continued to monitor their academic and socio-emotional development. We learned about their likes and dislikes, their family lives and their school experiences, through the many questionnaires that they and their parents filled out, through their academic results on Key Stage assessments and through evaluations filled out by their teachers. Recently, we met with them in person. Some boys and girls still looked, moved and talked much like children. At 14, 15 or 16 years of age the hormone surge of adolescence had not yet, or only partially, kicked in. Others had grown into tall young men with deep voices and into lanky, fashionable young women who talked and moved in ways that often reminded us of their parents. Usually the children and parents quickly felt at ease once we started our interviews, and talked about their family, learning experiences, lives and thoughts with little reserve. Others needed time before they were willing or able to open up and some remained reserved or acutely self-conscious throughout our meetings, carefully weighing every word. Once children and parents started talking, they often found themselves surprised at how much they felt they wanted to say, and could say, about the topic of academic success and academic difficulties. As a result, each of the fifty Case Studies tells a unique story about the learning life-course of a child and the supporting role that people and institutions in their lives may or may not have played during their ongoing journey through the educational system.

The four groups of children included in this study were created by combining the academic achievement of the child with the socio-economic characteristics of the family. Within each separate group we sampled and studied, children have similar levels of academic achievement for English and Maths and their parents have similar levels of education, and jobs that are comparable with regard to social status and pay – or at least they had when the children were starting school. All children in the first two groups, as stated in the foregoing methodology chapter, come from similar low socio-economic status (SES) families. The difference between Groups 1 and 2 lies in the academic results of these children: the children in Group 1 are doing very well in school, succeeding academically in an unexpected way, while the children in Group 2 are achieving the predicted low academic results. Similarly the children in Groups 3 and 4 have their privileged socio-economic background in common, but while the children in Group 3 are struggling to keep up academically, the children in Group 4 are doing very well, as expected, both for English and Maths. In this chapter we will describe the circumstances and experiences of one child from each of the four groups in our study through the use of an extensive in-depth case study. We have selected these particular children because their lives and circumstances have many aspects in common with those of their peers in each particular group. Thus their unique lives provide a template for life in each specific group; it is clearly beyond the scope of any book to add such detail for fifty case-study children. We hope these case studies will bring each group to life, making clear to the reader what it means, and takes, for a child to develop within each of these four groups, and provides the kind of detail which adds flesh and blood to the otherwise skeletal structure of our study. We hope the detail is compelling and draws attention to the depth of our knowledge of each child, their family and the trajectory of their learning life-course. As mentioned before, all names are fictional.

Succeeding against the odds of disadvantage: Steven Peterson

Group 1: Low SES, Steven's attainment is above prediction given the characteristics of his background.

14-year-old Steven Peterson is one of our students from a more disadvantaged family background who are 'succeeding against the odds'. When we first started to follow Steven's development at age 3, his early language and Maths skills were as expected, close to the low average of the full sample of children from low-SES families in the study. The home learning environment (HLE) Steven experienced at the age of 3 was rated as low, with a limited frequency and range of the activities that stimulate early cognitive development. Although his skills, particularly for Maths, improved during his time in pre-school and reception, he did poorly in his Key Stage 1 assessments for English. Because of this he was placed in special tuition for a nine-week period. By the end of primary school his academic achievements for English and Maths significantly surpassed the results that were predicted for him. The pre-school that Steven had attended was rated by our study to be high in quality on the Early Childhood Environment Rating Scales (ECERS) and the academic effectiveness of his primary school was rated one standard deviation above the mean for English, and as average for Maths. When we met with him for the interview he had just sat his Key Stage 3 exams. His results for English ranked among the highest 20 per cent in the full Effective Pre-School, Primary and Secondary Education (EPPSE) sample and only 5 per cent of the EPPSE children had managed higher results for Maths.

Meet the Petersons

Carol Peterson is a small, wiry woman in her late thirties. During the interview she deliberates her words and carefully registers every verbal and non-verbal response you give. But she speaks about her life and that of her son with disarming honesty and seems to greatly enjoy analysing their history. At 14 Steven is slender like Carol, but stands at least a head taller than his mum. His long limbs appear beyond his control. Whenever he gets excited his voice shoots up a register. His eyes, mouth, ears and nose all seem too big for his head but they somehow come together well and create an interesting face. People who first meet Steven Peterson often find him a bit odd, and Steven just feels awkward and clumsy and bored around people he does not really know. Even Carol, who probably knows and loves him better than anyone else, says Steven has always been a bit odd. He will often lose himself in activities or topics he finds interesting to the point of obsession; he will come up with unusual projects like figuring out how to brew beer; he even decided to start his own religion, Stevenism, because he thought it would be nice to have something to believe in. According to others his incessant question-asking at times can be annoying and even inappropriate and he sometimes tends to forget the simplest things, like putting on his trainers before he walks out of the door. But according to Carol, Steven will never forget to give his mum a kiss goodbye, and when she comes home after a long working day he will make her a nice cup of tea and tell her to sit down and relax for a bit. And he will add up the groceries for her or calculate the utilities bills in his head, and his poor attempts at telling a joke will often make you laugh until you have tears streaming down your face. So despite his oddities it's hard not to like Steven once you get to know him – and, perhaps more importantly, once he gets to know you.

When we met with Steven for the interview he was visibly nervous. He kept hopping from foot to foot and fumbling with his hands, while his eyes kept darting around the room. Despite his nerves, he said, he had been looking forward to the interview all week. And we believed him, because this was the boy who, as a 10 year old, wrote a note on his questionnaire asking if we could please send him more papers to fill out because he really, really enjoyed working on them. We found Steven to be bright, sweet-natured and witty in a slightly awkward way. He talks about himself and his experiences with disarming honesty and enthusiasm. Steven never brags about his academic achievements in school, but he clearly feels happy about his accomplishments. He looks back on the difficulties he experienced at the beginning of his time in school with slight wonderment. He gratefully recognizes how certain people, such as his mum, his teacher in the special education class for English and his friend Ethan, have helped him to overcome his difficulties and even taught him to love learning.

Steven lives with his mum Carol and older sister Gemma near the last stop on one of the longest and oldest lines of the London Underground. Sometimes his mum's boyfriend Tim stays over but usually it's just the three of them. The long street on which they live has few trees. Identical, small semi-detached two-story houses line the street on both sides. Most of the little front gardens are paved and are used to park cars or bicycles or store rubbish bins. The Petersons' house is well-kept and sparkling clean. Steven enjoys spending time at home with his family, but nowadays he is quite often on his own after school and in the evenings. At evening time when Steven is home alone he likes to watch cartoons or play his guitar, or sometimes read a book. His sister Gemma is 16. She comes home after school and quickly takes care of her school work. As soon as she is done, she is out of the door to meet up with her friends. On Tuesdays and Thursdays, Steven and Gemma spend the evening with their father John. Most days Carol is at work and does not come home until tea time. Recently, she and Tim have started going out every now and then in the evenings. She no longer wants to take Steven and Gemma along like she did before. Sometimes they will still all go out for pizza or a film but his mum says that he is old enough to take care of himself now for an evening and that he needs to see that she has a life outside of her work, home and children.

When the family do get together at home, they spend most of their time in the kitchen. Like the rest of the house, the kitchen is spotless and cosy. Carol, Gemma and Steven usually have their breakfast and tea together at the kitchen table. At weekends when Tim stays over, breakfast sessions can take a long time as Steven and Tim attempt to solve the crossword in the Daily Mail together. Steven spends much of his time at home at his computer. He uses it for school work but spends most of his time, he says, on far more interesting things, like computer games or research for his experiments. His mum insists on having his computer set up in the kitchen so she can monitor the websites he browses and keep time. Usually she will shoo him away from the computer after an hour or two, or whenever he gets all worked up over losing a game. Steven saved up the money he makes with his paper round to buy the computer. When they set up the desk, Tim put up two shelves above it so Steven would have his books and computer software at hand. The books, DVDs and computer games are sorted alphabetically and Steven keeps their spines perfectly aligned. Steven uses his tiny bedroom at the top of the house to sleep and sometimes to read or work on his experiments. The walls are decorated with posters of characters from picture books his mum used to read with him when he was much younger. Clothes spill out of a cupboard and parts of a model rocket take up most of the limited floor space. A book by Richard Branson on entrepreneurship and a thoroughly cuddled stuffed monkey lie propped on his bed.

The family background of the Petersons

Five days a week Carol takes the Underground line that runs behind their house into central London to work. Like her parents before her, she works as a cleaner. Before she had children she used to work in hotels in the mornings and offices in the evenings. But now she works school hours at private residences. Her parents, she says, were old-fashioned Irish immigrants with a strong work ethos. As a little girl she would spend her school holidays working alongside her mum cleaning hotel rooms. To her parents, school and education were inconveniences that kept their children from starting work 'proper'. Her parents might not have thought much of it, but Carol absolutely loved going to school. She enjoyed being with her friends and learning something new every day. Best of all, she loved listening to the teacher's stories about History and geography. Even though Carol loved school and never missed a day, she struggled to keep up with English and Maths, right from the start. Perhaps, she says, because she was quiet, polite and happy to be there nobody at school took notice of her problems. Once she had fallen behind, teachers simply seemed to forget about her and let her be. All through her remaining years in school she would quietly sit at the back of the class and listen. Despite her difficulties with reading and spelling Carol loved books. When she was 13, she started to use the little money her parents allowed her to keep to buy books. As a little girl she only ever had one book of her own and now any book on any subject would do. As she started to read her books her literacy skills improved substantially, but by then she had fallen so far behind at school on most of the subjects that it was impossible to catch up with her class.

Despite her avid reading and obvious enjoyment of school, staying on to go to sixth form or college was never an option as far as her parents and teachers were concerned. She left secondary school without any qualifications and soon she was cleaning classrooms rather than sitting in them to listen and learn. A few years after she left school Carol met Steven's father John. John too had left school at 16. He had found a job as a postman and loved walking his daily routes through the city. Soon they got married and moved into a tiny one-bedroom flat on a large inner-city council estate. Carol quit her job once their daughter was born and stayed home with the children until they started primary school. Gemma was an easy, independent little girl and Carol loved spending her days looking after her. Despite the fact that they now only had John's income as a postal worker, Carol and John carefully saved up every penny they could spare and managed to buy their flat.

The early years of Steven Peterson

Two years later, Steven was born, and suddenly life became more complicated for Carol. Steven never slept for more than twenty minutes at a time. If Carol was not holding him he would cry and scream. Although Steven was up and running well before his first birthday, according to his mum, he seemed different from other children, awkward even, in many respects. He never babbled or tried to talk, he would just grunt or scream whenever he wanted something and, other than his sister, he did not care to be with children at all. By the time he was 2 years old Carol was exhausted and frustrated. John was off to work during the day and in the evenings he would spend most of his time reading History books or painting toy soldiers. Sometimes he would read a bedtime story to the children and at weekends they would all go out for walks as a family, but mostly it was up to Carol to deal with Steven and his constant crying. Nothing she did or said seemed to help Steven calm down. He was always demanding her attention, clinging to her, wanting to be picked up and to be held. She thought maybe that was just who he was, that he was a clingy child. Despite everything she felt that it was probably not something she was doing wrong that made him so difficult. After all, his older sister was the complete opposite. Gemma had slept through the night after just three months, she never cried much, she started to talk well before her second birthday and she had always been very independent.

Despite the screaming and clinging, Steven started playgroup when he turned two. Carol thought maybe it would be good for him to interact with other children. And she said she had needed to get him out of the tiny flat to burn off some energy. Although the playgroup offered Steven lots of interesting things to do and his cousins went there as well, things did not improve much. Typically, when Steven saw another child he would either slap or bite. At first, Carol would follow Steven around as he wandered through the room. She would try to stop him from hurting other children. At one point the other adults at the playgroup told her to just chill out and let the children work it out by themselves. So she did and he bit a child so badly that he drew blood. She tells us that she got so upset with him that she bit him back. He would not hurt other children after that but he still did not care for their company. The only child he did seem comfortable with was Oliver, a severely autistic boy. The two of them would sit side by side for hours, each lining up their trains or cars or blocks, incidentally communicating without words.

With Oliver as his friend, Steven was calm and even seemed happy. Sometimes Carol wondered if Steven's difficulties perhaps were similar to Oliver's autism. But she never dared to voice her concern to anyone. She was afraid that once he had a disorder label attached to him, his teachers would no longer feel the need to help him overcome his difficulties. She was afraid he would be labelled and end up sitting quietly at the back of the class, listening but not really participating. But Carol did look for help, searching for ways to get a handle on Steven's awkward and difficult behaviour. Time and time again she took him to health clinics and general practitioners. Nobody was able to explain to her what was wrong or what she could do to make life easier for all of them. Finally, when Steven was two and a half years old, his hearing was tested. He was asked to point out pictures of familiar objects on a sheet of paper, such as aeroplane, car and pen. Steven was happy to respond to the questions, but he did not get a single answer right. After additional testing they found that Steven could barely hear and that he was probably guessing at what people were saying to him. An operation restoring his hearing followed just before his third birthday. The day Carol and John brought Steven home from the hospital he stopped screaming, and he slept straight through the night.

After the operation Steven's speech slowly started to develop. His aggressive behaviour towards other children subsided with his increasing ability to communicate through words. His tantrums receded and he became less demanding towards his mum. Carol found that having clear and strict rules about acceptable behaviour, as well as having regular daily routines, helped him control his temper and kept his more obsessive behaviours at bay.

Every morning the whole family would sit down together for breakfast and afterwards Carol would walk Gemma and Steven to school. Steven now attended a nursery school, five mornings a week. Carol hoped he would improve his social skills by watching and interacting with the other children in pre-school class. The nursery also offered a lot more structure than the playgroup had, and Steven seemed to feel comfortable with these routines and with a good structure. The teachers at the nursery were lovely with Steven and encouraged him to participate in every activity available. One of the teachers would accompany the singing of nursery songs with her guitar playing. Steven loved the music and insisted on having a little guitar of his own. His teacher happily encouraged him to strum along as she played. Most days Steven would come home covered in paint or mud and excited stories about his adventures. But Steven was still often the odd one out in class. Other than the sessions with the guitar, Carol says he never really seemed to care for group activities. After nursery Steven would come home for a snack and then he would have time to play.

Now that he was not distressed or crying all the time, Carol reports that Steven was actually good company. He still loved being cuddled and held but he would also play by himself or let Carol play games with him. Steven loved counting games and anything involving numbers. So they counted the cars in the street, they counted the ducks in the pond, they counted the blocks they were stacking. When Carol first had Gemma it had not even occurred to her to play with her, let alone talk to her. She usually left it to Gemma to entertain herself as she took care of her household chores. She thought children would just start talking one day because they heard adults talk to each other. But then she watched her own sister with her baby and she was talking and singing to the baby non-stop and playing little games like peek-a-boo. Even though the baby could not yet speak, Carol noticed, you could tell she was enjoying it because she was laughing and moving enthusiastically. So that is what Carol started doing with Gemma and soon Gemma started singing and using little words as well.

As Gemma developed, Carol discovered that to young children anything and everything could be a fun game or an interesting lesson, even tedious chores like putting laundry in the machine or going grocery shopping. Given Steven's initial difficult behaviour, playing these games had seemed impossible, so instead she had started talking to him, describing everything they did or saw or felt, to fill his silence or stop his screaming. When Steven's speech initially started to develop after the operation he was still slow to speak, and Carol just continued talking for the two of them – until one day at a speech therapy session they showed her a video recording of herself and Steven playing together. As she watched the tape of the two of them stacking blocks, she realized that she was talking so much that she never gave him a chance to get a word in. The therapist suggested that maybe Steven had become a bit lazy with his speech. Why would he make the effort to talk if he had somebody who did all the talking for him? Afterwards Carol consciously stopped trying to fill up the silences with words and soon she noticed that Steven started to talk more and more.

If the weather was pleasant they would leave the flat and find a safe place for Steven to run around, or ride a bike or kick a ball. After Gemma came home from school the children would play together for hours, lining up their teddy bears to have tea parties or embark on adventures with imaginary friends. Gemma had quickly learned to read and she too would often pick up a book and read to Steven whenever she felt like it or he asked for it. And there were plenty of books to choose from, as their mum would browse every bookstore she passed, hunting for interesting children's books. When Steven got older and his difficulties with reading became apparent, Carol sometimes wondered if maybe always having someone around to read to him had made him lazy, like the therapist had suggested about what happened with his speech. But then she thought about how books had helped her when she was younger, and she strongly felt that children could never have enough books read to them, because, to her, reading seemed the basis of their education, the perfect way to get their minds going. And now that Steven had started talking you could tell that his mind was definitely very active. He just talked and talked and talked. He would tell elaborate stories about the adventures he had with his imaginary friend Boot. He would scribble on a page and would 'read' elaborate stories about knights and dragons to her. And he loved asking questions. Like his father he would get interested in a certain topic and he would keep asking you questions until he had learned everything you knew about the topic. At the end of each day the children would watch half an hour of children's television while Carol prepared tea. Carol and the children would always have their meal together at the table and tell each other about their day. Steven loved it when his dad was home for tea, but according to Carol, John was often out pursuing one of his hobbies. And then after tea it would be a bath, a yoghurt, a bedtime story in the bunk bed, and then off to sleep.

The primary school years of Steven Peterson

After his fifth birthday Steven started at a local primary school that was a bit unusual. They had open plan instead of closed-off classrooms and children of different age groups sat together in class. The atmosphere was very informal and friendly. Carol did sometimes worry about the amount of noise in the school whenever she dropped him off. Because of the open plan the shouts and calls of the many young children carried to every corner of the building. Sometimes she wondered how any of them could concentrate on their actual school work, but Gemma was doing fine, so Carol thought things could not possibly be that bad. At first Steven seemed to be fine. He settled in well and he even made two new friends who he could sit with in class and play with during break. He was enthusiastic about every new thing he learned in class. But after a few months things started to change. Despite his enjoyment and interest in learning Steven was finding it difficult to concentrate on the lessons. Every time he was supposed to listen to the teacher his mind wandered. He would try to do the work but he never seemed to get it right. When he wrote, letters would turn and appear on the page backwards and jumbled up. Carol soon noticed the difference in progress between her two children. Gemma was always getting good marks and had been reading independently ever since reception. Although Steven liked books and stories, it became clear to Carol that when he was reading he often guessed at words and sometimes simply made up text in his mind. He now even seemed to be having difficulties with his Maths in class, even though he was still always doing more and more complicated sums at home and loved playing number games.

Carol dutifully attended every parent–teacher conference and regularly tried to talk to the teachers about Steven. None of the teachers seemed worried about his lack of progress. Carol trusted their judgement because after all, as she said, they were the ones who had been educated about these things. Carol hoped things would be all right once Steven had had a bit more time to mature. Perhaps boys just developed at a different pace from girls. But just to be on the safe side Carol consulted her sister who seemed to know a lot about how children develop their reading skills. She suggested that Carol should buy Steven some extra work books and help him practise. Carol and Steven sat together after school solving Maths problems, reading aloud to each other, playing spelling games and practising phonetics. Steven enjoyed their time together but despite their hard work his skills did not improve noticeably. Carol thought that maybe this was her fault; that perhaps she was not helping him properly, because after all she had never really understood what the teachers were saying when she was younger.

Throughout his first years in primary school Steven struggled to keep up. As the lessons became more complicated, his behaviour deteriorated. Carol encouraged him to ask for help, but Steven found that when he was stuck he could not find the words to explain his difficulties. Now, when Steven did not know what to do, he would start cracking jokes, goofing around, distracting others. Instead of receiving extra help with his school work and behaviour Steven was spending more and more time sitting by himself away from the class, to prevent him from disrupting the lessons. To Carol's relief the teachers finally acknowledged that Steven was not doing well when he and several other boys in his class performed very poorly on their Key Stage 1 assessments at age 7. The headmistress swiftly set up a special education class for the young boys. For a period of nine weeks they spent their school days going back to the basics of reading, writing and Maths. To Steven the class was a relief. Before each lesson the teacher would take them out to the playground and set them loose to burn off some of their excessive energy. Afterwards Steven would find it much easier to sit down calmly and concentrate on the task at hand. Unlike most of his other teachers, he reports that this teacher was strict, but fair. She took their questions seriously and taught them to patiently trace back their steps to determine what it was they found difficult or confusing. She would talk about subjects that Steven previously had come to think of as boring in a way that made him curious and excited to learn more about the topic. When Steven returned to his regular class after nine weeks, his teachers and Carol were amazed by how much his work and attitude had improved. This early intervention had worked for him.

During his remaining years in primary school, Steven's academic performance kept improving steadily. The teachers no longer complained about his behaviour in class. Now that Steven understood the basic concepts of English and Maths he felt that he was much better equipped to learn the more advanced topics as well. He discovered that he was actually good at solving Maths problems and that he loved science experiments. As his grades improved, his confidence grew. He no longer hesitated to raise his finger in class, to participate in class discussions or to cooperate with others on groups projects. He found that he could ask his teacher or classmates for help now that he could actually explain what it was that he did not understand about a topic. At home Carol made sure he kept up with his school work and she tried to help him out when he got stuck. As Steven progressed through primary school she found it more and more difficult to provide practical help with his school work. Often she had difficulty understanding the questions herself and the Maths problems seemed particularly daunting to her. But she kept encouraging him and she made sure he had extra books to work from. At first Gemma could help Steven out but soon the roles reversed and Steven was helping Gemma.

John seemed to become less and less involved with family life as the children got older. Most evenings he would go out to club meetings about one of his hobbies or would spend his time with his collection of toy soldiers. Although John was usually at home when Gemma and Steven sat down to undertake their school work, he was seldom willing to help out. Only when the questions concerned History did he get involved, and insisted on dictating them the answers. Carol sometimes wondered if maybe Steven's interest in History and wars were his way of trying to be close with his dad. She wanted to encourage him to do things that he liked, not just things that his dad enjoyed. She started to bring home extra ironing work to do in the evenings and managed to set aside enough money for him to take up guitar lessons and tap dance classes. Steven enjoyed the lessons and discovered that he was good at dancing and music. He even performed a few times in front of an audience and Carol could see how this boosted his confidence. So when he got older and his interest started to dwindle, she strongly encouraged him to stick with it and told him he would be grateful for it later on.

At weekends and during holidays, the Petersons enjoyed going on little excursions together. As money was always tight they found ways to enjoy themselves without having to spend much. When the weather was nice they would go on long walks through the city, visiting historical sites and looking at statues of famous people. They would go to one of the parks for a picnic or to listen to a free concert or watch a play performed in the open air. And many of the city's free museums were just a short walk or bus ride away. The four of them would spend hours wandering the galleries, particularly on rainy days. Carol and Gemma preferred the ones with paintings in, while John and Steven could spend hours in the Imperial War Museum. Particularly, Carol felt these outings were something she could offer her children that would make them happy and help them learn. As a little girl she never went anywhere with her family except to clean hotels, and after the school holidays she would have to make up stories about outings and holidays to tell in class. She wanted her children to learn about the world, their country, its history and about other people, not just through books, as she had, but through actual experiences.

By the time Steven was 10 years old his parents had saved up enough money to move to the small semi-detached house on the outskirts of London. Steven quickly settled in at his new primary school. Carol chose the school because it was an old-fashioned community school, where staff and students and parents all knew each other. Unlike his previous school, this one had classrooms with single age groups, and all staff members were quite strict with the students. Steven's grades continued to improve and now his academic performance was at the top of his class. Unfortunately the relationship between Carol and John started to deteriorate quickly after the family moved. John moved out of the new house and at the time Steven started secondary school the divorce became final. The break-up between Steven's parents was messy and violent, and difficult on everyone. Carol had to take out several injunctions against John, and only after extensive mediation did things calm down. According to Carol, Steven was the only one in the family who managed to keep it together throughout the whole ordeal. Steven seemed able to make sense of things that were way beyond his years. 12 years old, he calmly stood up to his raging father. He told John not to make him and his sister choose between their parents, and to stop putting his mum down.

The secondary school years of Steven Peterson

These days Steven and his sister visit their father on Tuesdays and Thursdays after school. John always insists on taking them out for a meal and then bowling or the cinema afterwards. He ends up driving Steven and Gemma home at ten in the evening with next day's school work still needing to be taken care of. But Steven manages to deal with these circumstances just as he adjusted to the new environment of secondary school, despite the difficulties at home. Steven says he tried to keep school and everything that was happening at home separate because he did not want the problems to interfere with him doing so well in school. He just wanted to keep that up so he had something to feel good about. Now that he is in secondary school Steven enjoys most of the subjects and classes. He soon made a new best friend and they are both top students. He and Ethan are always in competition for the highest grade, even for something they find silly, like sports. After class he will excitedly call his mum on her mobile phone to tell her about his marks and he feels disappointed with himself on the few occasions when his marks are below

80 per cent. He says he just always wants to achieve the best he can even though his mum tells him it's fine to fail every now and then and that there is more to life than getting one hundred per cent scores on your Maths test! But the fact that he is doing really well in school makes him feel proud, and want to do even better. That does not mean he always has his nose stuck in his school books. He usually does a quick assessment of his school assignments and then just puts them off as long as possible. He tries to spend the least possible time on each assignment without it negatively affecting his marks. He usually ends up doing his work in a slightly frantic mode on Sunday evenings or in the mornings before he has to leave for school. It is not that he hates the work or anything, it is just that there are so many other interesting things he could be doing, such as playing computer games, watching cartoons or talking to Ethan. Things that might not be part of his formal education, as he puts it, but that can be useful nonetheless.

Steven says he can learn something from everything he does. He loves playing tactical simulation games on the computer, like the one in which he takes on the role of Julius Caesar and has to plan for battle. It's not just fun he says, it also teaches him about the history of warfare and about Roman customs, and he has even picked up some Latin when he set out to translate the game's motto 'Veni, vidi, vici'. And not too long ago he started reading books for fun, on top of his required reading for school. Although the house has always been filled with books, and his mum and even his sister used to read loads of stories to him when he was little, he never really enjoyed reading by himself before. But then when they first became friends he noticed how Ethan always carried a book with him. And Steven thinks Ethan knows loads of cool things about any subject you can imagine. So now Steven reads too, and their discussions are becoming even more interesting than before. He enjoys books about History and biographies of public figures he admires, but best of all he likes to read fantasy fiction books that transpose him to exciting new worlds. Steven says that reading helps his imagination and his concentration. It also helps his mind to relax, which then makes it easier for him to learn in class.

Teachers at secondary school see that at times Steven needs additional encouragement to come out of himself a bit, to become part of the group. So they actively encourage him to answer questions in class. They say that one of the best things about Steven is that he is always willing to try to come up with an answer. He often gets the answer right but even when he does not, the answer is usually plausible and highly creative. The tenacity he shows when trying to solve a problem, or trying to figure out how something works, often sparks the class into interesting discussions. And whenever teachers' words are met by blank stares in class, they will look at Steven. If he is still following their line of thought they feel reassured that what they are saying actually does make sense. According to his teachers Steven is among the brightest students in school and should have no problem whatsoever getting into a good university and obtaining an advanced degree, particularly because of the strong support his is receiving from home.

Steven Peterson's future

When he grows up Steven wants to be an investment banker. He likes money. He does not particularly care to spend it but he does enjoy having it. He keeps the money he makes with his paper round and beer sales in a wallet, notes sorted by value, the queen facing upwards. After he finishes his education and is making 'loads of money', he plans to take care of his parents. He knows that, to be an investment banker, he will have to continue to do well in school and go on for his A levels and a university degree after that. He says he wants to try to get into a good university. His dream would be to go to either Cambridge or Oxford. But his mum told him about the daughters of one of her employers she cleans for who went to Oxford and how, apparently, besides being bright, you need to be very sociable and do a lot of extra-curricular things. And although he enjoys things like drama and music, he does not think he will be able to compete with other students, particularly because he is not that sociable. Carol wants him to go on to university if that is what he wants, and will do everything she can to support him financially. She feels that, at this point in his life, her role is more to help him develop his social and practical skills than to look after him academically. If he wants to do well academically, he will do well. She feel that she as a parent and person has learned some important lessons from watching Steven struggle through his early years and trying to find the help and answers he and she both needed. She has learned to trust her own intuition and judgement, no longer to shy away from speaking up to authority figures, to critically assess their judgement and to take matters into her own hands if necessary. At this stage of their lives these are the lessons and skills she has to offer. So she works hard to instil them into her son – that, and to be happy with himself and with his home life. And it appears that he is.

Not succeeding against the odds of disadvantage: Tom White

Group 2: Low SES, Tom's attainment is low as predicted by his background characteristics.

At 15, Tom White is not doing well in school. His grades are well below average, his coursework incomplete or late, and he is regularly being sent home in the middle of a school day because his behaviour is considered 'out of order'. Tom is one of our children from a socio-economically disadvantaged family background who is academically performing poorly, according to prediction. When we started to follow Tom's development at age 3, his emerging academic skills appeared fine. While his early Maths skills were as expected, close to the average of the full sample of children from low-SES families in the study, his early language skills were similar to the average of the children from socio-economically more privileged families. The early learning environment Tom experienced at home at this time was rated as medium. Tom's early academic development appeared to benefit from attending a (pre-)school environment even though this pre-school was rated low in quality on the ECERS. By the end of Reception, his skills for English and Maths both ranked among the highest 30 per cent of the EPPSE sample, well above the average for his low-SES peers. But as he progressed through primary school and the school curriculum became less playful, his academic achievements started to falter. Even though his primary school was rated academically effective (within one standard deviation of the mean of all primary schools in the EPPSE sample), Tom did not appear to benefit from their efforts aimed at raising his achievements. At the end of primary school, Tom's academic performance met the low predictions made for him based on his early disadvantaged socio-economic position. This decline in academic performance continued as he progressed through secondary school. The results of his Key Stage 3 assessments for English and Maths at age 14 were below the mean of his SES group, and ranked among the lowest 30 per cent in the EPPSE sample.

Meet the White family

Tom is a lean, small boy with spiky blond hair, rosy cheeks and bright blue eyes. He looks younger than his 15 years. Mr and Mrs White are both in their late thirties. Mrs White answers most questions about the time when Tom was young, but when the topic turns to his experiences in secondary school Mr White firmly takes the lead. While his parents talk Tom listens attentively. You can tell he wants to put in a word every now and then by the way he sits on his hands and wriggles, but he manages to keep quiet while they talk. When Tom is interviewed his parents walk in and out of the room, listening in on bits of the conversation, but they leave the talking to Tom. It is clear that the family members feel comfortable talking to each other and in each others' presence. Mrs White and Tom both talk quite quickly. Mr White on the other hand takes his time to carefully pick his words and to formulate his sentences. When he gets worked up about a topic he tends to lose the thread of his story.

The White family lives in a corner house in the outskirts of a large city in the West Midlands of England. Their neighbourhood was developed in the 1980s, aiming to attract young families. Along the winding streets, repetitive rows, each with six similar terraced houses, alternate with green patches of trees, flowers or play areas. A shopping centre, primary school and secondary school are located centrally in the neighbourhood. Tom's parents moved into the house soon after they got married, twenty-one years ago. They say they have done well for themselves over the years. The little front garden serves to park the painstakingly polished luxury family car and a number of motorcycles. A few years ago Mr and Mrs White secured a mortgage for the house, but before that they rented it. Mr White spends much of his spare time keeping the outside of the house in perfect condition, while Mrs White takes pride in having a sparkling clean house. Recently Mr White added an extension with a new kitchen to the downstairs living area, taking up most of the back garden. The L-shaped living room is spacious and light. It is filled with large, creamy white settees and matching creamy white wall-to-wall carpeting. A large flat-screen television is mounted on the wall facing the settees. Framed pictures of the family members decorate the other walls of the room. The windowsills are lined with neatly potted flowering orchids. The dinner table is at the back of the room, looking out on what is left of the garden. The wall next to the table is lined by a large book case, filled with a few books and long precise rows of magazines on cars and motor racing. In between the rows of magazines, shiny models of sports cars are displayed. There are three bedrooms and a bathroom on the first floor and attic. When Tom was born his grandmother and cousin were living with them. A few years ago his grandmother passed away, and his cousin moved back in with his parents. These days it is usually just Tom and his parents. His sister Charlene left school three years ago when she was 15. She has a job in the city centre, and recently started attending college two days a week. She usually stays over at one of her friends' houses during the week, and comes home at weekends.

Mrs White left school at 16 after completing her exams. She worked at odd jobs for a few years but stopped when she became pregnant with Charlene. When Tom was little, his mum stayed home with him and his sister. When Tom started primary school she went back to work part-time as a care assistant at a facility for handicapped adults. After a few years, she felt Tom and Charlene needed less of her time, and she decided to go to college for further qualifications. Now she works as a medical receptionist for twenty hours a week. By returning to study, Mrs White felt that she was setting a good example for her children. She always loved school and learning, but she feels she was never encouraged to take her education seriously as a child. She was one of the younger ones of a family of ten children and her father passed away when she was little. Her mother could simply not find the time or energy to be involved with her schooling. Mr White left school at 15 without obtaining any qualifications. He always found it difficult to keep up with the class, particularly with English. He too came from a large, fatherless family and none of his older siblings or family members seemed to notice how much he was struggling with his school work. For a while he received extra tuition in school. He felt embarrassed at having to sit in a separate class with much younger children and started truanting from class. Then he became ill with tuberculosis, and was in and out of hospitals for several years. Once he returned to school he had fallen behind so much that he found it impossible to catch up. He simply gave up on learning and instead developed numerous strategies to avoid anything related to literacy. Somehow none of the teachers caught on to the fact that he had not learned to read or write properly.

Mr White's greatest fear has been that his children would not learn to read and write. He can now manage short texts such as television listings, but Tom usually reads the interesting articles in the car magazines out loud to him. As for writing, he says he just does not bother with that any more. But he is good at Maths, so within their household he deals with anything related to numbers, and Mrs White takes care of anything involving letters. When Tom was younger Mr White worked as an industrial window cleaner. When his wife decided to continue her education he opted to try his hand at work-based vocational training. Despite his limited literacy skills, he managed to gain a number of qualifications, and now works as an industrial machine driver. Mr White has always worked long hours, but has always felt that it was important to make time for his family. According to Mr White, a man needs money to provide for everything his family needs and wants, but if he decides to put children into the world he also needs to make time for them. What with Mrs White going back to work, and both of them moving up several pay grades because of their additional qualifications, the family is now far better off financially than at the time Tom started participating in the EPPSE Project.

The early years of Tom White

Tom was a happy, chubby baby who developed into a happy, chubby little boy. Other than the odd asthma attack he was hardly ever ill, and he crossed each of the early years developmental milestones without a glitch. His language development always amazed Mrs White. He could hold a proper conversation at two, and the cheeky things he said often made people laugh. When he first started talking she did use flashcards for words and numbers with him because she wanted him to be more advanced, but he never really seemed to enjoy them and she soon gave up on that. At home Mrs White and his Nan were around to read him stories, sing him songs, draw pictures or play games with him. He enjoyed these activities, but just for a few minutes at a time, and only on rainy days. The only thing that kept him sitting still indoors for more than a few minutes at a time was the television. What he enjoyed above everything else was being outside. He loved riding his tricycle, playing rough-and-tumble games with his sister and cousin, kicking a ball around with other little boys who lived in the houses close by or 'just running around for hours at end and getting into mischief'. When he was little he was clumsy. He would fall over fresh air, as his mother put it, but would get up with a grin and just keep on running. After a few years you could really tell that always being out and about paid off: he became pretty good at any sport he tried, and his body changed from chubby to lean.

A few months before his third birthday he started at the same play-group his sister had attended, just for two mornings a week. Mrs White heard from other young mothers that playgroup was something that helped children to learn to mix with other children and that it stimulated their development. She felt that these were important skills for her children to learn. She chose the playgroup closest to home because it was convenient, and if they attended this playgroup her children could automatically get a place in the infant and junior school across the street from their home. Mrs White felt the staff at playgroup were very profes-sional; they were calm, organized and friendly. All the staff loved Tom, and he immediately made friends with the other children in his group. At playgroup Tom particularly enjoyed activities that he was not used to doing at home, like painting, or playing with water and sand, or doing group activities with other children and performing in little plays. His attention span for these indoor activities increased somewhat, but he still enjoyed being out and about most of all.

The primary school years of Tom White

After his experiences in playgroup the social side of the transition to Infant school posed no problem for Tom. He loved going to the 'big' school because this meant that he got to see his friends every day. What he did not like so much and found difficult to do was to sit down quietly and listen to the teacher or to other children talking. At home he was used to talking whenever he liked and about whatever he liked. And he definitely liked running around and physical activity better than sitting down. The teachers often had to remind him to sit still and pay attention. It took a while, but once he learned the 'do's' and 'don'ts' of the reception classroom he enjoyed participating in the lessons more, and his early literacy and numeracy skills improved notably.

As he progressed through the early years of primary school and the time came to really get serious about reading and writing, Tom's academic progress slowly started slipping. By the time Tom sat his Key Stage 1 assessments in Year 2, he was no longer one of the top students, but rather somewhere in the middle. Mr White fretted that Tom would end up like him, struggling with his schoolwork and unable to read and write properly. So during the following year of primary school, Tom and his parents would sit down at the kitchen table once a week for an hour or so and the television would even be switched off. Mr White would help Tom with his Maths and Mrs White would help him with his English. Tom would read a page out loud and his mum would correct his mistakes as he went along. She would read over his writing and spelling assignments and correct mistakes there as well. Although she usually knew the correct way to say or spell a word, she could not really explain rules about grammar or spelling to Tom. At the end of the year Tom mastered the basics of reading and writing and his parents no longer felt they really needed to worry about his academic performance. Soon the homework routine started to slip and after a while it was abandoned altogether. Rather than stay indoors and take care of homework, the family would go out after school and at weekends to parks, to ride bikes, kick around a ball or just for a stroll with the dog. Both Charlene and Tom were encouraged to take up any sport they liked. Their father firmly believed that if their body was healthy, their mind would be too.

During the primary school years Tom had private tuition for swimming, tap dancing and kick-boxing. Mr and Mrs White both felt that competing at individual sports such as kick-boxing would help Tom toughen up and develop the kind of mentality and self-discipline that would help him to move ahead in the world. Unlike his academic skills, the skills he learned through practising and competing in sports were a part of his education that they could provide for. Tom did really well with any sport he took up, winning medals and earning certificates. But after a while he would lose interest and would want to move on to something new. His father was always there to cheer him on and encourage him. He was disappointed when Tom gave up on a sport in which he was successful, but he did not see how he as a parent could do anything about that. To him Tom's loss of interest was just something that naturally happened as children got older.

Although Tom's reading skills were sufficient to keep up with the lessons and maintain average grades, he needed and received some additional tuition from teachers and teachers' assistants all through primary school for spelling. By the end of primary school when Tom sat his Key Stage 2 exams, his results approached the relatively low average level of children from socio-economically disadvantaged homes. In class the problem with Tom was not that he did not understand the lessons or instructions, but that he was simply not interested in paying attention and learning. There was always something more exciting to see or talk about with one of his friends. If he did get around to doing some work in class, he simply rushed through it in order to have time left for chatting. It came to the point that his incessant chatting was not just interfering with his own learning but with the learning of his classmates as well. Teachers tried to get him to stop talking time and time again. They moved him to the back of the class away from the other children; they moved him to the front, right at the teacher's table, but nothing seemed to stop the words from spilling out of his mouth. The things he said were often very funny, even if he could be a bit cheeky, and he would come up with the most amazing arguments as to why he could not possibly put off telling his friends a particular story. In the end nobody ever really stayed cross with Tom for long.

During the final years of primary school the amount of homework kept increasing. Tom found it more and more difficult to complete the assignments by himself once he got home. His parents felt they were unable to help him with his homework because the school curriculum seemed completely different from what they had learned, and as they said, they had forgotten most of that anyway. And while his sister had once been a source of help, she was now well on her way to dropping out of school. Tom decided that after spending six hours in school he was more than entitled to have some time off, so he stopped doing his homework altogether. Besides, he often had sports training to attend to, so by the time he got home he was frequently very tired and ready to slump down in front of the television. Teachers talked to Tom and to his parents about his attitude and lack of motivation for school work. They tried to convince them that his constant need to chat and his refusal to do his homework were negatively affecting all his school subjects and that he would have to suffer the consequences once he went to secondary school.

After meeting with his teachers, Tom's parents decided that even though they felt unable to help him with the content of his homework, they could try to see to it that he had done his homework. First, they tried bribing him with sweets and promises of family outings, but this had little effect. Then for a few weeks, he was grounded every time they got word that he had neglected his work. He would not be allowed to go out with his friends, his treasured Xbox would be locked away, and instead of watching television with the family he was to stay up in his room until he had taken care of his homework. But Tom soon discovered that if he spent ten minutes fiddling about with his books in his room after tea, he could go to his parents and say he was sorry and, in no time, there they would be watching television together. To Mr and Mrs White, going to battle with Tom about his homework every evening seemed fruitless. They felt they could talk until they were 'blue in the face', but in the end if he did not want to do it, then there really was nothing they could do about it. Some children are just like that, they explained: head-strong. And although they would never dare say this to Tom's teachers, they were somewhat proud, and as they put it 'quite chuffed', that their Tom could hold out against all the pressure from school and teachers.

So in the end Mr and Mrs White gave in to Tom. After all, they reasoned, if the teachers felt they needed to give him homework to do then it really was up to the teachers to make sure that Tom did it, not to them as parents. At school his teachers decided Tom would have to stay in during break time to complete his assignments for the following day. Tom figured that it was easier to give in to the teachers than argue with them and get detention after school as well. So now he would rush through his work at top speed during break time. He would skip any task that required a second thought and did not bother to check his work for mistakes. His grades did not improve but now at least, as he put it, the teachers stopped bothering him about not handing in his homework.

The secondary school years of Tom White

As the teachers had predicted, the change from primary school to second-ary school proved very difficult for Tom. Although the new school was located right next to his old primary school and just across the street from his home, he might as well have entered a new universe. All of a sudden he found that his position was no longer among the big and popular boys, but that he was part of the unknown masses that everybody looked down at or ignored. Having neglected his school work for so many years, Tom was unpleasantly surprised by the amount of subjects, tests and coursework that came his way. The sloppy work, chatting and cheekiness that he had 'got away with' at primary school, caught up with him in his first months of secondary school and soon earned him the reputation of being a troublemaker. To Tom and his parents, the teachers just seemed much stricter than they had been used to, and according to them that is what lies at the root of Tom's troubles with school. If Tom gets along with a teacher, he will be doing fine in the subject, for instance with auto mechanics and physical education. But if the teacher is unfair to him, he will not stand down without a fight. So now they find that he is spending more time in detention, or suspended, than in class. And to them that just seems unfair and inappropriate as well. The teachers, and particularly the head of school, seem to think they are 'running a military boot camp', instead of a secondary school. If teachers tell Tom he has not done his work properly and he talks back as he has been accustomed to, he finds himself in detention regularly. If he forgets to bring in his coursework, his school books, or even his pen, as happens almost on a daily basis, he finds himself sent home. If he chats with his friends he gets detention; if he gets in a fight he gets detention. And if he tells them he is not doing his work because he does not understand what he should be doing, they tell him he is lazy, and off to detention he goes. So ever since Tom started secondary school Mr White finds himself being called into the Principal's office at least once a week. He is not happy about that at all. To Mr White it seems that if they want to run a tight ship they need to get on with it but stop bothering him about it, and they need to stop sending out mixed messages. On some days Tom will be sent home for something and that same day they might receive a recommendation through the mail, praising Tom for his good work in a particular class. That just seems all wrong and confusing to Mr White. He feels angry and frustrated on behalf of his son, but he also feels angry and frustrated because he feels it is not his place as a parent to set the Principal or Tom's teachers straight.

But at home things are fine, according to Tom's parents. At weekends Tom and his parents visit relatives and attend motoring events or bike races together. During the week they spend their evenings watching television. When Tom and Charlene were little the family would often watch nature documentaries together and children's programmes, but as they got older their interests changed. These days Tom and Mr White refuse to miss out on any programme about cars, motorbikes and racing. Charlene and Mrs White need their daily doses of what they call 'soapies'. One of the things they all take an interest in is watching the news. Mr White holds strong opinions about any topic that will come along and enjoys voicing them.

The future for Tom White

For Tom, home and school are more and more becoming two separate worlds. He and his parents feel that at school he is wrongfully labelled a troublemaker with poor grades, who is not likely to amount to much. But at home and with his family Tom is perceived as one of the 'good lads'. His grades and behaviour in class have always been pretty much the same as those of his cousins and friends, and according to his parents none of their parents ever seemed overly worried. Unlike most of his friends, his cousins, his older relatives and his sister, Tom has not yet dropped out of school without any qualifications. He likes sports and does not get drunk or high at weekends. Although he gets into trouble at school, he has never been in any real trouble with the police. And, even more importantly, Tom is one of those boys who actually enjoys spending time with his family. Family life is what really matters. His eagerness to chat, that has got him into so much trouble at school, has never been a problem within the family, but rather a source of pleasure and pride. To his family and friends Tom is one of those boys that is funny and cheeky and makes you 'laugh until your stomach hurts'. According to his parents a boy who can hold an argument like Tom does must have a good head on him. The problem is that the teachers just don't seem to understand that some people are naturally chatty like that, like Tom – and his mother for that matter. They simply cannot prevent themselves from talking all the time, and there is really nothing anyone can do about it. Ever since they were little, Tom and Charlene have been encouraged to ask any question that popped into their mind. As far as Mr and Mrs White are concerned their children are entitled to speak their mind. The only limitation to speaking their mind is that they need to be respectful to their elders, particularly family and relatives. This lesson has been drummed into them as long as they can remember during the many family get-togethers at weekends and holidays. At the homes of aunts and uncles where the families meet up, children are allowed to participate in adult conversations, but they do better to quickly discover and respect the boundaries of what is permissible, or suffer the consequences. When he was younger Tom preferred to go roaming about with his countless cousins, while the adults sat around chatting, eating and drinking until late in the evenings. But now that he is more mature he enjoys being in the company of his adult relatives, chipping in to the conversation and holding his own.

As for him no longer doing that well in school, his parents feel that 'well that is just the way things go sometimes'. 'Not everybody is cut out for academics.' But then, his parents argue, not everybody can be good at sports and mechanics – and Tom is. As long as Tom will be able to go to a vocational college after secondary school and train for a proper profession that will help him to find a secure job, everything will be fine. Mr and Mrs White would be over the moon if their son became a police officer. In their view, someone as sociable as Tom is just what the police force needs. Tom says the thing he likes best about policing is that you can 'drive a car real fast without getting into trouble'. If they would just back off from Tom for a bit at school, he would be fine. So although Mr White regularly promises the Principal that he will deal with Tom at home, the truth of the matter is that when they talk about school Mr White rarely finds himself not siding with his son. He tells Tom to knuckle down, just hang in there and try not to let himself get worked up over the injustices that he faces at school. Just a few more years and then Tom is free to do as he pleases.

Failing to meet the high expectations of privileged circumstances: Marcy Stewart

Group 3: High SES, low attainment, 'performing against the odds' given Marcy's background characteristics.

15-year-old Marcy Stewart is one of our children from a more privileged family background who is not doing as well as predicted in her education. Although her attainment for Maths and English has always been close to or at the national average, her national assessment results have fallen short compared to those of her peers from similar backgrounds. Even though the learning environment Marcy experienced early on in life at home and in Nursery were high in quality, her early Numeracy skills were below the twentieth percentile and her early Literacy skills were comparable to the average ranking of children from less well-off backgrounds (fortieth percentile). By the time she started Reception her attainment levels had improved to the average level of her socio-economic peer group (sixtieth percentile) but when she had her first Key Stage assessments, at age 7, her rankings for English and Maths were again down to the average of her less privileged peers. Although the academic effectiveness of her primary school was within one standard deviation of the mean for English and even a standard deviation above the mean for Maths, her attainment levels at the Key Stage 2 national assessments at age 11 ranked just around the thirtieth percentile of the full EPPSE sample. At age 14 she again managed the nationally expected levels on her Key Stage assessments, but lagged behind her peers from homes with similar SES. Marcy and her parents were happy with these results and now feel fairly confident that she will probably manage to do well in her GCSEs next year.

Meet the Stewart family

The Stewart family lives in a semi-detached Edwardian house in a hilly suburban area of Greater London. The wide streets are filled with similar houses, each with a small front garden that continues along the side of the house and sprawls out around the back. Most of the front gardens are used to park one or two cars. At least six of the houses in their street have recently been sold and are now being thoroughly renovated by new owners. The Stewart house sits across from a little park with a pond and a playground. Marcy, her younger brother Daniel and their parents Lucinda and Edward share their house with six pedigree cats. In the living room at the front of the house two comfortable floral printed sofas are arranged around the large television. A large Scottish flag and a banner with the logo of the Scottish national soccer team are prominently displayed on the wall above the television. The remaining walls are lined with bookcases and small shelves. Everywhere you look there are stacks of books, magazines and little knick-knacks. Besides dozens of children's books there are hundreds of contemporary and classical novels. The small computer desk in one of the corners is covered with stacks of paper, more magazines and school books. Framed family photos, travel souvenirs and drawings and little pieces of artwork made by the children decorate any remaining shelf space. The cats are sprawled out across the top shelves of the bookcases and between the plants in the window sill. Every now and then one will jump up or down a shelf to find a more comfortable place to sleep, or wander off into the kitchen for a bite to eat. The house and the furniture are in good condition but everything is covered in cats' hairs. Facing the back garden are a spacious, light kitchen with a dining area and a separate office room. Marcy's mother Lucinda usually works from home at least three days a week. There are three large bedrooms and two bathrooms on the first and second floor of the house. Marcy's room is lined with shelves filled with sports trophies and prize ribbons. A large number of framed certificates testify to her accomplishments in a range of extra-curricular activities. A poster of the Scottish national soccer team decorates the wall above her bed. There are stacks of sports and fashion magazines everywhere. Aside from a few children's books, her course books for school are the only books in the room. Her desk with her computer is positioned in front of the window and gives her a view of the pond and playground.

Father Edward grew up in Scotland and came to England because he thought he would have a better chance of finding a job after completing his A levels at an esteemed private school. He soon found a job in business sales with a large corporation and married Lucinda. For the first ten years of their marriage he put in so many hours that Lucinda hardly ever saw him. After they had Marcy, Edward worked his way up to the managerial level. He changed jobs to a smaller business firm and found more time to spend with his young family. Despite having lived in England for the better part of his life, Edward sees himself as a Scottish nationalist. Marcy and Daniel have spent most of their holidays up in Scotland visiting their relatives, and are proud of their Scottish heritage. Lucinda grew up in England but has an Irish mother. Both her parents worked as school teachers. She had always done very well academically. She got admitted to a good grammar school and was heading straight for university when she decided she was fed up with what she perceived to be her father's relentless pushiness and suffocating aspirations. She left school before completing her A-levels. It was not until she was well into her twenties, working as a junior civil servant, married with a young child and a second one on the way, that she went back to study again for her A-levels. After she had successfully completed these, her employers paid for her to go to university where she earned degrees in English and History. She never stopped working when she had her children. When the children were little she worked three days a week but she went back to working full-time as soon as they were in the higher years of primary school. Marcy and Daniel both attended a nursery from when they were three months old. Over the years Lucinda steadily worked her way up the career ladder as a civil servant. These days she manages a large regional department and has enough seniority to work from home three days a week.

Marcy is a pretty, slim and mature-looking girl. She has long dark brown hair and large, bright blue eyes. She describes herself as bubbly and sociable. Her mother is a tall, large woman with striking features. They each stay in the room while the other is being interviewed. They treat each other as equals, rather than as a parent and child and seem used to talking in each others' presence. Most of the time when one of them is being interviewed the other stays quiet and listens intently. At times Marcy is visibly irritated by things her mother says and Lucinda seems agitated by her daughter's dismissive attitude towards her. They start rolling their eyes and object to what is being said. Twice these interruptions turn to fierce bickering. The atmosphere becomes tense and they verbally lash out at each other. Eventually they back off without resolving their disagreement. Lucinda says she often feels tired of all the bickering that goes on in the house. Marcy is chatty and boisterous with most people but at home with Lucinda she is often moody and argumentative. Marcy admits that pretty much anything her mother says puts her off and that she really only listens to her father. Lucinda says she hopes it is just a phase, that eventually they will find a way to be close again, like they were when Marcy was little, but Marcy just rolls her eyes.

The early years of Marcy Stewart

Before Marcy started primary school, life just seemed so much easier. Her mum had found her a wonderful local nursery that she attended three days a week. Until she turned two Marcy had a one-to-one carer, a sweet lady who cuddled her and comforted her and engaged with her in little games. When she moved on to a slightly older age group, Marcy loved playing with her friends and enjoyed the broad range of activities they were given. The staff at the nursery started introducing the children to letters and numbers from an early age through games and songs. When Lucinda was at home with her they would spend their days baking cookies, having tea parties, reading storybooks, going out for walks and feeding the ducks in the pond. Once Marcy started talking she hardly ever stopped to catch her breath. Lucinda loved listening to her talk about everything she saw and did. They would watch children's programmes on the BBC and think of new adventures for the characters in the shows. Lucinda observed how her nephew got hooked on American cartoons that were filled with fighting and poor language and vowed to keep her children away from these as long as possible. But they loved Disney films with songs and happy endings, and watched these cuddled up on the sofa whenever the weather stopped them from going out. They would sing songs together, making up new words to familiar melodies. When Edward was home from work he would take Marcy out. He started taking her swimming when she was just a baby and by the time she was 4 she was an accomplished swimmer and joined a swimming club. He also taught her to play soccer and to ride a bike.

The primary school years of Marcy Stewart

When Marcy started Reception everything seemed to be going very well. According to her mother, because of her experience with nursery school she never worried about being away from her mum like some of the other children. She was used to making new friends and looking out for herself. She was a confident, bubbly little girl who enjoyed everything about pre-school. She had no problem keeping up with the early academic activities at school, but she enjoyed physical games, performing in little drama productions and going on outings much more than sitting behind a desk working on her spelling and reading. As the emphasis of the curriculum gradually shifted from play to learning she enjoyed participating in class discussions and eagerly held up her hand to answer the teacher's questions. She especially liked the competitive number games they played during Maths lessons and usually managed to solve the little sums after a few tries.

According to her mum and Marcy, she ceased to enjoy her lessons in reading and spelling as time passed. She tried and tried but somehow every time she attempted to read or write a sentence the letters of the words became all jumbled. Marcy felt embarrassed and instead of asking for help she developed strategies to avoid being caught out struggling. Whenever she was asked to read out something she had written she would just make up sentences in her mind as she went along. Whenever she had to read from a book she found an excuse not to have to do it. Unfortunately Marcy's class teacher was away sick a lot and there was a succession of supply teachers who were easily taken in by Marcy's avoidance strategies. Because she was articulate and well behaved during class and hardly ever gave any indication that she was experiencing these difficulties, none of the adults around her seemed to realize the extent of her problems. But Marcy was acutely self-conscious about failing to keep up with her classmates, and her confidence diminished with every spelling and reading session. It was not until her poor Key Stage 1 assessments at the end of Year 2 that the school realized she was experiencing serious difficulties.

Once Marcy's problems with reading and spelling were formally acknowledged, the school stepped up with remedial classes. But Marcy hated being taken out from her regular lessons. She felt singled out and was afraid the other children in her class would tease her. So she sat through her remedial lessons reluctantly and achieved the new targets that were set in accordance with her abilities under sufferance rather than because she wanted to. Even though none of the children in her class ever made fun of her difficulties, Marcy still felt like a failure. According to her mother the standards in her year group were very high, and even if she had been an average reader she would still have been at the lower end of her class. At home her parents too noticed that something had changed. When she was little Marcy would eagerly approach the stacks of books she received for her birthday and Christmas, but as they changed from picture books to proper reading books they were simply discarded after a first quick glance. Once they became aware that Marcy struggled with her reading and that she felt very insecure about it her parents hoped to encourage her by taking time to read with her every day. At first these reading sessions seemed to help but soon they inevitably ended with Marcy shouting that she would never be able get the hang of it and bursting into tears.

As a result of her struggles with reading and spelling Marcy lost interest in much of the academic aspect of school. Instead she more and more focused her attention, abilities and ambitions on sports, drama and music. Edward encouraged her to be as active and competitive as possible. Whenever he could, their father would take Marcy and Daniel out camping. Even when they were very young they would go for walks through the woods, moors and mountains and Marcy soon joined the Brownies and later the Rangers. When it turned out that Marcy was a talented swimmer, Edward kept a close eye on her training schedules. He attended her practice sessions whenever he could and cheered her on at every match. As her room started to fill up with trophies and prize ribbons her self-confidence returned. Now she no longer minded going to school so much, not because she felt better about her school work but because her increased self-confidence made her happy to be around her friends again. Lucinda, too, encouraged Marcy to take up as many extra-curricular activities as she wanted because she could see how they helped to restore Marcy's self-confidence. Lucinda felt that by participating in a range of activities her daughter would develop a more rounded view of the world, instead of the more narrow outlook that would come from primarily focusing on academic subjects. As far as she was concerned there were other things in life apart from school that were equally important for her daughter's development. As a family, the Stewarts tried to spend their time doing things they all enjoyed. During their holidays they travelled to their relatives in Scotland, went on hikes, visited museums or historical sites and attended sports events. At weekends they would go shopping, have dinner at a restaurant and go and see a film at the cinema. On the few week nights that were not taken up by sports practice they would play board games or watch television together.

Marcy was reaching most of the lower targets set for her in school. She would complete a piece of work by herself if she could but as soon as she found that she did not understand a task she would set it aside without even trying. Because she never caused any real problems and was doing so well with her sports everybody seemed happy with the way things were. The only one who at times tried to encourage Marcy to perhaps put in a bit more effort was Lucinda. But whenever she tried to help Marcy with her school work or even just tried to talk to her about what she found difficult, things soon turned into discord. Marcy immediately felt pressured by her mother and insisted that Lucinda did not understand a thing about her school work. She would end up screaming at her mother and would turn to her father for support. At times she would accept Edward's help with her school work but he often felt as if she really did not need to spend as much time on it as her mother insisted. So often they would end up going out to do something nice, rather than sitting at the kitchen table trying to complete her school work.

During her final year in primary school Marcy at last had a class teacher who managed to help her improve her reading and spelling skills to the required national level on the Key Stage 2 assessments and helped her to restore some of her faded academic confidence. Over the years Marcy had come to approach any academic problem by simply giving up and doing nothing. Unlike the teachers she had had before, this one would not put up with such behaviour. He ran drama groups and encouraged her to communicate in other ways than through writing; to express herself through speech and movement. In class, he set her up with a spelling buddy, someone she could ask to look over her work before she handed it in. And he told her he did not care about her misspellings; that in fact he knew she had it in her to do well. A few months into Year 6, Marcy found it easier to spell, and whenever she did make a mistake she no longer felt embarrassed about it. When Marcy managed to achieve the national pass standard for English and Maths on her Key Stage 2 national assessment at the end of her time in primary school, Marcy and her parents were all more than happy with her results.

The secondary school years of Marcy Stewart

Marcy went to a local secondary school with more confidence than her family had ever felt possible. Marcy was placed in the middle sets and once she had adapted to the substantial increase in the amount of coursework and revision she had to do every week, Marcy managed to keep up with her peers in class. Much against the will of her parents she did decide to give up competitive swimming. She simply felt she had too little time and energy both to take care of her school work and to practise her swimming seriously and compete several evenings each week. Although she managed to achieve the targets that were set for her in most classes, her interest in the more academic subjects was usually still minimal. Instead, she chose to put more time towards Drama, both in and after school. Now that sports were no longer the focus of her life, it started to revolve around her girl friends who shared her interest in the performing arts. At times this caused problems, both in school and at home. At school she would get warnings because she would not stop chatting in class and because she put little effort towards subjects that were mandatory but that she did not enjoy, or for subjects that were taught by teachers that she did not care for. She was quick to form a negative opinion about her new teachers and once she decided she did not like someone she was hard to convince otherwise. At home her father was disappointed in her waning interest in sports, and her mother felt frustrated by her attitude towards her academic subjects. But while she kept a good rapport with her father by attending sports matches together and going for hikes at weekends, her relationship with her mother deteriorated. Marcy resented any effort Lucinda made to help her with her school work and even when they did something nice together, like going shopping for clothes, Marcy's attitude towards her mother was often dismissive.

The future for Marcy Stewart

Now that Marcy is preparing for her GCSEs she says that she realizes that she needs to become more serious with her school work. Marcy's attainment on her Key Stage 3 assessments at the end of Year 9 was on target for English, but her results for Maths and Science were not at the predicted level. Marcy felt that the difference between the subjects had been that she really liked her English teacher but did not feel so positively about her Science and Maths teachers, and therefore had worked harder for her English classes. She was placed in the lowest set for Science as a result, and was shocked by the lack of interest and the negative attitude of most of her peers in this class. Marcy's response to this was to stop attending the class altogether. It was not until Lucinda intervened on her behalf and negotiated for her to be moved up again to the middle set if she could pass a test, that Marcy started to seriously study for the subject. Marcy managed the test and was moved up again to the middle set. Marcy acknowledges that she would not have done so well if it had not been for her mother and this experience has had a somewhat positive effect on their relationship. Even though Marcy is still easily irritated by things her mother does or says, school is no longer a no-go area in their talks. Lucinda says she now primarily tries to help Marcy by talking to her about her future. She feels very strongly that Marcy can make things a lot easier for herself in life if her daughter decides to continue with her education, rather than take time off to work for a few years like she herself did. She encourages her daughter to focus on her drama and singing classes, because she feels Marcy is very talented and will have a good chance of finding a career in the performing arts. She does expect Marcy to go on to study at university, but is careful not to mention this too often. She is afraid that if she does, Marcy might decide not to attend, not because she does not want to go to university like her friends but as rebellion against Lucinda. Marcy says she has not decided yet, that the chances of her going to university are fifty-fifty. And yes, she would like a career in performing arts but maybe she will choose to go into catering and become a chef. When Lucinda hears her daughter say this, she looks mortified at the prospect, but perhaps wisely, keeps a quiet demeanour.

Doing well as expected: Imogene Woods

Group 4: High SES, predicted attainment, performing as expected, given Imogene's background characteristics.

At 14 Imogene Woods is one of the top students in her class, her school and of the EPPSE sample as well. In fact, ever since we started following Imogene's academic development she has been among the highest ranking 20 per cent for English and Maths, usually even among the ninetieth percentile. Imogene is one of our children who comes from a socio-economically privileged family background. The learning environment she experienced early on in life at home was high in quality. Initially she attended a playgroup three mornings a week that was rated no more than medium on the ECERS quality scale. As soon as she turned 3 she transferred to a Nursery class for the full five-session week. This nursery class not only had a very good reputation among the more highly educated parents in the neighbourhood; it was also connected to one of the best primary schools in the area. Towards the end of primary school she did very well in her Key Stage 2 national assessments and on the entry tests and interviews for several top, state-funded and privately funded academic secondary schools. After much deliberation, Imogene and her parents chose for her to attend a four-hundred-year-old, state-funded secondary school with a top academic rating and excellent overall reputation.

Meet the Woods family

Eleanor Woods is an immaculate-looking woman in her forties with a commanding presence. When Eleanor starts talking about her daughter she becomes emotional, laughing and crying at the same time. She feels that Imogene has always been an incredibly special girl. Imogene is a pretty and petite, young-looking girl. Her complexion is fair with a few light freckles scattered across her nose and cheeks. She wears her light brown hair wavy and long. Clear, large brown eyes pierce you from beneath her fringe. She is soft-spoken, polite and well-versed at conversing with adults. She says she generally feels more comfortable talking with adults than with her peers. With her peers she feels shy and finds it hard to think of a topic to discuss. But adults love hearing about her academic achievements, her goals in life and her view on politics, education and the state of the country in general. Imogene reminded us of a young Hermione from the Harry Potter films. It was not just her looks and obvious intellectual skills that resembled the heroine of so many girls of Imogene's generation, but also the way she seemed slightly haughty whenever she tried to mask her feelings of insecurity.

The Woods family lives in a well-off area just outside the centre of London. The neighbourhood is dominated by luxurious townhouses and rows of spacious terraced houses occupied by single families. The streets are clean, the front gardens have magnolia trees, their windows support blooming window boxes and the majority of cars that are parked in the streets and private parking docks are current models of luxury brands. The family owns a four-story Edwardian townhouse with a small front garden and a long garden at the back. The outside woodwork on the light yellow brick house is white and the front door is painted midnight blue. It is hard not to notice the baby grand piano in the music room to the right of the front door when you walk up the three stone steps and ring the copper doorbell. Inside, the walls of the house are painted in muted shades of grey and green. The high ceilings and doors are white. Behind the music room, a living room overlooking the garden offers comfortable sofas, chairs and ottomans arranged around an open fire place. Against one of the walls, a small wooden desk stands surrounded by wooden book cases filled to the brim with stacks of books on politics, sociology and psychology, as well as classic and contemporary literature. Large abstract paintings in subdued colours decorate the remaining walls. Dozens of silver-framed family portraits are arranged on a narrow side table. In the hallway one set of stairs leads up to the two top floors filled with bedrooms, bathrooms and studies, while a second stairwell takes you down to the garden level. The spacious kitchen takes up most of the ground floor level of the house. The room is dominated by a large Aga stove and a wooden table that could comfortably seat a dozen people.

During the week it is usually just Imogene, her younger brother William, their mum Eleanor and the live-in au pair who are around for dinner. Their father Mark is often home late on weekdays, but always clears his busy work schedule for family time over the weekends and holidays. Those are also the days that Imogene's 8-year-older half brother Lucian and 6-year-older half sister Ella come to spend a few nights at the house. Family life is centred around the kitchen where they come together to cook, bake, eat, chat and study. Imogene's room is right at the top of the house. Every single piece of wall along the stairwell is taken up by bookcases and framed family pictures. Imogene's room is large enough to accomodate her bed, her desk, a large antique wooden chest for her clothes and a sofa that can fold out into an extra bed. Bookshelves and reproductions of classical paintings are mounted on the walls. A bright pink laptop sits on her desk and piles of clothes are scattered around the floor.

Imogene's father Mark started working as a journalist after he received his degree at one of the country's top universities. Now he holds a position as a political editor for one of the national newspapers. He has written several well-received books on domestic politics and politicians. Imogene's mother Eleanor moved to the United Kingdom to complete her degree in Psychology when she was in her early twenties. She grew up in South Africa and spent most of her school years away from home at boarding school. Before she and Mark had children she was working full-time as a journalist. After Imogene was born she found she needed to keep working, at least part-time, to keep herself 'from going mad', as she puts it. As soon as Imogene and William were both well established in their primary school she went back to full-time work, but as she works freelance she finds it easy to arrange her work hours according to their schedules. From the time Imogene was born, the family has always had an au pair. Each year a new girl moves into the room next to Imogene's. She will help out with the child care and cooking, improve her English language skills and then move on again. Eleanor says that the au pairs have never played a significant role in the development of her children because of their limited English language skills. A cleaning lady comes in twice a week to take care of other household tasks. By bringing in help, Eleanor and Mark find they have been able to spend their time away from work doing interesting and fun things with their children, rather than having to busy themselves with domestic tasks like cleaning or laundry or grocery shopping.

The early years of Imogene Woods

Even when Imogene was tiny it was clear to anyone who met her that she was very bright and very sociable. Although she did not start speaking exceptionally early, the things she said made people notice her in a positive way. To Eleanor, the input she gave her daughter through activities and conversations when she was little seemed just the normal things to do with your children. She says she was never excessively focused on their development, like some of the other parents around her. They would just do nice things together, like bake cookies, paint pictures, go for strolls around the parks when the weather was nice, and through art galleries on rainy days. They would sing songs all the time and make up little games with everything they did. They would look for animals in the paintings in the galleries, point out the colours of the cars passing them by on the street, identify the magnetic letters on the fridge door. One thing she did do was always talk to her children, no matter how young they were. She felt that if you just talked to children simply enough there was nothing you could not say to them, nothing you should avoid discussing with them. And reading, as Eleanor put it 'endless reading'. As Eleanor says 'What else is there in life, really?' Eleanor was always scouring bookshops for new children's books. Imogene had her own membership card to the library even before she could speak and they would usually go there twice a week to collect a new set of books. When the children were young Mark was a very hands-on father. Whenever he was home he would take a share in caring for the children. He loved to play and joke with them. And he taught them to sail and ride horses, to play the piano and to hold their ground in a discussion. He would talk politics with them even when they were barely in primary school, or ask them a question about a random topic and encourage them to provide examples to support their views.

Although Eleanor loved spending time with Imogene and later with William too, she felt she also needed adult conversation, even if children were the topic. So she joined a local organization, mostly run by mothers, that provided social events and support for parents with young children. During most of Imogene's early childhood, Eleanor was joint chair and editor of the organization's magazine. By joining this organization as well as regularly attending meetings at walk-in centres run by the local authorities, Eleanor found she and Imogene were provided with a structure for their week. It also gave Imogene a chance to develop a nice group of little friends and Eleanor developed close relationships with some of the other mothers in her neighbourhood. Eleanor put Imogene on a waiting list for a local nursery school so that they would have a place for her as soon as she turned 3. In the meantime 2-year-old Imogene attended a local playgroup for two or three mornings a week. Eleanor felt that it would be good for Imogene to spend some time away from her and to learn to make friends by herself. Imogene always seemed comfortable around adults but was often shy around other children. It took Imogene a while to settle in but once she did she seemed to enjoy being at the playgroup and joining in with activities and games.

As anticipated, Imogene was given a place at the local Nursery class as soon as she turned 3. This Nursery class did not just have an excellent reputation among the local parents but, more importantly, was connected to the best local primary school. By attending the Nursery, Imogene was automatically assured of a place at this highly over-subscribed primary school. Although Imogene loved that she now got to see her friends every day, she missed Eleanor and baby William, and it took a few months for her to stop crying when she was dropped off at school. Eleanor never really worried because she knew the staff at the Nursery class were excellent. According to Eleanor they were insightful when it came to the children, creative when it came to the curriculum and professional when it came to dealing with the often quite demanding upper-middle-class parents. Imogene loved learning new things and her mother reflects that she was obviously one of the brightest children in class. Eleanor was pleasantly surprised to find that teachers did not hesitate to positively remark on this and willingly offered Imogene activities that matched her abilities and interests.

The primary school years of Imogene Woods

Because the Nursery class was part of the primary school, the transition from playful learning to formal schooling took place almost without Imogene noticing the difference. She just moved up in years with her friends and soon they were reading and writing, learning Maths and doing science experiments. She enjoyed the academic subjects as well as the more creative projects involving music and art. And again Imogene was always one of the best students in class, regardless of the subject. She was a conscientious student who would never consider submitting a piece of work that was not up to her personal, high standard. So at home her parents never needed to remind her that she had schoolwork to complete. But they always took time to ask her about her school day and made sure they were around to help her solve the few problems she encountered. In class she happily participated in lessons and teachers enjoyed having her in their class. She was in all the top sets, and often they would find her more challenging work to do after she had completed the standard curriculum. She enjoyed going on advanced computing courses and taking special art classes as part of the government's 'gifted and talented' scheme. During their final years in primary school the whole class was specially tutored to prepare for their Key Stage 2 national assessments and most importantly for their entry tests for the academic secondary schools.

As far as her parents were concerned, the school was wonderful. They appreciated the way the headmistress firmly ruled the school and how she set high academic and behaviour standards. But best of all they liked the peer group the school provided for Imogene, and to them as parents. Imogene's class seemed filled with children from families with similar values, and most of the parents shared their slightly left-of-centre political orientation. These children came to school well rested, well fed, packing healthy snacks and lunches. They were polite and sociable and academically ambitious. Their parents were well-educated professionals who often worked at creative and demanding jobs but who were nonetheless willing to invest their time in their child's school. It was never a problem to find enough parents to help organize a fundraising event for the school, to help out during celebrations and outings or to find someone who could teach a special workshop about dance or music or photography. Eleanor was always involved with some school project and Mark became chair of governors. By the time their children finished primary school Eleanor and Mark felt confident that through their involvement they made a positive contribution to the school and to Imogene and William's schooling.

When she was in primary school there were play dates with friends, piano practice and William to play with on week days after school. But she liked being by herself as well. If it rained, Imogene often snuggled up with one of the cats in a chair in front of the fireplace and read a book or attempted to write a story of her own. After she finished reading or writing, Eleanor would ask her questions about the plot lines and characters. She encouraged her to think about how the stories were written and how they might be improved on. At weekends Ella and Lucian, who lived with their mother, would join the household. Imogene would sit at the kitchen table with them and do her homework as they did their coursework and revision. They would tell her about their courses in Latin, triple science and advanced Maths, and they often made up little assignments for her to do. When the work was done, Ella loved to cook or bake and Imogene loved to assist her. After a few years she started to improve on Ella's recipes and now whenever Imogene feels she needs to unwind, she will fire up the Aga and think up a recipe for a cake or cookies. On Sundays the family would venture out into the countryside for a long walk, rain or shine. Mark always made sure there was a nice pub along the route to have a Sunday roast and some rest. Discussions were an important part of these walks, and every child, no matter how young, was encouraged to actively participate. Typically these talks revolved around subjects such as politics, art, social injustice and ethical or moral dilemmas. Imogene's parents felt it was extremely important for their children to develop a strong sense of morality and to learn that their privileged life was not a given, but something to be grateful for.

All through her years in primary school Mark would regularly take Imogene horse riding and sailing. Every week she went for piano lessons and ballet classes. Her parents also paid for additional private tutoring during her final year in primary school to help her prepare for the exams and entry tests that were coming her way. Not because they worried about her academic abilities or progress, but because that was what all parents they knew did. They feared that by not doing so for Imogene, she would find herself in an unnecessarily disadvantaged position compared to her peers. Her parents and Imogene feel that she has benefitted greatly from these additional academic and creative classes. Developing her musical and dance talents has, according to the family, stimulated her brain and formed her into a more cultured person. It has also helped build her self-confidence, helped her to overcome her shyness by performing in public and taught her how to deal with competitiveness. Perhaps most importantly it has showed her how rewarding it is to push through barriers and never to give up.

Over the years Imogene has developed a great relationship with her piano teacher. The piano teacher has become one of the few people Imogene confides in when she is struggling with school or friendships. Because she feels close to her teacher and she respects her opinion, she wants to do even better with her music. Every day she sits down at the piano for at least an hour and practises her scales and pieces. When Imogene was little, Eleanor would practise with her but as she became more advanced Mark took over. Over the years there were several occasions when she wanted to quit her music or dance classes, but her parents always insisted that she would come to regret it and firmly encouraged her to continue. During her admission interviews for secondary schools she realized for the first time how right her parents had been. As soon as she walked into a room people appreciatively commented on her 'ballet posture' and they made it clear that her musical credentials made her particularly suitable for the kind of education she was applying for. Of course 'it did not hurt' as her mother put it that she had achieved top marks in her entry tests and national assessments as well.

The secondary school years of Imogene Woods

Now that Imogene and William are both in secondary school, Eleanor is back to working full-time away from home and Mark often has social functions he needs to attend during the evenings. Ella and Lucian are both at university and come to stay less frequently. When the family does manage to find time to be together they will hang out at the kitchen table to eat, catch up on each others' lives and eventually have a heated discussion about some current news item. Eleanor feels saddened that they do not have more of this quality family time, but at the same time she realizes that it also good for the children to start developing their own lives. Imogene now travels for over an hour by public transport back and forth to her secondary school, and this has definitely made her more independent. When she has some time to spare she meets up with her friends for coffee or lunch or to wander around art galleries. Somehow every conversation they start turns to the topic of studying, school, teachers or grades. She and her friends are starting to feel the pressure to get even more serious about their school work. Otherwise they might lose out on their chance to get into one of the country's top universities.

And that is where most of their parents studied before them, where most of their older siblings are now and where they are explicitly or implicitly expected to go in the future.

Between school, coursework, revision, piano lessons, ballet classes and friends, Imogene finds there is little time left to just hang out at home and relax. Every few weeks she will just collapse and begs Eleanor to let her stay home for a day or two. Eleanor usually gives in because it seems to her that Imogene is under quite a lot of pressure. Not so much from her or her husband now, but mostly from herself. Eleanor sees how Imogene is struggling with the changes in her life now that she has become an adolescent. She makes sure to find time every day to have a quiet chat with her daughter. Usually they will cuddle up together and talk about their day after Imogene has prepared for bed. After they talk through the practicalities they usually turn to the Imogene's favourite subjects of the moment: human nature and human relations. Imogene has become fascinated with these topics ever since she found her life turned upside down when she started secondary school.

Things Imogene had taken for granted all her life, like being the best at everything, getting on with teachers and having friends to hang out with at school no longer were a given once she started secondary school. All of a sudden she found herself in an environment where most students were at least as bright as she was. The academic standards were much, much higher than before. So yes, she might have achieved top marks in her national assessments in Year 9, but compared to the school standards these results mean very little. Now she finds she really needs to work hard to stay on top of her Maths, and even then she is no longer the best student in her class. In fact she needs to work hard for nearly all her subjects, but then so does everybody else. The subjects she loves best are those given by teachers she finds clever and witty and who 'are straight with you and who do not make too big a fuss when you slip up once in a while'. But she no longer finds that she gets on with every teacher, or that every teacher gets on with her. She is no longer always the sweet little girl she used to be. When she feels she is being treated unfairly she will stand up to her teacher and demand an explanation. At home she often becomes furious and tearful with frustration when she tells her parents about these confrontations. But what changed her more than anything else were the people she became friends with. When she started at her new school she found herself immensely attracted to a group of particularly bright and popular girls. For months she tried her hardest to fit in by matching their competiveness and aspirations and by explicitly dismissing anyone who did not meet their standards. Her parents worried about her because she was turning into a completely different person. All of a sudden she talked disapprovingly about other students who were less bright, who did not dress according to the latest fashion or who were simply not from her part of town. This was not the kind of person they stated they had raised her to be. At home she would become furious whenever she felt criticized and any little setback would bring about a storm of tears. Eleanor and Ella talked and talked with her until finally as they say 'she came to her senses'. She realized she was feeling miserable because she was trying to be someone she was not. As soon as she realized this she started to feel better. It did not take long for her to find new friends. Now her friends, she feels, are girls who are bright, but like her for who she is, not as she puts it for 'how you look or what you have'. They care about having fun, and although they can be fiercely competitive they will always help each other out.

The future for Imogene Woods

Her form teacher says that Imogene is one of their top students in school, heading for A* all around. She is a pleasure to teach, bright, polite and hard working. The only problem seems to be her attendance, which slips every now and then. But then the pressure at school to achieve can be overwhelming, especially for top students like Imogene. At school they feel certain that Imogene will not have any problems securing a place at one of the top universities, if that is what she sets her mind to. After she finishes with school, Imogene says she definitely wants to go to university. She is thinking of becoming a barrister. She finds her parents' friends who are barristers immensely impressive. Eleanor has offered to arrange for her to have her work placement at one of their offices. Or she thinks she might work in journalism or politics like her parents or become a psychologist or maybe something different altogether. As far as her parents are concerned she is free to choose whatever subject makes her happy. But although they might not say so explicitly, they do expect her to go to a top university. They will support her to find her path in life in any way they can. They will pay for her tuition, they will use their social networks, they will offer her their own experiences, and through it all they will continue to encourage, praise and love her.

In the following chapters we refer to these four specific cases along with the other Case Studies to exemplify our findings and to draw attention to the richness of our data and the depth and complexity of family life. We particularly emphasize these four cases in the conclusions of our other chapters, and within the chapters, as the reader is more familiar with these four families, due to the full cases being written up here.

5   Children as active agents of their own learning

This chapter describes our findings on how children become, or fail to become, active agents in their own academic success. It combines protective and risk factors related to the Case Studies children based on the literature review, with factors explicitly identified by the children and their parents and teachers as having contributed to academic success or difficulties.

Introduction

No matter what their age, children will generally fully engage in cultural practices offered through the systems in their developmental context. Through their participation they develop culturally relevant skills and knowledge. But while all children will more or less actively participate in their learning processes, not all children go on to become active agents of their academic success. As they engage with others, all children contribute to their own processes of learning. This is not necessarily a conscious contribution. Rather, they contribute by simply being who they are and by how they are perceived by their social partners. They also contribute through what they do, what they bring into the inter-action, and by how these actions are perceived. Bronfenbrenner distinguishes three types of 'person characteristics' that influence children's proximal process experiences: demand, resource and force characteristics (Bronfenbrenner & Morris, 2006).

According to the bioecological theory of human development these characteristics influence the content of the proximal processes children encounter, how these processes play out and how effective they will eventually be to the child's academic achievements. In some ways all children in our Case Studies are active agents in their own learning processes; however, for some, the consequences are deliberately targeted to better attainment while for others their active engagement is expressed through more reactive and negative actions towards their academic success. For some children, person characteristics come together in such a way that they have a negative impact on the child's participation in learning processes. For these children their person characteristics can be a contributing factor to low attainment and these children might not reach predicted levels of academic achievement. For other children, person characteristics come together in such a way that they actually facilitate them in reaching their predicted high attainment or even make it possible for them to move beyond predicted levels of academic development. For these children, their person characteristics have facilitated a transition from being active participants in developmental processes to becoming active agents of development. As 'active agents' children not just actively contribute to their developmental processes, but become a force that spurs on their personal academic success. The question is: What sets apart children who become active agents from those who do not?

Academic achievement can be perceived as a function of cognitive and socio-emotional behaviour components of the child (Evans & Rosenbaum, 2008). The cognitive and socio-emotional characteristics and behaviours of the Case Studies children in relation to their academic achievement will be the focal point of this chapter. Special attention is given to the perceptions about 'force' and 'resource' characteristics of the child held by the children themselves, as well as by their parents, and in some cases by their secondary school teachers. Perceptions of characteristics and behaviours influence what people deem appropriate, expected and acceptable for a particular child. As a result, these perceptions influence how people will respond to proximal processes initiated by the child, and they influence the kind of proximal processes they will offer to the child. Similarly, children's self-perceptions will influence which proximal processes they choose to participate in and the extent and effectiveness of their participation. The influence is cyclical and reflexive to the participants engaged in the relationship, e.g., parent and child.

(Self-)perceptions of children

The Effective Pre-School, Primary and Secondary Education (EPPSE) project found that factors that influence children's self-perceptions differ, depending on which aspect of self-perception is measured. Information about children's self-perceptions and experiences of school was collected through a self-report questionnaire in Year 2 (age 7), Year 5 (age 10) and Year 9 (age 14). The items were derived from a study of existing measures (e.g., Teddlie & Stringfield, 1993) and adapted for use with the age groups. Students' perceptions of their learning environment were collected in Year 5 (age 10) and Year 9 (age 14).

The four dimensions of self-perception were broadly similar at both ages in primary school and referred to children's perception of their enjoyment of school (e.g., 'I like answering questions in class' or 'Lessons are interesting'), their academic self-image (e.g., 'I am clever' or 'I know how to cope with my school work'), their behaviour self-image (e.g., 'I try to do my best at school' or 'I talk to my friends when I should be doing my work') and anxiety and alienation (e.g., 'I get fed up at school' or 'Other children bully me') (see Sammons et al., 2008a, appendix 2; cf. Sylva et al., 2008). In Year 9, aside from two separate self-perception indicators for academic self-concept in English and Maths, self-perception indicators referred to the child's enjoyment in school, their popularity among their peers, their citizen values and anxiety behaviours (see the Sammons et al., 2012a, report for the technical research details).

The EPPSE study found that while gender, for instance, was the strongest precursor of how children perceived their own behaviours, children's self-image as learners was most strongly influenced by their father's highest qualification and the quality of the early home learning environment (HLE), i.e., before the age of 4. Towards the end of their time in primary school, children's self-perceptions were differentially associated with their developmental outcomes. Children who had more positive academic self-images did better on reading and Maths, but were also better at self-regulating their behaviours and emotions. Children's behavioural self-image had the strongest relationship with ratings of their behaviour by teachers, such as hyperactivity, pro-social behaviour and anti-social behaviour. Sylva et al. (2008, p. vi) concluded that

There appeared to be strong **reciprocal** relationships between 'Academic self-concept' and academic achievement and between 'Behavioral self-image' and social/behavioral outcomes, which might be expected because the student doing well may gain confidence and motivation that enhances later outcomes.

Although students became slightly less positive about themselves during adolescence, the majority still had a positive self-image at age 14. Children who reported enjoyment in school at this age showed greater development in the academic and social-behavioural domains during their first years in secondary school (Sylva et al., 2012).

The (self-)perceptions of the participants in the Case Studies were obtained by identifying references made during the interviews to characteristics, behaviours and experiences which were thought to have significantly influenced the academic trajectories of the children. Through this analysis we identified two mechanisms that explained *why* children did well or did not do well in school according to the participants from all four Case Studies groups. The first mechanism referred to the way children behaved and adjusted themselves to school and learning; the second to the way they were facilitated in their learning by other people within their microsystems. The children who were doing well in school were seen as having *successfully adapted* to the demands of school and as having been *consistently facilitated* in their learning by other people and the events in their lives. On the other hand, the problems experienced by the academically less successful children were attributed to the fact that they *were unable to adjust* to school and that their *learning was impeded* rather than facilitated by certain factors related to the child, their family and/or school environments and their peers.

In this chapter we focus specifically on characteristics and behaviours of the child that were thought to have significantly influenced their academic trajectories. In most cases these factors were similar for academically successful and less successful children, but while they functioned as a 'protective' factor for the successful children, they worked as 'risk' factors in the case of the 'vulnerable' children. For the children 'succeeding against the odds' (Group 1: Low socio-economic status (SES), higher attainment) and the high-SES children with predicted attainment (Group 4: High SES, predicted attainment), participants identified the following 'protective' factors related to the children: their perceived ability for learning, their strong motivation for educational success and their hobbies and interests. For the academically less successful children from Group 2 (Low SES, predicted attainment) and Group 3 (High SES, low attainment) identified 'risk' factors related to the children were limitations in their perceived natural ability, their lack of motivation for school and learning, their use of ineffective work processes and externalizing problem behaviour.

Children's mental resources

Children's cognitive abilities are part of their mental resource characteristics (Bronfenbrenner & Morris, 2006). During the Case Studies interviews children's cognitive abilities were commonly offered as explanation for children's academic success or for their lack thereof by the parents, children and teachers alike. These explanations referred to children's intelligence in general but also to specific cognitive abilities such as verbal abilities or their working memory capacity. They were mentioned for all but one of the boys, but only for 60 per cent of the girls. Ability was mentioned as a 'protective' factor for seven boys and six girls from Group 1, and for all three boys and two girls from Group 4. Ability was mentioned as a 'risk' factor for all ten boys and three girls from Group 2, and for all three boys and four girls from Group 3.

From a very young age onwards, children have their cognitive abilities scrutinized by the people around them. Parents, relatives and teachers closely consider and assess the progress of their development. They compare the child's development and his or her ability to learn to what they have observed for the child's older siblings, with their friends' children, with children they see on the street or in playgrounds, with children they read about or watch on television, or even with their own abilities as a child.

Carol Peterson used her older daughter Gemma's schedule of reaching developmental milestones such as walking and talking as a frame of reference for her son Steven's unusual developmental trajectory; Mr and Mrs White were proud of Tom's verbal language ability and compared his abilities to those of his cousins; Marcy Stewart's mother felt her daughter's difficulties with learning would have stood out less if her primary year group had not comprised so many academically gifted children; and although Imogene Woods' cognitive abilities might not have been all that exceptional within her family, they did stand out compared to those of her peers in playgroup and made other parents and teachers comment on them. Over time, these perceptions of children's cognitive abilities seem to become as much a part of their resources as their actual abilities are. For the children succeeding against the odds and for the academically successful middle-class children, cognitive ability seemed to have served as a protective factor that contributed towards their predicted or unpredicted academic success. These children were perceived as particularly bright, and learning new academic skills and knowledge was thought to come 'naturally' to them. Their parents took pride in their child's abilities, their teachers appreciated their understanding of the curricular subjects, and for these children being a 'good learner' became part of their identity.

Her intellectual development ... which was really early, you know. Her grammar school teachers were totally 'Look she's top of the class at everything' and they all liked her, you know? She's easy to like, she's easy to get on with, she's very positive in her outlook until very recently (laugh). She used to enjoy things, you know. Mother of Imogene, girl, Group 4 (high SES, attainment as predicted)

I was like one of the brightest in Maths ... I used to get third and second in the classroom when we were doing the test stuff. And English I was quite good as well, I was like in the top group so that way really was no problem for me to learn ... Cause it's, it just comes naturally to me but like other kids ... they've tried, used to find it hard at times so ... Abdi, boy, Group 1 (low SES, attainment above prediction)

For the academically less successful children on the other hand, their cognitive abilities, or lack thereof, were perceived by parents and students as having played an important role in their difficulties with school and learning. In some cases children's overall ability for learning was perceived as limited.

I don't find nothing easy, nothing's ever easy. Harry, boy, Group 2 (low SES, attainment as predicted)

Actually he was slow in everything. Yes, slower than others, walking wasn't, but the learning still is. You know, learning wise, I must say, he was slow. Mother of Hamid, boy, Group 2 (low SES, attainment as predicted)

But for most of these children, specific limitations in their ability concerning one or several academic subjects, primarily English or Maths, were perceived as having had a negative effect on their academic trajectories.

I just think like Maths, no matter how I'm taught it, it's not going to come naturally. Laurie, girl, Group 3 (high SES, attainment below prediction)

I think she was about 4. Yeah, 'cos all her letters were backwards as well and her writing was really, she was having issues with her writing, and it's something that because North West Primary did writing practice every day, that they noticed as well, y'know, this wasn't a 4 year old's writing, that the letter formation wasn't there, letters were back to front, letters were round the wrong way, upside down and ... y'know, even if she was asked to copy out letters, she'd miss out letters, because she just didn't see them, and it's like, that's not right. Mother of Susan, girl, Group 2 (low SES, attainment as predicted)

For one in three of these children, parents believed their child to suffer from learning disabilities, such as dyslexia or dyscalculia. However, formal assessments had rarely been undertaken. Parents felt that schools were reluctant to acknowledge the need for a formal diagnosis. Although most parents had considered undertaking these assessments privately at some point, only one parent actually did so. Some parents mentioned the high costs, and their fear that schools would not accept these diagnoses, as reasons that stopped them from pursuing these actions. But in most cases parents seemed to feel, or at least hope, that the problems would sort themselves out, somehow. This is how parents perceived their children:

I suppose we didn't really have any major concerns, we knew that she struggled with Maths but we weren't, you know, overly worried about it. I think because initially she'd done alright with it, then she wasn't doing so well with it, but then her dad is not very good at Maths or English, particular, and he's a bit dyslexic, but, you know, we were just very much like 'Oh well some people are good at this, and some people are good at that.' You can't be good at everything and you know, she was doing really well sort of in her English, and that, so I thought well maybe she's just going to be very much more

English orientated, I mean not everybody can do Maths. Mother of Laurie, girl, Group 3 (high SES, attainment below prediction)

[In primary] he didn't have a problem ... I was happy ... but I would have been a bit happier if it was ... I suppose you always want more for your child and as much as they feel they can do, but I think you always feel, you could do a little bit better. I think that was probably down to Tremaine really, lack of interest and ... I think just mainly that ... Mother of Tremaine, boy Group 2 (low SES, attainment as predicted)

During the Case Studies interviews we found that both parents and children generally perceived cognitive resources as inherent properties of the child. They believed these resources were not, or only to a small extent, susceptible to external influences such as parenting or teaching. Nonetheless, there was a difference in how these beliefs translated into actual practices and attitudes towards learning within the families. The in-depth interviews provided ample examples of how the academically successful children had in fact received abundant opportunities and stimulation to develop their cognitive skills, even though cognitive ability was perceived as a 'natural' part of the child. During their learning opportunities these children had experienced consistent, ongoing positive reinforcement by family members, teachers, peers and other significant adults that helped them develop a positive image of themselves as capable and clever.

She was a very active child, very active and she was always keen to learn things and she was always quick to pick up on things and that. My Mum and Dad they are always praising her up and they are always saying to her, you know 'You do well at school' and you know, if they have got a problem on the computer they always ask Charley, because she can just do it just like that. So yeah they all, everybody encourages Charley really. Mother of Charley, girl, Group 1 (low SES, attainment above prediction)

Research shows that developing a positive belief in your learning capabilities, i.e., developing a 'masterful' disposition, is closely related to academic achievement (Dweck, 1999). Moreover, there is strong evidence, from studies of academic self-concept, of the reciprocal relationships between attainment and academic self-concept that are mutually reinforcing (Marsh, 2006; Marsh et al., 1985). EPPSE 3–14 found that children's academic self-concept becomes somewhat less positive after their move from primary into secondary school and that gender differences appear. Adolescent girls have lower self-concepts than boys when it comes to Maths, and similar self-concepts in English. However, while girls overall achieve slightly less well than boys in Maths, their attainment in English is better than that of boys in general (Sylva et al., 2012).

Particularly during adolescence, family experiences appear to be strongly related to changes in self-esteem (Greene & Way, 2005). The parenting practices in families of children who were doing well, in particular, reflected a belief in the parent's efficacy to positively influence their child's learning. Although we cannot establish the direction of influence between this perceived efficacy and cognitive development, it is not unlikely that the positive association we observed between children's cognitive skills and the displayed parental efficacy is bidirectional: when children are cognitively successful, parents feel that their parenting has been successful and are reinforced to continue their parenting practices; when parents believe they can have an effect on their child's cognitive ability they might feel more inclined to provide the child with experiences that stimulate cognitive development such as a stimulating early HLE.

The parenting behaviours in the families of academically less successful children, on the other hand, mirrored the belief that difficulties with learning were hard to influence (Siraj-Blatchford et al., 2007). We found that although some families attempted to provide extra help with school learning, this was mostly short-lived as these children typically showed little motivation for extra school work and parents found it too demanding to keep pushing their child when the positive effects were not obvious. The negative perceptions of children's cognitive abilities and perceived failure or limitations in one's capacity to facilitate positive development of cognitive skills might lead to feelings of 'helplessness' (Dweck, 1999), both for parents and children.

I think it's in general in Maths I find it really hard to keep it in, like, because I just find it goes in one ear and straight out the other, because I don't have, I don't have any interest in it at all, so it's really hard to learn something that you don't find interesting. Laurie, girl, Group 3 (high SES, attainment below prediction)

Motivational dispositions and the force characteristics of the developing person

Force characteristics refer to the child's tendency towards particular behaviours that reflect his or her underlying dispositions, such as temperament, motivation or persistence (Bronfenbrenner & Morris, 2006). Dispositions were explicitly identified as explanatory factors by parents, children and teachers for children's successful or less successful academic achievement. Strong motivation was offered as explanation for academic achievement for four boys and nine girls from Group 1, and for all six children from Group 4. Lack of motivation was mentioned for eight boys and one girl from Group 2 and for all three boys and for four girls from Group 3. Children succeeding against the odds were typically described as 'inquisitive', 'curious' and 'interested', as 'liking to do well', 'wanting to achieve', 'wanting to learn' and as having a 'strong drive' and 'will power' to achieve. Many of the successful children showed a willingness to learn and an overall positive attitude to school and learning that seemed to 'come from within'. This internal drive to learn characterized them from a young age:

She has always been inquisitive, she is very into, um I know this from her, she's quite good at learning things, being curious about things. Mother of Ife, girl, Group 1 (low SES, attainment above prediction)

I liked school. Just, liked learning. Just liked everything about it really, counting, writing, stuff like that. Mark, Boy, Group 1 (low SES, attainment above prediction)

The fact that she's doing so well is kind of tribute to her, her ... a deep-down motivation I think, which she has ... Teacher of Sharlene, girl, Group 1 (low SES, attainment above prediction)

The dispositions described for children who were vulnerable to lower academic achievement (Group 2: Low SES, predicted attainment; Group 3: High SES, low attainment) were far less positive. These children were typically described as 'just not interested', 'never liked stuff like that', 'not keen', 'couldn't be bothered' and 'couldn't see the point'. Their lack of motivation for particular subjects or for learning in general was commonly perceived to have had a negative effect on their attainment in school.

Probably it's to do with confidence. I would think. He's afraid of making mistakes, even now ... even now. [In primary] well he got on with it, I suppose, as much as he could get away with. I suppose he probably did as least as possible. You know, whatever they said, well that's enough, that was enough. If he was told to do half a page, he'd never do a full page. So as long as he did what they asked him, I suppose it was OK. Mother of Christoper, boy, Group 2 (low SES, attainment as predicted)

Similar to the perception of cognitive abilities, these child dispositions were regarded as 'given' characteristics of the child. Children either were motivated towards school and learning or they were not, and if they were not it was perceived that there was little anyone could do to change their attitude.

Perceptions of vulnerable children's negative force characteristics

For the academically less successful children, several disruptive force characteristics were explicitly mentioned to explain their lack of academic success. Disruptive force characteristics can indicate a person's difficulties in maintaining control over emotions and behaviour, such as impulsiveness, explosiveness, distractibility or withdrawal (Bronfenbrenner & Morris, 2006). As part of EPPSE 3–14, measures of different aspects of children's social/behavioural outcomes throughout the primary and secondary years were obtained through the use of an extended version of the Strengths and Difficulties Questionnaire (Goodman, 1997). Teachers who knew the child well completed a social/behavioural child profile. Statistical analyses revealed four dimensions. These were self-regulation (e.g., 'Persists in the face of difficult tasks' or 'Shows leadership in group work'), pro-social behaviour (e.g., 'Considerate of other people's feelings' or 'Offers to help others having difficulties with a task'), hyperactivity (e.g., 'Restless, overactive, cannot stay still for long' or 'Can behave appropriately during less structured lessons') and anti-social behaviour (e.g., 'Often fights with other children or bullies them' or 'Often lies or cheats'). Throughout their years in school most children in the EPPSE project were rated positively for these features of social behaviour, and these results were in line with other research on social behaviour and with the distribution of scores for social/behavioural measures for the Effective Pre-School and Primary Education (EPPE 3–11) sample at younger ages (see Sammons et al., 2012a, 2008a; cf. Sylva et al., 2008, 2012).

For the academically vulnerable children in the Case Studies (Group 2: Low SES, predicted attainment; Group 3: High SES, low attainment) poor self-regulation skills typically seemed to have interfered with their learning. Their lack of ability to self-regulate their emotions and behaviours negatively affected their learning processes in and out of school. Use of ineffective work processes was mentioned for nine boys and all four girls from Group 2 and for all three boys and for four girls from Group 3. Their use of ineffective learning strategies, such as not reading carefully, not checking work over for possible mistakes and not revising, was most commonly mentioned to explain their disappointing academic achievement.

His way of learning, he's good verbally, so he can listen and take in information and then he can ask questions verbally. I think it really is difficult for him on the Literacy level, I think it's come back to that again. So if you ask him to, you know, fill in a worksheet where the questions on there of what they've actually been learning, he will struggle with that sometimes, and I think it is because he hasn't read the question properly, so the answers he gives rarely relate to what the question's about. Teacher of Subash, boy, Group 3 (high SES, attainment below prediction)

During their involvement in proximal learning processes these children would 'lose focus', 'get distracted', 'go off-track' or 'get bored'.

As a result they struggled more and more, which commonly resulted in them simply giving up.

When I was in primary school I kinda just stopped paying attention like when it was too hard or something like that I would just stop paying attention and talked to my friends. Alex, boy, Group 3 (high SES, attainment below prediction)

A further disruptive characteristic mentioned for these children was their reluctance to make use of help when offered. It appeared that somehow these children had not learned that they could benefit from the material and social resources that were available to them. The reasons most commonly given for this reluctance was that they 'just won't do it' and 'just don't want to'; but some were 'shy' and 'afraid' to ask for help.

In school they offered you after school clubs, but I never used to go to them ... Cos ... I dunno really, it's just ... ' cos ... I had to sense of like If I go now then I'd have, like, no free time, or time to do other homeworks for different subjects ... so I just, put it to one side, so ... which is kind of a regret now, 'cos I think if I went there I could've been getting better grades now. Christopher, boy, Group 2 (low SES, attainment as predicted)

I ran through sessions, we would be doing past papers, and I was very surprised that neither of them, erm, Ebun came to one, I have to admit, but Bunmi didn't. They just said 'Oh well', they didn't really have a reason, they just didn't want to. Teacher of Ebun and Bunmi, twin sisters, Group 2 (low SES, attainment as predicted)

In a few cases children's inability to maintain control of their emotions and behaviours resulted in externalizing problem behaviour. This behaviour usually developed as children approached puberty and mostly referred to children behaving in a way which was described as 'rude', 'lippy' and 'cheeky' in their communication, and to negative attention-seeking behaviour ('nag and nag'). Occasionally, problems became more serious and children became aggressive or would lose control, 'freak out' and get into fights.

He started going lippy, not just with me, but with his brothers ... sisters ... So yeah ... and he turned that ... took his turn in school as well ... y'know ... I dunno what happened. Mother of Tremaine, boy, Group 2 (low SES, attainment as predicted)

It's his nature I would of said, his nature is that he ... he's sort of that type of child, he is a child who wants to talk, would like to misbehave as much as he could, he's not a diligent sort of child, that will just put his head down and work, he's itching to do anything he can. Teacher of Sean, boy, Group 3 (high SES, attainment below prediction)

The consequence of these children's inability to control their behaviour and emotions was not just that their ongoing participation in proximal processes was interrupted (and that of their classmates as well) but that they missed out on further learning opportunities as well. Their behaviours often resulted in them being removed from class, put in detention or even being suspended altogether from school for a certain time period, or indefinitely.

Developmentally generative force characteristics

In contrast, for the academically successful children, their disposition towards high, intrinsically driven motivation for school and learning was associated with positive force characteristics such as children's self-regulation abilities, positive attitudes towards homework, positive perceptions of personal competencies and internal academic locus of control. Quantitative empirical research shows that these positive force characteristics of the developing child are associated with better achievement in school (Bursik & Martin, 2006; Hoover-Dempsey et al., 2001; McNeal, 2001). They appear to facilitate the child's adaptation to the school environment and to school learning and as such function as protective child factors. Their presence also enables the child to set in motion proximal processes and to prolong participation in ongoing learning experiences. During the interviews, these children were described as having dispositions which made them dedicated, hard-working and active problem-solvers. The children who succeeded against the odds were regarded by others and regarded themselves as good workers, who paid attention in class and focused on their school work from an early age onwards, and this perception was reinforced by parents and their schools. As with the successful low-SES children, the successful high-SES children were perceived as highly motivated to learn. However, while the high-SES girls showed this strong positive orientation to school and learning from an early age onwards, the high-SES boys generally needed a bit more time for this motivation to become apparent.

A study into ego development and adolescent academic achievement showed that children's excitement by opportunities to learn, their tendency to feel intrinsically motivated by the learning experience and by a regard for knowledge as a reward, are all indications of a strong positive learning orientation. These positive learning orientations tend to increase during adolescence and are associated with higher achievement (Bursik & Martin, 2006). The academically successful children said they felt happy and capable in school. They did not just enjoy learning, but the school experience as a whole, and therefore seemed able to make the most of what schools had to offer. For these children, the positive force characteristics associated with their person generated and sustained learning experiences that contributed to their further academic development.

The ability to self-regulate appears to be the joint result of external processes, such as parenting and education, and internal biological processes of maturation (Greene & Way, 2005). Although children from low-SES backgrounds are generally found to have more difficulties regulating their emotions and behaviour in comparison with wealthier peers, research shows that self-regulation mediates the effects of low income and poverty on achievement (Evans & Rosenbaum, 2008). The EPPSE project showed that early self-regulation skills had the strongest effect on children's academic 'resilience' at age 5 and later at age 10 (Sylva et al., 2007).

Furthermore, 'self-regulation' has been shown to be the dimension of social behaviour most closely linked with academic attainment for the EPPSE sample at ages 7 and 11 (Sammons et al., 2008a; Sylva et al., 2004). In secondary school, children who were rated by teachers as having higher levels of 'self-regulation' (a measure of autonomy, confidence and self-sufficiency in learning) had higher academic self-concepts, greater reported 'enjoyment of school' and more positive 'citizenship values' (Sammons et al., 2012b). These findings suggest that developing the ability to self-regulate their emotions and behaviours, to maintain control over what they do and how they feel, plays a particularly salient role in achieving academic success that exceeds expectations. The examples of successful children's use of self-regulation in the Case Studies show how these children used a range of strategies to control their emotions and behaviours, and that they were given opportunities and support by the people around them that allowed them to take responsibility for their learning processes.

First thing Shelly always done, she always used to come in from school and ... her homework had to be done there and then ... even if it didn't have to be in till next week, if she came home with it on a Wednesday, it had to be done on that Wednesday, but even to me now, touch wood, she's got homework, she comes home and does it straight away, so that's a really good thing. Mother of Shelly, girl, Group 1 (low SES, attainment above prediction)

The academically successful children (Group 1: Low SES, higher attainment; Group 4: High SES, predicted attainment) described how they managed to concentrate in difficult circumstances in class. For instance, when peers were trying to distract them in class they 'just focused', 'listened' or 'shut off' from distractions. They committed to school work even if they were not particularly interested in the subject or had other things they wanted to do.

Yeah, actually . . . I think it was half and half, half of my friends were and the other half weren't like me but I still got along with them. Just, it's only just like, in secondary school just their attitude towards school that where I would try my best to learn more in school, they would be more interested in other things, like football, computer games. I like those as well but just not in school. I can be interested in those kinds of things as well, but at school, I'd rather just be, have my head at school, than be concentrating on other things like that. Because it makes it easier. Shaquille, boy, Group 1 (low SES, attainment higher than predicted)

It's just like will power, I actually think to myself, you know, 'You've only got to sit behind the desk for an hour and concentrate for an hour, if you can do that, then you've got the rest of the day to enjoy yourself, and you've got the weekends and things like that.' I know that if there's something to be done I must do it. I can't just like let it build up and build up and if I don't understand something I'll ask for it. Anjali, girl, Group 1 (low SES, attainment above prediction)

If these academically successful students faced difficulties with a task, they would actively try to solve the problem by just 'trying', 'having a go at it', that is, they persevered in the face of difficulty and challenge rather than giving up.

If he got stuck on anything, he'd try and do it himself, and that's what makes him quite special really. It's something I couldn't do when I was little. Father of Mark, boy, Group 1 (low SES, attainment above prediction)

I just used to solve it myself, I didn't really ask anyone for help, just, find a way round it. Just, like, work it out from something else. Mark, boy Group 1 (low SES, attainment above prediction)

They regularly made use of material resources that were available in their homes, schools or communities. They used books such as dictionaries and encyclopaedias, but especially computers. Computers helped in several ways. Text-editing programmes, for instance, helped them to deal with handwriting difficulties and spelling difficulties, while the Internet helped them to research topics for assignments and provided them with on-line revision sources such as BBC Bitesize, and social networking sites gave them access to their peers so they could ask them for help. However, computers and books were sources of pleasure and relaxation as well. For the academically successful children, particular activities or hobbies were perceived to facilitate their learning and in some cases to stimulate them to apply themselves further to school and learning. Interests and hobbies were mentioned for eight girls and four boys from Group 1 and for all six children from Group 4 as explanation for their academic success. These hobbies and interests ranged from fashion to religion, but most frequently mentioned were reading and computers. Reading, writing and computers in particular were perceived by parents, children and teachers to have facilitated children's learning to the extent that it helped them perform better in school subjects such as ICT and English. Their language skills (vocabulary, grammar, syntax) in particular, appear to have benefitted from these activities. Engaging in these activities increased children's 'enthusiasm', 'motivation' and 'interest' for particular topics. But they also believed they served to increase their working memory and ability to concentrate during class. Steven describes how he started getting interested in books more and more over time, when asked if he thinks reading might have helped him with his learning he answers:

Yeah, I think it does, 'cause it also helps me concentrate ... I mean so, in class I could concentrate for fifty minutes, no, no problem ... like listen to the teacher and whereas ... everyone else seems to, you know, have to talk or ... so. Steven, boy, Group 1 (low SES, attainment above prediction)

The positive attitude towards traditional and computer literacy and their frequent use of books and computers clearly facilitated their learning. But it might even play a greater role in their future academic achievement. Computer literacy has become an essential part of today's society. According to Barron (2006) computers are often used to facilitate self-initiated learning by adolescents, as they are used to seek out text-based informational sources, for the creation of new interactive activities, the pursuit of structured learning opportunities, the exploration of media and the development of mentoring or knowledge-sharing relationships, and as such serve as a catalyst for learning. The importance of reading books as a well-loved hobby is illustrated by a review about who the people are that read and what reading offers them (Griswold et al., 2005). The review shows that although most people in the developed world are able to read and will read to some extent as part of their jobs, on-line activities and daily lives, only a minority will read books on a regular basis. Reading is now generally regarded as a 'good thing', but the growing division between reading as matter-of-fact practice and reading of literature, serious non-fiction and the quality press, suggests a 'reading class' is emerging, as these reading habits are considered prestigious and are seen as practices of social and cultural capital of an educated elite.

The academically successful children also actively used their social resources if they found they were unable to resolve a situation themselves, or encountered a serious setback. They were willing to ask and look for and accept external help from peers, teachers, parents, siblings or other adults.

He read me some work that he did, and I thought it was really, really good, his teacher gave him a mark that he didn't feel it was warranted and we spoke about that. I said 'I will sort it, if you like I will speak to the teacher about it', and Shaquille said 'No, I will speak to the teacher about it', and apparently he spoke to the teacher about it and they came to some sort of arrangement, and the teacher spoke to him and he was happy with the comments that the teacher had given him, because although the content was good, the fundamental things such as punctuation, the whole presentation, let him down. Mother of Shaquille, boy, Group 1 (low SES, attainment above prediction)

Particularly among our low-SES families, children frequently encountered negative life events such as unstable family situations or divorce, serious illness or loss of a loved one, or serious problems with peers or siblings. The academically less successful children (Group 2: Low SES, predicted attainment) often felt overwhelmed and unable to influence these negative events, and as a result expressed more anxiety and feelings of depression. The successful low-SES children (Group 1: Low SES, higher attainment), on the other hand, refused to let these experiences negatively affect their school achievement. Instead, these children used school and the focus required for learning as distractions from their troubles. As such these children did not only show educational 'resilience' but also psychological 'resilience'. The following examples were given by students when asked how they dealt respectively with a recent divorce, the loss of a mother and having had a very unstable early childhood resulting in adoption at the age of 6:

Well I did try and keep … school and … what was happening at home … separate 'cause I didn't want it to interfere 'cause I was doing well so … didn't wanna loose that. Steven, boy, Group 1 (low SES, attainment above prediction)

Nah, just stuck in at school and covered it up really. So if I had something to do, I wouldn't really think about it. Mark, boy, Group 1 (low SES, attainment above prediction)

Just like 'cause I did not have an easy time when I was younger, if I can get through that I can get through anything, I am not going to give up. Natalie, girl, Group 1 (low SES, attainment above prediction)

For the majority of children 'succeeding against the odds' their self-regulation appeared to be further motivated by their goal-orientation and aspirations. External motivation for learning, including a strong focus on earning high grades and aiming to please teachers in order to receive positive feedback, is typically negatively associated with academic success and usually diminishes with maturation during adolescence (Bursik & Martin, 2006). Interestingly, in the Case Studies, we found that successful boys in particular were spurred on by a competitive, strong grade orientation. A possible explanation might be that the actual motivation underlying this external orientation was indeed intrinsic. Steven, for instance, had a very strong grade orientation, but this seemed primarily intrinsically motivated: he described having a 'sort of natural urge to be above 80 per cent' in tests. His mother says the following:

> He's just got the drive in him, he's got this ... he's got natural ability as well for Maths and sciences but eh ... he's got this drive. He wants to be the best at everything that he puts his hand to. And he's not happy unless he is ... and so the more he's trying, the more he's getting better. The exam results coming in and he's getting in the eighties and nineties ... he's like 'Yes!' ... and that drives him on. Mother of Steven, boy, Group 1 (low SES, attainment above prediction)

The children 'succeeding against the odds' also expressed ambitious future goals, such as going to college or university, and aiming for professional careers in law, engineering, medicine, teaching or finance. Anjali was doing her GCSEs, and aims to become a barrister:

> Well first I'm gonna get, make sure I do well in my GCSEs. I don't want to focus too much on the future, 'cos I can't have a future if I haven't got this like done, so I'm going to revise as much as I can for my GCSEs, make sure I do well in them. Then obviously I'm setting up to go into sixth-form and some universities that I've looked at, that I'd like to go to and things like that and seeing what grades they want and what they expect from people who want to join up, so now I know what it's like, I know what sort of goals and targets I've got to achieve to become a barrister, so ... Anjali, girl, Group 1 (low SES, attainment above prediction)

This goal orientation seemed primarily instrumental, as they perceived these futures as ways to achieve economic security, independence and employment opportunities, and was related to the value placed by their parents on education and their high expectations and aspirations for their children. A longitudinal study that followed up the job aspirations of teenagers in the United Kingdom at age 33 showed that these early aspirations predicted specific professional occupational attainments in adulthood. Occupational attainment at a later age was not only significantly related to aspirations at 16, but also to children's belief in their own ability and their Maths performance at age 16 (Schoon, 2001). This suggests that these children's goal orientation, which was reinforced by parents and schools, might help them to follow up their educational achievements with future occupational achievements.

Transition into active agency

Although all children actively participate in their developmental processes from the moment they are born, there appear to be considerable

differences in the extent and effectiveness of their participation in proximal processes relevant to their academic learning and development.
Children's person characteristics play an important role when it comes
to their participation. These demand, resource and force characteristics
create a system of reciprocal feedback between the child and the social
partners with whom the child engages. They seem to function as 'filters'
between the child and the context in which the child develops. Much of
their effect will depend on how these characteristics are perceived and
valued by the people within their particular context of development, but
also by the child.

Through their interactions with other people, children gradually learn
to interpret other people's valuations of their behaviour, abilities and
appearance. In response to these perceptions, they might change their
behaviours and beliefs, although not necessarily in the way expected or
intended by their social environment or even by themselves. Through
these changes in individual characteristics, they also change the system of
person characteristics and the dynamics between themselves as learners
and their social learning environment. For some, these changes enhance
their chances for academic failure; for others, they seem to promote
chances of academic success and even resilience. As such, person characteristics, real or perceived, will function as risk factors or as protective
factors with regard to the child's development in general and their
academic achievement in particular.

The way their social partners – their parents, friends, teachers –
initially respond to or approach a child is influenced by observable
'demand characteristics' that are typically beyond the control of the
child. People act differently towards children of different ages, towards
boys and girls, and towards children with distinctive physical appear-
ances, and they are often unaware that they do so. In the Case Studies no
explicit references were made to demand characteristics of the children
as a way to explain children's academic achievements. We found no
indication that parents, children or teachers believed that academic
success or failure was in any way related to, for instance, their gender
or their skin colour. But that is not to say that these demand characteristics have not in some way exerted their influence on children's identities
or academic trajectories. This might be because people base inferences
about the availability of mental, emotional, social and material resources
to children on the demand characteristics of the child.

Sometimes assumptions about such 'resource characteristics' are
correct; sometimes they are not. Regardless, these assumptions have
implications for the child because they influence people's understanding
of the child. They influence what people deem appropriate, expected and

acceptable for a particular child. And as a result this influences how people will respond to proximal processes initiated by the child, and they influence the kind of proximal processes they will offer to the child. It is not just other people's perceptions of these resources that matter, but the child's perceptions of and experiences with these resources as well. Children develop assumptions and expectations about themselves and others on their perceptions of and experiences with available resources. And these assumptions and expectations, for instance about their ability to learn or about what to expect from others when encountering a problem, will influence their actual behaviour during (future) proximal processes.

This seemed potentially to be the case with the demand characteristic 'gender' and the mental resource characteristic 'cognitive ability'. The Case Studies revealed that parents, students and teachers believed that children's cognitive abilities played an important role in their academic achievement. Cognitive ability as explanation for academic achievement was offered regardless of whether these achievements were expected or unexpected, or more or less successful. But while this explanation was offered in relation to the academic achievement of a small majority of the girls, it was offered for virtually all of the boys. Parents and children also generally believed that these cognitive abilities were a 'natural' part of the child; that is to say, beyond the control of others such as parents and teachers. The beliefs of parents (and children) regarding cognitive abilities as part of the natural characteristics of the child that could not easily be affected by external influences such as parenting or practice could potentially have serious negative consequences for the academic development of children.

How important the perceptions of children's abilities might be for children's academic development is illustrated by a study with 7-year-old twins (Turkheimer et al., 2003). This study suggests that the influences of experiences through proximal processes in microsystems are particularly important for the child's general abilities such as IQ, and this appears more important in impoverished, low socio-economic status, environments than in affluent, high-SES families. The study found that for children from poor families, shared environment accounted for 60 per cent of the variance in IQ (Full Scale IQ and Performance IQ), while the proportion of variance explained by genes was virtually none. For children from wealthier backgrounds, by contrast, genes accounted for a high proportion of variance in IQ measures (Turkheimer et al., 2003). The implication seems to be that particularly for those children who grow up in disadvantaged circumstances, learning environments and experiences play an important role when it comes to actualizing genetic potential into cognitive functioning. So what parents do with their child matters for the cognitive abilities they develop, particularly for children growing up in disadvantaged circumstances (Melhuish et al., 2001).

For children whose cognitive abilities are perceived as sufficient to deal with the demands of learning processes, it might mean that their genetic potential is greater than what is being actualized through their proximal process experiences, due to limited involvement from, and stimulation from, more skilled partners such as their parents and teachers. For children whose cognitive abilities prove problematic in meeting the academic expectations and demands of society, the consequences are likely to be even more severe. For these children such beliefs could mean that they might not only miss out on vital opportunities for learning, but also that their repeated experiences with failure to meet requirements enforces negative perceptions of themselves as learners. The gender differentiation we observed in our data regarding the perceived relation between academic success and cognitive abilities suggests that the consequences of fatalistic beliefs about self-efficacy of parents and of children to influence cognitive abilities, might be particularly serious for boys and perhaps even more so for boys from disadvantaged families.

Children's motivational disposition was also perceived as an important factor in explaining children's academic achievements. Their dispositions became manifest in actual behaviours that appeared to have facilitated or impeded their learning processes. These 'force characteristics' of the child influence both how the child acts and how social partners anticipate and respond to the child during proximal processes. They translate into differences between children, the effectiveness of their learning strategies, their perseverance with tasks in difficult circumstances, their problem-solving strategies, their interests in activities that facilitate academic achievement in their time away from school, but also in their future goals and aspirations. Similar to their beliefs about cognitive abilities, parents and children in the Case Studies seemed to regard dispositions such as motivation for school and learning, or lack thereof, as a 'given' characteristic of the child. Children were either motivated towards school and learning or they were not, and if they were not there was little anyone could do to change their attitude. Again, these beliefs about the nature of children's attitudes and the perception of these attitudes and behaviours by the child and by others can have far reaching consequences, as they will likely influence not just how these children come to perceive and value themselves as learners and as persons, but how and if they will be able to put these characteristics to use when it comes to achieving academic success.

Conclusions

The experiences of children such Anjali, Mark, Shaquille, Charley and Steven, who succeeded against the odds, provide us with case-study evidence that person characteristics such as cognitive ability and motivation can change, even though they might be perceived as static. These changes can have dramatic consequences for children's abilities and for their possibilities to engage in proximal processes and to develop their academic potential, skills and knowledge. Take Steven, for example. As a little boy he did nothing but scream and cry, and his mother felt it was nearly impossible to engage him in the little games and activities that typically stimulate the development of early academic skills and knowledge. But after his hearing operation their lives changed completely. The quality of his interactions with his mother, his sister, his pre-school teachers and even some other children improved dramatically. His skills and knowledge improved substantially but nonetheless he struggled to keep up with his class once interaction processes in class became more formal and explicitly aimed at academic skill development. He found it hard to make sense of what was being taught in class. Because he did not understand what it was he was struggling with, he could not ask for appropriate help. He lost interest in the lessons and his behaviour became disruptive to the point that he was spending a lot of his time away from the classroom. But then he was placed in an intensive remedial programme that offered him a chance to come to terms with the basics of academic learning. Because of the way the teacher in his remedial class explained and discussed the subjects during these classes, he became interested and even excited about school subjects that he previously had discarded as uninteresting. His attitude towards school and learning became more positive. He learned to identify problems and how to ask for help. His change in attitude altered his behaviour in class, and these changes were duly noted by his teachers. He went from being 'special needs' to the top of the class over a relatively short period of time, and as his results improved his perception of himself as a learner changed. He no longer felt like a failure but grew confident in his own academic abilities.

These days Steven is highly motivated towards learning and school. He is ambitious and cannot tolerate getting a poor result, even for subjects that he finds less interesting. He actively participates in classes and he will attempt to solve any academic problem he encounters. He actively seeks out new opportunities for learning, through his friends, his hobbies, the media or adults in his life. Steven has become a driving force behind his own, personal academic success. That is to say, he has become an active agent of his academic development. Although he himself has played a crucial role in this process, he has not done this by himself. Children like Steven depend on opportunities to participate in proximal processes that stimulate and facilitate the development of the particular skills, attitudes, behaviours and self-perceptions that contribute to spurring on their academic success, and his mother played an instrumental role in fostering this.

6   Powerful parenting and home learning

In this chapter we describe the parenting practices in our four groups and include sections on the home learning environment (HLE) through the early, primary and secondary years. We relate these practices to empirical evidence for educational success as well as to their educational effect as perceived by children and parents' and the parents' reasons for providing these learning environments.

Introduction

Throughout a child's life, and particularly in the early years, family life is widely recognized as one of the primary microsystems, if not the most important microsystem, for children's cognitive and socio-emotional development. Not only do parents provide a substantial amount of the actual proximal processes, they also influence children's proximal processes outside the family context, by managing and regulating their access to other socio-cultural contexts such as (pre-)school, peers, and community (Parke, 2004; cf. Bradley & Corwyn, 2002; Feinstein et al., 2008; Harkness & Super, 1992; Rogoff et al., 1995; Tomasello, 1999) and set the child's trajectory on their learning life-course.

The findings from the previously mentioned study by Turkheimer and colleagues (Turkheimer et al., 2003) with 7-year-old twins suggest that the influences and experiences through proximal processes in microsystems such as the family are of particular importance for children's academic success when children grow up in disadvantaged social circumstances. This conclusion is further supported by evidence from the Effective Pre-School, Primary and Secondary Education project (EPPSE 3–14), which showed that what parents did at home through the early HLE was more important in terms of the children's outcomes than who they were in terms of socio-economic status (SES) or income (Melhuish et al., 2001). This chapter looks closely at family factors that act as protective influences in combating poor outcomes and factors that increase the risk of poor academic outcomes of children. More specifically, we discuss what it is that families and particularly parents (and families) do that helps children succeed, and why they do this. We start by describing academically effective proximal process experiences among our families during the early years, primary years and secondary years of the children. As in the previous chapter, we investigate the perceptions of parents, children and teachers about how the family microsystem has influenced children's academic trajectories. In addition to the perceptions about effective parenting, we include findings from the interview analysis, from the EPPSE project and from research literature in general about characteristics of the family microsystem and of parents that are found to influence parenting and academic achievement associated with this parenting.

Perceived 'protective' and 'risk' factors related to the family microsystem

The Case Studies participants felt that differences in how well children had adapted to the demands of school were related to whether they had been consistently facilitated in their learning or whether their learning was impeded by factors related to the family microsystem.

Practical and emotional support from people and through activities within the home was identified as critical and important protective factors for academic success while *lack of such support* was seen as having contributed to less successful academic attainment.

Practical and emotional support in the parent–child relationship was perceived to have facilitated learning and to have stimulated students to apply themselves to school and learning. The extent of the emotional and practical support, and what constituted this support, was not necessarily the same for each Case Studies child and every family within each of the groups. It also changed as children matured and developed. Despite these differences, there were notable patterns that characterized and distinguished children's family microsystem experiences in the different sub-groups of Case Studies participants. For the children succeeding against the odds, and for successful high-SES children, effective support was attributed to their parents, and in some cases to siblings. *Effective practical and emotional support* was mentioned as a reason for academic success for eleven girls and seven boys from Group 1, and for all six children from Group 4. For over two-thirds of the children who were not 'succeeding against the odds', or were doing less well than predicted, lack of, or ineffective, practical and emotional support were seen as having significantly impeded their academic attainment. *Ineffective practical and emotional support* was mentioned to explain lack of academic success for eight boys and two girls from Group 2 and for all three boys and for four girls from Group 3.

Academically effective family microsystems during the early years

Provision of educational experiences as part of everyday family life and relations is perhaps the most well-established pattern of influence between the family microsystem and children's academic achievement. Studies with pre-school-aged children and children in the first years of primary school show that differences in early home learning experiences result in substantial differences in English and Maths abilities at the start of school (Sylva et al., 2004, 2008; cf. Brooks-Gunn & Markman, 2005; Hoff et al., 2002; Hoff & Tian, 2005; Stipek, 2001; Tudge et al., 2006). This effect of what is termed the early HLE, that is to say early experiences with academically relevant proximal processes in the family microsystem, continues to influence children's academic achievement as they progress through primary school, and through secondary school too. Longitudinal research, such as the EPPSE project, has provided evidence that the effect of these experiences on both cognitive and social/behavioural development of children is both strong and lasting (Sylva et al., 2008, 2012; cf. Sammons et al., 2008a, 2008b, 2012a, 2012b).

A wide range of activities related to the home environment have been identified as having a positive effect on children's developmental outcomes at different life-stages. At the pre-school age, activities such as joint storybook reading, oral storytelling, mealtime conversations, games with numbers and words, painting and drawing, and also visits to the library, or teaching and playing with children with letters and numbers, are important (Melhuish et al., 2008; see further Bradley, 2002; Bus et al., 1995; Duursma et al., 2007; Leseman et al., 2007). EPPSE 3–14 has shown that early HLE continued to function as a powerful predictor of academic success at age 14, after children had in fact experienced six years in primary school and three years in secondary school. Although effect sizes decrease with time, they are still substantial, and seem to indicate that high-quality early learning experiences in the home provide children with an academic head start that continues to positively affect their academic achievements even after eleven years (Sylva et al., 2008, 2012). One could also argue that such experiences facilitate a relational bonding for both parent and child around learning and support for learning, and set such positive expectations for the future.

Measures of early home learning environments

The early HLE index was based on data collected during the parent interviews conducted at the beginning of the Effective Provision of Pre-School Education (EPPE) project, when the children were between 3 and 4 years old. Parents were first asked to think back over the previous six months and to describe the kinds of things they did together with their child. After this, parents were asked to indicate if and how frequently their child had participated in a pre-described list of activities. From these answers an early HLE index was derived, based on seven educationally orientated learning experiences: going to the library, being read to, learning activities involving the alphabet, learning activities with numbers and shapes, learning activities with songs, poems or nursery rhymes, playing with letters and/or numbers and painting and/or drawing. The HLE scale ran from 0 to 49 (the frequency of each of the activities being coded on a scale of 0–7 with 0 = not occurring and 7 = occurring very frequently) and was normally distributed with a mean of 23.42 (sd = 7.71) (Melhuish et al., 2008). It was found to correlate .38 with children's total British Ability Scales II (BAS II) score at pre-school entry, .32 with family SES, and .35 with parents' educational levels (Melhuish et al., 2001).

A five-point scale (in quintiles) was used to describe the early HLEs in the EPPSE sample: HLE 1 (0 to 13 points), HLE 2 (14 to 19 points), HLE 3 (20 to 24 points), HLE 4 (25 to 32 points) and HLE 5 (33 to 45 points). The highest level of early HLE indicates that these children experience the full range of educational activities and that they do so very frequently. The lowest level indicates a more or less complete absence of experiences with educationally relevant activities. The levels in between can indicate a range of scenarios of children's early experiences with educational activities with their parents. For instance, for some children an HLE level 3 might mean that they are being read to every day before bed, that they are regularly taken to the library to pick out new books and that they often play Literacy-related games. At the same time, this child's parents might never sing to them or engage them in Numeracy-related activities. For other children a similar level might mean that their parents engage them in the full range of educational activities, but just not very regularly. In this book we refer to three general patterns of early HLEs rather than to scale points. Low early HLE combines the first two scale points and indicates that educational activities are not typically part of the parent–child inter-action in the home. That is not to say that these parents do not interact with their child in many other ways, but it does indicate that their interactions generally do not focus on activities that are associated with preparing children for future academic learning. Medium early HLE refers to the third scale point (20–24 points) and indicates that although some educational activities certainly are part of parent–child routines, others are likely not, or only haphazardly. In the high early HLE pattern, combining the two highest scale points, educational activities are firmly rooted in children's everyday experiences with their parents.

Differences in early home learning experiences

Frequency patterns of early learning experiences have been found to differ between cultures (industrialized world vs majority world), between cultural sub-groups (working class vs middle class; cultural majority vs ethnic cultural minority groups), but also in relation to demand characteristics of the child, such as age or gender. We did not find any clear indications in the Case Studies that differences in early HLE experiences were related to ethnicity: high and low early HLEs were found among white UK families and among families from different ethnic heritage. Neither did we find any indications of ethnic-cultural differences in explanations about why parents provided a highly stimulating or less educationally stimulating home environment. In general, parents who provided a high early HLE felt that by doing so they were preparing their child for school, helping them 'get a head start'. In our Case Studies sample we did find SES differences, and we also found indications of gender differences in early HLE experiences.

Figure 6.1 shows patterns of early HLE for boys and girls in the full Effective Pre-School and Primary Education (EPPE 3–11) sample and patterns by gender combined with SES for the children from the Case Studies. The percentages of early HLE patterns by gender in the full EPPE 3–11 sample are based on Siraj-Blatchford and Siraj-Blatchford (2009). EPPE 3–11 found that that early HLE varied between boys and girls similarly across all SES groups, with more girls having higher overall early HLE scores than boys (Sylva et al., 2008). As with EPPE 3–11, the findings from the Case Studies showed that marked gender differences in early HLEs favoured girls. Considerably more girls than boys experience high stimulating early HLEs, and more boys experience low early HLEs. But for our Case Studies sample we also found that these gender differences were not necessarily the same between the SES groups. In our sample from low-SES families we found that about two-thirds of the girls had medium to high experiences compared to only one-third of the boys. In the high-SES sample of the Case Studies,

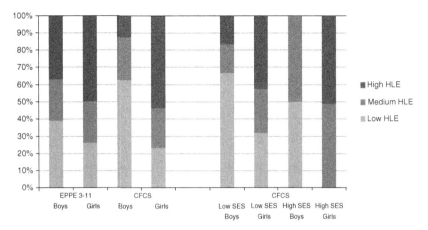

Figure 6.1 Gender differences in the early home learning environment
(HLE) of the EPPE 3–11 and the Case Studies sample, and by SES
background for the Case Studies sample

half of the boys and girls experienced medium early HLEs. But while
the other half of the high-SES girls experienced high early HLEs, the
other half of the boys experienced low early HLEs.

Patterns of early HLEs in high–SES families

Research shows that early learning activities are more commonly part of
childrearing practices in the home environment of middle-class families
(Hart & Risley, 1995; Hoff, 2003; Molfese et al., 2003; Tudge et al.,
2003). Typically, middle-class parents 'cultivate' skills and attitudes that
prepare their children for a successful academic school career. The
middle-class parents in our Case Studies were generally no different. In
the middle-class families in the Case Studies, school-relevant early learning activities such as book reading were typically regarded as an inherent
aspect of child rearing. As Imogene's mother put it when asked why she
felt it was important to read with her child: 'What else is there in life
really?' The following Case Studies example describes how Abby, one of
the children from a high-SES home who has been doing well all through
her school years, was surrounded by books and reading from birth. Her
mother explains why she felt it was important for her to read with Abby
from a young age:

Because I think that's the base, the root of all education, if you can't read then
you can't get an appreciation of books and so forth, right from the word go.

How would you get Abby to appreciate books at that age?

Erm, well we just had so many, because I mean, from the first the boys, and all my family are into books and there're a lot of book club things that I used to go to. You know, coffee mornings and that sort of thing? And just because I like them and they're beautiful, they're so lovely, children's books. And in the Nursery as well, they always have the lovely little reading corners and things like that, they did take books out, they did have the little library thing. Yes, and it's just a nice thing to sit down and do, I suppose. I mean, if they're showing interest and want to do it as well, it makes it easier, but to me it was important, and all my family are a bit like that, and you know, I suppose that's just how it sort of, transferred down to me. I mean I can't say I'm a big reader at the moment. Their stepfather, he's an avid reader but I don't actually feel that it's made them want to read books as they've grown up, it was there and that was my bit as Mum that you should be doing that and encouraging that. Mother of Abby, girl, Group 4 (high SES, attainment as predicted)

Although a higher prevalence of educationally relevant early learning experiences in the home context is more common among high-SES families, it is by no means absent in less affluent homes, nor is it present to the same degree in all high-SES families. In EPPE 3–11 the early HLE was only moderately associated with SES and parents' educational levels (correlations = .28–.33) indicating that low-SES homes sometimes scored highly and, conversely, high-SES homes at times scored poorly on the early HLE measure (Sylva et al., 2008). EPPE 3–11concluded that

In terms of the statistical model, the early years HLE and parents' qualification level work as two independent predictors indicating that some parents can provide a high-scoring early years HLE irrespective of their own qualification levels, and support the development of their children in this way. (Sylva et al., 2008, p. 25)

While we did not find any indication that ethnic heritage had in any way influenced the presence or absence of high early HLEs among high-SES families in the Case Studies, we did find a notable gender difference in early HLEs. It should be noted that our high-SES Case Studies sample includes only fifteen children, of whom six were boys and of whom only four had a non-White ethnic heritage, and that therefore these findings should not be interpreted as being representative of patterns in high-SES populations in general. Nonetheless, we found that while half of the girls from high-SES families had high-quality early HLE experiences, the other half experienced medium-quality early HLEs. So although not all these middle-class girls might have had the opportunity to experience the full range of educational experiences on a daily basis, these educational activities certainly were a normal and reoccurring part of their inter-actions with their parents and would certainly have impacted on their relationship. In contrast, none of the high-SES boys experienced high and only half experienced medium early HLEs. The other half of these boys had low early HLEs and experienced few early learning activities during their interactions with their parents.

Although all the middle-class parents stressed their awareness of the importance of providing early learning activities to their child, not all these parents had translated these beliefs into actual parenting practices that are considered part of a high-quality HLE. While the absence of high early HLEs for boys was commonly related to aspects of their gender, the explanations offered by the parents at least suggested that this had not been the case for instances where early HLEs were low. Parents who provided medium HLEs for their sons typically mentioned that although they regularly offered educational activities, their child's interest was often limited. They felt their sons, and boys in general, were more inclined towards indoor and outdoor activities that allowed them to burn off lots of energy, such as riding tricycles, ball games and rough-and-tumble games.

Although the middle-class parents who had provided low early HLEs for their sons also mentioned their sons' preference for typical 'boy' activities, they felt their work situation at the time had been the primary reason. Parents in the high-SES sample nearly all worked but there were considerable differences in working hours. Fourteen of the fifteen high-SES mothers worked before the child went to school, mostly part-time (nine); nearly all fathers worked full-time. The three children from high-SES families who had low early HLEs all had two working parents. These parents had jobs as entrepreneurs and medical professionals, which meant that they worked extremely long hours and as a result, they felt, had little time to personally engage with their child in early educational experiences.

I didn't play with him, because when he was at an age where I should have been doing little words, making blocks and things, I was extremely busy in the business ... We were all involved in the business, there was no spare time, we left all of that to the other children to do, you know ... His cousins did colouring and stuff like that. I should have done it, but it's just, it was out of our, you know, it wasn't, we couldn't do it at the time ... it was impossible ...

I saw in the case notes that he attended playgroup for over fifty hours a week?

That's right ... yeah, he was almost living there ... we'd drop him off early in the morning, pick him up late at night ... it was a nightmare for him as well, I'm sure it was. Father of Subash, boy, Group 3 (high SES, attainment below prediction)

Although nearly all high-SES parents felt that their work had impinged on the time they actually spent interacting with their child, most of them, often mothers, managed to provide a stimulating early HLE environment for their child. In fact, four of the five high-SES families that provided a high early HLE for their daughters had mothers who worked, but none worked full-time. These high-SES working mothers generally felt that at the time it had been important for them as an individual to work, and also that by doing so they had provided an important role model to their daughters.

Mother: I think she respects that I'm busy as well. I've got things that I have to do and I think that also, that sort of, well it gives a work ethic doesn't it? That there is a work ethic within this family, she's gonna know that she's . . . in fact she wants a part-time job now, doesn't she? She keeps going on about she wants a part-time job . . . but her father said to her she can't have one yet . . . (laughs)

Father: Well she's too busy, she's too busy . . .

Mother: She's a bit young but she probably will get one in the summer. I don't think they've been deprived really by the fact of me working, or both of us working. I've only just started full-time actually, just last year so . . . it's always been sort of four days, three or four days a week. I think it's quite good, it's good the kids know that there's an ambition . . . that gives them a bit of ambition to do something and . . . yeah I think it's good. Parents of Chloe, girl, Group 3 (high SES, attainment below prediction)

Patterns of early home learning environments in low-SES families

In the Case Studies sample we found that half of the children from low-SES backgrounds had experienced medium to high early HLEs. Qualitative and quantitative analyses from the EPPE 3–11 research (Melhuish et al., 2008; Siraj-Blatchford, 2010a) showed that children from disadvantaged backgrounds with high attainment typically came from families that provided them with a highly favourable early HLE in combination with attendance at a high-quality pre-school setting. These children and families were found across different minority ethnic groups. In our Case Studies we found medium or high early HLEs for eleven of the twenty children from low-SES families who were succeeding against the odds and six out of fifteen low-SES children who attained as predicted. These children, for instance, had been given ample opportunities to experience early Literacy activities, which helped them develop school-relevant skills.

Games, yeah I know she liked the round circles, you put one, they build up to the small circle. Stack, stack the circles up. Yeah, she liked that game, I bought her that game. I still remember that. Yeah.

And would you read with her?

Yes. Just easy books, the books with sounds and lots and lots of pictures. She'd learn, I think ... they pick, pick it up don't they? The sounds and the letters and and ... you know, I don't know. Everything really, to learn how to turn the page of a book, how to respect a book. Children they need to know that don't they? Several colours, everything, I used to teach her all that. Mother of Fareeda, girl, Group 2 (low SES, attainment as predicted)

Although Fareeda was part of Group 2 (low SES, predicted attainment) her trajectory showed a significant improvement from the time she started school. At the end of primary she was still doing as predicted but by the time she was 14 years old the ranking based on her Key Stage 3 attainment put her among the children succeeding against the odds of disadvantage.

Often these less advantaged parents were very creative at finding enjoyable and stimulating activities for their child that would not put an extra strain on the often limited household budget.

'Cos we didn't have a lot of money, so we made things ... Used to make all sorts (laughing).We used to walk up the city and walk to parks, and we used to do art stuff didn't we? We used to make a lot of things. Anything out of nothing (laughing). We made this big dolls' house out of toilet roll and glue and cardboard. We had this big cardboard box (laughing) we put a wooden plank on the bottom, and we made it into a dolls' house. And it was really big, it was just out of toilet roll. It's brilliant (laughing). Mother of Martha, girl, Group 1 (low SES, attainment above prediction)

The other half of the children from our disadvantaged sample (five girls and four boys who were succeeding against the odds, and eight boys and one girl who were attaining as predicted) had lower early HLEs. In some cases this low early HLE indicated that although these children did experience a wide range of activities, they only got them every so often and not frequently. For other children it meant that perhaps they only experienced one or two kinds of educational activities, but that these frequently reoccurred. Despite their lower early HLE, the analysis of the Case Studies interviews showed that for all children who were 'succeeding against the odds' except one (a girl who had been adopted at age 6), stimulating early HLE activities involving parents and children, such as book reading and teaching letters and numbers, were in fact provided. The mother of one of the boys describes an elaborate ritual she and her son shared before bedtime, when he was little, that actually involved reading, rhymes and storytelling, despite the overall lower early HLE that had been reported earlier during her EPPE interview when the child was 3 years old:

I used to read to him every night when he was little, we used to have a little bedtime story, a bit of animation and a bedtime prayer, every night. He had a little bunny, he had a little bunny and it was the … y'know we'd do the little 'hop little bunny, hop, hop, hop' nursery-rhyme sort of things … so yeah and we … we made, we tried to make it come to life and if the story, wanted to put some action in the story … I thought perhaps reading to him, because it would help him gain an interest for books … yeah, for his education. Mother of Jarell, boy, Group 1 (low SES, attainment above prediction)

Besides reading to him, Jarell's mother also engaged him in learning activities involving songs, poems and nursery rhymes, because that was something they both enjoyed, and it was something they could do while she was for instance preparing tea, when they were out shopping for groceries or when she was doing the laundry. But taking him to the library or engaging him in learning activities involving the alphabet, or numbers and shapes, playing with letters and numbers or painting and drawing were not part of their regular routine. The foregoing example showed that despite the fact that this mother had a job and had a disabled older child to take care of, she made the effort to spend quality time with her son because she felt this would benefit his education.

Less effective early home learning environments

For the children who did not go on to be academically successful, examples of frequently reoccurring, high quality, educationally oriented learning experiences in the home context, that were enjoyed by parent and child together, were rare. This is perhaps most clearly visible when we look at activities that characterized the early years experiences of boys from the low-SES group who did not succeed against the odds, but it was also apparent in the experiences of the academically less successful boys from high-SES family backgrounds. Nearly all these boys had experienced low early HLEs. For these boys, interactions in and through the home environment consisted, for a large part, of outdoor activities with other children, such as siblings, nephews and children who lived on their street. Although these boys did sometimes play games with their parents or read books together, their parents often felt they were not particularly interested in these activities, and perhaps as a result these were not a regular part of family interactions. It seemed that for these boys and their parents, engaging in educational activities had not given the kind of enjoyment described by other parents and children.

He wasn't really much into the letters and number things as a child, to be honest, more into playing with toys and …Yeah, cars and stuff like that. Yeah, stuff like that. He wouldn't actually bother to do that kind of stuff at an early age. But then at school, it became fun ... you know teachers do that ... they get away with working with the kids and all that but he'd still do it here and there but it wasn't home as much as when he went to school. But when he went to school, he loved it there ... it was nice watching him.

And what about bedtime stories?

Yeah we'd ... get a few ... I couldn't say it was all the time, no, it was a few times here and there over the years. It was never a routine, every other night, it was just ... say, whenever you want to do ... and a lot of times he'd just get to bed himself and ... 'I'm going to bed now, Mum.' He was a good little fellow, no mistaking. We couldn't understand how he'd worked out that way. Like I say: he's a self-made man in a way ... Whatever he's doing now it was all in him to do when he was young. Father of Harry, boy, Group 2 (low SES, attainment as predicted)

Nope ... Never been interested in books at all. He can read. He's never ... he's a lot like me in that respect. I hated reading when I was a child, I could read before I went to school, my mum was very good and taught me to read before I went to school, but I didn't with him, he learned at school.

Why didn't you do that with him?

'Cos he hated books! We could do like, sort of flash cards and certain things if you were just out and about. You know, little things he'd pick up, but I never actually sat and taught him to read as such, 'cos he wasn't interested. He'd rather be doing something, rather than sitting with a book. I'm not even sure if he can do it now, but I don't think he's got the ability to make up the pictures? You know when you read a book you make up the people's faces and the situation that they're in, you have a mental picture of what's goin' on? He just reads the words and I don't think they really absorb and mean anything.

How did you discover that?

Because I think he's like me and I hated books when I was at school. I read because I had to. Mother of Edward, boy, Group 2 (low SES, attainment as predicted)

For these boys in particular the home environment and attitude of parents towards early learning seemed much more oriented towards what Lareau (2003) has termed 'accomplishment of natural growth', with much child-initiated peer play, long stretches of leisure time and frequent interaction with members of the extended family:

He'd always be nattering away to himself, talking and making these little men and say that they were talking to each other (laughs). I could always hear him nattering away to himself.

Would you play with him?

Sometimes if he asked us to, but sometimes he was like more independent, he weren't gonna do anything you tell him, sometimes he would let you play, sometimes he wouldn't. He had loads of friends ... he grew up with the next door neighbour, 'cos he's the same age as him and they grew up like, since they was little, right to the end. [He played outside with cousins] all the time really, but we didn't have to go far because we're a close family and we're all like living in the street (laughs). Mother of Richard, boy, Group 2 (low SES, attainment as predicted)

Parents offered several reasons for not being able to provide a high early HLE. As with high-SES parents, work was mentioned as an explanation for not being able to spend much time with the child in working-class families. Of the thirty-five low-SES mothers, twelve had jobs outside the house, either full-time (five) or part-time (seven). In cases where mothers worked full-time, irregular shifts were part of their job routine. In seven of these families the early HLE was low. In fact, four of the six girls who had a low early HLE had working mothers. Although some mothers took pleasure and pride in their work, for most of these mothers from low-SES families staying at home was simply not an option. Nearly half of them were lone parents (compared to only one single mother from the high-SES sample) and in four cases the fathers were unemployed (none of the high-SES fathers were unemployed). Although having an (additional) income through work helped parents to provide material resources for their child, they felt it made it harder for them to provide a highly stimulating early HLE.

Many mothers in the low-SES sample mentioned that they also felt they had not had enough time due to family circumstances. In several of these families, children had siblings or relatives (such as grandparents) who were severely ill or disabled, or the mothers themselves had health issues. This not only required a lot of time from mothers, it also often brought about stress and feelings of sadness and guilt. The Centre for Excellence and Outcomes (C4EO) Early Years Knowledge Review (2009) discusses at length the empirical evidence that supports the conclusion that putting in place new policies aimed at supporting these families dealing with multiple disadvantages could make an important contribution to improve children's attainment (Siraj-Blatchford & Siraj-Blatchford, 2009). Often these parents felt they perhaps were not spending enough time with their child, and tried to provide the child with alternative learning opportunities, for instance by enrolling them in a pre-school or by accepting support from their family and extended social networks, such as their religious community.

What made you decide that Christopher would attend a nursery?

'Cos I just thought it would be better for him really. They're probably getting more stimulation at school than what I would have been able to give him

Mayo & Leseman, 2008; Stipek, 2001; Tudge et al., 2006). Our Case Studies sample, and particularly the sub-samples, are relatively small, so it is hard to draw any firm conclusions about patterns of association of early HLEs and their early Literacy and Numeracy skills within and between the four groups. Purely based on visual inspection, we observed a positive association between higher HLEs and higher initial rankings, but only among our sub-sample of children from low-SES families, and more so among the ones who would go on to succeed against the odds. The children from Group 1 who had experienced medium or high early HLEs had initial rankings, typically on both domains, that were above their SES group's average.

Among the SES peers who did not go on to succeed against the odds, this association was observed for two-thirds of the children with medium or high early HLEs. In contrast, among the children from wealthier backgrounds who had experienced similar medium to high early HLEs, initial rankings were just as often below average as above average. An association between low early HLEs and initial rankings below average was observed for the high-SES sample, where none of the children (three boys) who experienced low early HLEs had initial rankings above average. This association was visible, but weaker, in the low-SES sample, where initial rankings below or at average for at least one domain were found for two-thirds of the children who had experienced low early HLEs. In line with quantitative results of analyses for the full EPPSE sample at younger ages (Melhuish et al., 2008; Sammons et al., 2004, 2008d) the foregoing patterns of association among the Case Studies sample seem to suggest that, particularly for low-SES children, the effect of high vs low early HLEs plays a substantial role in the development of early numeracy and literacy skills. If they are given an opportunity to participate frequently in educational experiences in the home environment, these children are more likely to start their learning trajectories in school with early numeracy and literacy skills that are developed beyond the averages of their low-SES peers.

For children from more advantageous backgrounds, the relation between a more highly stimulating HLE and initial literacy and numeracy skills is less evident. The finding that medium or high early HLEs did not necessarily coincide with above average or even average initial rankings for the children from middle-class families, but that it did for children from disadvantaged backgrounds, could be an indication that in these wealthier families, as was shown for IQ in the Turkheimer study, perhaps genes accounted for a greater proportion of variance in earlier Literacy and Numeracy skills than environment, and that the reverse might be true for disadvantaged families (Turkheimer et al., 2003).

On the other hand, missing out on early educational experiences in the HLE seems negatively to affect children's initial literacy and numeracy skills, regardless of whether they come from wealthy or disadvantaged families.

Interestingly, the effect of low vs high early HLE appears to be particularly visible for the low-SES boys in our Case Studies sample, showing that when early HLE experiences are high they not only start off with higher initial rankings but also have a better chance of 'succeeding against the odds' at a later age. It might be that the effect of low vs high early SES has a significant impact on boys in general, but we cannot tell based on the Case Studies data alone. In our sample, none of the middle-class boys had experienced high early HLEs, and only three of the boys had low early HLEs. But for these three particular boys their initial rankings were below those of their high-SES peers, and by the time of their Key Stage 3 assessments in secondary school, two of them ranked among the lowest achieving children of the EPPSE sample.

Effective early practical support in family microsystems with children succeeding against the odds

For children succeeding against the odds of disadvantage, even those with low early HLEs, the practical support they had received through their family microsystem had several characteristics that are worth exploring, as these set them apart from the support in other families.

For one thing, although the frequency and range of early learning activities these children got to experience with their parents were often limited, the quality of the interactions during these activities when they did occur seemed to positively set them apart from the experiences of children in similar circumstances who did not academically succeed. For instance, the early learning experiences Jarell's mother described during her interview had many of the characteristics positively associated with children's cognitive and socio-emotional development. When they were reading together she would talk to her son about his thoughts and feelings. By doing this she was supporting him to develop the ability to reflect on his own actions as well as on those of others. She was also stimulating and modelling the use of abstract language. Extensive research in patterns of language use with young children shows that these quality characteristics are common for interactions in high-SES families, but are less typical for interactions between low-SES parents and their young children, particularly among mothers with low educational quali- fications (Hart & Risley, 1995; Hoff, 2003; Tudge et al., 2003).

However, there was more that set apart the early learning experiences of children who would go on to succeed against the odds of disadvantage. In these families HLE activities, such as reading, were seen from an early age onwards as something that was naturally enjoyable for both parent and child. These shared activities provided them with opportunities to bond, and as such supported a good social and emotional relationship between them. Although this enjoyment and bonding was mentioned for some of the less academically successful girls, it seemed to have played less of a role in the interactions between parents and academically less successful children, particularly boys.

Furthermore, regardless of the actual early HLE they provided, parents of children who succeeded against the odds explicitly regarded early HLE activities as valuable opportunities for the child to develop cognitive skills that would help and prepare the child to do well in school, but also to develop a positive attitude to and interest in school-related activities. They valued education.

[I learned] like what school was and maybe like helped me with my like work we were doing in school before like doing . . . Yeah, or like just so we can have a bit of a better understanding, so it's not like totally new to them. Because then like, you're going to school and if you learn so many things new at the same time, you don't, you don't get them all. Asya, girl, Group 1 (low SES, attainment above prediction)

These parents felt it was important to help their child to develop school-relevant skills and behaviours. Aware that they could not always provide these experiences to the extent they felt would have been necessary, these parents tried to find alternative ways to offer their children stimulating early learning experiences. For some, this meant that older siblings read to them or played (computer) games with them. For others, there were other adults, often family members such as grandparents, but also family friends, neighbours or members of their religious community, that provided learning experiences for the child. This suggests that at least for some of these children, the limited learning experiences they might have had (and reported on during the interviews) with their parents were compensated for to a certain extent by other people in their environment. Charley was one of the girls with the lowest HLE at age 3. The following excerpt from the parent interview shows that although Charley's mother did not feel comfortable undertaking activities that are part of a high early HLE, she did provide Charley with many other experiences through which she could develop school-relevant skills and furthermore made sure that Charley had a rich network of significant others that did provide her with high early HLE activities.

Can you tell me a bit about what Charley was like when she was a little girl?

(Laughing) She was a very active child, very active and she was always keen to learn things and she was always quick to pick up on things and that.

What kind of things did she enjoy learning?

Everything really, she would always pick a book up, she would always amuse herself with ... toys um ... yeah, she was definitely ...

What kind of things would you do with her?

I would do things with her, her Dad used to read more with her than what I used to, I used to play with her a lot but her Dad would be the one who would sit down, and who would read with her and her Nana as well.

Did they have a regular reading routine?

Umm, not so much regular but Charley would always pick books up for you to read quite ... quite a lot.

And you said you played with her ...

A lot yeah ... All sorts of things really, I can't sort of really remember what ... she used to love jigsaws, floor puzzles, that sort of things she used to like doing ... and the park ... really.

Do you remember teaching her letters and numbers?

Her Dad was more that than what I was.

Why do you think that was?

I don't know, her Dad just ... her Dad's very clever (laughing) and he always sort of really used to do all of that sort of things with her. He'd sit down with her and her Dad would do all of that with her more than me. Mother of Charley, girl, Group 1 (low SES, attainment above prediction)

By personally engaging the child in early learning experiences, or by facilitating opportunities for the child to have these experiences with other people, these parents from low-SES families created a structure of effective practical support that stimulates the development of school-relevant skills and knowledge by their children. Children bring the skills, abilities and competencies they develop during early proximal processes in the family context with them, once they start participating in (pre-)school classrooms. The linguistic features of the language used during activities that are part of the early HLE resemble the academic language register that will be used later on in classroom instruction and textbooks (Leseman et al., 2007). As such, activities that are part of the early HLEs, particularly Literacy activities, provide children with the necessary opportunities to encounter and develop a vocabulary that will allow them to actively participate in classroom activities and facilitate their understanding of classroom instructions (Forget-Dubois et al., 2009; cf. Bus et al., 1995; Mayo & Leseman, 2008). But other activities, such as elaborate storytelling, shared fantasy play, following a recipe while cooking together, talking about a child's feelings, discussing things that happen when taking a walk outside, all potentially offer opportunities for children to develop their language abilities. For instance when these activities facilitate and stimulate the use of aspects of child-directed speech that are positive predictors of language development, such as high quantity of speech, lexical richness of the language, high rates of question asking, long length of their utterances, syntactic and grammatical complexity and metalinguistic references (Alexander Pan et al., 2005). A study by Tudge and colleagues (2003) for instance found that children who were more familiar with decontextualized conversations, because of their earlier family experiences, initiated and engaged in more conversations in reception and were subsequently perceived by their teachers as being more competent.

The home learning environment during the primary years

As children moved from the pre-school years into their primary years, the nature of effective, practical support changed with the increasing abilities of the child. Differences found in the early HLE of children from different socio-economic backgrounds tend to persist as children get older and the HLE shifts to include more school-related activities (Bradley, 2002; Bradley et al., 2000, 2001; Feinstein et al., 2008; Parke, 2004).

Two kinds of effective practical support were most commonly mentioned for the academically successful children in the Case Studies: learning activities and help with homework. Effective *practical support* was explicitly mentioned to explain academic success for six boys and seven girls from Group 1 and for all six students from Group 4. Academically effective HLEs during the primary years continued to offer children a range of learning experiences that gave them a chance to practise and develop school-related skills and knowledge. Children watched educational programmes on television, such as *Sesame Street* and *Art Attack*, they played board games with their parents and siblings, were read to and went on holidays and outings. Sometimes the HLE activities were the same as they had been during the early years, but typically their form changed; as parents and children sat together with a picture book, reading by parents was gradually replaced by the parents listening to the child reading out loud. But that did not mean that this new form replaced the old form all together. Particularly during the first years of primary school, bedtime stories were still commonly part of the evening ritual, but the complexity of the books of course changed.

In contrast to what is usually found for low-SES families, informal learning activities that support children's academic achievement in school were mentioned for all of the children from low-SES families 'succeeding against the odds'. In nearly all these families, children were actively stimulated to read. Parents took them to libraries, bought them books or would read books with them that the child brought home from school. They also listened to their child read.

He's read every possible version of things like Robin Hood to compare which one he likes best (laugh).

Would you and he talk about that?

Yeah, 'cause I also enjoy reading kids' books ... so he'll read a good book and he'll say: 'Mum read that, you'll love it', or, 'Don't read that you'll hate it.' We'd compare notes on it. Yeah, we would discuss a lot ... and my mother would have read most of them as well so ... (laugh) he'd know a lot of outlets on that. He's definitely got a lot of books ... I mean, he's one of the only teenagers I know who will actually go out and buy books for the fun of it. A lot of his friends look at his books 'What the hell, why have you got the book?' and he says then: 'Why haven't you got the book?' (laughing). I mean books are so much a part of our life that to have kids who sort of sit there and go 'You're strange, you read', you don't understand why they wouldn't want to. Mother of Robert, boy Group 1 (low SES, attainment above prediction)

We would normally do that [buy extra books or get books from the library] mostly during the holidays, because we want to keep it easy and it's a learning process and you can't just stop learning at one point, you have to keep going. If, during the holidays, if you sit down idle and then you go back to school starting from square one again, and we made it compulsory for them, two hours of library twice a week during the holidays and it has to be done. They will read there or bring it home, whichever way pleases so ... The library is just round the corner from us as well, yeah. Mother of Ife, girl, Group 1 (low SES, attainment above prediction)

These parents and children alike felt that these activities in and through the home environment had continued to play an important role in facilitating children's academic achievement throughout their years in primary school. But as children were becoming less dependent on their parents for regulation of emotions and behaviour, the role of parents became less prominent in many of these activities. Now, instead of taking the lead, parents rather followed the initiatives of the child. They facilitated opportunities for children to play by themselves, with other children or other adults. Typically they continued to monitor these activities and offered advice and guidance. Charley described how she and her cousins would go to a market with their mother over the weekend when she was 7 years old:

> Every Sunday my mum would give me ten pound and me auntie would give my two cousins ten pound each and they'd take us to the market so we could buy things what we wanted. Yeah, like that helped me with my Maths a lot, 'cos like, I could, I could work out how much I spent and 'cos my mum and my auntie used to say to us, 'Make sure you get the right change', so we could like work out ourselves, before they give it to us, how much we were gonna get. Things like the make-up, we had to read what the spelling, say on the front. So that was quite good yeah. Charley, girl, Group 1 (low SES, attainment above prediction)

In families where practical home support was perceived as having been insufficient to effectively support children's academic achievement, parents regretted not having taken the time to read more with the child or engage them in informal learning activities, such as educational computer games. For many of the 'vulnerable' children particularly, reading activities became less frequent during the primary years. For most of the Case Studies children from high-SES families who did not do as well as expected academically (Group 3: High SES, low attainment), parents indicated that their child had experienced learning difficulties at a certain point in their development. In most cases these difficulties were preceded by children's loss of interest in related educational activities that had previously been part of the HLE. As a result, these children tended not to participate in particular aspects of the HLE even though it was offered to them. As the stacks of books in the home of Marcy Stewart testified, books and reading had been given a prominent place in her high early HLE and continued to do so when she was in primary school. But while Marcy initially enjoyed these interactions, she lost interest once she started struggling with reading by herself.

> She still used to be read to, but she seemed to lose interest in books in a big way. Y'know, she wasn't so keen? We used to go to the library fairly often and she wasn't interested in going any more. Books she got for her birthday or Christmas weren't really given much attention. We still used to try to read with her, but you could tell it was something she wasn't enjoying. It was quite a frustrating period. Mother of Marcy, girl, Group 3 (high SES, attainment below prediction)

Although the low-SES children who did not succeed against the odds (Group 2) also experienced a range of activities with their family, the nature and perception of the activities was typically different from the activities experienced by their academically successful low-SES peers. The perceived lack of interest in educational activities such as reading, that had been present during the early years among many of the academically less successful low-SES boys, became even more obvious once they started school. These children seemed to lose interest in books all together. Instead they filled their out-of-school time with outdoor activities and particularly computer games. Many of these boys spent substantial parts of their out-of-school time playing computer games on consoles, which was often perceived as having had a negative effect on their behaviour. It is interesting that the use of computers can be both beneficial, as reported earlier, when it is used in moderation to support learning and some relaxation through games, but also a problem when the computer is used largely for games and entertainment, often less well supervised.

In many of these working-class families, but particularly in families without an income from work, parents felt limited in the kind of experiences and support they could provide for their children, because of financial difficulties. In our Case Studies sample, many of these working-class parents who left education at a young age took up unskilled or semi-skilled manual jobs in the lower pay-grades. When their children started pre-school, the majority of their parents (twenty-two) had, at the most, only worked in semi-skilled jobs (like Steven's father who worked as a postman). In two families, fathers worked as skilled manual labours (both worked in construction) and in two other families parents had worked in unskilled manual jobs only. When children were in reception, less than half of these families received incomes from at least one full-time job (eight families in Group 1 and six families in Group 2). Five additional families (four from Group 1) only had one part-time income to support the family.

At the end of the first decade of the twenty-first century, nearly 30 per cent of children and over 20 per cent of working adults in the United Kingdom were living in households with incomes below 60 per cent of the median net disposable income after deduction of housing costs; effectively this means that 3.8 million children are living in relative poverty according to income standards for the United Kingdom (Department for Work and Pensions, 2011a, 2011b). In families where no one earns an income from work, financial situations are even worse. When the Case Studies children attended reception, fifteen out of the thirty-five low-SES families received no income through work (seven families from Group 1 and eight from Group 2). Even with everything society has to offer in terms of economic support, many of these low-SES families found it difficult to make ends meet.

As children grew up, nearly half of the working-class parents found a route that took them away from poverty or socio-economic hardship. These parents found their way into skilled labour or even professional jobs, for instance in the areas of construction, as mechanics or in the health care profession. They took up craft apprenticeships, went back to college to obtain the qualifications they needed to gain access to forms of further or higher education or took up opportunities to obtain additional work-based qualifications. As a result of their efforts they experienced a steady increase in their work-related responsibilities and earnings. But in other families, job levels had not improved substantially as children moved to the higher grades of primary school and into secondary school. In half of the low-SES families with children doing poorly as predicted, and in 20 per cent of the low-SES families with children succeeding against the odds of disadvantage, parents found themselves without jobs or had never worked. In these families, parents had difficulties providing for basic living conditions such as housing, heating, food and clothes.

During the primary years, family outings at weekends and holidays, or family vacations over extended periods of time, became more common, even in the poorest low-SES families. These outings offered parents and children prolonged opportunities to share experiences. But while family holidays and outings were often a normal aspect of family life in middle-class homes, many of the low-SES families had to save up for a family holiday or trips. It was not uncommon for them to be supported with loans or donations by relatives or friends. Family outings and holidays were generally perceived as a way for the family to have a nice time together and to 'relax' together. Although amusement parks, visiting relatives and trips to the coast were commonly mentioned as favourite outings, some of the families also took the child on outings to historical sites, to museums or to theatres. Particularly in low-SES families with children succeeding against the odds and in high-SES families, parents and children felt these experiences were also helpful for their school and learning because it taught the child about other cultures, History, languages and sometimes about their cultural heritage. Parents often expressed the belief that they were supporting their child academically by offering their child these educational experiences.

Just take them to museums and treats, they've been to every museum, they've done it. I mean their dad's gone to a lot of those as well in school holidays. 'Cause I think you can't just learn everything in the classroom ... I think that's important, I think it's good to have experiences out ... It just broadens your mind ... so when you're asked to write a story you've got experience in this, you've something to write about, you've ... There's nothing worse than going back to school after the school holidays and they ask you to write what did you do in the school holidays. And it's like we used to nothing, go work for your mum as a job ehm ... you would lie (laughing). And, and they can tell you lie (laughing) and you can suffer the humiliation. Mother of Steven, boy, Group 1 (low SES, attainment above prediction)

Stonehenge and all sorts of historic sites and things like that, and we used to take him to Warwick and ... culturally he went out and about in that respect. You would buy the Roman books at the Roman Villas so he could read up on it and understand it 'cause it was a fascination and it still is in that respect a fascination. Mother of Robert, boy, Group 1 (low SES, attainment above prediction)

While the out-of-home experiences provided by low-SES families with academically less successful children also aimed for pleasure and enjoyment, they were not typically expected to provide opportunities for additional learning or cultural capital. For instance, family outings for these children from low-SES families were less often educational and more often of a purely social nature, such as visiting friends and relatives.

Places like the zoo and parks and stuff like that, not like museums ... no, 'cos they was never interested in that, the older ones weren't interested in that either so ... Yeah, more outside, sort of outdoors, bikes and things like that, picnics and that sort of thing. We used to go abroad to Spain every year, 'cos my family and I lived there. So we used to do the sun holidays over there every year. It was nice! Three weeks in the sun it was lovely. Mother of Christopher, boy, Group 2 (low SES, attainment as predicted)

Yeah, yeah, we travelled to Germany, to Scotland, London, Nigeria. If I find the money to buy the tickets. They first say: 'Oh we want to go to Germany.' I will try to find a way for the tickets, sometimes it's very cheap to buy. So I buy the tickets and we go there one week holiday. One year ago. So we have fun. We all go visiting friends. London, sometimes we have the holiday, maybe two weeks, we go to London. We spend one week there. We go shopping, we go around to McDonalds, to have fun, to park, we went to park in London, have fun. My wish to make them happy, so ... then I can see they are OK. Mother of Ebun and Bunmi, twin girls, Group 2 (low SES, attainment as predicted)

The home learning environment during the secondary years

In early adolescence, what constitutes an effective HLE again shifts further away from shared activities to facilitation of the child's experiences in additional microsystems, such as peer groups, religious communities or sports clubs (Bradley et al., 2000). The goal for adolescents is to emerge as healthy, well-functioning adults who can fulfil their potential and meet the requirements of society, and effective home environments facilitate this process (Bradley et al., 2000; Steinberg et al., 1991). They can achieve this by developing the ability to form meaningful attachments to others, a positive and coherent sense of self, learn to make informed decisions, attain skills to successfully participate in institutions such as school or work environments and to develop a value system that forms the basis for socially responsive participation in society (Steinberg et al., 1991). The instrument developed to measure the home environments of children in adolescence (i.e., Bradley et al., 2000) indicates that an effective HLE provides a healthy physical environment, learning materials (such as books, a library card, access to a computer) and a variety of experiences (for instance, cultural or sports outings, visits to relatives, shared meals).

After the children in the Case Studies sample started secondary school, activities with family members were mostly limited to television watching, family meals and the occasional shopping or cinema outing and holidays. Across high- and low-SES families, parents and children felt that the frequency of these shared activities was not very high. This was not something they necessarily regretted or worried about, rather, it was just what happened when children got older. When asked about the things they now did as a family, 15-year-old Imogene answered:

> We don't go to so many art galleries any more but I think that's because we're so busy at the moment 'cause we, we're all a lot older, we do a lot more by ourselves. Obviously my brother and sister are at university so we don't see them as much. We still go on walks, we go to the park quite a lot. I think we're left to our own devices more, which is nice, you know. The day is so busy normally that the only time you get to talk about that kind of thing is when you actually sit down and you're forced to sit down and talk about it, you know. I think also because we all work hard now every one's more tired, y'know? My mum she didn't use to work [when I was] in primary school, I'd come home and she'd be happy to sit down and talk about stuff, and now I get home later, my parents get home later and there's just not so much time, you know. Imogene, girl, Group 4 (high SES, attainment as predicted)

> But as they get older that [playing games] kind of wears off which is a shame really ... perhaps you should still do it [laughing]. But they become independent and they don't want to do it and you don't want to do it and ... it just stops. Mother of Martha, girl, Group 1 (low SES, attainment above prediction)

Regulating children's behaviours and experiences

According to Bradley and colleagues (2000), the role of the parents during early adolescence is to regulate the child by setting boundaries to, for instance, computer/game console use and television watching, by discussing possible hazardous activities (e.g., drugs and alcohol abuse, sexual activity), or by giving the child household responsibilities (cf. Mounts, 2000). Many parents feel that the regulating aspects of their childrearing practices play an important role in their children's school success. When asked about the reason for her daughter's school success, Leanna's mother answered:

Because, basically when she comes home, I do not let up on her. I do exactly the same thing as she did when she was at primary school. She has to do her homework ... she has to do her chores around the home. I do give her free time ... and ... I don't think I put much pressure on her. Maybe if you ask her she may say something else but ... (laughs), I think that is it. Mother of Leanna, girl, Group 1 (low SES, attainment above prediction)

Interestingly, examples of such regulatory behaviours were given for nearly all girls, but only for half of the boys that were 'succeeding against the odds'. These kinds of regulatory activities were hardly mentioned for low-SES boys who were attaining as predicted, at least not as occurring on a regular basis. Household chores were a regular part of the lives of most girls and some boys from low-SES families, particularly of those 'succeeding against the odds'. Chores were seen as a necessary part of the child's daily life. They functioned to teach children to take responsibility for their own needs, but also as a way to prepare them for their future life at college or in marriage. Particularly among families with African or Caribbean heritage, children were expected to contribute to family life by doing laundry, vacuuming and cooking.

[He did those chores] because, I wasn't (laughing) going to be a slave ... which now sometimes I feel like as if I am. It's important for him to have the jobs because he needed to grow and to fend for himself and learn how to care for himself and how to live, basically. If you give a man a fish he eats for a day, but if you teach him to fish, he'll eat for the rest of his life ... and this was the life skills that he'd need, for the rest of his life. Mother of Jarell, boy, Group 1 (low SES, attainment above prediction)

I think I introduced her to the kitchen from when she was about 10. I think it's a tradition that's just been passed on through generations of my family, umm. My mum would cook and I would come in the kitchen and then right when I was 10 she just chucked me in and left the kitchen for me. I haven't done it that way. I've let her into the kitchen with me an' when I come back from work an' I'm in the kitchen, she's with me. We do the cooking together, she does the chopping, she does this, and gradually, she's learning new things. She still do, she can't do everything, but she can still cook quite a lot right now an' ... if I'm coming from work an' I'm calling in late, I can say, 'Ife, can you cook this or cook that?' she'll do it brilliantly, not a problem. Mother of Ife, girl, Group 1 (low SES, attainment above prediction)

Many of the high-SES parents, regardless of their child's attainment, felt that they had not done well with regard to making chores a regular part of children's lives. Most commonly mentioned reasons referred to them just being tired of having to negotiate the chores time and time again. They often added that there had not really been a need for the children to do these chores and that they would have plenty of time to develop these practical skills once they matured.

He doesn't have any jobs around the house now, so ... I mean I do nag him to empty the dishwasher and tidy the room up a bit and stuff like that ... but no ... I don't think he ever did.

Why is that?

Well ... (sighs) I ... oh ... I might have tried to encourage him and his brother to do some ... things maybe but ... I suppose ... in the end it seemed easier and quicker to do it myself. But I do think they have got a bit better as they got older. Mother of Alex, boy, Group 3 (high SES, attainment below prediction)

No, none of them do chores. Because they won't, they won't. I don't, oh because they've got too much homework, they'll only do it for money, really, it's true though, and it's my fault for not having got them to do things. I don't know why I've failed in that department, they can all cook, I think they can put the washing on. Abby does do cleaning for reward. I mean I've drawn up in the past rotas for them to do, chores, but then it never works, because they play one another off: 'Dave didn't do it and if he's not doing it ...' and then there's three of them, three to one, and then I'll do it myself, but it's not fair really because especially when they've been lolling around all through the holidays, and they wonder why I get, you know, slightly irritated. But no, that's been their weakness, 'cause it's skills. It's developing skills for when they have their own homes or when they go off to uni. I feel, they should be doing it, without being prompted perhaps. Mother of Abby, Girl, Group 4 (high SES, attainment as predicted)

However, talking about what was going on in the lives of their children and educating them about sex or drugs were part of the regulatory activities that many of the high-SES parents provided. While these conversations were far less often mentioned for low-SES families with children who were not 'succeeding against the odds', many of the low-SES families with children 'succeeding against the odds' for instance regularly held family meetings in which they discussed how each family member was doing and negotiating necessary changes in children's behaviour and activities.

We just, we just sit down. We have what we call family meetings. We all just sit down, we just switch off tellies, switch off radio, sit down and talk. I think at some point Dad introduced that egg timer. So we'll take the time out, turn it over, talk to which ever member of the family you wanna talk to, whatever you wanna talk about ... All of that five minutes or however long that is. Generally we will have a kind of 'Brain pick' with just the four of us or five, if the cousin's around, just to sit down and talk through things: 'We don't like this, we don't like that, we don't want you doing that, this is what you're good at, this is what you're getting better at, this is what you've been doing that's great.' That's just it.

Why did you feel it was important to have that ritual?

Well ... in this day and age where no one has time for each other you're always just, you know ... scattered around the whole place, every time. I mean for instance, now Dad is not in yet. By the time he comes in it might be getting ready to go up to bed and things like that, so, I think it's very important that we have a kind of family time, if you like, be it thirty minutes or so, or an hour depending. Mother of Ife, girl, Group 1 (low SES, attainment above prediction)

[I discuss] ... erm ... sex ... periods. I don't push her too much. I've explained periods right from when she was sort of 10 onwards. I've just explained it biologically, but not going into technical detail ... and more recently as she's started her periods and stuff, I've explained that she can get pregnant and how she can become pregnant, but without going too ... I think you give too ... deep into it ... but just explaining that, you know, that you can get pregnant now, but she's adamant she don't want children, so ...

Why do you feel it's important to have those talks with her?

Well they need to know [laughing]. I mean you can't ... a little girl wakes up one day and she's got blood coming out of her, she'd panic like hell if she didn't know nothing about it [laughing] wouldn't she? I mean I wasn't told anything ... I was just told you may have a period ... and one day I woke up and there was blood everywhere I like, 'Oh my god I'm dying' [laughing]. You panic don't you? She said she don't want kids, she's not having sex. OK that subject's left for now ... it's on the back burner, until perhaps she does find a steady boyfriend and decides and then we'll talk again, but I don't push it. If she doesn't want to talk about it we don't talk about it. They do do it at school, they do cover that at school, the more biological side of it which is yeah, yeah, good. But 'cos it's all a laugh when you're sort of 13, 14 ... they just sit and giggle, I can remember doing it myself [laughing]. Mother of Martha, girl, Group 1 (low SES, attainment above prediction)

Through these kinds of conversations parents were not only teaching their child about their values and beliefs, they were also exposing them to what Bernstein (1971) referred to as the 'elaborated code'. The language use referred to as the elaborated code is typically more often found in middle-class families and in many ways is more similar to language that is used in schooling. The elaborated code can stand on its own: it does not necessarily assume that the listener holds the same assumptions or understandings as the speaker, and is therefore more explicit, more thorough, and does not require the listener to read between the lines. The elaborated code is contrasted with the 'restricted code', typically associated with communications in working-class families. This restricted code is suitable for insiders who share assumptions and under-standing on the topic; it is shorter, condensed, and requires background information and prior knowledge. By using the elaborated code in their interactions with their child, parents model the use of 'academic' lan-guage, and help their child to practise and prepare for the kind of communications they will, for instance, need to successfully write school papers. Later studies, however, have cast doubt on whether some of these findings are universal truths (Tizard & Hughes, 1984). The issue of the type or form and content of language across social classes is one of great contention. What is clear to us is that parents model and set patterns of language development at an early age and children enter pre-school and school with vastly different experiences of the amount and type of language which has been modelled to them. All of which has a bearing on their ability to gain from, or be ready for, participating in educational activities.

7   Parenting towards higher aspirations

This chapter is closely linked to the foregoing chapter on effective and adaptive home learning environments (HLEs). It describes parenting characteristics and practices in our four groups regarding 'family involvement with school and learning' and relates these characteristics and practices to empirical evidence for children's educational success as well as to their educational effect as perceived by children and parents, and the parents' reasons for providing these parenting repertoires.

Introduction

The parenting characteristics of the family microsystem are likely to have an important effect on the support children experience through the family microsystem with school and learning. Evidence for this hypothesis comes from studies that show that caregivers' beliefs about their role in children's academic development, their perceived self-efficacy in fulfilling this role, their parenting style and their academic expectations for their child, predict the activities they provide in the out-of-school context (Eccles & Harold, 1996; Green et al., 2007; Jeynes, 2005). However, child-rearing characteristics, such as parenting style, differ between ethnic-cultural and socio-economic groups (Coleman & Hildebrandt Karraker, 2000; Driessen & Valkenberg, 2000) and parenting context characteristics that are positively associated with socio-emotional and educational support in one of these groups are not necessarily positive for children with a different family background (Okagaki & French, 1998). For instance, studies in the US that related parental beliefs to cognitive development and school achievement showed that more traditional authoritarian beliefs were positively correlated with cognitive delays, lower IQ, psycho-social problems, lower school achievement and less successful social integration (Palacios et al., 1992; Okagaki & Sternberg, 1993; Stoolmiller et al., 2000). On the other hand, Okagaki and French (1998) found that for children from Asian-American communities, authoritarian parenting was associated with higher achievement in school.

This chapter focuses on differences in parenting style in the fifty families in the four groups and looks at how these parenting styles and parenting practices are influenced by parents' interactions within the more distal contexts of the developmental system. The ability of parents to provide effective support within and through the family context has a history. Long before these children started their actual learning life-courses, conditions for parenting and children's learning through the family microsystem were being shaped through the life-experiences of their parents and the beliefs their parents developed through these experiences.

Family involvement with school and learning

Once school becomes a prominent fixture in children's everyday lives, help with school and homework constitutes an important part of support that children might experience in and through the family microsystem. Typically, this kind of practical support comes from parents, and is referred to as parental involvement. This was the case in the families of all our academically successful, high socio-economic status (SES) children and in most of the families of our children succeeding against the odds. In this second group, siblings and other relatives, in addition to parents, also played an important role in providing children with practical support for school and learning, particularly in the higher grades of primary school and in secondary school, as school work became more advanced.

Parental involvement includes a broad range of activities that are situated in the home context or at school. Epstein (1992) for instance refers to two types of parental involvement: 'basic obligations' and 'involvement with learning activities at home'. 'Basic obligations' include providing a home environment that facilitates the child actually doing their homework, such as providing a quiet space to work, or materials such as books or computer software, and interacting with school and teachers about homework (cf. Sampson, 2007). 'Involvement with learning activities at home' includes engaging in homework processes and tasks with the child, as well as interactive processes supporting the child's understanding of homework. In the Effective Pre-School and Primary Education (EPPE 3–11) project, parental involvement as perceived and reported by teachers was related to children's academic and socio-emotional development. For instance, when teachers reported more consistent homework practices, better school communication with parents and parental support for children's learning, children showed better progress in Maths and on some socio-emotional outcomes. Where teachers reported strong parental support for their child's learning, children made better progress in reading and pro-social behaviour (Sylva et al., 2008).

A meta-analysis of forty-one studies among urban primary school children in the United States (Jeynes, 2005) found the extent to which parents read to their child to be the strongest predictor among parenting practices. A much smaller effect size was found for the extent to which parents communicated with their child about school activities and reported a high level of overall communication. Although it is possible that talking with children has a smaller impact on their academic achievement than reading, this smaller effect might be due to the fact that, in the analyses, all types of communication were treated as equally important for school achievement in the communication measure. Following the literature on pre-school activities, it might be that communications requiring use of the academic language register (such as talks about what the child has heard and seen on the news) have a stronger effect on academic achievement than informal communications about aspects of everyday life. A third commonly included measure, homework supervision, did not have any effect at all. This does not necessarily mean that homework supervision is a negative thing. Rather it might be that high levels of homework supervision are indicative of underlying difficulties that a child experiences with academic learning and/or with their social behaviour. For instance, it is possible that homework in the early grades of primary school is extra work, indicating difficulties experienced by children with learning (Fan & Chen, 2001).

This seemed to be the case for those Case Studies children who experienced difficulties with reading, such as Steven, but also for Tom and Marcy. The Effective Pre-School, Primary and Secondary Education (EPPSE 3–14) study showed that in secondary school, after controlling for SES, children spending two or more hours a night on homework, compared to none, had a particularly strong effect on progress for Maths and a slightly less pronounced, but still substantial, positive effect for English. It also had a positive effect on social-behavioural outcomes and on positive changes in these between ages 11 and 14 (Sylva et al., 2012). So children who actually took time to do their homework did better academically and social-behaviourally than children who did not. In our Case Studies we found that at this age children who did their homework did not generally depend on parental supervision to do so. Rather than depending on external supervision and motivation, they were intrinsically motivated, in the sense that they wanted to do well in school and therefore took the responsibility of their school work seriously. Only in those cases that children were doing poorly academically did parents report that they increased supervision on occasion but usually not structurally.

A review of studies examining the reasons for, and effects of, parents' involvement with homework in primary and secondary school revealed that other types of involvement, that go beyond simply making sure that a child has done the assignment and checking for mistakes, do influence student outcomes through modelling, reinforcement and instruction (Hoover-Dempsey et al., 2001). This review indicated that if involvement with homework was characterized by parental behaviours aiming to enhance the child's understanding of homework and of general learning processes, their involvement was positively related to achievement and particularly to student attributes such as attitudes towards homework, perceptions of personal competencies and self-regulation abilities (cf. McNeal, 2001).

Meeting basic obligations of parental involvement

Basic obligations usually posed little problem in middle-class families. Children had their own rooms, and often even had a personal computer with internet access that they could use for homework. In their home environment they usually had access to a wide range of reference books, work materials or commercially available revision books for Key Stage exams. Extra tutoring for exams was regularly provided, even when children were doing very well in school.

In low-SES families, meeting basic obligations for their children's learning more often posed a challenge. Living conditions were less spacious than in middle-class families, and often it was not easy for children to find a quiet place to work on school assignments or study. Personal computers became part of the household setup somewhere during the child's primary years for nearly all of the families who were part of the Case Studies. Again, for many of the low-SES families, buying a computer meant having to make financial sacrifices. Once a computer was available in the house, it was usually shared with all family members, and internet connection was not a given. In the Case Studies, in families with children who 'succeeded against the odds', parents provided a space for homework and would often make sure that the environment did not offer too many distractions such as television or loud conversations. They stimulated their children to go to the library, and often bought them commercial Key Stage books to practise for exams, or simply made up extra sums to get the child to practise Maths.

My dad probably gave me more work than the school did, like the Maths book and things, I used to do like an hour every day I think, that would help me as well. And just knowing that like if I hadn't done that, I don't think I'd be as good as I was at Maths now, 'cos it's nice to know that like when you're out of school even your parents want to help you, and it makes you more enthusiastic at school. Anjali, girl, Group 1 (low SES, attainment above prediction)

Even parents who themselves had never learned to use a computer felt the need to provide their child with access to a computer. Children and parents believed that having a computer in the home had offered the child playful opportunities to develop practical skills that had helped the child do well in school.

And I think she actually also started on a bit of the computer as well because of her older sister. Again, this was again something I believed in, that as soon as computers came out and my oldest daughter, I knew that 'Yes, OK, this is the right time for her to sit down on the computer and sort of start learning about computers' so I brought her a computer. Then at the same time obviously Anjali was growing up and she was doing bits and bobs, just basically playing games, and then when she grew up she demanded her own computer, and I said: 'Ok fine, fine', because looking fifteen, twenty years ahead … this is what life's gonna be, y'know, full of these youngsters basically at a desk and computers. Anjali was fortunate to have a computer in her room as well, so they both had a computer each and she is very good with computers … as we speak … so it's always sort of been my encouraging. Father of Anjali, girl, Group 1 (low SES, attainment above prediction)

ICT's very easy. Because I've been, like, I went on computers nearly all my life, so I know what to do on 'em, and when you know what to do, it makes it a lot more easier, 'cos you want to do it more.

When did you start using a computer?

Probably when I was about 7. Play games and like if I had, when I was in middle school, sometimes I'd write my stories on the computer. Or they'd give you Internet sites to go on that'd help you with your work so I could go on them.

And how did that help?

Because, when I'd write my stories like I'd do Word, I'd do it in Word, and I could like use all the different sorts of fonts and things, so now I am doing it at GCSE a lot of the things is about using, like to send an email and all that sort of thing, because I've done it before I know it's easy. Charley, girl, Group 1 (low SES, attainment above prediction)

Most of these parents also diligently attended school functions and parent evenings in school. In some cases they had additional meetings with teachers to resolve problems experienced by their child as they had strong emotional relationships with their children and were willing to advocate on their behalf where necessary.

All through primary school we had parents' evening. We had reports, every end of term, and ummm, once you had the report you could request to see the teacher and the teacher would talk you through the report and we've always done that. Any time we can talk to them because we've always been of the opinion that we needed to know what's going on in school on a termly basis, that's every three months, and we still do that, even now. Mother of Ife, girl, Group 1 (low SES, attainment above prediction)

I think it was Year 2 or 3 and one of the teachers didn't feel that he was doing as well as he should have been doing and was questioning whether Shaquille could do any numbers or anything. And I thought 'Well he's been counting for ages' and I knew some of the stuff that he was doing at home. He said: 'Well for example Shaquille can't count to seventeen' and I was really baffled by it. I gave Shaquille a couple of Maths and he answered it. Yeah, he probably was about 7, 8, I don't know why that was because everybody thought this teacher was very, very good, and he had a good reputation for being very good, but my experience was, because Shaquille, we would do work with him outside of school, I kind of got a sense of where he was at, and what the teacher was telling me about his ability, I just thought, I didn't believe that and once the teacher knew that, actually, he does learn something then that kind of was OK. Mother of Shaquille, boy, Group 1 (low SES, attainment above prediction)

Parental involvement with school learning activities

Engaging in homework processes with the child and supporting their understanding of homework was something that happened in nearly all the middle-class families and in low-SES families with children succeeding against the odds. It was less common in low-SES families with children succeeding as predicted. For the successful low-SES children, this kind of support was explicitly mentioned to explain their academic success. Particularly during the primary years, parents and children generally felt that the degree of support parents would and could offer with school work was not only helpful, but also effective.

Well my mum would help me then [during primary] and sometimes my brothers would, but that's it really. I think I just used to do the questions that I did know and then I would call her for the ones I didn't know. I think she would help me find it. She would talk through the questions with me and go through it step by step. Leanna, girl, Group 1 (low SES, attainment above prediction)

I needed a little bit of encouragement, yeah. I would sit down, get a snack or something. Then have a bit of dinner and then go and do my homework after dinner. I would sit at the table and work, but it is like if I did not understand it I would get my mum or dad to come and help me and then they'd talk me through it and then I would get it. They will get another piece of paper and like write it out in a different way until I understand that way. They'd take it step by step. Natalie, girl, Group 1 (low SES, attainment above prediction)

I remember when I first started doing division, long division, and it was him [my dad] that gave me, kind of, methods to do which I always found really helpful. I found his method much more helpful, for me, than the others. [I use it] to the day. Shaquille, boy, Group 1 (low SES, attainment above prediction)

Particularly for the children succeeding against the odds, having a parent, sibling or relative sit down with them and explain difficult homework was believed to have helped them achieve academically. It had helped them to develop new or alternative learning strategies and practical and emotional skills to cope with future difficulties, and it had made them feel supported and cared for.

For the academically successful children from low- and high-SES families, high emotional support and encouragement by parents or siblings was seen as an important 'protective' factor in addition to the practical support described in the previous paragraphs. Effective *emotional support* was mentioned as an explanation for academic success for six boys and eight girls from Group 1, and for all six students from Group 4. In high-SES families, particularly those with children doing well as predicted, parents also talked extensively with the children about their experiences in school throughout the years. During these talks parents clearly communicated to the child that although the children might not always do as well as they possibly could in school, they would eventually be fine and go to university. This seemed to reinforce these children's confidence in their future.

I think he's not interested enough, he's more interested in, like the social side of things and doing, messing around with his mates, I know he's bright, I know he's switched on, he's definitely not, he doesn't put enough effort in . . . I think he does a bit of class clown stuff. I think he, I don't think he deliberately, erm, disrupts it, but I think he tries to make the others laugh. Yeah, I think 'cause he is amusing, so I think the others will probably sort of, go along with it.

Is that something you talk about with him, about his motivation and how he conducts himself in the classroom?

After he came home with this report, I went into one of my spiels, 'Oh God, he's going to be unemployed and he's never going to go to university', and he said, 'Mum, I'm on report for Science, that's it.' It's like me going and thinking the whole world was going to end because he was on report for one subject, which he then corrected and he said he was fine again. But we had a long chat at that and how about, you know, I do expect you to be attentive, and I expect you not to be rude in the class, and I wouldn't like to think you were being disruptive and all this kind of thing, so he knows, what I expect of him, and what his Dad expects of him as well. I think he wanted the shouting thing again, so, 'Oh please bellow at me', so I think that's what he wanted. Mother of Benjamin, boy, Group 4 (high SES, attainment as predicted)

Having parents who had emotionally strong relationships with their children, who asked them about school, took an interest in how they were doing and talked to them about their future made children feel 'happy', 'encouraged' and 'supported'. They felt 'inspired' and wanted to 'push to

make a future' and 'be successful in life'. These parents also kept emphasizing the importance of school for the child's future, and kept encouraging
the children to apply themselves to homework, lessons and tests.

I liked school. Except when I argued with friends, but everyone has that . . . it is just
normal things happening. They [my parents] used to say that if I came and said
I hated school that I'd just have to accept that. You have to persevere, you can't
leave school. You just gotta go to it no matter what, and like they would just help
me and push me further, but not like push push me, just like encouraging me.

Do you think these talks were important for you?

Yeah, because I never felt like I was under too much pressure to do well and
I always tried my best and I realize that my best will be good enough. Natalie, girl,
Group 1 (low SES, attainment above prediction)

Abdi was one of the boys who mentioned that his parents would often
speak to him about school and his future even at a young age. When
asked if he felt this might have helped him do well in school, he answered:

Yeah, when . . . er, yeah it did because it shows that they're interested as well . . .
and . . . it helped but I'm not really sure how like . . . Yeah, when I used to be
doing good in school and they used to ask like or if you told them like, it makes
your children feel, makes your kids feel proud. Proud of themselves and that in
turn builds up your confidence, self-esteem. Abdi, boy, Group 1 (low SES,
attainment above prediction)

Particularly for children from low-SES families who were doing as predicted, this kind of support was far less common. Many of the parents felt
unable to provide support with homework as they did not feel they had
the necessary skills, and as a result it was often left to the children to find
alternative help, for instance from teachers or peers. These parents
displayed a form of helplessness and were unable to encourage their
children.

Sometimes he'll come home with homework, and I'll ask: 'What's that then?'
He'll explain to me and, my God, we never done that when we were at school, the
way they do the Maths and everythin' it's all totally different. It's like, I can see
that they're doing Maths, like the way they do that, like the sums now, haven't got
a clue, we used to just gets adds and take away, times and divide, never end up
with these big sums like that, and you think 'How do they do all this?' We had to
just write the answer . . . sort of, quick little sums. Mother of Richard, boy, Group
2 (low SES, attainment as predicted)

In families where home support was perceived as having been insufficient, parents and children indicated that parental involvement with
school and learning had either been too little or too much. Ineffective
practical support was mentioned as explanation for lack of academic

success for seven boys and two girls from Group 2 and for all three boys and for four girls from Group 3. Looking back, many of these parents regretted not having attended (all) parent evenings, or not having pushed the school and teachers for additional help for their struggling child. Although the parents of Subash implemented an intensive home programme to help him with his reading and school work once they realized how serious his problems really were, his father reflected:

> What could have helped was if we would have done it sooner, but we didn't know we had to do it ... as parents. We're not teachers, like I said earlier, we only realized we had to do it because it wasn't being done in the school ... I'd say he was about 7 ... maybe 8 or 9 and then he was still being ... Now he's up to speed with his peers at school, but he was about two-and-a-half years behind them and we've struggled like hell to get him up there. Father of Subash, boy, Group 3 (high SES, attainment below prediction)

Some parents felt they had done too much for their child and as a result the child was not getting the help it needed in school. Christopher's mother talked about how her son refuses to work in school even when he is offered help by a teaching assistant. When asked what she felt might be the reason for his behaviour she stated:

> He was never sort of left to, you know, he used to come and say: 'I can't do that!' We'd never sort of say to him 'Just have a go.' Someone would be like 'Alright, I'll do it for you', whether it be me, one of the other girls, or ... really, it was like he had another two mums there, at 9 and 7 ... everybody did everything for him, so he's grown up with that. Mother of Christopher, boy, Group 2 (low SES, attainment as predicted)

The influence of parents' learning histories on parental involvement

During their child's first years at secondary school, most parents in the Case Studies, regardless of their SES, kept on providing practical support with school and learning by supplying materials such as computers, books and revision guides. However, particularly in low-SES families, the actual help the child received with homework decreased strongly. For some children, not only did this form of practical support with school and learning diminish, but so did the emotional support they received as they progressed through secondary school. For children who experienced this decrease in support during early adolescence, this was likely to negatively affect their academic achievement at the time and their future achievement.

Similar to the effects found for parental involvement during the primary years, effects of parental involvement on achievement are found for early adolescence with a meta-analysis of fifty studies (Hill & Tyson, 2009). This meta-analysis showed no effects of assistance, supervising or checking of homework, but positive effects from involvement that reflected academic socialization. Academic socialization referred to involvement with school and learning by parents that created understanding about purposes, goals and meaning of academic performance in the students and provided them with effective strategies. A study by Sheldon and Epstein (2005) illustrated the importance of this particular kind of parental involvement for children's achievement in Maths. They found that when homework assignments required the student to discuss mathematical skills with a family member, in combination with the provision of Maths game packets for home use, children's Maths achievement improved.

Parents and children provided several sets of reasons for diminished practical and emotional support during the secondary school years. The first set, primarily given by the families with academically successful children, was that parents trusted their child to ask for help when needed, but that in fact the children no longer needed their help. The children were more than capable of doing the work, and if they encountered a problem they had plenty of additional resources, particularly friends, that would help them come up with a solution. A second set of reasons, mainly given for children who were academically less successful, was that children did not ask for help and parents did not feel it was their role to check if help was needed. Although more common in working-class families, these first two sets of reasons were also given in some of the middle-class families. A third set of reasons was given in low-SES families only, and was given by families regardless of the child's academic success. In these families children and parents felt that these parents would not actually be able to help even when they were willing to do so, and if this help had been needed. These parents doubted their ability to provide actual academic support due to their personal experiences, or rather lack of experiences, with the educational system. In some cases they said the curriculum had changed so much since they had been in school themselves that they could no longer relate the things they had learned to what their child was learning. But often they felt that the education they had personally experienced had been insufficient to teach them enough to provide more than basic academic help to their child. In many cases these children had reached a grade level in school that their parents had never experienced.

Differences in the educational experiences of parents were considerable between middle-class and working-class parents in our Case Studies sample (see Appendix 5). Sixteen of the thirty-five mothers from low-SES homes had left education without obtaining any qualifications; i.e.,

65 per cent of mothers with academically less successful children and 40 per cent in the group succeeding against the odds. Eleven of the nineteen fathers living with the family at the start of the EPPE project had left school without qualifications; i.e., nine out of twelve fathers in the academically successful group and two out of seven in the academically less successful group. A number of these parents grew up in circumstances or countries that did not allow them the opportunity to obtain even the most basic educational qualifications, but others who were given these opportunities simply could not wait to be freed from what they perceived as the pressures of education and school.

In working-class families with children achieving as predicted, parents who had stayed on to earn a qualification had left school after their general exams at age 16 (six mothers and three fathers) or had left with a vocational diploma (one mother, two fathers). In the families of children succeeding against the odds, four parents who had stayed on to obtain an educational qualification received a vocational diploma (three mothers, one father), seven (one father) had successfully sat their exams at 16, and one set of parents had stayed in education until they were 18 in their country of birth, which they fled immediately after receiving their diplomas. One working-class mother had stayed on in education after age 18 and had earned a degree in nursing.

The parental educational situation was very different in our middle-class groups. The middle-class children were generally born into families with parents who had stayed in education until they completed the compulsory stages. Of the families with academically less successful children, four parents had obtained vocational diplomas, three had obtained general qualifications at age 16, six left education after they sat their exams at 18, and only one parent, a mother who grew up in India, had left education without qualifications. Four of these parents and eight parents of the academically successful children went on to attend university, and few of these had left education without degrees from prestigious universities. The three remaining parents in the successful middle-class group had left education with qualifications obtained at age 16 (one father, one mother) or 18 (one father).

Empirical Studies, including EPPE 3–11, have shown that parental qualifications, particularly mothers' qualifications, are strong predictors for children's educational attainment up to the end of primary school. Particularly mothers' education shows a consistent pattern of strong and positive effects for children's achievement in English and Maths at age 11, as well as for their social and behavioural outcomes at this age. The effects were strongest when comparing mothers who had obtained a degree with mothers who had not obtained any qualifications.

Fathers' education also had a statistically significant effect on English and Maths attainment, and for children's self-direction and hyperactivity, but was less strong than mothers' education (Sammons et al., 2008b).

But like the relation between family SES in general and children's academic achievement, the relation between parental education and children's academic achievement is substantially determined by how these educational experiences influence parenting practices and goals. In the Case Studies, for instance, we found that differences in educational experiences of middle-class and working-class parents (and other family members as well) led to differences in the way they used these experiences as examples for the children in our study. For children from high-SES families the educational experiences of their parents, family members and siblings usually provided them with examples that encouraged them to set their educational aims high. Many of these children had plenty of examples of people who went to university, and it was often simply assumed that the child would go to university as well. Imogene had parents who had both earned a degree at a good university, but also had her two older half-siblings, who were attending top universities. When her mother was asked what kind of qualifications she would like her daughter to have she initially said she did not feel strongly about qualifications, but then went on to say:

I think she would have a wonderful time if she goes to university and of course she'll go to university 'cause that's what she wants to do. Mother of Imogene, girl, Group 4 (high SES, attainment as predicted)

When asked about her future after her planned GCSEs and A levels, Abby answered:

Then university, get a degree. I don't know [where], Cambridge (laughs), no . . .

Have you visited any universities?

It was only because my Grandpa went to Cambridge, and he was showing us the bit where he was and it was really nice, I liked it and I've seen where my brother's university is, but I haven't been like, around. Abby, girl, Group 4 (high SES, attainment as predicted)

Although positive role models existed for children from low-SES families, they were far less common, and the assumption that obtaining a university-level qualification would be a matter of course was not common. In contrast, it was often not the educational success of parents that was used as an example, but their lack of success. But although these low-SES parents shared a limited experience with education in general, and with higher levels of education in particular, there were notable differences in the way these experiences influenced their parenting practices and goals.

Educational experiences of parents and differences in parental involvement in low-SES families

For one thing, although low-SES parents with children succeeding against the odds were often just as acutely aware as the other low-SES parents of their limitations to help the child with actual school work, and as a result rarely helped children with their actual work, this did not stop them from continuing to carefully and actively monitor their child's progression through school. Contrary to many of the parents of low-SES children who attained as predicted, these parents continued to monitor homework and communicated with the school about the child's progress.

I don't [help] ... No, because I am not very clever and I don't understand it. She will sort of show me her homework or I will sort of say to her, 'Are you doing your homework?' and, 'Yeah I am doing my homework mum'. Some things she will ask me for school, but nine times out of ten she does it herself. Her textile books and that she will always show me, but like her English and Maths and that she always does it herself. Mother of Charley, girl, Group 1 (low SES, attainment above prediction)

[They ask] 'How am I doing?, What do you want to do?, Do I need any help?, If they can help us?, 'ave I done my homework?, Am I doing OK?' Just like, stuff like that. Sometimes they're hard. Like: 'Have you done your homework?', 'No', 'Why haven't you done it?' 'I'm just not doing it yet' but they just make sure that I have done it, and that I'm not, like, forgetting to do it, and I have done it and things. Yeah, it helps because like if I'm being told to do it, I have to do it, or there would be repercussions. Like grounded, books taken away. Brenda, Girl, Group 1 (low SES, attainment above prediction)

Although unable to provide much actual help, these parents made sure to provide emotional support by regularly talking to the children about their school work and by encouraging them to do the work and apply themselves. If parents could not provide the necessary help to solve a problem, they encouraged children to look for alternative sources of help. They facilitated and encouraged them to solve the problems they encountered by going online to consult websites or friends or to wait until they could ask a teacher for help. In the low-SES families with children achieving poorly academically, parents were perceived not to have sufficiently stimulated the children to apply themselves, by not asking about school or school work and having low aspirations for the child, or not making it clear to the child that even in primary school doing the work in class and at home and paying attention in class were important.

I mean, my husband's a manual worker, my dad was a manual worker, so none of us have been a doctor or a lawyer, or ... I, I think you just ... you don't expect much more of them than what you know of your ... close family already.

There's no common example to follow, if you like ... or no competition, if that's the best word to use perhaps. So, I just want him to be happy in what he's doing ... You don't know, maybe in several years time he might change and think: 'Well I really want to do that now' and go and do what we thought maybe he'd never do. Mother of Christopher, boy, Group 2 (low SES, attainment as predicted)

Parents who had experienced difficulties while they were in school, for instance with Literacy, often feared their child would have to face similar hardships. When they had gone through those experiences they did not have the benefit of support from people around them, such as their parents or teachers. But while these experiences caused anxiety for parents such as Tom's father, who had never properly learned to read or write, and seemed to diminish the effectiveness of the support and encouragement he felt he could provide for Tom, other parents found ways for their child to benefit from their problematic educational histories. In quite a few of the families with children succeeding against the odds, parents were actually spurred on to help their child by the difficulties they personally experienced during their school years. Through their experiences they had been made aware that difficulties children experienced were not something they would simply grow out of, but rather that they required active help from as many people around them as possible. They therefore kept a keen eye on their child's progress and were ready to find ways to provide additional help when needed.

[My education was] ... not too bad, but I would say I'm not really good at reading and that was really not picked up on me until I went to like the top school and to me that is too late and that's why I have always made sure that they can, or if they were struggling they got help with that. But I didn't do very well in school and I would say that they are doing a lot better than I am. No I didn't do that well. Mother of Peter, boy, Group 1 (low SES, attainment above prediction)

Many parents felt that lack of encouragement and emotional support had been an important factor in their own lack of educational success as a child. But especially parents whose children went on to succeed academically were determined not to let this happen to their child. They had been raised in traditional working-class families and poor families. Like Steven's mother Carol, many of their own parents and carers regarded education as a luxury that kept their child from making a proper contribution to the household. Like many of her peers, Carol had been pulled from school at the earliest possible time and had been sent to work as a cleaner. Other parents, particularly mothers from minority ethnic families, had left school to be married. Some parents had left education because the people around them had instilled in them a firm belief that they were unsuited to achieve anything if they stayed on. But instead of continuing this inter-generational transmission of lack of academic success and qualifications, these parents used their experiences to break the family cycle of disadvantage, sometimes for themselves but more often for their child.

Even then, when I went to study [as an adult], it was, 'Well you should leave it to people who know what they're doing', it was always that kind of ... and it raises its ugly head with me as well. So it was why, when I saw especially in my children they are so much brighter than I was, that's where I was coming from encouraging them. You know I lacked encouragement. You have doubt anyway, you don't always feel that you're good at everything all the time, it's natural to think you want to strive for better. So that was my experience at school so I would say, you know, I didn't do as well as I could have done. Mother of Shaquille, boy, Group 1 (low SES, attainment above prediction)

They used the adversities they had experienced as an example for their children, encouraging them to excel beyond what they had achieved. Brenda's mother left school at age 16:

Well, I say to them, 'You want to get a good job at the end of it. You don't want to end up like your Dad.' You know the postman and postwoman. But you know, if you want to do something, anything in your life, you've got to do something that you enjoy doing. Then if you've got more or less the qualifications, you can more or less go into anything. When I was at school, you could literally walk out of school, get a job, not a good job, but you could just go from job to job, and that's what we did. I can't remember anybody from my school ever going to university. I think a couple went to college but nobody ever really, you know, they never encouraged you. I know it was just a case of the teachers had to be there, we had to be there, and we eventually left. Mother of Brenda, girl, Group 1 (low SES, attainment above prediction)

Particularly in the homes of children succeeding against the odds, parents worked hard at continuing their personal development through work-related courses, NVQs and even academic degrees. Often these parents had made considerable steps along the career ladder. Their personal development increased their confidence as parents, and they were very much aware of the positive example they were setting for their child. Charley's mother left education at sixteen, without any qualifications:

Did you ever consider going to college?

No, no, no. Because I wasn't very clever, I haven't got any GCSEs or City and Guilds, or anything, not until two years ago, I have got a NVQ 2 in nursing, which is the only qualification I have got since I left school.

Was that something your work required or something you chose to do?

I was really adamant you know that I didn't want to do it. And I was sort of ... pushed a little bit, but I am glad I was, pushed, now because at the time, I was you know coming home and having to do some work but they were very good at the college and I am glad that I did do it.

Do you think that in any way set an example for Charley?

I think so yeah, yeah, she was pleased when I sort of got my certificate, yeah she was. Mother of Charley, girl, Group 1 (low SES, attainment above prediction)

Particularly for those minority ethnic parents who had received their schooling as children in their country of origin, these further qualifications brought them important personal knowledge about the British educational system and the necessity of qualifications in the United Kingdom. Ife's mother, who grew up in Nigeria and moved to the United Kingdom in her early twenties, had earned a degree and made a career in nursing. She was now Head Nurse of an Intensive Care Unit. When asked if she felt it had been important for Ife to see her and her husband in (professional) jobs, she answered:

I think that it's very important. I think that's very important for any child. I think it's a kind of a positive influence. It's what you see … I used to have a neighbour who didn't used to work 'cause she had health problems and her daughter at age 14 wanted to have a child. And then she said to me, 'But can you please talk to her?' and you know, she's helpless. And I did sit with her and I said: 'Look at me, I'm like, your mum's age, I've got the job, I've got the house, I've got a car. Do you want that or do you wanna just be on the streets, only 16 with a child on your hands?' And she said, 'Oh, yeah, definitely, I definitely want that.' I found that she felt that it was much better than just sitting down there, but I've always known that anyway. It's one of the reasons why I decided I wanted when my children start school, that I'm gonna go to work because, I don't want them thinking that it's the norm, an' that mums don't do anything. Mums do it if they can. Mother of Ife, girl, Group 1 (low SES, attainment above prediction)

Although such examples of continued personal development were also found in the low-SES homes with children achieving as predicted, they were far more common among the parents of children succeeding against the odds of disadvantage.

Parenting style, interactive and strong relationships

The examples provided about parenting and emotional support in families with academically successful children clearly show that the parenting style of these parents had many of the characteristics of the authoritative parenting style in Baumrind's typology: the parents were emotionally supportive, set and held high standards, granted autonomy at appropriate moments and used clear bidirectional communication with their child (see for instance Bradley, 2002; Bradley et al., 2000; Darling & Steinberg,

1993; Steinberg, 2001; Steinberg & Morris, 2001). This parenting style is typically associated with parenting in middle-class families and it is far less common among working-class parents. Nonetheless, it was clearly present in the parenting style of the parents from working-class families who had children who succeeded against the odds of disadvantage, but it was not identical.

For the children from disadvantaged backgrounds who managed to succeed against the odds, parents for instance had encouraged them to do well in school, gave them positive feedback on achievements and behaviour without pressuring them and talked to them about social-emotional issues. They had worked on building strong relationships based on encouragement and support for their child.

He was always confident, he was always, his reading and writing, for me he did that fairly early, with his talking so, we all used to say how clever he was and I think that he really grew from that and he liked to feel good, that someone was telling him how good he was and what he did. Mother of Shaquille, boy, Group 1 (low SES, attainment above prediction)

Just encourage her really. In her past we have tried to open her mind to what it will be like, make her aware she has to fit the work in. Yeah we encourage her, we praise her for all the good things she does and equally the negative ones we try and explain them to her really. Yes encouragement. If she feels she is doing good and doing well and achieving, you know, hopefully she will just want to carry on doing that. Mother of Natalie, girl, Group 1 (low SES, attainment above prediction)

These parents felt they needed to provide the children with regulation by setting clear standards and boundaries for behaviour (Bradley et al., 2000), particularly by offering verbal explanations.

I think it's me giving her the freedom to play with her friends, not being very strict and that, although I did have sort of strict guidelines to say, 'Look, if you're gonna go out with your friends, you need to be back at this time. If you're going outside the house I wanna know where you are' ... right. So that worked over the years. I don't really believe in shouting at children, don't believe in hitting them, I don't think I've ever hit you have I? How old are you now, you're coming up to 16 years old, probably smacked her bottom or something for being naughty, but I believe that if a child is doing something wrong, and to punish them is to obviously say not to do it again and give them something to do that they realize, that, 'Oh if I do that again I've got to do this, this and that' ... you see what I mean, so I punished her in that way ... Father of Anjali, girl, Group 1 (low SES, attainment above prediction)

As children matured, parents recognized their agency and showed them respect; they also granted the child more autonomy with regard to school and choices about education.

She is really good at subjects but those are not the ones she actually wants to do for her GCSE's and ... I would like her to do them because she is good at it. But she is not willing to take that path and obviously it is down to her in the end. So we discuss it with her, but in the end it is her choice what she wants to do. Yes it is important [to talk to her], because if you don't talk you don't know basically what she is thinking, what she would like to or what she wouldn't like to do. And later on she would probably say 'You weren't there to guide me or to tell me or ask me what my interests were' and things like that so yeah I do think it is important. Mother of Leanna, girl, Group 1 (low SES, attainment above prediction)

Whereas before they [mum and dad] were very sort of involved in helping me choose, they sort of, they've started to back off a bit as time's gone by as I've got older. So ... letting me make my own decisions. I mean my mum still advised me [for my GCSE subjects] but ... at the end of the day I've chosen. I suppose I enjoy this sort of freedom to make my own decisions eh ... I do like other people making them for me, it's sort of easier but ... ehm ... yeah. Yeah I know it is [important] 'cause when you grow up and you know, they're not always there. You've gotta make your own decisions. Steven, boy, Group 1 (low SES, attainment above prediction)

The parents had high aspirations and expectations for their child and made their child aware of these expectations. These expectations referred to school work and the way children behaved in class, but also to their future education and working life.

I would like her to be an accountant. I don't know [why] because it's just a good job, and you know not somewhere where she is in a shop or anything like that because she is very clever and I would like her to make use of it, definitely. Mother of Charley, girl, Group 1 (low SES, attainment above prediction)

I mean, not now but I used to say to her, I said: 'Anjali, with the brain you've got, you can run this country' (laughs) ... But we got a very good talk didn't we? 'What you wanna be, where do you wanna be?' ... because her sister's graduated ... Now Anjali's own thinking is quite bright and quite sort of spread out. She knows what she wants in life, to have that she's got very good goals. I said to her 'Look, what you wanna be?' She said 'I've decided, I wanna be a barrister', 'A what?' I didn't even know what a barrister was. 'Oh one of them who wears wigs and courts and they're really high up.' 'Well why do you want to be a barrister?' 'Oh, because... ' She gave me her own reasons, which were damn good reasons. I said: 'OK, that's fine, if that's what you wanna do, then I'll support you, yeah, no problem.' Father of Anjali, girl, Group 1 (low SES, attainment above prediction)

Parental self-efficacy

Perhaps the most obvious difference between the low-SES parents whose children succeeded against the odds and those whose children attained as predicted was their strong sense of responsibility for their child's learning and development, and the value they placed on education. Contrary to many of the parents of the less successful children, the parents of the children succeeding against the odds felt they had to, and could, play an active part in their child's development, even when the child was typically spending more time in school than at home. They generally felt that schools and teachers did whatever they could but that ultimately it was up to them as parents to help their children become the best they could, to live up to their potential. In other words, these parents had a sense of self-efficacy, they believed in their own capabilities to organize and execute the courses of action required to manage their child's education (Bandura, 1995). Ife's mother, for instance, said she felt that school had done all it could to help her daughter reach her potential, as Ife had left primary school with her predictive grades. When asked: 'What about reaching beyond her predicted potential?' she answered:

Ummm, that would be something that we've always thought was our own jobs rather than the school. The school can only do so much, but we're supposed to put the extra input into it. We normally try to do that, we try to push her as much as we could bearing in mind that we have to be a bit careful about the pushing and so . . . Ummm, when we do homework with her, I don't do the Maths, 'cause I'm not very good at Maths. Dad does Maths with her and Dad would say to her, 'So you've done that already if you can do these ones', and of course we have all educational books and things like that that we bought with her, we go through with her, things like that. Mother of Ife, girl, Group 1 (low SES, attainment above prediction)

This sense of efficacy with regard to educational success seemed to lead to effective parenting practices that helped children progress through school and supported them in achieving higher grades. These children (Group 1: Low SES, higher attainment) managed grades that were similar to those of the successful high-SES children and it might be that these parenting practices, in turn, are reinforced by the child's success.

For the low-SES parents with children who were achieving as predicted, this kind of belief in their ability to help their child succeed and awareness of the importance of their support was less often expressed.

Well, I suppose you could say in a way I didn't really [get involved]. Because I probably feel that all the support comes from the school, I thought like that way really. Not that I was not there but probably as I got more involved . . . as I didn't with Tremaine. Mother of Tremaine, boy, Group 2 (low SES, attainment as predicted)

The strong sense of self-efficacy with regard to their children's educational experiences that we witnessed among low-SES parents with children succeeding against the odds was perhaps even stronger among high-SES parents. The high-SES parents of children with some kind of learning difficulties commonly organized private tuition for their child. Generally the high-SES parents made sure their child was prepped for national assessments, that they could take the eleven-plus exams to get into the best state schools or private schools, and that they thought about life after A-levels. Despite the fact that Imogene had always been at the top of her class, her parents had provided her with private extra tuition at the end of primary school:

Because, I mean, at that stage a lot of kids in North London do that, at that stage before the [SATs], 'cause a lot of them are moving from the state sector to the private sector say, so they need to ... well they need to learn a different way of doing things and they need to up their game a lot of them, like, getting into somewhere like the place she's at now ... you know quite challenging entry tests.
Mother of Imogene, girl, Group 4 (high SES, attainment as predicted)

Abby went to a local public primary school but she and her two brothers attended private secondary schools. Their mother had made sure not to leave it to chance whether or not her children would be admitted.

You did have extra coaching, with Mrs Pickett, to do St Martha's and Our Mother's Convent, which really I think you didn't need. It was a lady called Mrs Pickett, who is an old lady, and old-fashioned teacher, and she coached, this is my paranoia, and she coached all of them, in Year Six, and she coached entrance exams to all the private schools, which was really more old-fashioned teaching, erm ... and they used to have to do extra, God I was horrible, extra homework for her every week.

Was that something that you instigated?

Yes, absolutely, nobody ever said to me to do it.

Why do you feel it was important for them to do that?

For getting into these schools and things like that, they needed to be tutored in a different way, shall we say, to the [primary school way], because a lot of them [other children] come from prep schools, and with their coach it would be the exam technique from Year 5 and Year 6, whereas in the primary school it is only Key Stage, then that [extra tuition] is key to them.

What kind of things would they have to learn to get into that school?

Erm, it was just how best to talk, to use a word, like they weren't always like more difficulty, they just had words that you wouldn't usually come across, and then, just have ... It was a bit more old-fashioned really. When I look back, I don't know now, with hindsight and experience, I don't know why I was worrying about that, but ... Mother of Abby, girl, Group 4 (high SES, attainment as predicted)

The support of these middle-class parents with school and learning was in line with what Lareau (2003) described as their 'concerted cultivation' of the child.

Conclusions

What parents of academically successful children effectively do is create a home environment for the child in which they have clear goals towards which they direct the socialization of their child. They provide activities they feel are important to reach these goals and they do so in a family climate that prioritizes relationships and is emotionally supportive (Darling & Steinberg, 1993) and open to regular communication about learning. They are actively involved with their child's learning within the family context: they both provide stimulating home learning activities and become actively involved with the child's learning process through their advocacy in school.

Through their verbal communications and interactions with their child they convey to the child that they can and must take joint responsibility for their own academic trajectories. At the same time they show their child that they are willing and able to provide the necessary support for the child to achieve becoming an active agent of his or her future. This kind of parenting might have come naturally to many middle-class families because they had experienced these practices at first hand in the families and schools in which they themselves had developed. Through their childhood experiences and their educational trajectories they had developed a strong sense of self-worth and belief in their ability to provide similar experiences for their child. Their current professional positions reinforced the great value these parents placed on opportunities and abilities to exercise self-direction and intellectual flexibility in life, both for themselves and their children (Kohn & Schooler, 1983). But for the working-class parents with children succeeding against the odds of disadvantage these parenting practices were much less a given. Their personal experiences as children with parenting and education had rarely been aimed at instilling in them a sense of self-direction. But they had taken their experiences, good and bad, and nonetheless had found ways to use these to this effect. They had developed a strong sense of agency towards their personal lives and towards their roles as parents as well.

Through their roles as parents, through the activities they engaged their children in, through the activities they facilitated, through the unrelenting practical and emotional support they offered towards school and learning, they provided their child with academically effective proximal processes. By recognizing their ability to support their child as well as limitations to this ability, by communicating high standards for their child and keeping to these high standards themselves, by the examples they were setting through their jobs and continuing development, they were transmitting their beliefs about self-direction and the value of education to their children. Despite their disadvantages they, as parents, had found ways to facilitate their child in his or her process of becoming an active agent of academic success.

8   Inspiring success in the early years and school environment

This chapter discusses our findings on how the school environment supports academic success and relates it to the wider literature. We look at factors at the school level, factors related to teachers and factors related to peers and friends. Again we provide additional perceptions of Case Studies children, parents and their secondary school teachers, of how schools and teachers have contributed to academic achievement.

Introduction

There is an increasing interest in researching the vital connection between learning and teaching. Learning can be defined as the process of acquiring knowledge, skills, habits and values through study and teaching, experience and experimentation, interaction with others, observation, engagement, involvement and reflection (Siraj-Blatchford & Mayo, 2012). All learning occurs within a social environment that can impede or aid this process, depending on the quality of interactions experienced (Bronfenbrenner & Ceci, 1994; Bronfenbrenner & Morris, 2006; Moriarty & Siraj-Blatchford, 1998). Most children start their learning trajectories within the context of the family microsystem. Within this system, in the early years, most learning will occur as the result of children's active participation in everyday activities and through playful interactions that might or might not be specifically educational. During their interactions with the child, parents and other more knowledgeable people who interact with the child in the family microsystem help children develop culturally appropriate skills, knowledge and behaviour.

Within the family context these processes are referred to as 'parenting' or 'socialization'. But children will sooner or later expand their learning experiences to other microsystems that include more people than just their parents or primary carers. Once children in England enter the year of their fifth birthday, they have to be enrolled in a primary school reception class. But for the vast majority of children, regular participation in institutions of care and education will start much earlier in life.

Children can attend private or state-run day care centres, sometimes from as young as three months old. Most children above the age of 2 will have had a play-based introduction to the educational system through playgroup or nursery before they start the reception class of a primary school. For many children these settings will provide substantial sources of proximal processes in addition to those experienced in the family microsystem. Particularly during early childhood, the interactions and activities that children engage in with staff and teachers will be fairly similar to those they might experience in their home environments. They read storybooks together, they share meals together, they are consoled when they are sad or hurt, they sing songs together and they go outside to run, climb, hide and play ball. In these institutionalized contexts we refer to these processes not as parenting and socialization but as teaching and pedagogy.

Teaching involves appropriate interaction with learners, using a number of strategies to enable learning to take place. As with parenting, these interactions will be affected by practices implicit in the social context in which the learning is taking place (Wood, 1986). Pedagogy is that set of strategies which enables learning to take place and provides opportunities for the acquisition of knowledge, skills, attitudes and dispositions within a social and material context. It refers to the interactive process between teacher and learner and the learning environment (which includes family and community). In order to consider what constitutes effective pedagogy and teaching in care or education settings, it is important to have an understanding of how learning takes place. There is much evidence within the psychological literature that learning is usually an interactive event, where the child actively constructs his or her own understandings within a social, cultural and physical environment (see for instance Rogoff, 1993, 2003; cf. Bronfenbrenner & Morris, 2006; Tudge, 2008). Effective learning environments for young children provide the children with opportunities to be active and take the initiative to learn. The role of the adult is to provide these opportunities and experiences by setting the environment and through consistent planning and rigorous assessment so that appropriate opportunities may be given. Adult support is also important to encourage children to learn in an active and participatory way (Siraj-Blatchford & Mayo, 2012). In order to define effective teaching, it is also necessary to take into account the educational objectives of the context in which this teaching is situated (Ko & Sammons, 2011).

Unfortunately, not all educational microsystems, or all teaching that is provided through these microsystems, is equally effective for children's learning. Therefore, the choices that parents make about their children's participation in these learning environments can have significant effects on their child's academic achievement, their socio-emotional development and their future life.

Pre-school environments

Parents face important choices about their child's participation in pre-school settings. In the first place they need to decide whether they will enrol their child in pre-school or keep the child at home. By enrolling their child in a pre-school setting, regardless of whether this setting is a full-day nursery or a half-day play group, parents transfer part of their control over proximal process experiences of their child to the realm and responsibility of other adults. For some parents it might seem that they have little choice in the matter, as their job situation or family circumstances make it impossible to keep the child at home full-time during the early years. Some of these parents might choose to seek alternative, informal options of additional care through people they know well and trust, such as relatives, family friends or neighbours, rather than enrolling their child in a formal, group childcare institution. The majority of children in England will have had some experience in early years care and education institutions prior to their enrolment in primary school. For these children parents will have to make additional choices about the type of pre-school setting, such as playgroups with limited hours and sessions or nurseries that offer daily part-time or full-time day care, they will have to decide from what age their child will attend a pre-school setting and need to make choices about the amount of hours their child will be in care each week, or even each day. Many of these choices have important consequences for their child's development and well-being in general and for their future academic achievement in particular.

Childcare and early-years education has a long history. In many countries, care and education for young children was split up among government departments, policies, programmes and types of pre-school centres. In some cases even the populations of children varied, with more disadvantaged children often attending provision provided by a social services government department, while their wealthier counterparts attended private provision. However, many countries, including England, are now seeing that, from the child's perspective, any separation of care from education is both unachievable and wrong. Every setting educates and provides care, whether the aims for either are explicit or not (Siraj-Blatchford & Mayo, 2012). In the last three decades the value of high-quality early education and care programmes has been recognized as an important feature and stage in enhancing children's development and well-being. It has also been equated with better economic returns for society and for providing individuals with a good start to their schooling (Heckman, 2006; Schweinhart & Weikart, 1997) and better academic progress throughout primary education (Sylva et al., 2008).

The Effective Pre-School, Primary and Secondary Education (EPPSE 3–16) research provides an extensive overview of how parents' choices regarding pre-school affect their child even up to the end of secondary school. Attending a pre-school continues to have a positive influence on children's academic and social-behavioural outcomes at age 11 at the end of primary school and beyond that, as well as on their self-perceptions. But the positive effect of pre-school experiences is strongest at entry into the formal educational system. Pre-school experience, compared to none, enhances all-round development in children at entry to primary school, which helps these children deal with the transition from playful learning to the formal curriculum. Particularly those children who started attending pre-school before the age of 3 showed better intellectual development than their peers who did not attend a pre-school at this time. Whether children attended pre-school on a full-time or part-time basis did not matter for their emergent Literacy and Numeracy skills (Sylva et al., 2004, 2006, 2008; cf. Sammons et al., 2002a, 2003, 2008d). These findings have compelled the government of the day to offer fifteen hours of free pre-school education from 2014 to 40 per cent of the most disadvantaged families in the England, some 260,000 children.

All but two children in the Case Studies had attended a pre-school setting before they started reception. For almost all parents in the Case Studies, the question had not been *if* their child would attend a pre-school but rather *when* they would start. Particularly for low socio-economic status (SES) parents, pre-school was just something children went to at a certain age:

So what made you decide that Richard would attend pre-school?

I don't ... it's just a thing that you had to do, you had a go to pre-school. He had to go. Everybody had to do it. Mother of Richard, boy, Group 2 (low SES, attainment as predicted)

It was across the road ... I don't know, it's just ... assumed that was where you go, don't know ... what you do (laughing). Mother of Martha, girl, Group 1 (low SES, attainment above prediction)

The majority of parents, regardless of their SES, felt that pre-schools offered children the opportunity to learn to socialize with other children, a skill they believed would help once their child started school. However, parents with successful low-SES children and high-SES parents also stressed the importance of pre-school for preparing their child for the more intellectual side of school, that is, make them more 'school ready'.

These parents felt that pre-school helped their child to get used to school routines and rules and offered the child an opportunity to further develop emerging Literacy and Numeracy skills. This positive perception of the value of pre-school education seemed to be indicative of a more generally positive attitude to education, school and learning in these families.

> I think it is good that they interact with other children really because at the end of the day that's what they are going to do, isn't it? The earlier they learn to be with other children I think the better because they will be not so selfish I think and getting their own way. Sort of being with you around sometimes you would just give in whereas if they are in a nursery they wouldn't get that because there is other children there. Its learning isn't it – so they do different things. Even though you would do things like painting and drawing and that things with them, it is different, isn't it in a different environment with loads of them doing it because they see another person doing it and they think: 'Oh, I want to do that a bit better' and that is better. I think that is part of the learning, it's a challenge and I think they want to do that better. Mother of Peter, boy, Group 1 (low SES, attainment above prediction)

> I think it was very good for her socially and I was a bit worried that you know, she would be socially disadvantaged if she wasn't doing a bit of interaction with other kids and learning her place in those hierarchies and learning to deal with strange teachers and that kind of thing really and learn to be independent and away from your mummy sometimes. Mother of Imogene, girl, Group 4 (high SES, attainment as predicted)

For many parents childcare and early education was also a necessity because of their work. In the high-SES families all but one of the parents (a mother) was in part-time or full-time work when children were at pre-school age. Nearly half of the low-SES mothers with children who would be academically successful also needed childcare as they had full-time or part-time jobs and they were either lone parents or had a spouse who also worked. This was the case in only three of the low-SES families with children attaining as predicted; they worked before the children started school.

However, two-thirds of the low-SES mothers were stay-at-home mums before their children started primary school. Although these mothers too valued pre-school as an opportunity for children to develop their social skills through interactions with other children and other adults, having their child attend pre-school also offered them a short break from their role as full-time parent. In quite a few cases, particularly in low-SES families with children who succeeded as predicted, these mothers had to deal with difficult family situations, due to their own health problems or those of a dependent. Although neither of the mothers of the two children who did not attend a pre-school worked outside the home, they had initially tried to find a pre-school place for their child, but either none was available or it was too complicated to combine logistically with their family routine. Both children were of Asian heritage, and neither of their parents spoke English with their children at home. Nonetheless, both mothers felt they had provided their children with sufficient educational experiences at home to prepare their child for starting school. They had for instance helped their child practise the English alphabet and both children had older sisters who attended primary school and spoke English.

Choices for particular pre-school settings were most often based on practical reasons, particularly in the low-SES families. They chose to enrol their child in settings that were within walking distance of the home, in settings that provided free or inexpensive care. Other parents, typically those of children who would go on to succeed against the odds, also evaluated the suitability of the setting for their child. They visited these settings personally and talked to other parents about their experiences with staff and children in the setting; they were more discriminating.

The reason I chose this nursery over the other one I looked at, I felt that there was more, it just met the requirements that I felt were necessary for looking after a child. There was more space, the staff seemed more committed to the children and it's cheaper, wasn't the main issue, the issue was about whether or not she would be OK. Mother of Reanna, girl, Group 1 (low SES, attainment above prediction)

Ife first attended Anansi Playgroup, initiated by a group of parents who had immigrated to England from Africa, for a few mornings a week. After a year, she moved on to a full-time free place in a regular state-funded nursery school.

Anansi was like umm ... it was like a stepping stone for her and I found that she would be able relate more with children of the same ethnic origin and nation. Yes, but, umm when it got to a certain stage I thought, okay now she's probably ready to mix with children from all over, and umm, she needs to integrate. I mean we all live in a kind of integrated society so umm, plus the fact I got a job, with Gillespie, I could have longer hours for her with extended time, ya know, so I thought, okay, now's the time for her to do so 'cause she's a big girl now. She can move to mainstream; she's going to go to mainstream school anyway, so ... Mother of Ife, girl, Group 1 (low SES, attainment above prediction)

These kinds of evaluations, that take into consideration the pedagogy of the setting, were also mentioned by all the middle-class parents in our sample. Evaluating a setting before deciding on a pre-school helped these parents to find settings that provided the kind of care and educational experiences that parents valued and deemed suitable for their child, and increased their chances of experiencing interactions with staff that reassured them that their child was well taken care of and supported. Like parenting in the home environment, activities and experiences that are planned and carried out in early-years settings are a practical interpretation of the values of the adults providing these experiences, in this case the staff in those settings (Siraj-Blatchford & Mayo, 2012). Bennett and colleagues (1996, p. 157) have suggested that early-years educators make decisions about the curriculum they provide based on their consideration of the knowledge, skills, values and attitudes they understand to be the most worthwhile for children to acquire. These decisions may also be based on early-years educators' knowledge and understanding of children's cognitive, psycho-motor and affective development, disciplined ways of knowing, reasoning and understanding, cognitive skills and processes.

What most obviously distinguished the choices for pre-school settings by middle-class parents from choices of working-class parents, was that the middle-class parents actively selected a pre-school with the aim of getting their child enrolled in an affiliated primary school. They appeared to be planning their child's educational trajectory from a very early age, recognizing the power of educational experiences on later outcomes.

Yes his brother had not been able to get into it and had gone somewhere else and then got into Bury at the reception class ... hmmm so yes it is obviously because his brother was there it was easier and the two at the same place and it is a very popular school. Because of the Head Mistress I think really – she has quite a strong personality and you know, it's kind of oversubscribed hmmm quite you have to live quite close in the catchment area and Edward just got in and then just because Alex was in the Nursery class did not automatically mean we will get a place in reception but he did and I think, you know, by that time we established kind of a relationship with other parents of kinds ... Mother of Alex, boy, Group 3 (high SES, attainment below prediction)

Imogene's mother had put her daughter on a waiting list for a local nursery that had a very good reputation and was affiliated with one of the most highly regarded primary schools in the area. As soon as a place became available Imogene transferred to this nursery from the playgroup she was already attending.

Did you have a particular reason for choosing this particular nursery?

Well we, it's just at the top of the road and it has very fantastic reputation.

Were there any staff at the play-group or at the nursery who were particularly helpful for Imogene's learning?

Not at play-group. Maybe for kids that went a lot, every day and so they were close to them, we didn't make such strong bonds there. At the nursery there'd been fantastic staff all the way through, you know.

What made them great?

The relationship with the mother eh (laughs). Some people ... are able to address you, reflect on your child in the way that's insightful and that's always interesting ... eh ... it, it makes you feel as though they've noticed, they are paying attention. Staff at the nursery were always very kind ... eh usually. There was one woman I've seen teaching kids there and I just dreaded her having any of my kids, a complete witch, but everyone else, thank God, everyone we had was fantastic! We were very lucky.

Can you give me maybe an example of the kind of things they would do that you feel has been very helpful?

Their compassion, I think. More friendly to Imogene, because she needed more compassion (laugh). Eh you know, they were honest with you and they would say things to you like ... I think a lot of teachers they don't want ... I'm sure at a place like this they get a lot of pressure from articulate middle-class parents who think their children are ... gifted ... and you would expect that they should be given a special provision eh ... and so I was quite surprised that they would be so honest with me about Imogene and her abilities and tell it to you straight.

What kinds of things did they say to you?

Imogene is the cleverest, you, well not the cleverest not but eh Imogene is the best in the class at all subjects, you know ... Eh ... with her it wasn't ... she just loved the teachers and they loved her, so that was nice. Mother of Imogene, girl, Group 4 (high SES, attainment as predicted)

These high-SES parents showed 'concerted cultivation' child rearing, as they were already carefully planning the educational career of their child, trying to make sure that the best schools would be available to their child.

Quality of pre-school settings

Although pre-school attendance generally has a positive effect on children's development, the extent and persistence of these effects depends to a great deal on the quality of these experiences. The Effective Pre-School and Primary Education (EPPE 3–11) study has shown the persistent effect of pre-school quality on children's academic, social and behavioural outcomes, as well as on their self-perceptions, net of all other influences. These positive effects are particularly persistent for children who attended high quality pre-school settings (Sylva et al., 2004, 2006, 2008, 2012; cf. Hall et al., 2009; Sammons et al., 2002a, 2002b, 2003, 2008d, 2012a,

2012b). For all social outcomes, the benefits of pre-school were greater for boys, for students with special educational needs (SEN) and for students from disadvantaged backgrounds. However, for some of the outcomes, notably English, Mathematics and 'Hyperactivity', only pre-schools of medium or high quality had lasting effects. Overall, children who did not attend pre-school, and those who attended low-quality pre-school, showed a range of poorer outcomes at the end of primary school, and even in secondary school.

In the EPPE project, quality of pre-school settings was measured on the Early Childhood Environment Rating Scales (ECERS-R, see Harms et al., 1998; ECERS-E, see Sylva et al., 2003, 2006). The ECERS-R is an American observational instrument for assessment of quality of early childhood education and care. It is one of the most widely used instruments in the United States, the United Kingdom and other European countries and measures a diverse set of quality aspects, ranging from furnishing to the quality of children's interactions with caregivers. The instrument consists of forty-three items divided into seven sub-scales: *Space and furnishings, Personal care routines, Language reasoning, Activities, Interaction, Program structure* and *Parents and Staff*. ECERS-E was developed as an additional scale for the EPPE project, to do better justice to the assessment of educational curriculum and processes in English pre-school settings (Sylva et al., 2003).

The English pre-school curriculum puts greater emphasis on 'emergent skills', particularly the emergence of Literacy, Numeracy and scientific thinking, than is covered by the concept of 'Developmentally Appropriate Practices' (Bredekamp & Copple, 1997) on which the ECERS-R is based (Soucacou & Sylva, 2010). After wide consultation with experts in Early Childhood and piloting in the field, the EPPE team created three curricular sub-scales related to *Literacy, Numeracy*, and *Science*, each covering a specific cognitive domain in the English curriculum but also in pre-school curricula emerging across the international scene (Communication, Language and Literacy; Numeracy; Knowledge and understanding of the world). The English curriculum was revised in 2000 and 2008. It has three additional areas of development (aside from the three included in the ECERS-E): Creative development; Physical development; and Personal, social and emotional development. These non-cognitive domains were considered to be adequately covered by the ECERS-R. A fourth *Diversity* sub-scale was included to assess the extent to which the first three are implemented with respect to children of different genders, cultural/ethnic groups and varying levels of ability. Assessments involved approximately half a day of observation and conversations with the staff about aspects of the routine that were not visible during the observation session (e.g., weekly sport sessions). Each item is rated on a seven-point scale, ranging from inadequate to excellent. The psychometric strength of both ECERS instruments is good, and for both scales high inter-rater reliability was established between senior research officers of the EPPE study in the different participating regions (Kappas ranging from .75 to .90 for the ECERS-R and between .83 to .97 for the ECERS-E). Taken together, the two observational measures assessed not only the structural elements of the pre-school centres, but also the educational and care processes that children experience on a daily basis (Sylva et al., 2003).

The EPPE study showed that settings that had more qualified staff, especially with a good proportion of graduate, trained teachers, showed higher quality and their children made more progress and better social/behavioural gains compared to those attending centres of low quality (Sylva et al., 2004). Good quality can be found across all types of early years settings, but, overall, quality was higher in settings integrating care and education and in those prioritizing educational experiences such as nursery schools (Sylva et al., 2004). These integrated settings run by local government were found to be exciting places, where children were challenged and supported in their learning by staff that were well qualified and responded sensitively, attending to the educational needs and abilities of the children. Unfortunately, other centres such as some playgroups and private day nurseries were typically characterized by more hasty planning and poorer implementation of the curriculum, and these characteristics interfered with the quality of care experienced by children.

By extending the EPPE project's quantitative data with qualitative data on pre-school settings, the Researching Effective Pedagogy in the Early Years (REPEY; Siraj-Blatchford et al., 2002) research has shown that the most effective pre-school settings (in terms of intellectual, social and dispositional outcomes) achieved a better balance between the opportunities provided for children to benefit from teacher-initiated small group work and the provision of freely chosen, yet potentially instructive, play activities. The REPEY study also showed a positive association between higher scores on dimensions of pedagogic practice such as curriculum differentiation and matching in terms of cognitive challenge and 'sustained shared thinking' and its effectiveness. The most effective settings also adopted social/behaviour policies that involved staff in supporting children in rationalizing and talking through their conflicts (Siraj-Blatchford et al., 2002).

Aside from the overall positive effect of good-quality pre-school experiences, the EPPSE project has made it clear that disadvantaged children in particular benefit significantly from higher-quality pre-school experiences, and that these experiences carry on to positively affect these children's outcomes up to the end of primary school (Sylva et al., 2004, 2006, 2008; see also Sammons, 2010a, 2010b) and beyond this to secondary. Taken together these findings suggest that high-quality pre-school education not only can provide children with a better start to school but can help to alleviate some of the effects of social disadvantage (Siraj-Blatchford et al., 2003; Sylva et al., 2006, 2008).

Quality of pre-school setting in the Case Studies

Nearly all the Case Studies parents positively evaluated the pre-school setting(s) their child had attended. In most cases their positive perceptions were supported by the formal quality assessment conducted by EPPE (see Sylva et al., 2004, 2006). The majority of Case Studies children attended pre-school settings that provided medium-quality experiences. These settings were mostly Local Authority day nurseries, and the quality of provision they provided was average but satisfactory. Although none of the children from high-SES families were enrolled in low-quality centres, only two high-SES children attended high-quality centres. We did find that half of the boys and two girls who succeeded against the odds attended high quality pre-schools. Of the vulnerable children (Group 2: Low SES, predicted attainment; Group 3: High SES, low attainment) only one boy but three girls attended a high-quality setting. Nine of these eleven high-quality pre-schools were nursery classes; the other two were Local Authority day nurseries. So the majority of high-quality settings were from the state-funded, maintained sector, led by graduate teachers.

Particularly the low-SES parents of children succeeding against the odds believed that pre-school offered their child something in addition to what they were able to offer at home.

I thought it just be good for him. I thought when we went ... I just thought ... be mixed inside of things. I think children learn much quicker with their peers than they do with their parents, you know, I can only be at a certain level. Mother of Steven, boy, Group 1 (low SES, attainment above prediction)

I've always been of the opinion that children cannot learn everything from home, so they have to mix with other children, especially for the first one. She was the first child and it was only me and dad and we wouldn't necessarily have the kind of vocabulary to speak with her, you know, talk like all her peers will have in school. She needed that social interaction. I went to a pre-school as well in Nigeria and we've always known of the advantage of that plus the fact it gets the children out of the house and you can go and do your own thing (laughs).

It was a gentle way of getting her into school without all the hassle and we called up, as I was working part-time then, only the days that she goes to nursery, so it sort of like served two purposes. Mother of Ife, girl, Group 1 (low SES, attainment above prediction)

Parents, and in some cases children, from the successful low-SES group looked back on the pre-school period as a positive experience that had been valuable for later academic achievement. They were happy about the way the pre-school setting communicated with the parents, but even more so they mentioned the pleasant atmosphere created by the staff, that made their children feel at home and provided them with a wide range of playful learning experiences. For the majority of the girls and nearly all boys who succeeded against the odds, references were made to how the pre-school setting had helped them develop socially and cognitively, and in some cases had helped them develop a positive attitude towards school and learning.

They learn how to interact with other children ... definitely, erm ... and I think they do pick up a ... it ... slowly ... gets them into going to proper school, rather than just shove 'em in ... into school full-time, and then you're, 'Oh my God', you know, they slowly learn ... because it's very few hours to start with, and then they increase it until they go to proper school, so they do ... and I think they do teach them a lot, they teach them songs and ... urm ... well they teach them things that you wouldn't believe that they're teaching 'em. 'Cos they do it all through play to start with, in nursery. Mother of Martha, girl, Group 1 (low SES, attainment above prediction)

The nursery that ... he absolutely loved that, absolutely loved it. It was quite a big class but it was so full of life, I mean they did everything, painting, the lot. I mean they were never given the chance to be bored ... and it was, you know, big area as well, it wasn't a small, enclosed porch cabin like at the playgroup. It was good size, you know, double of size of the classroom that had loads of room to move around ... good teachers ... I don't remember them having ... the formality, they had their routine but it was much more free play ... I mean obviously it was free play and then you had gym, music and all that. Mother of Robert, boy, Group 1 (low SES, attainment above prediction)

Despite the overall positive perception of the pre-school settings by parents and children, pre-schools were not always evaluated positively with regard to their effectiveness for children's development on the formal EPPE ratings. This was particularly the case for low-SES boys who would continue to develop as predicted; five out of the ten boys in this group attended a low-quality pre-school centre. Only one girl succeeding against the odds attended a low-quality pre-school. All low-quality settings attended by Case Studies children were playgroups, but this does not follow that all playgroups in EPPE were of low quality.

The differences between the quality of provision of pre-school experiences were reflected in the learning trajectories of the children during the early years. All children from low-SES families who had a medium- or high-quality pre-school experience showed substantial progress as measured by rankings on at least one of the developmental domains during their pre-school period. But for nearly all low-SES boys with low-quality pre-school experiences, their rankings showed regression during this time. In our Case Studies sample, which is large in number of cases compared to other case-studies researches but modest in terms of general representation, it appears that the importance of high- vs low-quality pre-school settings seems particularly great for low-SES boys. First of all, these boys appear to have a greater chance of enrolling in a low-quality pre-school setting than boys from middle-class families and girls from equally disadvantaged backgrounds. For nearly all these boys their rankings regressed during their pre-school years. Secondly, when boys from disadvantaged families do find themselves in an excellent pre-school setting they seem to experience long-term benefits, as all these boys went on to succeed against the odds. As such, it appears that while good or even excellent quality pre-school helps low-SES children develop school-relevant numeracy and language skills and helps them to prepare for future educational experiences, low quality pre-school might be an additional risk factor for boys from disadvantaged backgrounds.

Combined effects of pre-schools and early home learning environment

The main quantitative EPPE analyses of attainment outcomes at age 11 pointed to the benefits of medium- and especially high-quality pre-school. It also showed important interactions with the early home learning environment (early HLE). In particular, it showed that children who had little or no pre-school experience who also experienced low early HLEs had the worst outcomes of all children in the sample. For children who did attend pre-school, high-quality pre-school offered some protection against the adverse effects of a low early HLE (Melhuish et al., 2008; Sammons et al., 2008a, 2008b; Siraj-Blatchford, 2010a). When combining the early HLE index with pre-school effectiveness and quality, none of the boys in the Case Studies and only three girls (one from low-SES, two from high-SES backgrounds) experienced the benefit of a high early HLE in combination with highly effective pre-school. The working-class girl who had experienced the combination of high early HLE and high-quality pre-school was not one of the low-SES children who succeeded against the odds by the end of primary school. However, her trajectory rankings showed a steady increase from the moment she started to attend pre-school. While Fareeda started among the lowest 30 per cent of the children in the EPPE sample, her rankings had improved to slightly above the low-SES sample average by the end of primary school. Once in secondary school her rankings improved considerably to the top 20 per cent of the EPPSE sample by Key Stage 3 (at age 14) and she was in effect succeeding against the odds of disadvantage at this point of her learning life-course. For two other children from low-SES backgrounds, highly effective pre-school was combined with medium-level early HLEs, and this boy and girl had succeeded against the odds by the end of primary school.

Despite a near absence of the most favourable combination of high-quality pre-school and high early HLE, the combination of early HLE and pre-school effectiveness generally seemed more favourable for low-SES children who succeeded against the odds than for those who did not. Only one girl succeeding against the odds had the disadvantage of a low early HLE combined with a low-quality pre-school experience, compared to four boys who attained as predicted. On the other hand, seven of the children who succeeded against the odds (three boys) who had low early HLEs had high- (four) or medium- (three) quality pre-school experiences, compared to five of the children who did not exceed predictions (four boys; two children attended high- and three attended medium-quality pre-schools). Furthermore, ten successful low-SES children combined medium- or high-quality pre-school with a medium or high early HLE (four boys). This was the case for only five of the less successful low-SES children, only one of whom was a boy.

These findings from the Case Studies indicate that, unfortunately, few low-SES children have the combined benefit of experiencing a high early HLE and excellent pre-school education, in our modest Case Studies sample. However, the relatively high occurrence of medium or high HLEs with good or excellent pre-school experiences among the children succeeding against the odds once again confirms the importance of the combination of good-quality experiences in the home and the pre-school to help children succeed against the odds of disadvantage. Furthermore, it seems that for low-SES boys, who generally have a greater chance of experiencing a lower early HLE, good or excellent quality pre-school settings indeed can function as an important protective factor.

Choices regarding primary and secondary school environments

The transition into formal schooling marks an important developmental milestone for young children. For most children in the Case Studies, as well as for their parents, starting primary school was an event they had happily anticipated. Nearly all children mentioned how they had looked forward to spending more time with their friends, how their teachers in the lower grades of primary school had seemed particularly helpful and pleasant, and some children had looked forward to learning new skills such as reading, writing and Maths. Their transition into primary school generally caused few problems, although for some children it took some time to settle in and adapt to the rules and demands of the primary school classroom.

Some parents felt that the transition into formal schooling demanded that they would carefully consider their options. For instance, they weighed options for schools with specific didactical philosophies, such as Montessori schools, or faith-based schools, single-sex schools or private schools.

There are times when I think, maybe we should have considered private school or given them that, 'cause I had private education through my whole schooling, and maybe they've missed out on some of the things that I've experienced, but they feel, we talk about it, and they feel that they've benefitted in other ways, by having a wider exposure to different people and a less narrow view. I think they feel happier with what they had, they don't ever wish for that, they've got a sort of inverted snobbery actually, they actually sort of think that people at private schools are all posh and this and that.

What do you think they would have gained from private schooling?

I think probably smaller classes and maybe more opportunity to develop their potential. My oldest daughter is at Cambridge doing English, and sometimes she feels that she's at a disadvantage just because the other, she feels that public school children have got more self-confidence than she has. I'm not sure quite whether she's right or not, but maybe instilling a sense of your worth. Maybe that's what they do, give them some sense they are somehow special and I've always thought that wasn't necessarily the right thing to do anyway, but she is encountering that now. Mother of Lucas, boy, Group 4 (high SES, attainment as predicted)

Abby and her two brothers went to a local state primary school, St Barth's, but then went on to private secondary schools. When asked if many of her friends did the same with their children, Abby's mother said:

I suppose in my clique of people that it was common. [The primary school], never made a comment whatsoever, they knew that they were going into these exams. I think they honestly felt that they would all three of them would have done well wherever they went, but there was a family thing that was set when John was like, 2 or 3. I mean a long, long time before we came [to that age], about you know, the grandparents supporting them to go through private education at secondary level. And John sat his entrance exam, a couple of weeks after his

Dad and I had split, and he passed you see. And well ... he was going to be going, that was me driving for it really. And then I, as a child, didn't go to private school, and my brother did, and I always used to feel that I was second rate, and I used to say this to the kids and they were [saying] 'Ooh God Mum' but I wanted them all to have the same opportunity, up to GCSE's anyway, and then in sixth form, you know, they could go somewhere else.

What do you think private education adds to their experience?

I think there's a lot more educationally, and I can compare directly with my friend whose kids were all at St Barth's and they're still very close friends, and most of them went off to the comprehensive in town and they've done very well, exam wise. It's the sports, it's the extra-curricular side of things, which gives a broader horizon of things, the facilities. I mean it sounds terrible, but they are fantastic. You know, they've got their own swimming pool, and all sorts of things, that you could get by doing it yourself outside school I suppose. But then, I'm working and I want them to have a really brilliant education and go somewhere that I think might just give them a little bit of an edge, and prepares them better for exams. I think if you're in the state system, if you're in the top set, this is absolutely reflected in the results and at present there isn't a problem, at our local comprehensive anyway. Whereas if you're elsewhere, it's the luck of the draw, whereas I feel I've got more clout. This sounds terrible doesn't it, you know, paying for your education, I expected them to deliver and if there's problem, I expect them to come to me very quickly, I didn't get that with my eldest's school, at his private school, because I was a different, I was a weaker person I think and now I won't stand for a thing if they're not going quite right at the other two schools. Mother of Abby, girl, Group 4 (high SES, attainment as predicted)

These parents based their choices on their research of the schools through publicly available reports, talked to other parents with children who were enrolled in the schools, visited the schools and met with teachers and heads of schools. The high-SES parents had usually carefully chosen the school their child attended, and perceived these schools as having been academically effective and well managed.

Fantastic peer group, aspiring staff, fantastic leadership! The head is a scary woman, she would never be a friend, very good head, you know, ruled with a rod of iron ... zero tolerance of bad behaviour but still with great compassion, you know with very high standards, very aspiring and none of the stuff about 'Oh the national curriculum makes it impossible for us to do extras.' Mother of Imogene, girl, Group 4 (high SES, attainment as predicted)

Considering alternative options and researching schools was less common for working-class parents. Only a few parents of children who would succeed against the odds used any available means to gather information to base their choices on. Abdi's father explained how he had chosen a secondary school for his son.

Why did you choose that particular school?

It was the best school in the area . . . Internet and meetings I ask the school, which the school with best result from last years . . . and it was a foundation boys school . . . yeah all boys . . .

Did you think going to an all-boy school was important for him as well?

Hm, no . . . no, but it was because it was a good school, that's why I chose it . . . Father of Abdi, Boy, Group 1 (low SES, attainment above prediction)

In some of the working-class families, parents and children were willing to go to great lengths to secure a school they felt was suitable for the child. Particularly in low-SES families from ethnic minority backgrounds, religion was an important factor for consideration in their school choices. Parents, and sometimes children, were keen on finding schools, particularly secondary schools, that instilled values and norms similar to those of the home. Ife's parents moved to a new area, outside of the city they had lived in, to find a more suitable faith-based school for their daughter, even though attending this school meant they now had longer commutes to their place of work, and though none of the children Ife previously knew from primary school would be there with her.

Did you feel it was important for her to go to Christian schools?

Yes, we thought it was. It was part of our own ethos and it was something that we strongly believed in. And I believe that if we bring her up the right way and in that kind of environment: good both for ourselves and her as well. Mother of Ife, girl, Group 1 (low SES, attainment above prediction)

But most children in the Case Studies, particularly those from working-class families, simply went on to attend primary schools and later secondary schools that were closely allocated, based on their postcode catchment area. Often these schools were affiliated to the local pre-school the children had attended. Many parents were not even aware that they had some sort of choice in the matter. When they could choose, they usually selected schools because of their proximity to the home, or because of familiarity with the school through experiences of older siblings or children from friends or relatives. Research shows that these choices, or lack of choices, regarding the primary or secondary schools children will attend can have significant consequences for children's academic trajectories.

Most children from working-class families will live in neighbourhoods and attend schools with children from families with similarly disadvantaged backgrounds. Besides structural characteristics of school environments such as overall poverty levels, that affect children's academic progress, distal characteristics of the classroom microsystem also influence progress.

The age of the children, number of students, socio-economic background of the students and the language skills of the other children in the class positively or negatively affect children's academic achievement over the course of their school trajectories (NICHD ECCRN, 2002; cf. Lee et al., 1998; Pianta et al., 2002). For instance, children's classroom experiences are less effective when the concentration of poverty, as indicated, for example, by eligibility for free school meals (FSM) in the school is high (see for instance Lee et al., 1998; Pianta et al., 2002).

In the EPPSE sample, schools with few students who were entitled to FSM were more likely to report that they encouraged students to take responsibility for and evaluate their own learning, involved students in decision-making, developed leadership skills and targeted high achievers (Sylva et al., 2012). For the children in EPPSE 3–14, analyses showed that children who were eligible for FSM showed substantially less progress across all subjects during primary and secondary school up to age 14. As these children typically had lower Key Stage 1 attainment, the gap was widening between them and others over time (Melhuish et al., 2006; Sylva et al., 2008, 2012). At age 14, EPPSE children who received FSM also reported substantially more negative perceptions about their schools than other children (Sylva et al., 2012). In our low-SES sample a little over 30 per cent of the children received FSM during Reception. In Year 9 in secondary school their number had gone down to less than 20 per cent. As expected, none of the children from middle-class families received FSM. But even those children in our low-SES sample who themselves were not considered disadvantaged enough to receive FSM were likely to have many peers in their classrooms and in school who were vulnerable with regard to their family background and abilities.

Academic effectiveness of schools

Overall academic effectiveness of a school is an important factor of influence on children's academic attainment. In EPPE 3–11, the academic effectiveness of the primary school was measured between Key Stage 1 and 2 independently of the longitudinal EPPE sample, by analysing national assessments for all students (600,000+) in all state primary schools (15,000+) in England, across three successive cohorts from 2002 to 2004 (Melhuish et al., 2006). For the children in EPPE 3–11, the research showed that students who attended an academically more effective primary school had significantly better outcomes for English and Maths, over and above child and family background. Not only was the effectiveness of the primary school linked to students' absolute attainment at age 11, it also predicted the amount of progress the EPPE 3–11 students made between the ages of 7 and 11. But while all children benefitted from being in a more academically effective school rather than an ineffective one, the consequences were markedly greater for vulnerable groups, such as low-ability children. Although academic effectiveness did not have a generally significant effect for children's social-behavioural outcomes, certain groups of vulnerable children, such as those with special educational needs (SEN), or whose mothers had low educational qualifications, had better social/behavioural outcomes if they attended schools that were more academically effective. There was no evidence that children who attended these academically effective primary schools enjoyed school less or were negatively influenced in their self-image or social outcomes. Instead, for children from more vulnerable groups it seems to be beneficial (Melhuish et al., 2006; Sammons et al., 2008c; Sylva et al., 2008). In secondary schools, similar measures of academic effectiveness did not predict children's progress and attainment, but judgements of the quality of student learning in inspection reports by the Office for Standards in Education (Ofsted, the English standards regulation body) did (Sylva et al., 2012).

In the Case Studies sample we found that the majority of children, both from low- and high-SES backgrounds, attended primary schools that had average to good academic effectiveness for both English and Maths. Simultaneous good academic effectiveness for English and Maths was rare for all four groups. Interestingly, the one high-SES boy who did have this experience, Alex, was dyslexic. His ranking trajectory showed a strong dip in English attainment from baseline (age 3) to Key Stage 1 (age 7). However, after this his attainment improved considerably. Although he was still below the high-SES average at the end of primary school (age 11), he continued his progression during secondary school and by Key Stage 3 (age 14) managed rankings around the mean of the high-SES group.

Although there were a few high-SES children who attended a primary school that was less effective on one subject, it was only in the low-SES samples that we found examples of children who attended schools that were substantially less effective for both English and Maths. Interestingly, four out of the five children for whom this was the case had managed to succeed against the odds and the poor effectiveness of their schools was in no way visible in their trajectories during their time there. However, for Tremaine, one of the boys from the low-SES sample who did not succeed against the odds, the low effectiveness of his school went together with a steep decline in ranking during the early years of primary that stabilized at a very low level. In general, very few clear patterns of association could be discerned between primary school effectiveness and development of rankings on trajectories of the Case Studies sample. In order to understand more about how schools might have supported our children to succeed, we need to consider a range of factors at classroom and school level.

Additional school-level factors that influence academic achievement

For the parents and the children in the Case Studies, perceptions of the academic effectiveness of the schools these children attended were highly personal. The one school-level factor that seemed to most clearly set apart the Case Studies children who succeeded against the odds from those who were vulnerable was the help they received from school when they were experiencing difficulties with academic subjects or behaviour. Although difficulties were reported by respondents from all groups, the parents and children who succeeded against the odds felt schools had effectively helped them to deal with these difficulties, through extra intervention such as booster, remedial, homework, revision or behavioural classes. These additional classes helped children to catch up with their peers and (re)establish and reinforce a positive perception of school and learning and of students' efficacy to deal with difficult situations.

For nearly half of the children in the 'resilient' group, school policies of providing additional (remedial) classes or mentors were perceived to have played an important role in helping these children overcome possible difficulties with school and learning. For six girls and three boys from Group 1, some type of *remedial event* was mentioned as having helped them succeed in school. In primary school this help generally consisted of 'booster' classes which offered additional help with one or more of their core subjects (English, Maths or Science). Interestingly, this included all three children from Group 1 (Low SES, higher attainment) whose trajectories showed a steady improvement over time. The children who had attended booster classes mentioned how these had facilitated their learning by helping them grasp the basic concepts and skills of the subject, which provided them with a foundation for further learning. The following student provided a particularly clear description of the benefits the booster class offered her:

The only subject that I ever really struggled with was Maths that is like my weak point, but going to the booster classes it really made me enthusiastic about Maths, more, so the more I did it, the more I got used to it and now it's like a routine, if I find something difficult, like in Maths, I'll look it up, and then I'll, read over it again until I understand it.

What was it about Maths that you found difficult at the time?

I don't think it's numbers, I just overall, I didn't really understand, didn't really find it easy to add up numbers and divide and things, and also, trying to keep up with the other students, it's like you didn't want to be left behind, so it was like, if I didn't understand it, like sometimes I wouldn't say, because I knew that I didn't want to be behind everyone else, so I used to ... but having the booster classes, with other children who were just like you, so it made it easier for you to, erm say if you didn't understand this, didn't understand that it was like, you could just say it and it wouldn't matter.

Did they teach things differently in the booster classes?

It's more erm, one on one like the classes were much smaller, like five or six students instead of like ten, fifteen like much smaller classes, so it made it easier for the teacher to like pinpoint which student was lagging behind, which student needed more help, then it was easier to learn, if there's less people in the class asking for help. Anjali, girl, Group 1 (low SES, attainment above prediction)

In secondary school the additional help came in the form of after-school classes to deal with coursework and revision, and also mentors to help the students deal with behavioural and any socio-emotional difficulties they were encountering. The fact that they were offered help made them feel supported and increased their motivation to apply themselves. Jarell was experiencing difficulties with bullying, which was in turn affecting his performance and behaviour in school. His behaviour became progressively worse and eventually he got into a fight with one of the bullies and was suspended, as the fight was caught on a security camera. His mother asked the school to intervene:

I was concerned in Year 9 where then he was doing things to wind children up ... erm, and erm when I went to the parents evening, I just couldn't believe I was listening to ... [I was shocked] Yeah ... so then I said, 'He needs, he needs some help!'

Is that when he got the mentor?

Yeah. Erm, it did help. He said he enjoyed it, it was every so often ... it did help ... I think it did help ... Yeah, it cleared the air ... it cleared the air perhaps and how he was feeling ... and he's just done exceptional work ... Mother of Jarell, boy, Group 1 (low SES, attainment above prediction)

Although remedial and revision classes were available for the high-SES children who succeeded as predicted, these were hardly used by these children. Only one boy attended remedial classes for spelling in primary school. Rather, if on occasion children encountered difficulties with school subjects, or needed some additional help with revision, their middle-class parents could draw upon their personal resources of cultural and social capital, which enabled them to take matters in their own hands and deal with their child's needs outside of school (Allatt, 1993).

The vulnerable children and parents, on the other hand, felt let down by schools and head teachers. Their lack of academic success was attributed to the overall way schools were run, including policies on student behaviour, policies regarding help with learning difficulties and lack of continuity in the teaching staff. Ko and Sammons (2011) describe how

In England the Office for Standards in Education (Ofsted) was introduced in 1993 to change more traditional quality assurance functions of inspection (where previously inspection reports were never published at the school level and inspection occurred only very infrequently) to a high profile accountability mechanism that involved regular inspection of all schools on a three-year cycle. This publicly identified and graded school performance and involved sanctions for schools deemed to be failing, showing serious weaknesses or needing to improve. The threat of closure was introduced for schools deemed to be failing that did not improve sufficiently within a short period of time (2 years). Ofsted's self-selected aim was 'improvement through inspection' (Matthews & Sammons, 2004, 2005) as well as publishing individual schools' inspection reports to inform parents, an annual report commenting on standards of attainment, the quality of education, school leadership and of teaching and learning was published based on an analysis of all the inspections conducted in a year. (Ko & Sammons, 2011, p. 9)

Ineffective policies were mentioned for four boys and two girls from Group 2 and for two boys and two girls from Group 3. This pattern was most prevalent for students who showed problematic behaviour and learning difficulties. In the EPPE 3–11 sample, quality of school leadership, higher overall school effectiveness and improvement since last inspection, as determined through Ofsted inspections, all predicted better progress in Maths. These last two measures also predicted better development of self-regulation skills for children. In the executive summary of their final report on the primary phase of the EPPE 3–11 project, Sylva et al. concluded that

This indicates that students who attended a higher-quality school (as judged by inspectors) made more progress and had better development, taking into account their background and prior attainment, confirming the importance of primary school influences in shaping students' outcomes during Key Stage 2. (Sylva et al., 2008, p. v)

Better academic and social-behavioural outcomes and progress from age 11 to 14 were predicted by better quality of teaching (including a strong emphasis on learning by teachers) and where teachers were more supportive with learning and positively valued their students. Students also did better in schools where head teachers showed better leadership qualities, in schools that were clean, safe and well equipped and had substantial learning resources available. Finally, a positive behaviour climate in the school also significantly predicted attainment and progress (Sylva et al., 2012; cf. Ofsted, 2009).

Although certainly not all schools that were judged poorly by parents and children would have had negative Ofsted evaluations, the negative perceptions of parents and children of these schools certainly seemed to interfere with children's learning processes and parents' ability and willingness to cooperate with the school in efforts to improve children's learning. This process was described in the extensive case study on Tom White in Chapter 4. Tom was being sent home from school very regularly because of his behaviour. Tom's father, Mr White, felt the school policies were both ineffective and unfair.

To put it quite frankly, I think they run it [the school] like a boot camp really, and I think if some of the children are finding it difficult, their way is to send them home, send them home. Yeah, send them home. He [the head teacher] did say, they don't want to see, they don't want to deal with the issue that's going on, they just want to send them home. Father of Tom, boy, Group 2 (low SES, attainment as predicted)

According to parents and students, the willingness of students to apply themselves was compromised when (head) teachers did not communicate clearly how they expected students to behave, and imposed unreasonable rules. The EPPE 3–11 study found that in schools where teachers reported active communication with parents by, for instance, teachers or head teachers, students showed better progress in their ability to self-regulate (Sylva et al., 2008). Where communication between school and homes failed, as in the case of Tom White, this often resulted in misgivings about the school on the side of the families. Parents and students felt they were treated unfairly and that schools did not want to have to deal with the more problematic students. When asked how he looked back on secondary school (before getting permanently excluded), this student remarked:

I didn't really like it that much. 'Cos, I don't like ... See everything that I did ... teachers would be on your back ... every step, everywhere ... teachers are saying 'I don't want you here', to me and a few other people. The Head is always trying to get you out of the school. Tremaine, boy, Group 2 (low SES, attainment as predicted)

Many of the less academically successful students had experienced difficulties with one or more school subjects. Mostly, parents and students felt that schools had offered sufficient support. Some of the parents who believed the support insufficient, particularly those from middle-class backgrounds, had resolved their issues with the school by privately organizing additional help for their child after school. But others felt frustrated and even angry with school policies and head teachers for not dealing effectively with their child. These parents, like Tom's father, felt badly let down by the school and insisted that schools had not offered their children the support they had needed to overcome their difficulties with school and learning:

She was 5, 6 then and I started to say something then, and they just said, 'We don't do dyslexia until they get to Key Stage 2', and I'm like ... 'No, it doesn't matter when you do dyslexia, it's when the child has it.' And they're like, 'Yes but we don't have dyslexia, children don't show signs of dyslexia until Key Stage 2', and I'm like 'I don't know where you've done your teacher training, but that's not true.' It was difficult, it was just ... made me very angry. Because I knew my child wasn't stupid, you only have to talk to her and y'know, we go to museums, we go to discussions, we used to come here [Institute of Education] to things and it's sort of ... the child's not stupid. Because she can't get her words down on paper, you don't need to penalize her for it. But the school started to treat her like she was stupid. Mother of Susan, girl, Group 2 (low SES, attainment as predicted)

I had to fight with the governors and the council people to get him statemented. Subash has been statemented because he's dyslexic you see and they didn't pick it up, I had to identify it to them. I had to go in end of Year 2, I had to go to them and say, 'My son's not being able to read, what's happening?' You know, and that head teacher said 'You're a paranoid parent' to me ... so ... It did upset me, I'm saying 'Well I'm pretty certain this child is not running in line with the other children, yet he's being pulled along, he's being dragged along, he's not holding his own ground' and she said I was a paranoid parent ... Father of Subash, boy, Group 3 (high SES, attainment below prediction)

Insufficient support was mentioned for two boys and two girls from Group 2 and for two boys and one girl from Group 3. It seems likely that these negative perceptions of parents were at least to some degree transmitted to their children, and in some cases might have reinforced a negative attitude to school and learning and to their teachers, perhaps even to themselves as learners. Children who do not feel supported by their teachers show less self-regulation in class and less pro-social behaviour (Sylva et al., 2008). Susan's mother had tried to no avail to convince Susan's teachers to offer her daughter additional support with reading and writing because she was convinced that her daughter was dyslexic. Instead of providing her with specific help for her reading and spelling problems they pulled her out of the regular class and placed her in a booster class for children who were learning English as an additional language.

They said she was stupid and they told her she was stupid. She kept coming home and telling us that, y'know she was stupid ... No you're not stupid Susan and she used to get dragged to school screaming. She wouldn't go to school because they treated her like that. As I said, they put her in the class with the ... English as a different language. Erm ... and that wasn't appropriate so she was in with the kids that, y'know everyone else said was stupid. They put Susan in [that class] then of course she got labelled as being stupid, which ... caused her problems. Mother of Susan, girl, Group 2 (low SES, attainment as predicted)

Susan seemed just as angry and frustrated as her mother. She was relieved when her mother finally decided to find a different school for her. When asked why she had disliked her school she said:

'Cos of the teacher.

In what way didn't you like her?

Well, first of all she put me in these stupid booster classes, where they had this puppet called Po ... teaching me about letter formation and it's like duh! It is as a connective. Duhhh ... no it's not. Or 'the' is used as ... it's like, I'm not thick, I'm not 2 years old, I just couldn't write it down and they were just treating me like I didn't know what I was saying or doing ... so that's kind of ...

Did you get frustrated with that?

Yes. What did I use to say about the evil puppet? Not a very polite thing ... I used to hate it, I used to come home going, oh that bloody puppet ... It was annoying ... more than anything, 'cos all these kids were like, English was their second language, yet they seemed to be getting it more than I was. They seemed to be understanding it or being able to do it more than I was. Susan, girl, Group 2 (low SES, attainment as predicted)

It seems quite a laid-back school. I don't think they put a great deal of pressure on the kids to do more, if you like. I think if they see that he's getting where he's getting, then that's ... OK, but they don't push either. I don't think this works with him ... might work better with other children, but it won't work with him. If it's left ... if it's left to his choice, then it won't work with him. Mother of Christopher, boy, Group 2 (low SES, attainment as predicted)

The EPPE 3–11 study found that children who felt safe in school and felt supported by school staff, such as teachers and head teachers, showed better overall development than children who had negative perceptions of the social school environment. Not only did these children do better academically towards the end of primary school but they were also perceived as better behaved and more socially adapted by their teachers (Sylva et al., 2008).

In secondary schools students who rated their secondary school more favourably in terms of behavioural climate and emphasis on learning had significantly better attainment for English and Maths (Sylva et al., 2012). But while school level characteristics are important, teacher characteristics seem to be even more relevant to children's academic and social-behavioural development in school. In their review of teacher effect-iveness research, Ko and Sammons (2011) conclude that the evidence on educational effectiveness suggests that while schools can make a difference to student achievement, the most substantial portion of that difference may be attributed to teachers. According to their synthesis, schools account for around 5 to 15 per cent of the variation in student progress over a school year, after taking account of student prior attainment and background, while teacher effects are generally much larger at 20 to 40 per cent.

The classroom microsystem

Although parents of vulnerable children often felt let down by their children's school as a whole, they appeared particularly bothered by the fact that they felt the child's teachers had not taken their concerns as parents seriously. To them this seemed to communicate that these schools and particularly the teachers expected very little from and for their child.

Yeah ... because some teachers have favourite students to another, and I think, I don't ... I like, in Year 8 there was an English teacher who blatantly showed it and had all of her favourites in the back line, and then everyone else like that [in front]. Everyone used to hate the lesson even if you were at the back, because it would show. Because the teacher wouldn't have faith in you, and because you wasn't the favourite you'd put up your hand ... immediately they'd pick the back row, and ... things like that, like even if you, if it was the same ability as another student then they would still mark you down, so ... Marcy, girl, Group 3 (high SES, attainment below prediction)

Reviews of school effectiveness research have consistently drawn attention to the importance of high teacher expectations as a characteristic of effective schools and teachers (Teddlie & Reynolds, 2000; Sammons, 2007). This is particularly the case for effective schools serving disadvantaged communities (Muijs et al., 2004; Harris et al., 2006).

But there are other teacher characteristics that also influence children's academic achievement in school, such as teachers' qualifications, beliefs that teachers have regarding the goals of education and their classroom curriculum (NICHD ECCRN, 2002; cf. Lee et al., 1998; Pianta et al., 2002). The EPPE 3–11 research showed that proximal characteristics of the classroom such as teaching style affect children's attainment. Observed quality of students' educational experiences during Year 5 (age 10) was significantly higher in classes where teachers closely adhered to the English Literacy and Numeracy strategies. Although this influence of teaching quality on reading and Maths outcomes at the end of primary school is stronger than the net influence of some background factors, such as gender and family disadvantage, influences of the early HLE and mothers' highest qualification level show stronger effects (Sammons et al., 2008c).

Studies that included both teacher demographics and teacher beliefs show that the frequency of effective teaching practices, such as engaging children in cognitively challenging talk, including early literacy talk, conversations about past or future events, personal narratives and scientific talk, is positively associated with a strong pedagogical orientation of the teacher towards literacy development. These practices are also associated with higher levels of teacher qualification, but not with years of experience (NICHD ECCRN, 2002; Pianta et al., 2002; Smith & Dickinson, 1994). The Effective Primary Pedagogical Strategies in English and Maths (EPPSEM) study in Key Stage 2 showed that, of the primary schools that participated in the EPPE research, the most academically effective primary schools with the highest teacher quality scores for classrooms were characterized by the fact that the teacher showed respect, social support and concern for students – not dissimilar to the characteristics of more successful parenting in homes. The teachers made sure students' individual needs were recognized. They established routines so students knew what was expected of them, conducted end-of-lesson plenaries and used group work and peer tutoring. They also engaged students in dialogic learning and teaching, and built on students' prior knowledge, interests and experiences. During lessons they identified key learning concepts and lesson objectives and provided assessment for learning, questioning and feedback to class/groups/individuals. Teachers also made cross-subject links explicit (Siraj-Blatchford et al., 2011b).

Wider research on effective teaching has demonstrated the importance of teacher behaviour as an influence on student progress and suggested that school and teacher influences may be especially important for disadvantaged student groups (Mortimore et al., 1988; Sanders, 1998; Scheerens & Bosker, 1997; Van der Werf, 2006). In our Case Studies we found considerable differences in the way academically successful and academically vulnerable children perceived their relations with their teachers, as well as the effectiveness of the teaching they had experienced. The academically successful children, regardless of their SES background, generally described having positive relationships with at least some of their teachers.

All my teachers were my favourites really. There was Miss Jophal, she was my favourite primary school teacher. She was quite young and she was really like, enthusiastic about things and really like nice to children and used to help me whenever I needed help and things like that. When we used to have like free time at the end of the day, she used to play music and make it fun and let us relax and things like that, which really like helped me want to go school more, because it made you more excited about going to school knowing there's something to look forward to at the end of the day. Anjali, girl, Group 1 (low SES, attainment above prediction)

Imogene described how she felt she had benefitted from building a good relationship with her teachers in the lower grades of primary school.

They [my primary teachers] were always very approachable like we, we never called our teachers by their second names, it was always the first names which, which made it a lot easier to talk to them and I think because we had the circle times and stuff like that and because when we were working we weren't just taking notes from a board we were all discussing it and stuff. You really got thinking about it a lot more and if there were any problems there would be no hesitation. You'd just ask, you know, it wouldn't be embarrassing (laugh). Imogene, girl, Group 4 (high SES, attainment as predicted)

Ko and Sammons (2011) provide general profiles of effective and ineffective teachers based on a number of review studies. Effective teachers set clear instructional goals and clearly communicate these to their students, including what is expected of them and why. They are knowledgeable about curriculum content and the strategies for teaching the curriculum and they make expert use of existing instructional materials in order to devote more time to practices that enrich and clarify the content. Good teaching is also characterized by teachers who are knowledgeable about their students, adapting instruction to their needs and anticipating misconceptions in their existing knowledge. They are able and willing to integrate their instruction with instruction in other subject areas. During their teaching they address higher- as well as lower-level cognitive objectives, and carefully monitor students' understanding by offering regular, appropriate feedback. In addition, effective staff teach students meta-cognitive strategies and give them opportunities to master these strategies. Finally, they accept responsibility for student outcomes.

In contrast, ineffective teachers and classroom practices include inconsistent approaches to the curriculum and teaching and more frequent use of negative criticism and negative feedback. These teachers emphasize supervision. They infrequently interact with students and in their communication refer to classroom routines. In these classes students show low levels of involvement with their work and they perceive their teachers as not caring, unhelpful, under-appreciating the importance of learning and their work. These teachers have inconsistent expectations for different learners, that are lower for disadvantaged students from low-SES families (Ko & Sammons, 2011).

Perceptions of teacher quality

The majority of positive and negative explanations by children about their success or failure in school referred to particular characteristics of the teachers and the way they taught their classes. References to teachers as 'protective' influences were made for eight boys and ten girls from Group 1 and for all six students from Group 4; references to teachers as having contributed to less successful school attainment were made for five boys and one girl from Group 2 and for five girls and two boys from Group 3. When children talked about teachers that had been particularly helpful, three patterns of teacher characteristics emerged. Firstly, teachers were perceived as being particularly helpful when they were *sensitive* to the child's particular needs and responding to the child in accordance to these needs. *Sensitive responsiveness* was mentioned for seven boys and nine girls from Group 1 and for three boys and two girls from Group 4. These teachers, for instance, provided the children with extra help when needed, but were also willing to offer additional, more difficult, work to challenge children to stretch their development.

Yeah, Miss McDonald. I don't know, she had a personality that, and she was always willing to help me, and that, if I don't understand something, and then I told her, 'I don't understand it', then she would just have a good attitude about it. I can't explain it to be honest. It would just be the way that she was willing to help. Because there is some teachers who some would prefer and they would help you in the end but it's their attitude they'll have about it, but with her, she would always give me answer straight, not the answer but help me figure things out straight away ... Hmm punctuation, because she really helped me with it. Just the exercise. She'd give me separate exercises as well with it, because I was already good at the stuff that we were doing in the class, she'd give me separate exercises from other children so that, instead of spending time doing things like reading notes, I did work on the punctuation. Shaquille, boy, Group 1 (low SES, attainment above prediction)

A second pattern showed that teachers who were perceived to have helped the students do well were characterized as being 'strict' and 'in control', but simultaneously as 'calm', 'nice', 'enthusiastic' and 'friendly'. References to *authoritative teaching* as a 'protective' factor were made for five boys and seven girls from Group 1 and for all six students from Group 4. By being *authoritative*, rather than authoritarian or permissive in the way they approached and taught students, these teachers inspired students to apply themselves during the lessons and in their school work. The following example was given by a 15-year-old girl when asked how teachers would help her do well in school. She refers to the Religious Education teacher in her secondary school:

She can be strict but she is very calm and relaxed about everything and she will let you say what you think and she don't criticize you for it because it is your own opinion and it is what you believe in. She tries to give constructive criticisms but she also really praises you if you are doing really well. And she's seen your reports and after the exams she will come up to you and say, 'You have done really well.' [It's important] because instead of that negative criticism all the time, like, 'You have to do this and that', like, 'You don't understand that', you can like work at it. Natalie, girl, Group 1 (low SES, attainment above prediction)

These children often described their teachers as having been enthusiastic about the subjects they taught, as approachable when children experienced difficulties, as generally friendly and as having clearly communicated their expectations and boundaries. They felt they had learned most from teachers who had been knowledgeable on the subject, who managed the class well, who could and would use interactive teaching strategies and who made learning a pleasant experience.

I've got a History teacher who wants us to do good, and we're all, she's focused us lots on learning and getting good grades in History, and it's because of her teaching. Good way of teaching is just taking time with the class, making sure that everyone is alright and that, like, everyone's, like some people are doing good and some are struggling and just help everyone and people who are distracting others, do something about them 'cause some people want to learn and some people who don't and the people who don't want to learn, take away the teacher's attention, and we want to learn but they claim all the attention because they're being rude so we're not going to learn anything so they've got to discipline out the children who are not really, don't want to learn and some people do. Breona, girl, Group 4 (high SES, attainment as predicted)

A final teacher characteristic that was mentioned was the teacher's use of *interactive teaching*. *Interactive teaching* as a 'protective' factor was mentioned for five boys and six girls from Group 1 and for all three boys and one girl from Group 4. According to the students, the use of ball games to learn about numbers and Maths, films to illustrate social and moral dilemmas during Religious Education or attending the theatre to learn about English Literature made lessons 'less boring' and easier to 'pay attention' to, but also made it easier for the student to recall what they had learned later on, for instance during a test or exam.

I like practical classes 'cos I like to get involved in doing things. 'Cos when you ... like sometimes when the teacher is just talking to you like it goes in one ear and out the other and you can't remember it all, but if you do it then the teacher will say oh, something and I'll think, 'Oh yeah I did that' with that experiment. Erm, like at school now in Science I'm doing about radiation and like we do things with microwaves and things like that, so when you need to talk about radiation it's easier to remember the things 'cos you've done experiments with 'em. Charley, girl, Group 1 (low SES, attainment above prediction)

Martha's Maths teacher felt his teaching style helped students do well. He described his classroom practices in the following way:

Just the explanation at the start, again, you think how you're going to explain something, you emphasize the key points. You start off easily and graduate up in their level of difficulty. You ask a lot of questions. You get an atmosphere where they don't mind getting things wrong in front of a class, if you ask such and such what the answer is and they get things wrong, they don't feel like gutted, that's just fine, that's allowed sort of thing, and you allow pupils to ask you for when they're stuck and they feel happy to do that. Teacher of Martha, girl, Group 1 (low SES, attainment above prediction)

With these teachers, students felt they not only enjoyed the classes and could achieve the standards set for them, but they could actually extend themselves beyond their predicted attainment. When asked about this Maths teacher Martha said:

The best! [laughing] Oh, he made Maths really fun and he didn't have favourites, but he was nice to everyone ... but er ... I dunno he treated everyone like the same and he was just generally nice to people and he made loads of people like him, so that they enjoy the lesson more, which I think helped. 'Cos like mum said he's quite good looking for a teacher, which was annoying sometimes [laughing] but like, I think the more people like the teacher, the more, well any teacher ... if you like the teacher you enjoy the lesson ... well most of the time. If people were naughty, he'd send them out so they don't disrupt the lesson, but he'd still make them work, he wouldn't like just let them sit outside, he'd make them do work still ... which I thought was good.

And you just said that he managed to make Maths fun? How would he do that?

Well ... he'd ask us like quite a lot like ... if it was getting boring, and if someone said it was getting boring he'd just change the subject completely and he always did like ... quizzes and stuff, like Maths quizzes and that made it quite fun. Martha, girl, Group 1 (low SES, attainment above prediction)

I discovered I was like quite good at Maths like, in like Year 8, Year 9, 'cos I've got a really good Maths teacher and like he's proper friendly and he's always helping me out with stuff like ... If I need extra help on homework he'd do it for me ... so he's a good teacher. Rajnesh, boy, Group 1 (low SES, attainment above prediction)

Up until Year 3 I couldn't seem to sort of function with numbers and then I moved to Hutton's and suddenly I went from being bottom of the class, in fact I think I was in special needs class, to actually being top of class, so ...

Do you remember what it was you found difficult?

No, all I remember is that I couldn't solve them. I suppose the [teacher of the] special needs class, I think she actually sort of helped me and actually gave me sort of love for numbers.

How did she do that?

The way she taught or . . . you know, actually maybe enjoy it rather than looking at it as like sort of a chore. To be honest I don't think I really enjoyed a lot, English, Maths, Science, all of that seemed like a mystery to me. I'm not sure if it was right at the start I didn't understand the basics so when I got into Year 2 and Year 3 and it started becoming harder, I sort of, 'cause I didn't know the basics I couldn't learn more advanced stuff . . . I mean, she did the basics which I didn't understand and once I got those . . . then I think it was easy. Steven, boy, Group 1 (low SES, attainment above prediction)

For the children who had been less successful academically, lack of school success was commonly attributed to the teachers, or rather the mismatch between the needs of the students and what the teacher could or would offer. They also felt that the lessons and school work were perceived as 'boring', 'unchallenging' and 'just not right' for the students in question. According to students and parents, the teachers who had been least helpful in the child's learning process, supply teachers in particular, had difficulties with keeping order and were 'uninterested in teaching' and unable to motivate the students. The EPPE 3–11 study found teachers' ability to control the classroom to be positively related with emotional and behavioural conduct of children, which in turn was associated with achievement (reduced 'Hyperactivity' and increased 'Pro-social' behaviour and 'Self-regulation'). But disorganized classrooms predicted poorer progress in both English and Maths and increased hyperactive behaviour in children (Sylva et al., 2008). So the vulnerable children in the Case Studies, who felt that the high quantity of supply teachers, and the disorganized lessons that came with them, contributed significantly to their low attainment, seemed to have a valid point.

It's the way the school is I think, the discipline. I don't think they have good teachers there, that's the problem, the teachers are always changing, and they're very young and inexperienced teachers. I talked to one of his teachers the other day, and he's a science teacher, and he said to me that Hamid knows what to do to do his project. He can't just ask him all the time. He says he's just here to just watch them. So what kind of teacher would you say that is? Mother of Hamid, boy, Group 2 (low SES, attainment as predicted)

Conclusion

Perceptions about schools, teachers and education of children who were academically successful and their parents on one hand and of children who were less successful and their parents on the other hand, seemed to be fundamentally different. The successful children seemed to have been able to build a good rapport with teachers in general and with certain teachers in particular. These children enjoyed their lessons and learning and felt confident about themselves as learners. They felt supported by teachers and by their school environment. They respected their teachers and felt motivated by them to achieve well, sometimes even better than expected. These positive perceptions contrasted strongly with the perceptions of children who struggled academically. These children and their parents typically felt let down by the educational system and by individual teachers. They had become frustrated because they felt their concerns had not been dealt with adequately or because they felt that the child had unjustly been stereotyped in a negative way. As a result, school and academic learning were perceived as necessary evils in the eyes of both parents and children. Although they knew they needed to comply with the rules of society and stick with it, they almost all looked forward to the moment that schools would no longer be a part of their lives.

Teachers played an important role in children's perceptions of school and learning. Effective teaching was associated with teachers who were sensitive towards the needs of their students, who used an authoritative teaching style with their students and who encouraged active participation from their students through their use of interaction in lessons and assignments. With these teachers in particular, children enjoyed participating in lessons, they were willing to work hard for these teachers and often achieved more than they had believed possible (see also Sylva et al., 2012). These teachers seemed to encourage children to use what Kohn and Schooler have termed 'educational self-direction', that is, to show initiative, to think for themselves and to rely on their personal judgement – just as many of the parents of the academically successful children had done in their home environment.

This concept of educational self-direction is analogous to the concept of self-direction that Kohn and Schooler (1983) used in their research into differences in workplace experiences between adults from middle-class and working-class backgrounds. They found that work environments that allowed for self-direction, such as were commonly experienced by adults who had completed higher levels of education and worked in more professional jobs, created and reinforced differences in adult personalities and orientations. Parallel to what they found for adults, their research showed reciprocity between self-direction and intellectual flexibility in adolescents. Intellectual flexibility referred to a person's ability to cope with the demands of a complex situation. Children and adults who were facilitated and encouraged to exercise self-direction in their (school)work showed greater intellectual flexibility; and greater intellectual flexibility, in turn, positively affected their exercise of self-direction in (school)work.

Even when controlling for parents' intellectual flexibility, they found that students' intellectual flexibility was positively influenced by complexity of schoolwork, not by closeness of supervision by teachers (Kohn, 1995). For our academically successful Case Studies children it seemed that those teachers who set high academic standards and challenged their students beyond their intellectual comfort zone facilitated them to become more effective problem solvers.

When they extended their analyses to include non-cognitive aspects of personality, Kohn and Schooler (1983) found that greater self-direction in schoolwork increased students' self-directedness of orientation and decreased their sense of distress. Distress, in turn, negatively affected educational self-direction. Self-directedness of orientation was reflected in not having authoritarian-conservative beliefs, having personally responsible standards of morality, being trustful of others, not being self-deprecatory, not being fatalistic, and not being conformist in one's ideas. Distress was reflected in anxiety, self-deprecation, lack of self-confidence, nonconformity in one's ideas and distress. While self-directedness of orientations seemed to characterize many of our successful children and their parents, examples of such distress related to education and learning were effectively what we found in many of the vulnerable children, and in their parents for that matter.

Kohn and Schooler further found that greater educational self-direction increased students' self-directedness of orientation, and this greater self-directedness of orientation then increased intellectual flexibility. As in the case of many of the academically successful children, particularly those succeeding against the odds, and in accordance with what their parents and their teachers had said, Kohn and Schooler concluded that success was in fact a matter of motivation:

Wanting to think for yourself helps you to think. To put the matter most simply, education matters for personality for much the same reason as does occupation: People learn from their experiences, and learn most of all from having to cope with complex and demanding experiences. There is more to education than attuning people to the printed page, important though that is. (Kohn, 1995, p. 152)

9 Gateways to enhanced social, cultural and emotional capital

This chapter examines learning experiences through additional microsystems in the child's developmental system. It provides descriptions from the Case Studies on how educational success was supported through children's engagement with the wider community, for instance by participating in extra-curricular activities, through hobbies, religious activities or involvement with support networks of extended family and friends of the families. Again, the findings are related to the literature as well as to the perceptions of our participants.

Parents as active agents of socialization

The finding that parents can positively affect academic achievement by more frequently providing certain activities and support in the family microsystem is consistent across different socio-economic and ethnic-cultural groups (Dearing et al., 2004; Fan & Chen, 2001; Jeynes, 2005).

Views of parenting and the parent–child relationship have expanded over the last decades to include parents as active managers of the child's social environment outside the family. It is now widely recognized that parents not only provide a substantial amount of the actual proximal processes, they also influence children's proximal processes outside the family context, by purposefully managing and regulating their access to other socio-cultural contexts such as (pre-)school, peers and community, or extra-curricular activities and classes, such as music lessons or sports classes (see Bradley & Corwyn, 2002; Bradley et al., 2000; Feinstein et al., 2008; Harkness & Super, 1992; Parke, 2004; Rogoff, 1993; Rogoff et al., 1995, 2003; Steinberg et al., 1991; Tomasello, 1999). In their capacity as active managers, parents actively regulate the access that children have to physical and social resources outside of the family microsystem (Parke, 2004). Particularly when children are young, these learning experiences are typically still strongly regulated and facilitated by their parents. Parents arrange play-dates for their child with other children (and parents) who they feel comfortable for their child to interact with. They take the child along when they meet up with friends and relatives or when they attend events in their wider social, cultural and religious communities.

Parents will likely have their own preferences and interests, and this will influence which experiences they value and deem appropriate for their child. Initially it is often parents who suggest that a child will play with a particular friend, or that the child will try a particular class or lesson. Sometimes parents will simply encourage and facilitate an activity or experience; in other cases they might even make a certain activity or experience mandatory if they feel very strongly about it.

During their extra-curricular activities and experiences outside of the family and school context, children often have the opportunity to engage with a wider range of peers and adults. As the realm of their experiences expands beyond the direct control of their parents, children gain more autonomy to form and maintain relationships with these peers and other adults. But even then, most parents continue to play an important regulatory role as gatekeepers and monitor children's social contacts and choices (Mounts, 2000).

Extra-curricular activities facilitated or stimulated by the family context

When Steven became fascinated with the teacher who accompanied the singing sessions on her guitar during circle time in his reception class, his mother bought him a tiny guitar so that he could play along. As he got older and continued his interest in the instrument, his mother found him an after-school music class. She bought him a proper guitar so that he could practise and play it for enjoyment at home, and she encouraged him to practise and take exams that earned him certificates.

After Tom gave up on kickboxing, his disappointed father was pleased to find this sport replaced by one they were both passionate about. Tom and his father both loved cars and motor racing. So Tom's father bought him a quad to race and a small motorbike and made sure he had a trailer to transport Tom's wheels to races and training sessions. They would scrutinize the pages of motoring magazines, and watch any motor-related television programmes they could find; and when Tom was not himself racing at weekends, they would find other motor-races and car shows to attend.

Marcy's father introduced her to swimming at a very young age. Even before she started school he enrolled her in swimming classes. He diligently attended her training sessions and competitions. When she showed great talent at swimming he encouraged her to increase the frequency of her training from weekly to almost daily. He drove her all over the country to attend competitions and provided substantial financial support for her when her competitions started taking her abroad. He was extremely disappointed when Marcy decided to give up swimming competitively because she could no longer manage her practice and competitions in combination with her increased workload in secondary school. He tried his hardest to persuade her not to give it up, but in the end accepted and respected her decision.

For Imogene, her piano lessons have been an important part of her life, almost as long as she can remember. Every day she practises at home in the music room. When she was little her mother would come along to her lessons and help her study at home. But as she progressed, her father, who had learned to play when he was young and is a proficient musician, took over the practise sessions at home. Over the years Imogene has built a close relationship with her music teacher. She has come to see this teacher as one of the most important adults in her life, and she regularly seeks her advice about her life and future.

Parents are usually the ones who pay for sports classes, music lessons or other activities outside of the home and the school. Often the child will depend on the parents to provide transport to and from these activities. In some cases parents will become actively involved. They will come along to classes and training sessions, to matches and performances. They are there to watch and support their child emotionally. But when they attend these activities they also communicate with teachers and coaches. They talk about their child's development and often about what they as parents can do to support their child to do well. They provide their services to the team or organization. They drive their children and their teammates to out-of-town sports matches, they wash uniforms, they organize fundraising events. At home they will make sure the child takes time to practise when this is required, or will even help their child during these practice sessions. By actively participating, these parents not only communicate to the child their appreciation of these experiences, but also that they value spending time together. Even when children mature and become more autonomous in their choices for extra-curricular activities and less dependent on their parents for their actual participation, they generally still need their parents' permission to take part in these activities, and often depend on their practical and financial support as well. By providing this support, whether financial, practical or emotional, parents communicate to the child that they value these experiences for the child but perhaps even more importantly that they value the child. Their child is worth investing in.

For the Case Studies children from high socio-economic status (SES) families, extra-curricular activities, such as dance classes, private music tuition and sports activities were simply a given. All of these children participated in a number of such activities, and had done so from a young age. In nearly all cases these activities were paid for privately.

Laurie had been taking dance classes ever since she was 2 years old. At the age of 16, she was taking dance as part of her GCSEs. Laurie was one of the high-SES children who were failing to meet the predicted attainment. Laurie and her mother said the following:

Erm, I think it [dance] lets me express myself in like the best way I can, because I love doing it. It comes quite naturally, and it's really good to have like a subject that's like a hobby and you really like it, and it's really good to have something you like. Because, because for dance, I won like an A star, and for Maths I'm on, well I'm on a G, and you can tell the difference between something I enjoy and like and something that I don't enjoy, it's just a really big difference like, of why I would want to do it and why I wouldn't want to do it. Laurie, girl, Group 3 (high SES, attainment below prediction)

Do you feel there is anything she learned from dance lessons that might have helped?

Probably her confidence, definitely her co-ordination.

Why do you think that the dancing increased her confidence?

Just because she felt she was good at it, you know, and also because it was something a bit different and not everyone was doing so it was something a bit special to her you know. Mother of Laurie, girl, Group 3 (high SES, attainment below prediction)

The parents felt it was important and even necessary to provide and facilitate these activities for their child. They valued the experience for their child to become accomplished at something other than the regular curriculum subjects in school. They believed it would help their child become confident in his or her abilities as a learner, but also to develop social skills through their interaction with children and adults outside of the familiar environments of home and school. Often they had had similar experiences during their childhood and as a result they were aware of the benefits these extra-curricular experiences would provide in society. As a result they emphasized their importance and value during their parenting practices and communications with their child. These attitudes were gradually transferred and instilled into their children. Imogene became aware of the extent of their value during her admission interviews for secondary schools.

I tried for a lot of private schools and I got into them and ehm ... I just didn't [like] the whole interview process. I remember walking into one and it seems like they take you ... ehm ... they take you as a certain kind of person when you walk in. I can remember walking into one and someone said: 'Oh you walk like a ballerina, do you do ballet?' and I said 'Yeah', and they seemed to take that as like a big step up, you know … I was gonna say I don't particularly want to be judged for what I do out of school, but I guess it's important (laughs). Imogene, girl, Group 4 (high SES, attainment as predicted)

For other middle-class children, this awareness particularly started to sink in once they started to orientate themselves towards their future education in college and university and discovered that these experiences would benefit them in their application processes. But for many children from low-SES families, learning to play a musical instrument or attending ballet classes was not something that was seen as a normal, let alone necessary, part of a child's upbringing. Financially, practically and emotionally supporting a child to have these experiences can place too much of a burden on the limited resources of the family. Nonetheless, many of the children from the Case Studies working-class families were given opportunities to experience a range of extra-curricular activities, although not necessarily similar to the activities experienced by their wealthier middle-class counterparts.

The children who were succeeding against the odds in the Case Studies were typically the low-SES children most commonly encouraged and facilitated by parents to participate in extra-curricular activities. But as private tuition was often too expensive, children in most cases participated in after-school sports or music programmes sponsored by their school or community. They also often joined organizations such as the Sea Cadets that were sponsored nationally.

Reanna liked to try everything, she did try the dancing, and she got bored, she tried the modern dancing, she got bored, er, she went to Brownies as well, she was a Brownie as well, she got bored. If she sees something she wants it 'I want it, I want it now', but she doesn't think ahead. I'm always trying to get her to look at what she could gain from it, whether it's going to take commitment, because if something takes commitment … she's not very good at commitment over a long-term basis. That's what amazes me [about the Sea Cadets] because the Sea Cadets involves discipline, commitment, all the things that she shies away from normally. The Sea Cadets demands it of her and she does it, even though she comes home and moans and moans and moans at me. Mother of Reanna, girl, Group 1 (low SES, attainment above prediction)

He did tap dancing. Yeah … yeah. Confidence ehm … he was good at tap dancing. He only did it for a year, he did one exam, he got a B. It was only him and another girl who got a B out of the class. It was a talent class so it was, they were by the ballet school, it was proper people examining them so that he was really chuffed with that and he really liked that. He was the only boy in the class as well … so … eh … I don't know. Mother of Steven, boy, Group 1 (low SES, attainment above prediction)

Some children attended classes or activities related to the family's ethnic-cultural or religious heritage, such as language classes, Sunday church school or Qur'an lessons.

> Going to church helps with R.E. again. And at the youth group we socialize a lot and then we talk about what God is doing in our lives and stuff. It makes me happy because like I have someone to talk to and things like that. Ife, girl, Group 1 (low SES, attainment above prediction)

> I think one, it's her background I mean our religion, and I believe and I have strong values that we shouldn't really forget our own language, keep Panjabi alive. I did encourage both of them to go to Panjabi classes, her older sister as well as Anjali when she was young, and they did attend Panjabi classes just to keep up the Panjabi, because it's something I didn't want them to completely loose and just be with the English language only. I think if you look, I think the more languages nowadays you know, the better person you are, the better opportunities you got outside as well, so it's something that I think any parents whose background is whatever, I'm sure they, deep down in their heart they do want their children to have the language perhaps they were born with or the parents were born with. Heritage, yeah. Father of Anjali, girl, Group 1 (low SES, attainment above prediction)

In some families the parents in our sample did not necessarily feel they had had a particular educational or developmental motive to provide these experiences, they just regarded them as a normal part of life, something they themselves might have enjoyed, and just felt their child might do as well. This was particularly the case in low-SES families with children who were developing as predicted. In these families, and also in the high-SES families with children who were vulnerable, children who wanted to stop participating in a class or activity were often not encouraged to give it another try when they lost interest. As the activity was mainly regarded as 'fun' or 'something to enjoy' and not so much as a learning experience, it was often left to the child to decide whether or not they wanted to join a class or to continue an extra-curricular activity. The parents of these children were more passive and accepting of their children 'giving up'.

However, in many other families, particularly those with children who were succeeding, parents, and sometimes children too, recognized that extra-curricular activities provide children with learning opportunities. For instance, to experience and experiment with roles that were not otherwise a common part of their experiences in life. Children are typically used to the role of being the novice, especially during inter-actions with adults. But when these children became better accomplished in a skill or they learned something during their extra-curricular activities there was often room for them to take on a different role. For instance, the role of leader, peer tutor or expert, when participating in discussions during religious classes, when playing computer games with their friends, or when earning merits and certificates as part of music classes or cadet programmes. As such, these activities allow for expertise development while simultaneously supporting aspects of identity development, such as sense of belonging in a community, feelings of competence and interest development (Barron, 2006; Rogoff, 1993; Rogoff et al., 2003).

In many cases these children and parents were, or became, very much aware of the educational implications of these experiences, and felt their child's development and perhaps even school achievement would benefit. These activities seem to be part of a more 'concerted cultivation' socialization strategy that is typically employed by middle-class parents to help their children develop social skills and confidence from which they will benefit in later life (Lareau, 2003). According to Vincent and Ball (2006)

'Education' does not, for our middle-class parents, only describe what goes on in nurseries, schools and universities. Instead education is an all-encompassing engagement with the child. As part of this the children have access to a wide range of 'extra-curricular' activities, chosen from the options offered by burgeoning local markets. (Vincent & Ball, 2006, p.137)

However, our study shows that it is not only middle-class parents who do this. Many working-class parents 'actively' do so too, and are able and willing to draw upon the social and cultural capital they know will benefit their child.

Relationships with peers and friendships as 'protective' or 'risk' factors

The review of research on adolescent development by Steinberg and Morris (2001) shows that peers tend to choose friends with similar behaviours, attitudes and identities. They influence each others' academic and pro-social behaviours because they admire and respect each others' opinions. A study of nine hundred students entering middle school showed that how well friends do in school has a substantial effect on students' grades and academic self-efficacy (Cook et al., 2007).

The children in the Case Studies offered explanations about the mechanisms through which peers affect attainment. For the successful children, peers, especially their friends, offered practical, social and emotional support. The social and emotional support helped them to enjoy school and to deal with any difficulties they encountered. Practical support was often mutual, as children helped each other out during lessons and with homework and revision. Not only did this offer children opportunities to take on the role of teacher, it also provided them with opportunities to deepen their understanding of subjects, either by rephrasing the teacher's explanations to clarify things for their friends or by receiving alternative explanations from their friends. These 'peer-tutoring' experiences seem to have contributed positively to children's positive self-perception, sense of efficacy and use of effective learning strategies. A study into self-esteem trajectories among minority ethnic, low income adolescents in the US provided evidence that supportive family and peer environments are particularly important contributors to psychological well-being (Greene & Way, 2005).

Peers were thought to have had a positive effect on school success for nearly all children who were 'succeeding against the odds' and for the successful high-SES children. *Positive influence from peers* was mentioned for all eight boys and for twelve girls from Group 1 and for all six students from Group 4. In almost all cases these positive influences came from their friends in school, and more specifically their classmates. These peers seemed to have a 'protective' influence through the practical support they offered which facilitated children's learning, but also offered encouragement and set a positive example through the way they applied themselves to school, which in turn stimulated the children in our sample to apply themselves as well.

From an early age onwards friends offered practical support in class and with homework. Often, students felt it was easier to ask a friend for help than it was to ask the teacher. Charley describes how one of her friends helped her to do well in primary school:

Sometimes one of my friends, who weren't in my group, like I'd go round her house after school when I got older and we'd do our homework together and things so we could help each other. Like explain what to do.

Do you think that helped you with your learning?

Yeah. Cos then like, if you didn't understand then you'd be able ... your friend would, 'cos they're in the different group, then they'd explain the different way how they're doing, how they're doing, sort of things like that. Charley, girl, Group 1 (low SES, attainment above prediction)

However, students also benefitted from explaining things to their peers. The following example comes from Asya, a 15-year-old girl, who has been doing extremely well ever since she started reception. When asked if she revised in a particular way to prepare for her Key Stage 3 national assessment tests she answered:

No, not really, it's just like, it was, it wasn't exactly like revising, but it was more like, 'cos other people would ask me a question 'How do you do something?' and I suppose that was almost me revising, 'cos I was telling them what to do ... so I was like ... learning and with helping everyone else, helping each other so in a way even though I wasn't actually technically revising, I was like relearning my stuff that I already knew ...'cos I was helping others. Asya, girl, Group 1 (low SES, attainment above prediction)

Peers were also an important source of emotional support. According to the students, having friends around in school made them feel 'comfortable', 'confident', 'supported' and 'not alone' and made them want to be in school, all of which made it easier for them to apply themselves to the learning process. Reanna had a difficult time making new friends when she went to secondary school and didn't do so well academically initially, but once she did make friends this started to improve:

And I suppose that's ... me becoming closer to them, people in my school and class, I kind of, settled in more and I didn't have to worry about what people were thinking or anyone else in the class. It made me kind of relax and so I suppose that made me kind of focus more on my work instead of the people around me. Reanna, girl, Group 1 (low SES, attainment above prediction)

Finally, friends offered motivational support as they stimulated students to apply themselves by 'encouraging' them, wanting them 'to do well' and 'praising' them and friends who were doing well in school stimulated these students to do even better. Friends could further reinforce positive attitudes towards school, and the learning of these through a more positive perception of education, and stimulated them to be the best they could by providing positive role models and friendly competition.

They're all quite clever and they're all quite thoughtful, you know? So I think there is the part of, you know, the teenage culture now which, which praises not being clever, you know (laugh). And my friends were never like that so if there's something that I was considering or something like that, I'd, I never have a problem to my friends about it 'cause I, I would not be spurned for thinking about things, you know. Imogene, girl, Group 4 (high SES, attainment as predicted)

They do help me quite a bit, I mean ... as I said Ethan is the one who likes to read a lot, he seems to be sort of naturally gifted in pretty much every subject and like A and A stars in everything. It sort of made me work harder and harder 'cause so, sort of reach his level and he always seems to sort rise it so ... I always have to keep ... [up with him]. Steven, boy, Group 1 (low SES, attainment above prediction)

For some students, friends or siblings who were doing particularly well or had done well in school in the past triggered them to do even better.

Like even at my school and stuff my teacher was saying you know like, 'Your sister's smart and like you should get help off her and like you could be', like my Maths teacher he said how I could be better at Maths than my sister was … and so … Yeah, yeah it does like, it gives you like confidence and stuff so you wanna do better. Rajnish, boy, Group 1 (low SES, attainment above prediction)

Towards the end of primary school, around national assessment test time, Year 6 SATs, I was in a group of people who got like fives. So I was, it helped me because, had I been around people who had got fours or threes, I thought, there weren't that many people that did, but I felt better about getting them [fives]. So I thought it was better for me to be in a more pressured environment, so I think my, well my five in English was like a five c, a low one, so I had to work quite hard at that, so I'm glad I was in the group of people who got higher marks. We didn't really talk about the work an awful lot, but we always knew what kind of marks that people got in the SAT test papers, which we did quite a lot of, which I found quite helpful, because you knew what format the stuff was in. I wouldn't say so much a competition, but I would have been embarrassed if I'd got, one mark lower than a couple of my friends, 'cause yeah, I think the majority of my friends got five, five, five, and I was glad I did. Lucas, boy, Group 4 (high SES, attainment as predicted)

Boys more than girls mentioned that they would have little competitions with their friends that pushed them to work harder and faster.

That's what I did with Maths, I wanted to learn quick because I wanted to be first to finish it. Peter, boy, Group 1 (low SES, attainment above prediction)

Mark talked about how having competition with his friends in class helped him do better in school:

Just building me self-esteem, and stuff like that.

How does having good self esteem help you to do well in school?

Just, more mature, like, and get more work done instead of faffing on, stuff like that. Mark, boy, Group 1 (low SES, attainment above prediction)

In contrast, some peers were thought to have had a negative influence on the majority of the students who were not doing particularly well, particularly on how they applied themselves to schoolwork and learning in class. Peers were perceived to have had a *negative effect* on three girls and seven boys from Group 2 and four girls and two boys from Group 3. Although some of the vulnerable children in the Case Studies experienced positive peer influences, these students often had friends and peers with negative attitudes to school and learning. When asked about encouragement for school and learning Edward remarked:

I don't … I don't necessarily get encouraged, but I mean I know my best mate over the road, he's meant to be really smart, well he is really smart, and he's been getting in a lot of trouble at school and being sent home and stuff. I've tried encouraging him, but I haven't, apart from sort of mum and my stepdad now and again, I haven't really had any encouragement about it.

What about discouragement?

I think you get that all the time. Just idiots around school. You get the paper throwing around the classroom, which is distracting, you get, like I said, loud noises and stuff like that, I just think, I think it happens every day, to everyone. Edward, boy, Group 2 (low SES, attainment as predicted)

For all these students, examples were provided of how their peers interfered with their learning processes, particularly by distracting them. Other examples referred to the fact that peers interfered with the way they applied themselves, as it was not considered 'cool' to do well. This is in line with findings from the Effective Pre-School and Primary Education (EPPE 3–11) study, that showed that where teachers reported higher levels of anti-academic ethos in their school, children made less academic and social/behavioural progress (Sylva et al., 2008). The following example comes from a teacher who explained that Hamid's slow progress in the first years of his all-boys secondary school had to do with the fact that he got distracted in class and tended to get a bit 'chatty' with his friends. He then continued to say:

There was another bit of image there, you see, they can't be seen to be too keen, but quietly he'll get on with some of his work if you set a project or independently work to be done at home. It's that boy thing isn't it? In front of their peers, they don't want to be seen to be doing brilliantly sort of thing. But he'll do it in his book, quietly, but then when you get his homework, or his project work, his independent learning, you'll see that he really has put an effort into it, particularly this year, since he's started his GCSEs. Teacher of Hamid, boy, Group 2 (low SES, attainment as predicted)

A second, although less common, way for peers to negatively affect students' learning processes, was by stimulating problem behaviour. Children, parents and teachers felt that certain children were particularly susceptible to negative peer influences that resulted in them 'acting up' towards authority figures, getting into fights or 'getting them to do stupid things' (three girls, four boys). These children seemed particularly vulnerable in their behaviour in school and in class. For some children this problem behaviour followed from being bullied by their peers. Susan ended up changing secondary schools because of the bullying. Her mother believed that the stress her daughter had experienced and endured had negatively influenced her attitude to school and her behaviour in class.

Was she bullied?

Yes, yes, that's why she had to leave Paxton. She was beaten up by fifteen girls, and this one particular one threatened to pull a knife on her … We got the police involved … and this young lady … in the broadest sense of the term, got cautioned, because of beating Susan up, and it took us, three months to get her another school. But I didn't pull her out of school, because I thought, once I do, because of the seriousness of the bullying, if I pulled her out of school, then she'd never go back in school. She wouldn't, she wouldn't feel safe in school, it would be a big phobia thing. So … what we did was, for the whole time that she stayed at Paxton she left school, they finished at half three, she left at three o'clock … that gave her enough time to get to the bus stop and get on a bus and get away from the school, before the rest of the school came out. Mother of Susan, girl, Group 2 (low SES, attainment as predicted)

In other cases it was their friends that negatively influenced them:

I think on the whole he probably got into [trouble] because, people, kids there would dare him, because he's reached the age, where as he was really tall for his age, there was always challenge for him to fight or get into arguments … and I don't think he knew how to deal with that, and he wouldn't ask for help … to deal with it, he would more or less deal with it himself … so yes he did [get suspended]. Mother of Tremaine, boy, Group 2 (low SES, attainment as predicted)

I think he is quite controlled by what he does outside of school in a negative way. Tremaine is involved with the gang culture. Let me have a look [in his file]. They've actually said, yeah he's got a physical assault, yeah he got into a physical assault with hospital treatment and police involvement so … he was permanently excluded. Teacher of Tremaine, boy, Group 2 (low SES, attainment as predicted)

Additional support networks for the family microsystem

The social network of parents may include other adults as well as children who all might function as possible play and learning partners for their children (Parke, 2004). Support networks of friends and extended family played an important role in the lives of many of the Case Studies respondents. Similar to Lareau's qualitative study (2003) we found that extended family and kinship networks generally play a greater role in the lives of low-SES families than in high-SES families. Grandparents and aunts and uncles were frequently mentioned by low-SES parents as having provided important practical and emotional support for parents.

In the low-SES families of children with predicted attainment these family and kinship networks were important for their sense of well-being but generally did not seem to provide children with additional extended social and cultural capital that might help them do well in school and later in life, as they entered situations different from their personal and family sphere of influence. Many of these extended family members looked after the children when parents were at work, particularly in single-parent households. In many cases family members lived close by. When asked if she and her son spent time with their family, Richard's mother said:

All the time really, but we didn't have to go far because we're a close family and we're all like living in the street (laughs).

Is this where you grew up?

Yeah, I've always lived here. Mother of Richard, boy, Group 2 (low SES, attainment as predicted)

FATHER: His nan ... his nan ... she's been, she's worked miracles over the years to be honest.
MOTHER: I don't know if she's helped him with the schooling but she's always been there.
FATHER: No, but, but she's been an important person in his life.
MOTHER: Yeah but not helped him with his schooling.

Parents of Harry, boy, Group 2 (low SES, attainment as predicted)

However, in the low-SES families with children succeeding against the odds, family and kinship networks were also often mentioned as providing important practical support, but also as having provided additional learning experiences for the child, both through activities and through the example they might have set.

My Mum and Dad are very helpful to Charley. Because they want her to do so well and they are always encouraging her for things, and they have got her a place for her [work placement]. My Mum and Dad sorted all of that out for her, and they are always praising her up and they are always saying to her, you know, 'You do well at school' and you know, if they have got a problem on the computer they always ask Charley, because she can just do it just like that. So yeah they all, everybody encourages Charley really. Mother of Charley, girl, Group 1 (low SES, attainment above prediction)

Their granddad is very good with them as well. He is here as well. Well doesn't do anything with them but he just speaks to them, they know he is there and they can speak to him and he can speak to them, he is always asking those things about themselves, how they are progressing. Yeah he has been an influence in their life. Mother of Leanna, girl, Group 1 (low SES, attainment above prediction)

For the successful low-SES children, a range of adults besides their parents had played an important part in facilitating their learning and stimulating them to apply themselves by offering them emotional and practical support with their school work. *Significant others* were mentioned as a 'protective' factor for nine girls and six boys from Group 1. In most cases the adults were family members, such as a grandparent, aunt or uncle, or older cousin; and in some cases a friend of the family.

My auntie ... and ... my uncle, my mum's brother not my dad's. My dad's brothers are from Pakistan so my mum's brothers were a big help ... 'cos they're from England and their wives are from England so ... it's just like, they understand more about schools and they're more into education. So if you were stuck you would just phone them and ask and they would help you by explaining it to you. They were all like in university, getting their jobs then so it ... I dunno like, it was easier but it still was there. They'd had like ... just say I was doing tables ... adding, they'd be like, 'Well I've got two chocolates, and I've got two more chocolates, how many chocolates', like that, stuff like, how I explain it to my little brother now, I've learnt off them, so it's easier, a lot easier. Fareeda, girl, Group 1 (low SES, attainment above prediction)

The pilot study with working-class children from homes with a high early home learning environment (HLE) who were 'succeeding against the odds' (Siraj-Blatchford, 2010a) found that transnational family and kinship networks and relationships were particularly important for Caribbean families in terms of social and material resources (cf. Reynolds, 2006a, 2006b). The Case Studies found examples of such transnational relationships for families with Caribbean heritage but also for some of the Asian families with children who were succeeding against the odds. Rajnesh's family would 'save up' so they could visit their relatives in India every three or four years.

I love going India though ... Yeah ... I love chillin' with like my Grandma and stuff, and just like talking about how school is and all that, and like we phone them every week ... yeah ... They just ask like 'how's like school and stuff', and like, like ... 'Do you have homework?' and they make sure I'm doing my work ... Yeah, they're always asking if I've like, if I've grown like big and strong or whatever and I know they care about me ... and I love like all my family in India. Rajnesh, boy, Group 1 (low SES, attainment above prediction)

Particularly in families with Asian, Caribbean and African heritage, religious communities and spiritual leaders were mentioned as additional sources for emotional and practical support with parenting.

The mother of the twin girls Ebun and Bunmi had fled her war-torn country in Africa when she was six months pregnant and her husband had been killed. In England she had managed to build a social life for herself and her daughters filled with people who shared her beliefs and traditions. While she herself had had little experience with formal education and as a result found it hard to offer educational support to her daughters now that they were in secondary school, she tried her best to support them in different ways.

I can't do more than this I am doing to change them ... I look after them ... their work. I do what mother does. This is the way I am supposed to help them ... Stand by them, for they are my children. Talk to them about school education, talk to them about home, home to me is the most important. Take them to church, help them to know about God. I think this is what the best I can do. Mother of Ebun and Bunmi, twin girls, Group 2 (low SES, attainment as predicted)

When asked if she felt supported by her community in raising her daughters, she said:

Yes. There is one of my friends, family friends and her sister, yeah. They teach them that we are from Africa. Even when she's born here, she's 46 now. When she comes here she teach. She come in calling 'O ya, everybody should get pen and paper' and starts calling some things from the dictionary, spelling and these kind of things. She's very good at that. When she come like this, ohhh this place will be fun (laughs) and activity, which I quite enjoy so ... Mother of Ebun and Bunmi, girls, Group 2 (low SES, attainment as predicted)

Ife's mother talked about how religion and their Christian faith played an important role in Ife's upbringing:

What about church, do you feel that's been important for her?

It has been very important. She's been to two camps in the summer now, and she's really enjoyed herself. It gives her time away from everyone else for her to do her own thing with her friends ... in a safe environment, where rest assured, everything, ya know... Ummm, in church, she sings with the worship team. And then she's a member of the youth team, and they do all sorts of different, have a youth group an' they have a meeting on a Monday evening. It's all religion based. Anyway, whatever she learns in those places were based on her, on our own religious beliefs, just Christian belief, so ... It might not have any effect on what she learns in school but there might be some aspects of it that she might be able to use. You talk of faith, you talk of religion, in school, as well as told all the religious knowledge and things like that. And umm, sometimes she thinks the things that she's learnt in church pop up, 'Oh yeah, I know that story', or things like that. And she's able to express herself and to express what her own beliefs are. Mother of Ife, girl, Group 1 (low SES, attainment above prediction)

Although support from family members was mentioned by some of the high-SES families, these parents more often mentioned their friends when asked who had supported them in bringing up their children. These high-SES parents had generally less often needed practical support, but valued the emotional support their friends gave them.

I spend a lot of time with my friends and the children. We do a lot of stuff together. I suppose that it takes a lot of ability to raise a child. I think that we're alike and my friends are very good friends and they're more like some sort of family, and especially the closest ones, wouldn't think twice about telling one of the kids off, whoever it was, if they were doing something wrong, or just picking one up and cuddling one up, and throwing them about, and, it just doesn't matter who the child belongs to, everyone jumps in, so in that respect we're like an extended family, who aren't related I suppose. Mother of Laurie, girl, Group 3 (high SES, attainment below prediction)

Can you tell me a bit about the things that you do as a family now?

We do see a lot of friends like, my Mum does like dinners and has her friends round, because they have all got kids about the same age as my sisters, or a little bit older, so they like play and my Mum has her friends round or we'll go out for the day. In the summer we went to safari parks with them and just to the park maybe, just out and about, just to make sure we don't sit inside all the time. But we do see a lot of friends, and it's good to have people around. I just think, 'cause my Mums friend, he said when he was little he can't remember his parents having anybody around, I just think that it's boring, and you need to communicate with people, and if I didn't meet anybody, then I would be really scared to go to a job, or go to the world and find what I wanted to do, and I think it just gives you a bit of a head start doing that. Laurie, girl, Group 3 (high SES, attainment below prediction)

All the high-SES children succeeding as predicted, and their parents, felt well supported by the people around them, such as family members or family friends. However, this support was not usually of a practical or emotional nature, but rather came in the form of providing a good role model.

I think there's quite a few of the family that have, like, gone to university and have got, you know, Masters in things as well, so he's seen that learning is continual. I mean I got my degree part-time at work, and his dad's got two, and there is that, you know, uncles have got degrees and things, so he's definitely seen that it doesn't just finish. You know, it doesn't stop at 16 and then you just go and work in Morrison's for the rest of your life so he does know that, I mean, he also knows that you can change direction, which I think is a very useful lesson to be learned. Mother of Benjamin, boy, Group 4 (high SES, attainment as predicted)

Conclusions

The foregoing paragraphs in this chapter have shown how important it is to consider the child's developmental niche with all its facets when trying to determine what leads children to unexpected academic success in school. We see that the social, cultural and emotional capital gained by the middle-class children due to their families' resources and 'concerted cultivation' (Lareau, 2003) can be partially matched by the schools for the working-class children. This illustrates the important role that schools can play in bridging the cultural capital gap between the social classes and contributing to the social mobility of less well-off children.

In addition, this chapter highlights the importance of encouraging working-class parents to provide what they can through their active cultivation of educational and cultural pursuits, as Steven's parents did through day trips to free museums and historic sites or through using their limited resources in purchasing a guitar for him. Many working-class parents actively seek out and support their children in gaining wider social and cultural capital.

The extension of educational and cultural experiences are worthwhile for any child, but might be particularly valuable to children from homes with limited HLEs or with limited emotional and practical support with school, homework and learning. While these experiences will likely supplement and extend experiences children generally have with parents and teachers in their homes and at school, for children from disadvantaged homes who lack, or seldom engage in, educational experiences through the home environment, participating in interaction with other adults or peers in their community might offer them extremely valuable alternative sources of support for their development.

Peer relationships and school behaviour play an important part in sustaining or constraining learning. The ability to make friends and sustain friendships was good for children's well-being, and mixing with more academically successful peers helped all children. Boys in particular valued a slightly more competitive edge to their school experiences and lessons with their friends and peers. Supporting children in pro-social behaviour and forming and maintaining friendships is a valuable concern for both parents and schools. At the same time, teachers and schools need fair and transparent behaviour management and policies for dealing with bullying, to protect children who might be vulnerable and face adverse relationships.

Finally, who the parents bring into their sphere of influence also impacts on their children. Mixing with people who have a similar background, and experiences such as extended family, adds much to the richness of life. However, mixing with a wider circle of friends with different backgrounds and higher educational backgrounds, and socializing and getting support from them, also helps. Our families experienced a wide range of social and cultural practices, and some of these acted as strong protective factors in supporting our children through their learning life-course.

10 Concluding discussion: promoting agency and advocacy

In the final section of the book we summarize the main findings from the Case Studies, followed by the conclusions that can be drawn regarding when and why some 'at-risk' children, given their background characteristics, 'succeed against the odds' while others fall further behind. This book synthesizes our findings on what we have termed 'active cultivation' as cultural practice of childrearing with our findings on effective support from significant others in schools, classrooms, families and the wider community in the form of cultural, social and emotional capital. Together these factors inspire children to become active agents in their learning life-courses. In this final chapter some implications of the study for practitioners and policy makers will be discussed.

Introduction

In this book we have described the mixed-methods Case Studies that were conducted as a sub-study and part of the Effective Pre-School, Primary and Secondary Education (EPPSE) study. We have based the Case Studies on qualitative data and analyses that are supplemented and backed by the extensive quantitative data from the EPPSE study's full sample and multilevel analyses. As well as an innovative mixed-theory and mixed-methods approach we have used a grounded theory method, which does not aim for the 'truth', but to conceptualize what is going on by using empirical evidence alongside large, quantitative data sets of our individual case study children's assessments and questionnaires. We used this information to go back and forth from our data on all the children to the case study children, both to inform and test emerging findings and to iteratively use qualitative and quantitative methods and data to interrogate our findings – and indeed the methods! We have already referred to papers that go into far more detail about the methodology of the EPPSE study and associated projects (Sammons et al., 2005; Siraj-Blatchford et al., 2006).

With the Case Studies we have aimed to fill a gap in the existing literature on children *succeeding against the odds* of disadvantage, by providing 'thick' descriptions of practices and beliefs of students and parents, and some additional perceptions from secondary school teachers about children's academic success (or failure). These thick descriptions were based on the interviews we conducted with children, their parents and their teachers. Throughout the book we have aimed to let their voices speak for themselves as they gave us their perceptions of why children became academically successful or struggled to keep up. They have told us what the children were like from a very early age onwards; they told us about the way these children felt about learning and school; they talked about the things they did as a family that might have helped them do well in school; they have told us about their experiences with teachers, peers and schools in general; they have told us about other people, activities and events in their lives that they felt have had an impact on the child's learning experiences. These descriptions of their experiences and beliefs have also provided us with illustrations of developmental mechanisms that have been determined using complex statistical analyses on large samples such as by the EPPSE project. For instance, the powerful positive effect that qualitatively high early home learning environments (HLEs) have on children's development or the effect of poor schooling and lack of personalized teaching.

Our interviews have provided information about the *what*, *how*, and *why* of this mechanism of development. Parents and children offered us a broad range of descriptions of what high-quality HLE (or any quality HLE for that matter) actually looks like in the everyday lives of children from different socio-economic backgrounds. But the interviews also allowed us to move beyond descriptions of activities, as children and parents told us how their early HLEs shaped their self-perceptions, their motivation, their school-relevant skills and knowledge, which in turn, they felt, had influenced children's academic attainment in the school environment. These descriptions have also told us why parents provided a certain level of quality of early learning experiences in the home environment.

The Case Studies have clearly shown that any educational success, but particularly unexpected educational success, requires some effort and determination from the children themselves as well as from the people and institutions around them; children are active agents. This is not to lay success and failure at the door of the child, but to emphasize how schools and parents provided successive experiences which positively or negatively impacted upon a child's sense of self-efficacy and their concept of their own ability. Our data were strongly driven by child and parent perceptions, and in this we learnt a great deal about good and less-effective parenting to support learning and good and bad teaching and schooling. Schools are the second chance many children get to support their learning when they come from poor homes, and the drive to improve schooling is critical; but it cannot be undertaken without attention to working with parents and understanding the backgrounds children come from and, where appropriate, offering the support children need.

When do success and vulnerability become apparent?

The findings from the trajectory analysis of children's learning in their life-course described as part of Chapter 3 showed that differences between children who go on to 'succeed against the odds' and children who remain 'vulnerable' are often already apparent from a very young age. The children succeeding against the odds started their academic trajectories with higher rankings than their low socio-economic status (SES) peers, indicating that already at this age they appeared to have a better grasp of school-relevant skills and knowledge, or indeed, 'readiness to learn'. This readiness is often associated with the beginning of school but it is interesting to us that children can be supported in ways to assist them for readiness to pre-school and many parents, regardless of SES, manage to do this successfully by providing a stronger HLE and emotional support. For many years in the UK, schools have emphasized the importance of reading with children, and many initiatives encourage educational support at home by parents. For instance, from the 1970s onwards, children were encouraged to choose and take books home daily to read with their parents. Many parents now, regardless of social class, assume that this is good child-rearing practice, and because they enjoyed books and reading they want to pass this love of stories on to their children. Early experiences can transcend social class and affect inter-generational behaviours. However, our work shows that this impact is patchy, as some parents show this behaviour, learned from schools or from others such as their own parents, while others do not. This, to us, means that we need a number of initiatives to support parenting and schooling for success, aimed at all citizens, but particularly at those whose children might follow a cycle of disadvantage.

Once in pre-school, the trajectories of the children from socio-economically disadvantaged homes often showed substantial progress, indicating that they particularly benefitted from the learning experiences these settings offered. During their years in primary school, and even well into secondary school, the children succeeding against the odds managed to academically keep up with, or even surpass, their peers from more privileged families. However, the general pattern of regression observed for 'vulnerable' children, both from working- and middle-class families, particularly during the primary years, suggested a poor 'goodness-of-fit' between the specific needs of many children and the ability of pre-schools,

schools, teachers and parents to tailor to their needs (Thomas & Chess, 1977). Interestingly, these same children quite regularly showed substantial improvement during the early secondary years. This could indicate that these years in which children are often offered time for reinforcement of the curriculum and concepts addressed at the end of primary school, provide children who previously struggled with a chance to fill in certain gaps in their existing skills and knowledge, at least for Maths and English. Analyses on trajectories with larger samples of children, such as the full EPPSE sample, are necessary to determine whether these findings are specific to our Case Studies sample or might apply to children in general.

Why do some children 'succeed against the odds'?

Children as active agents of their academic success

Our literature review (Chapter 2) and interview analyses (Chapters 4, 5, 6, 7, 8 and 9) on what set apart the children who 'succeeded against the odds' from those who proved to be 'vulnerable' to low attainment in school, showed that academic achievement can be perceived as a function of cognitive and socio-emotional behaviour components of the child (Evans & Rosenbaum, 2008). In terms of the bioecological model, we found patterns of particular constellations of person characteristics (e.g., demand, resource and force characteristics) which set apart the children who succeeded academically, regardless of whether they succeeded against the odds or did well as predicted, from those children who struggled academically (Bronfenbrenner & Morris, 2006). Children bring their person characteristics into any proximal process, and by doing so they actively or passively shape the nature of these processes. When these person characteristics come together in a constellation that offers protection from negative experiences and creates positive experiences, such as seems to have been the case for the academically successful children in the Case Studies, these person characteristics support the child to do well and effectively support them to become active agents of their academic success.

We found that while perceived cognitive ability functioned as a 'protective' factor for children who were particularly successful in school, it brought the danger of functioning as a risk factor for 'vulnerable' children. For the academically successful children, their intelligence or intellectual ability was perceived as a strong mental resource that stood out positively from a young age onwards. As a result, many of these children experienced positive feedback from, and stimulating experiences with, more knowledgeable others, such as parents, older peers, family friends and teachers. Children like Imogene were offered additional work in class, from a young age onwards, that allowed them to interact with people or materials beyond the zone of their current development and to move into the zone of their proximal development, thus stimulating their cognitive development even more. Being perceived as smart and bright, and having this perception regularly reinforced at home and school, helped children to establish and strengthen a positive academic self-image: they developed a strong sense of self-efficacy with regard to school, education and learning, or a 'masterful' disposition (Dweck, 1999) which encouraged them to stretch their learning beyond what might be expected. In other words, other people expected them to achieve, and they did; even if it meant applying themselves to their school work, working hard and not going out so much with their friends.

In contrast, children who experienced learning difficulties or were not seen as particularly bright often developed a negative academic self-image. This negative self-image resulted in, or at least reinforced, the use of ineffective problem-solving strategies, diminished their motivation for school and learning and instilled a sense of helplessness (Dweck, 1999). It seemed that, as a result, many experiences involving (emergent) academic learning became sources of stress and anxiety instead of sources of enjoyment and opportunities for learning and development. While Steven became a highly appreciated participant in classroom interactions once he went through remedial classes and started to enjoy learning, his behaviour in class before that time had become more and more disruptive as he felt unable to keep up with the lessons; while Marcy had loved picture books and being read to by her parents, she came to disregard her newly acquired books once she was expected to read them for herself, and she developed a range of strategies to avoid having to read out loud in class; Tom was never one for reading or sitting quietly behind a desk but as his class work became more demanding he used every resource available, including his parents, to avoid having to actually do the work. The 'risk' aspect of this negative perception of children's abilities was increased by the fact that parents and children often felt that their children's ability to learn was inherent in the child rather than something that could be influenced through, for instance, parenting (see Siraj-Blatchford et al., 2007); that is, there was often negative reinforcement at home. However, while it might be the case that general cognitive ability is partly determined by genetic factors for children who grow up in affluent circumstances, research shows that cognitive ability in poorer families depends heavily on what parents do and on environmental influences (Turkheimer et al., 2003).

In our Case Studies sample, particularly in low-SES families, this perception of ability as 'innate' and 'static' often seemed to result in the abandonment of attempts by parents and school to remedy the difficulties children experienced and therefore offer appropriate support. The potentially negative consequences of such beliefs are underlined by the experiences of children such as Steven Peterson, who struggled severely with all academic subjects during the first years of formal schooling, but who was fortunate enough to have a parent who would not give up on him. After many fruitless attempts his mother eventually managed to rally effective support from his teachers, and after this intervention Steven went on to succeed academically against very poor initial odds. We are learning about the way genes interact with the environment, and the importance of the environment in shaping children's learning successes and failures. It is the business of education to support children in their learning. Our work shows that schools and teachers need to find out about what is happening at home, and where necessary to provide children from poorer educational home environments with more stable emotional support and more educational support. In the UK, some schools and local authorities have caught on to this concept and provided breakfast clubs, intervention classes and out-of-school homework clubs and activities to boost support for children's learning.

Furthermore, child characteristics that are typically associated with better achievement in school, such as self-regulation abilities, positive attitudes towards homework, positive perceptions of personal competencies and internal academic locus of control at school (Bursik & Martin, 2006; Evans & Rosenbaum, 2008; Hoover-Dempsey et al., 2001; McNeal, 2001; Sylva et al., 2007), were commonly attributed to academically successful children in the Case Studies sample, but not to the 'vulnerable' ones. These particular combinations of positive cognitive and socio-behavioural child characteristics we found for children who succeeded academically functioned as developmentally generative force characteristics that set proximal processes in motion or sustained their operation. In contrast, for the academically less successful children their constellation of force characteristics often disrupted their proximal process experiences and made it harder for them to adapt to the school environment and to school learning. Furthermore, they seemed to reinforce the (self-)images of children, either as being 'good' students or 'just not academic'. As a result the children 'succeeding against the odds' and the children from high-SES families who were doing well in school seemed to enjoy the school experience more than their 'vulnerable' peers and were therefore able and willing to make the most of what schools had to offer.

Parenting towards academic achievement

The early home learning environment

The importance of the very early home environment for children's learning is well established through national and international research. In the Case Studies sample we found that more than half of the children 'succeeding against the odds' had experienced good-quality early HLEs, which helped them develop (pre-)school-relevant skills. The parents of these children were often very creative at finding enjoyable and stimulating activities for their child that would not put them under extra strain, given their limited household budget. Although a substantial number of successful children experienced low early HLEs indicating that they experienced fewer stimulating educational activities, the quality of the interactions these successful children experienced was still generally high. The early learning experiences these children and parents described during the interviews had many of the characteristics positively associated with children's cognitive and socio-emotional development (Hart & Risley, 1995; Hoff, 2003; Tudge et al., 2003). This apparent quality despite low early HLEs was not found for the children with low early HLEs who did not 'succeed against the odds'. Nearly all boys from low-SES families who did not 'succeed against the odds' had low early HLEs. For these boys in particular, the home environment and attitude of parents towards early learning was not particularly aimed at developing early educational skills, but instead seemed much more oriented towards what Lareau (2003) termed 'accomplishment of natural growth'.

Demand or 'personal stimulus' characteristics, such as gender, age, skin colour and physical appearance, that trigger instantaneous expectations about a child and as a result can influence initial interaction between the developing child and the social partner, were not typically mentioned as having had an effect on how well children developed academically. Despite nearly half our sample coming from minority ethnic backgrounds, parents and children did not report, and we did not find, ethnic-cultural differences in early HLE experiences in our Case Studies sample. We did find several patterns in parenting practices that appeared in response to, or at least related to, for instance, children's gender. Far more girls than boys from the Case Studies sample experienced medium and high stimulating early HLEs; they also went on to experience better self-regulation activities in the home (such as experiencing transfer of responsibilities and a greater share in household chores) in later years which supported their self-regulation, perseverance and ability to feel competent with school and learning.

This gender differentiation with regard to early HLE did not result because parents felt they were unable to provide such activities, or were unaware of the importance of the HLE as a source to develop early school-relevant skills and knowledge, but rather because many felt these activities were not particularly suited to the preferences of their child. Many boys were simply perceived to have been less interested in activities such as joint storybook reading or drawing, singing and playing letter-games that are typically and frequently part of a high-quality early HLE. Instead they were thought to prefer, and in fact indicated themselves that they had preferred, outdoor and gross motor-skill activities above indoor and fine motor-skill activities. Although this finding might not seem surprising given what we know about boys in general, it does once more underline a serious implication of the way our schools and learning systems are set up: classroom practices and learning environments are often simply better tailored towards the person characteristics of girls than towards those of boys. Because children are being prepared for these classroom practices and learning experiences through the particular activities that constitute the early HLE, and typically girls experience more of these activities and experience them more often than boys, in many instances girls seem to start their formal schooling better prepared, and as a result might be able to benefit more from the early learning experiences in the classroom.

Perceptions of the early home learning environment

The Case Studies further showed that, regardless of the actual early HLE index score, these families, parents and students who 'succeeded against the odds' regarded early HLE activities as valuable opportunities for the child to develop cognitive skills that would help and prepare the child do well in (pre-)school. They also felt it helped to develop a positive attitude and interest regarding school-related activities. From an early age onwards HLE activities such as reading were seen as something that was not just useful, but naturally enjoyable as well for both parent and child. These activities provided parents and children with opportunities to bond, and supported a good relationship between them.

Although this also seemed to be the case for the 'vulnerable' girls from the low-SES families, it appeared to be less so for the 'vulnerable' boys. Nearly all these boys had low early HLEs. An enjoyment of these 'bonding' activities was noticeably absent from their responses. For many of the Case Studies children from high-SES families who did not do as well as expected academically, parents indicated that their child had experienced learning difficulties at a certain point early in their schooling and developmental trajectory. In most cases no formal diagnosis or statement was provided, but the effect seemed to be that children lost interest in the subject domain they were experiencing difficulties with. As a result, these children tended not to participate in certain aspects of the early HLE, even though it was offered to them.

Parents offered several reasons for not being able to provide a high early HLE, such as difficult family circumstances and parental work. However, these perceived limitations were often turned to strengths by parents of children 'succeeding against the odds'. Because these parents felt it was important to help their child develop school-relevant skills and behaviour, and because they were aware that they could not always provide these experiences to the extent they felt necessary, they made sure they found alternative ways to offer stimulating early learning experiences, for instance through their personal social networks. They actively sought support to further enhance their child's learning and well-being for future educational success. Furthermore, mothers often felt that by working they were providing their child with a good role model, particularly for their daughters.

The home learning environment during the primary and secondary years

In contrast to what is usually found for low-SES families (see Bradley, 2002; Bradley et al., 2000; Feinstein et al., 2008; Parke, 2004), we found that all our successful low-SES children regularly experienced informal learning activities outside school that supported their academic achievement in school. Parents listened to the child reading aloud, played board and computer games with them and were involved in outdoor activities such as sports or educational visits to museums. These parents felt they were supporting their child academically, and went to great lengths to provide these educational experiences.

Reading in particular was highly valued and encouraged in low-SES homes of successful children and in high-SES homes with children doing well. For many of the 'vulnerable' children, reading activities became less frequent during the primary years. Particularly the 'vulnerable' low-SES boys seemed to lose interest in books and instead were more interested in outdoor activities, and particularly computer games. Many of these boys spent substantial parts of their out-of-school time playing computer games on consoles, which was often perceived by parents as having a negative effect on their behaviour.

Although shared family activities became less frequent as children got older, particularly after the children started secondary school, this was

not perceived as a negative development by the Case Studies participants, and many examples of effective HLEs could be found, particularly
in the families of children 'succeeding against the odds' and in high-SES
families in general. For instance, conversations about the child's progress
in school and their future, topics that caused the child some anxiety or
worry, or topics of general interest, were a regular part of the daily
conversations of these families. These conversations were a way of
transferring to children beliefs and values that supported an academic
attitude, but also of socializing children to gain social and cultural capital
and to use the 'elaborated code' that plays an important role in schooling
(Bernstein, 1971). This was not the case in the low-SES families with
children attaining as predicted. Furthermore, parents of successful low-
SES children, particularly parents with girls, and parents with African or
Caribbean heritage, felt that during adolescence the regulating aspects of
their child-rearing practices played an important role in children's school
success. As a result they often provided clear expectations about behaviour and educational goals, and allocated household responsibilities to
the child, i.e., relied on parenting practices that typically facilitated
further development of self-regulation skills in children (see also Bradley
et al., 2000; Mounts, 2000).

Family involvement with school and learning

Effective parental involvement with school and learning includes a broad
range of activities that are situated in the home context or at school
(Epstein, 1992; Sampson, 2007). In the Case Studies families with academically successful children, parents showed strong involvement with
school and learning by providing materials, attending school meetings
and engaging in homework with the child, as well as strong relationships
and interactive processes supporting the child's understanding of
homework. During the primary years, parents and children generally felt
that the degree of support parents would and could offer with school work
was not only helpful, but also effective. During secondary school, most
parents kept on providing practical support with school and learning by
supplying materials such as computers, books and revision guides.

Although actual help with school work became less frequent, parents
still took an active interest in the child's progress and continued to
encourage their children and to offer relational and emotional support.
These parents aimed to enhance their child's understanding of homework and the general learning process. Research shows that this kind of
parenting is positively related to achievement, and particularly to positive
student attributes (Hill & Tyson, 2009; Hoover-Dempsey et al., 2001;

McNeal, 2001). This kind of support was far less common for children from low-SES families who were achieving as predicted. Many parents felt unable to provide support with homework, as they did not feel they had the necessary skills, and as a result it was often left to the children to find alternative help, for instance from teachers or peers. Often, these parents displayed a form of helplessness, and felt unable to encourage their children.

The quality of the relationships within homes that supported children's learning was generally higher in terms of the parents' willingness to offer continued emotional and practical support to their children. They not only continuously expected to be involved with their children's learning, they offered their advocacy and love when things were not going well, making special efforts to speak to teachers and garner further intervention for their child. Interestingly, children often referred to the teachers they liked and did well with as having very similar characteristics in offering this emotional as well as good, instructional support.

The role of the school and teachers in supporting children's academic success

Laying foundations for learning in the early years

The Effective Provision of Pre-School Education (EPPE) research has shown that pre-school education can help to alleviate the effects of social disadvantage and can provide children with a better start to school (Siraj-Blatchford & Sylva, 2004), particularly when pre-school settings are assessed as highly effective (Siraj-Blatchford & Sylva, 2004; Sylva et al., 2004). In our modest sample the importance of high vs low quality pre-school settings seemed particularly important for low-SES boys. First of all, these boys appeared to have had a greater chance of enrolling in a low quality pre-school setting than boys from more advantaged families, or girls from equally disadvantaged backgrounds. Secondly, when boys from disadvantaged families did find themselves in an excellent pre-school setting they seemed to experience long-term benefits, as all these boys went on to 'succeed against the odds'.

While nearly all families in the Case Studies sample needed some form of child care during the pre-school years due to their family situation, the majority of parents, regardless of their SES, felt that pre-schools offered children the opportunity to learn to socialize with other children, a skill that would help them once they started school. However, parents with successful low-SES children and high-SES parents also stressed the importance of pre-school for preparing their child for the more intellectual side of formal schooling. Pre-school offered them the chance to get used to school routines and rules and to further develop their emergent and basic Literacy and Numeracy skills, and reinforced their positive attitude to school and learning. The low-SES parents of children 'succeeding against the odds' in particular, felt that pre-school offered their child something in addition to what they were able to offer them at home. Although low-SES parents generally enrolled their child in a particular setting for reasons of convenience, e.g., proximity to the home, the parents of the successful children did evaluate the suitability of the setting. They did not however resort to assertive 'concerted cultivation' as was sometimes found with the high-SES families who were already carefully planning the educational career of their child by making sure that the pre-school choice would open the path to the best primary schools for their child (Allatt, 1993; Vincent & Ball, 2006).

In our Case Studies sample of fifty, we found that, unfortunately, very few low-SES children had the combined benefit of experiencing a high early HLE and an excellent (high-quality and effective) pre-school education. However, the relatively high occurrence of medium- or high-quality home experiences, with good or excellent pre-school experiences among the children 'succeeding against the odds', once again confirms the importance of the combination of good quality in home and pre-school settings to help children overcome disadvantage (Melhuish et al., 2008; Siraj-Blatchford, 2010a) and get a good start in life. Furthermore, it seems that for low-SES boys, who generally have a greater chance of experiencing a low early HLE, good or excellent quality pre-school settings function as an important 'protective' factor. Given the growing initiatives such as Sure Start in England, Flying Start in Wales and Early Start in the US, families with disadvantaged under 3s should be given advice on higher quality providers in their area. Parents sometimes need support at this very early stage to allow in more protective factors such as high-quality pre-school.

Primary school academic effectiveness

The Effective Pre-School and Primary Education (EPPE 3–11) study showed that students who attended an academically more effective primary school had significantly better outcomes for English and Maths, over and above what was expected on the basis of child and family background (Sylva et al., 2008; see further Sammons et al., 2008c). In the Case Studies sample we found that the majority of children, both from low- and high-SES backgrounds, attended primary schools that had average to good academic effectiveness for both English and Maths. Simultaneous experiences of good academic effectiveness for Maths and English was rare for all four groups. Although there were a few high-SES children who attended a primary school that was less effective on one subject, it was only in the low-SES samples that we found examples of children who attended schools that were substantially less effective for both Maths and English. As we did not find any clear relations between the child trajectories during primary years and the primary academic effectiveness, it seems that in order to understand more about how primary schools might support children to succeed, we need to consider a range of structural and process factors at classroom and school level, such as teacher quality (Sammons et al., 2008c; Sylva et al., 2008). Schools and teachers do make a difference, and our families told us this over and over again. However, unsurprisingly, the teachers in secondary schools knew their students less well and their home circumstances even less. For vulnerable children this is a particular problem, because so much of what we heard from our Case Studies children was predicated on the quality of the relationships they perceived themselves to have with significant others, such as teachers and peers.

Teaching to inspire success

The early observed differences in mental resources (such as cognitive ability) and differences in patterns of constellations of force characteristics also seemed to affect the emotional resources that children developed, particularly in the way of child–teacher relationships. The academically successful children and parents typically commented positively on experiences with teachers, both for the child and the parents. These positive teacher–child and teacher–family relationships were usually not one-off, but were mentioned for pre-schools, primary schools and (to a somewhat lesser extent, at least for parents) for secondary schools. Parents and children felt that many teachers had been knowledgeable, warm, responsive and supportive, and had taken their needs seriously. For these children, relationships that they were able to build with (at least certain) teachers seemed to have functioned as a protective factor in their learning life-course. Children and parents from low-SES families 'succeeding against the odds', as well as from successful high-SES families attributed (part of their) success in school to the quality of their teachers. To them, good-quality teaching, for instance, meant that teachers were able to explain topics and lessons clearly, were enthusiastic about the subject they taught, were approachable when things were difficult to understand, were generally friendly, had control over the class, and clearly communicated their expectations and boundaries. They liked and listened to children, and they cared about whether children understood a subject or not. Children bonded with these teachers, and not only enjoyed the classes, but actually felt encouraged to work to achieve beyond their predicted attainment (see Siraj-Blatchford et al., 2014).

The academically vulnerable children and parents, on the other hand, often felt let down by teachers and schools. That is not to say that they never had positive experiences with teachers or schools. Rather, negative experiences that often tied in with the difficulties children experienced with learning in general or with specific subject matters, gradually started to dominate in their actual relationships with and perceptions of teachers and learning, and soured their expectations of future relationships and experiences, as they prepared themselves for negativity. These children and their parents in particular mentioned that they felt that the high number of supply teachers, and the consequently disorganized lessons that came with this, contributed significantly to their low attainment. In the work we have undertaken in eighty-two primary schools with excellent, good and poor quality and outcomes, we identified several strands of practice that impact on children's outcomes (Siraj-Blatchford et al., 2011b), including:

> Organisation;
> Teachers shared their objectives;
> Meaningful homework;
> Positive classroom climate;
> Behaviour management;
> Collaborative learning;
> Personalized teaching and learning;
> Making links explicit;
> Dialogic teaching and learning;
> Assessment for learning.

From our feedback from parents and children, these were precisely the kinds of areas in which schools failed more disadvantaged children. More careful attention, particularly by secondary schools, to getting to know and supporting children vulnerable to school failure is needed. Yet, sadly as children go up in age, and by the time they get to secondary education, there is less known about individual children's circumstances, and therefore less attention given to differences in support that a child might receive or benefit from.

Schools' helping hands

The one school-level factor that seemed most clearly to set apart the Case Studies children who 'succeeded against the odds' from those who were 'vulnerable' was the help they received from school when they were experiencing difficulties with academic work or behaviour. Although such difficulties were reported by respondents from all groups, the parents and children who 'succeed against the odds' felt that schools had effectively helped them to deal with these difficulties, through interventions such as booster, remedial, homework, revision or behavioural classes. These additional classes helped children to catch up with their peers and (re)establish and reinforce a positive perception of school and learning and of students' efficacy to deal with difficult situations. The 'vulnerable' working-class children and their parents on the other hand often felt let down by schools and teachers. While some of the parents, particularly those from high-SES families, had organized additional help for the child after school, many felt frustrated and even angry with school policies and head teachers for not dealing effectively with their child. It seemed that these negative perceptions of parents were to some degree transmitted to their children, and in some cases might have reinforced a negative attitude to school and learning. The role of schools and teachers is vital in supporting working-class children to succeed.

Social and cultural capital in the environment external to school and family

Building social and cultural capital through extra-curricular activities

Extra-curricular activities provide children with opportunities to experience and experiment with different roles, for instance that of leader or expert when participating in discussions during out-of-school religious classes, when playing computer games with their friends or when earning merits and certificates as part of their participation in music classes or cadet programmes. These activities allow for development of expertise while simultaneously supporting aspects of identity development, such as a sense of belonging in a community and feelings of competence and interest development (Barron, 2006; Rogoff, 1993; Rogoff et al., 2003). For children from high-SES families, privately paid extra-curricular activities, such as dance classes, private music tuition and sports activities were an essential part of the 'concerted cultivation' they experienced (Lareau, 2003). Although extra-curricular activities were also common for low-SES children in our sample, they were usually offered through the school, or parents sought less costly or free opportunities. However, the children who were 'succeeding against the odds' in the Case Studies sample were also widely encouraged and facilitated by parents to participate in extra-curricular activities such as the Sea Cadets or activities related to a family's ethnic-cultural or religious heritage.

The difference between successful and 'vulnerable' children seemed to be the way these activities were perceived and valued by parents, and as a result, by the children. Low-SES parents with children who did not 'succeed against the odds' usually regarded the activities as fun and relaxing, but did not consider any educational aspects or benefits that might follow from participating. When children wanted to give up on an activity, these parents and high-SES parents with 'vulnerable' children were less likely to encourage them to persevere. On the other hand, families with children who were succeeding were very much aware of the educational implications of these experiences and felt their child's development and perhaps even school achievement would benefit, and, perhaps as a result, strongly encouraged them to continue with these activities even when they became less interested in participating.

Valuable relationships with peers and friends

The children in the Case Studies offered explanations about the mechanisms through which peers affected their attainment. For the successful children, peers, especially their friends, offered practical and emotional support. These friendships and this emotional support helped them to enjoy school and to deal with any difficulties they encountered. Practical support was often mutual, as children helped each other out during lessons and with homework and revision. Not only did this offer children opportunities to take on the role of teacher, it also provided them with opportunities to deepen their understanding of subjects either by rephrasing the teacher's explanations to clarify things for their friends or by receiving alternative explanations from their friends. These experiences seem to have contributed positively to children's positive self-perception, sense of efficacy and use of effective learning strategies (Greene & Way, 2005).

Friends also further reinforced the positive attitude towards school and learning through their positive perception of education, and stimulated the successful children to be the best they could by providing positive role models and offering friendly competition. Although some of the 'vulnerable' children from the Case Studies experienced positive peer influence, these students often had friends and peers in general with more negative attitudes to school and learning, and often with behaviour problems (Cook et al., 2007; Steinberg & Morris, 2001).

Gateways to additional cultural capital

Bourdieu (1986) has argued that in order to understand how power is applied in society we need to consider those resources drawn from social relationships: 'social capital', as well as the 'symbolic and cultural capital' that individuals deploy. We found that relationships were vital in how our Case Studies families operated within and outside the family. Each of these forms of capital plays a part in the reproduction of class and class relationships. Individuals draw upon cultural, social and symbolic resources to maintain or enhance their positions in the social order. 'Aspiration' may be considered a feature of cultural capacity, and it is in this light that we should recognize that aspirations are especially important. Efforts to improve aspirations have therefore been central to recent government efforts to combat social exclusion (Siraj-Blatchford, 2010a).

The low-SES children who 'succeeded against the odds' and the successful high-SES children made good use of external sources to help them with school work: written materials, computers, but also peers, siblings and adults in their social environment. Their positive attitude and frequent use of books and computers as vehicles to support their work for school or as hobbies facilitated their previous and current learning, and is likely to be beneficial for their future education (Barron, 2006; Griswold et al., 2005).

But many low-SES children fail to thrive academically. For those parents suffering poverty and multiple disadvantages, efforts to sustain what Lareau (2003) called their children's natural growth may be seen as a significant achievement in itself, but less obviously, both the 'sustaining natural growth' and the 'concerted cultivation' approaches provide advantages and disadvantages, and for many parents across the social spectrum they increasingly present clear alternative choices. It would seem that concerted cultivation makes as significant a contribution to the social capital and reproduction of the middle classes in the UK as it does in the USA (Lareau, 2003).

Support networks as sources of capital

Support networks of extended family, family friends and religious communities played an important role in supporting parents when raising their children. Although practical help, such as minding the child when parents had to work, was useful, there were other support networks which went beyond this. For instance, offering opportunities for parents to discuss parenting issues or providing encouragement to children about school and learning. These friends and support networks were available in many low-SES families with children who 'succeeded against the odds' and high-SES families in general. Family support networks offered additional social and cultural capital that could benefit the child's educational attainment.

Final remarks and implications for policy and practice

Particularly, children who 'succeeded against the odds' had managed to adapt very well to educational processes. In part, this process of adaptation appeared to be facilitated by their perceived good general ability for learning. However, what made them stand out even more when we compared them to children who were less successful was their apparent positive perception of themselves as successful learners, their appreciation of what school and education could bring them and their willingness and ability to build and sustain meaningful relationships with the people around them that actually served to facilitate their learning. These children actively engaged with activities and people that could help them develop their skills and knowledge. For example, they read books for pleasure, joined the Sea Cadets or youth groups, explained Maths problems to their friends, felt encouraged by their friends' success in school, discussed their lives and interests with family members and turned to their teachers for guidance and help. They not only reciprocated offers from others to engage in learning experiences, but actively initiated these experiences; in fact actively regulating their own behaviour. As such, these children had learnt to be agents of their academic success and had the self-regulation skills to do this.

Schools, teachers, peers and other adults in children's lives can all contribute significantly to children's chances of 'succeeding against the odds' of disadvantage by facilitating children's interest in, and adaptation to, education. Teachers who are able and willing to meet the specific needs of their students, and who are capable and inspiring, not only teach them as teachers but contribute to their positive perception of school and learning. Peers and siblings can inspire high aspirations and help children do well by supporting school work and by offering emotional support that reinforces their positive perceptions of themselves as learners and of school in general. Adults, such as family members or members from their wider community, can provide practical help that parents might not be able to give, due to their financial or time situation or their limited experience with education or the education system in the United Kingdom. They can also serve as positive role models to which a child can aspire, and they can offer encouragement. By supporting children in these ways, these teachers, peers, siblings, family members and community members become 'significant others' to the child, in that they help them maintain and even reinforce their positive perceptions of themselves as learners and of education as enjoyable and valuable.

However, the Case Studies clearly show that parents in particular play a pivotal role in helping their child 'succeed against the odds'. Parents hold the key to many of their children's experiences, not just through their own interaction with the child and their involvement with school and learning but also for the learning opportunities they facilitate through their choices about children's schools, extra-curricular activities, community involvement and contact with extended family. Through their own behaviour, parents set examples that show children how to conduct themselves in a good way but also of what to value and how to achieve goals. Through their own example they model, reinforce and facilitate successful adaptation to school and learning. In some ways, the activities and experiences of these children and the beliefs of their parents are similar to activities that are typically associated with success in family life in middle or higher socio-economic status families, and reflect the socialization pattern of 'concerted cultivation' rather than the pattern of 'accomplishment through natural growth' that is more common among lower SES families (Lareau, 2003). However, effective parenting in low-SES families was by no means a mirror image of 'concerted cultivation'.

The children who 'succeeded against the odds' were definitely 'culti-vated', in the sense that they were 'educated' and 'cultured' by their parents in a way that 'fitted' the educational system. Their socialization experiences helped them to benefit from the educational system in a way that allowed them to make the most of their potential and extend their cultural capital. Nonetheless, this socialization process of 'cultivation' was in many respects far less 'concerted', or rather 'assertive', than in high-SES families, and as such is perhaps better described as 'active cultivation'. Partly, the child-rearing practices of these parents were less obviously concerted because parents simply did not have similar financial means or the same economic capital as high-SES parents, so they could not provide their children with the same amount of private tuition and extra-curricular activities. However, the fact that these low-SES parents also did not necessarily have equivalence in social and cultural capital to their high-SES counterparts seems to be of equal importance.

The low-SES parents generally had little personal knowledge or family experience of the cultivation routes that lead children to higher education in general and into the top schools and universities in particular. This for instance meant that parents were often unaware of entry exams that children would need to pass to enrol in particular schools, or that additional preparation through private tutoring had become 'the norm' for children sitting the entry exams for the best secondary schools. However, the fact that these parents managed to help their children 'succeed against the odds' even without these means, and without long-standing reference points to educational achievement that were typically available to middle-class parents, underlines the strength of their deter-mination to help their child move ahead. Unlike the middle-class families who were helping their child to aspire to something that they as parents had already achieved, these working-class parents were helping their child to aspire to something more than they had managed for themselves: in effect, to move upwards on the social mobility ladder. These parents were cultivating their children for educational success by staying true to their own values and beliefs, while simultaneously stimulating their child to make a better life for her or himself.

Therefore the child-rearing practices seen in the low-SES families with children 'succeeding against the odds' could perhaps be more appropriately described as 'active cultivation'. Children become part of society's culture at first by participating in family practices. Through participation they learn what is accepted and expected (Rogoff, 1998). The practices with which the parents of children 'succeeding against the odds' familiarized their children during their day-to-day interaction, included reading together, conversations over shared meals, routines for children to help out with the housework or modelling going out to work and acquiring additional qualifications. These behaviours socialized the children in a way that resulted in them developing skills and beliefs that matched the expectations of society, and as a result helped them to benefit from what society had to offer through schools, teachers, friends and others in their communities. Parents built on their personal experiences (good and bad) to help their children move ahead, and in this way made the most of the cultural capital they had available. These parents were setting good examples for their children through their own efforts in the work place, through efforts to better their social and financial position through additional learning and qualifications, and by taking responsibility for their lives and that of their children. By doing so they provided valuable role models to their children, demonstrating the value of cultural capital for social and economic status and personal well-being.

Like their children, who showed educational resilience to disadvantages, these parents too seemed particularly resilient to the hardships they encountered in their lives. They used their own experiences, resources and strengths to cultivate their child, but often in a less obvious way than the high-SES parents. They were aware of limitations in their ability to facilitate the child's learning process. They did not move away from close family ties or religious communities as is often the case in more affluent families, but instead tried to make use of these social networks to find additional sources of support for their child. Additionally, these financially less affluent parents were willing to make substantial personal sacrifices in order for their children to have the opportunity to go on educational outings and family holidays, to have extra tuition for subjects the child struggled with, to have out-of-school classes, to have additional books, a computer and Internet access, and sometimes even to provide a school uniform. By doing so they once more relayed to the child how much they valued education.

In some of the households we visited, heating was turned off despite the winter cold, walls, windows and floors were bare, and light bulbs or tea bags were a luxury. Nonetheless, these families welcomed us into their homes and seemed to enjoy the opportunity to talk about their child, their experiences as parents, their beliefs about parenting and education and their aspirations and hopes for their child. They were proud of their children and often also about what they themselves as parents had achieved. This testifies to the determination of these parents to help their child succeed and make a good future for themselves.

To date, the existing body of literature has identified a broad range of characteristics at the level of society, community, family, school and individual which contribute to children's success or lack of success during their learning life-course and their academic career. Models such as Bronfenbrenner's bioecological model of human development, Harkness' and Super's proposed concept of the developmental niche and Lareau's conceptualization of socialization in different socio-economic classes provide us with theoretical frameworks to study how these characteristics shape the lives and academic outcomes of children (see Chapter 2 of this book). Our aim has been to provide clear examples of how these features are complex and work to promote success or failure, and why these characteristics are of importance for academic and social success. We have attempted to give 'voice' to how the participants in these successful and less-successful learning trajectories perceive, understand and explain what they think are the reasons behind their experiences.

Although our data does not allow inferences about causality or generalization to the overall population in England, the quantitative data available through the EPPSE project does seem to confirm that such differences in agency, as for instance captured in variables such as the early HLE and the social/behavioural child measures, are not just apparent and influential when children start their academic careers, but that their effect also carries on and is compounded as the children progress through their academic trajectories and through their life-course as learners, and will no doubt have an enduring impact on the future lives of these citizens and their children.

Some of our findings contradict Annette Lareau's study (2003). This might be because her sample of twelve children is very small compared to our fifty children and their extensive data sets, especially outcomes over time. She did supplement her case-study children with a further sample of interviews, but these did not alter her main conclusions. Lareau emphasizes that working-class families tend to use these *natural growth* strategies, where their children determine control over their own time and friendships and activities. The parents cannot send their children to extra-curricular clubs because of the expense and time, as most working-class parents have less flexibility in their work schedules. They are more deferential to professionals, and they are less likely to disagree or question such professionals. In our study this was certainly not so much the case; many of our working-class parents were advocates for their children, they questioned teachers and schools and they sought out cheap but valuable educational activities for their children.

Lareau finds that working-class families tend to be more family-oriented, with the children playing mainly with extended-family relatives. She makes the case that working-class parents were less likely to engage in discussions with their children and more likely to issue directives; again this was not the case for most of our working-class parents, especially in the 'succeeding against the odds' group.

Lareau explains that there are advantages and disadvantages to both styles. Working-class children in her study are less bored: they are happier, and learn how to be creative; and they are far more relaxed and energetic. Middle-class children tend to learn to negotiate with institutions; they pick up more and better vocabulary and they learn a sense of entitlement that helps them to negotiate their way through institutions. Our findings do show that stress levels were higher for some middle-class children, but only the girls, and we did find many working-class families that supported their children's language development, reading and other educational activities and provided them with emotional and social and cultural support.

Our analyses clearly confirm the premises of the theoretical models we applied, i.e., that it is never 'just' the one factor of child, family or school or broader social context that brings about success or failure in an academic trajectory. Rather, it appears to be the particular ecological niches that arise through the active reciprocal interactions between these factors that determine the parameters for children's pathways to academic success. In other words, the real world context of development is complex, but while characteristics at macro- or meso-level, such as school policies and curriculum or parental jobs, exert some influence on children's day-to-day learning experiences, the best opportunities to help children are within reach right there on the micro level. What becomes evident from our Case Studies is that unexpected academic success, i.e., academic achievement that defies the odds of disadvantage, requires effort and determination from the children themselves as 'active agents', as well as from the people around them. By having people around them that believe in them, encourage them, challenge them and support them, children develop a strong sense of self-efficacy with regard to academic success. Through their interactions with these people, children learn to build and sustain relationships (i.e., develop social capital) that support and facilitate academic success. As a result, these relationships with 'significant others' help children to develop their cultural capital.

Parents in particular have the opportunity to play a pivotal role in facilitating academic success. Our analyses of parenting in families with children 'succeeding against the odds' of disadvantage show that parents can encourage and facilitate academic success directly through the proximal learning processes they choose to offer their children, as well as more indirectly through the opportunities they create for their children to engage in learning processes with others, and through the example they set their children through their own life. They offer their personal economic, cultural and social capital to their children. These parents develop and foster meaningful relationships with their children through the support and guidance they offer during the developmental process. Through a process of 'active cultivation' they can teach their children to develop and sustain meaningful relationships with the people around them and with learning and education. Although they are aware of, and acknowledge, the limitations to their resources, they inventively find ways to turn such 'weaknesses' into strengths.

Our bottom-up analysis of the qualitative data showed that in families with children 'succeeding against the odds', parents and students not only actively created and seized a broad range of learning opportunities in the home, at school and in the broader community, but also felt confident about their abilities to have a positive effect on the child's academic success, and nurtured more sustainable and successful emotional and social relations in their child. Through their example, these parents helped children become active agents in their own educational processes. That is not to say that there is not more that could be done for these children. For instance, schools could play a much more active role in 'supplementing' the cultural and social capital that is available to these children and to their families. For instance, although most schools provide information about GCSE choices, and some schools provide information or even excursions to universities, many children and parents are not aware of the often implicit expectations that these institutions have that need to be met before children can become part of their culture. Starting to offer such information before children choose their GCSE subjects, or even before they start secondary school, might offer these children better chances of continuing their unexpected academic success beyond their compulsory schooling.

Understanding how we can support children through their learning life-course has become a policy imperative, particularly for those children from poor homes who would normally be facing a low achiever trajectory. The Case Studies provide information that can be of use both to policymakers and practitioners. It has implications for parenting and home–school relations, and may serve to inform policies and practices that aim to increase the chances of 'at risk' children, and help in closing the gap between those who are academically and socially advantaged and disadvantaged (See Siraj-Blatchford et al., 2013). The implications include:

- The implications of 'active cultivation' for parenting programmes/ initiatives are substantial, as our study shows that in these cases the home as an institution is a very powerful 'proximal' context. It helps children to establish masterful learning dispositions towards school and learning, and stimulates the development of self-efficacy;
- Parents who show active cultivation provide strong, child-centred emotional support that is sensitive to the child's developing needs. They do so, even in the face of difficulties, by being encouraging, persistent and consistent;
- As children who succeed start school with a better grasp of school-relevant skills and knowledge, there are implications for the early assessment of children entering school or pre-school, in order that appropriate curriculum and pedagogy is personalized and adopted;
- The importance of teachers and schools in supporting and encouraging vulnerable children and avoiding negative expectations and stereotypes has implications for recruiting the best teachers into schools in disadvantaged communities;
- The importance of relationships with peers and friends has implications for teachers in promoting 'communities of learning' in classrooms in which students can take some responsibility for their own and others' learning, and work towards shared goals;
- The importance of schools conducting early assessments and providing additional support classes has implications for early diagnostic assessment and individualized support and intervention in Key Stage 1. Later support through to secondary education has a vital role;
- The importance of social and cultural capital has implications for schools and communities in fostering 'learning to learn' dispositions by providing support with educational experiences, especially for vulnerable children.

The sense of active agency that the Case Studies show among families with children 'succeeding against the odds' of disadvantage is in stark contrast to the helplessness that was commonly observed and expressed by parents and students who were not 'succeeding against the odds'.

However, for these children, opportunities too might be created by enhancing their social and cultural capital with the help of 'significant others', such as teachers or members from their broader social or cultural communities. Unlike the children 'succeeding against the odds', these children and parents found it hard to remember any teachers that had been particularly helpful to their learning. Instead, they often felt let down by schools and teachers alike and frustrated by their lack of academic success. In many cases, these parents could or would not help their children to develop academic aspirations. Sadly neither did the children's schools. Generally, low targets were set for these children with regard to national assessments and GCSEs, and children were all too aware that little was expected of them. As long as these targets were met, teachers, parents and students felt that things were as they should be. Because of this, children missed out on the experience of having someone believe in them and of being challenged to succeed beyond the low expectations. We know from our Case Studies that there are good schools and good teachers. They offered short-term interventions to correct the problem of low expectations, and listened to the child and parent to offer appropriate support. And as a result, some of our children and families experienced a turnaround in their educational trajectory, when schools intervened with appropriate recognition of a child struggling with a behavioural or educational problem. Both schools and parents have a profound impact on children's learning, and the way the two interact with each other often determines how well the child is equipped to deal with the challenges during their learning life-course.

Appendix 1 Example of personalized student interview

Semi-Structured Student Interviews

Name student: Steven Peterson (ID xxxx)
Interview date: 14–1–2009
Name interviewer: A.Y.M.

Introduction

I'm really happy that we are going to have this chat. I just want to tell you a few things before we get started. First of all, I want you to know that the things you tell me are confidential. That means that I won't tell your parents or anyone else about the things you say to me. However, a part of doing research like this is writing about what I learn from you. Just to let you know, when I write about things, I always make sure that you and your parents stay anonymous, that is: I'll use different names for you, so nobody will know it's you. Can you think of a name you would like me to use? I can't guarantee that I'll use it, but I'll certainly keep it in mind! . . . .

Now, as you know, the reason we are having this chat is because I want to learn more about what things and which people you feel are important to help you learn since you were very little to now, and how you think they influence how you do in school. I would also really like to hear about when you were younger and maybe if things were different from how they are now. So I'll be asking you questions about school, home, friends and other important people in your life. And you can help me by giving me examples of things that have happened recently and when you were little. I have a paper here with information that I got from the questionnaires that you and your parents filled out since you were in Nursery class. It also has information about your school and names of the schools you went to. We'll keep that in front of us, as it might help you to remember things. Furthermore, you can probably hear my funny accent. That is because I grew up in Holland.

So I might use words you don't know and you might use words that I don't know. So I'll ask you to explain to me what those words mean and you can ask me to do the same.

We'll start with when you were really young ...

Pre-school

1. Can you tell me about your first memories? How old were you?
2. Can you remember what kind of things you learned when you were very little, under 5? Who or what did you learn them from?
3. *Possible follow up* Do you remember any of the things you did at home at that time? Who did you do them with and what did you learn from them?[1] ➔*HLE=2; no set bedtime; no TV watching; did not play with friends; no family meals; book = every day (no library), looking at books, pointing at letters, play writing, singing abc-songs; counting games during daily grinds; singing songs together.*
4. Do you remember what it was like at *Happy Park*? Do you remember your teacher at Nursery? Can you give me some examples of things you used to do there?
5. Do you remember any of your friends from Nursery? Can you think of something that you learned from them?
6. How did people make you feel about learning? Why?

Primary school

7. So then you went to *Prior Preston Primary School*. How easy did you find it to learn in primary school? Can you give me some examples of what you found hard and what was easier? *What about at Tuttons Primary School? Why did you change schools?* ➔*Y5: liked school, coped well.*
8. Did you have a favourite teacher? Why was that? Can you give me an example of the things s/he did that helped you to learn? *What about at Tuttons Primary School?*
9. Can you give me an example of the kinds of things other teachers or adults at *Prior Preston Primary school* did to help you with school and learning? *What about at Tuttons Primary School?*

---

[1] The notes in italics, following this and some of the other questions in Appendices 1 and 2, refer to information previously supplied in the form of answers to questionnaires (referred to in the introductions to the interviews) during the years of the longitudinal survey.

10. Can you tell me about the friends you had at *Prior Preston and Tuttons*? Do you think they influenced how you did in school? Can you give me an example? ➔*Y5 had a lot of friends & best friend in class.*

11. What happened when you worked on your homework after school? Can you tell me where, how and when you did it? ➔*occasionally got homework.*

12. Was there anyone around to help you with your homework if you needed it? Can you give me an example of how they helped you? ➔*Mum helped 2–3 times per week / later once a week/Y5: help some of the time.*

13. What kind of things did you do as a family before you were 11, that you think helped you with primary school? ➔*often: play computer games, listen to his reading, read to, shopping; 3–4 hrs TV; occasionally: games, educational computer, educational visits outside the home; hardly ever: sports, library. Plays pretend games and computer games.*

14. Can you give me an example of what used to happen if you disagreed with your parents about something, for instance their rules about jobs around the house, television or bedtime? ➔*shout / tell off.*

15. When you were at *Prior Preston* and *Tuttons*, what kind of things did your parents say to you about learning and school? Can you give me any examples? ➔*parents asked about what he did in school.*

16. Do you feel these talks were important for how well you did in *Prior Preston* and *Tuttons*? Can you give me an example?

17. How about discussions and activities with other adults who are important to you, e.g., another family member, a sports coach, or a religious person. Do you think these helped you with learning? How?

Secondary school

18. Can you tell me a bit about how you think you are doing in school right now? ➔*excellent in Maths, Science, ICT, Arts; pretty good in English, average in PE.*

19. How did you do in your Key Stage 3 SATs? What were the results for English, Maths and Science? ➔*expected 7 for E, Sc. & M.*

20. How did you choose your GCSE subjects? Who or what influenced you? ➔*interest, useful for job, do well; not: like teacher, friends, parents.*

21. Can you give me some examples of things you find hard and things you find easier in secondary school? How do you deal with things you find hard?

22. What do you think is the reason that you are doing well in school? Can you give me an example? ➔*above prediction.*

23. Why do you think some children do better in school than others?
24. Have you got a favourite teacher? What is it that s/he does that helps you most with school? →*likes most classes; positive about teachers.*
25. What about homework? Can you tell me what happens when you work on your homework after school? →*homework room at school; revision for SATs computer; 2–3 hrs homework; parents check homework.*
26. Tell me a bit about the things you do as a family. What do you feel you learn from these experiences? →*3–5 meals together, discuss current events/TV, shopping, visit relatives.*
27. What kind of things do you do in your free time now? How does this influence your experience in school? →*going out with friends; reading; dance class; 2–3 hrs computer games; spend with family.*
28. How do you feel your friends influence you? How does this impact on how you're doing in school? Why? →*no problem behaviour; support from friends; makes friends easily, popular.*
29. What usually happens if you disagree with your parents about any of the rules at home, for instance about computer time or how long you can stay out with friends? →*hardly ever falls out; never breaks rules; shout / tell off.*
30. What kinds of things do your parents say to you about school, education, or learning? Do you feel these discussions are important for how well you do in school and learning? →*most days ask about school, sometimes friends and teachers.*
31. How about discussions and activities with other adults who are important to you, e.g., another family member, a sports coach, or even a religious person. Do you think these help you with learning now? How?
32. Which people do you think have given you the most help with school and learning so far and what did they do to help you?

Future

33. What job you would like to have when you leave school? How did/ will you decide on that? →*university.*
34. What will you need to do to make sure you can have that job?
35. What do you feel are the most important things for your future that you have learned so far from school, home and friends?
36. Do you think there are things that happened in your life that have influenced how well you've done in school, that we haven't talked about? Can you give me an example? →*family violence, new partner for parent; religion.*

Closing

Well, we are almost done. Thank you so much for telling me all about your life. As I said at the beginning, the reason I wanted to talk to you was to get a better idea of what you think is and has been important in helping you learn and dealing with school. This talk has been very helpful. We have talked about school, teachers, your home and parents, about friends and about your future plans. But maybe you feel that someone or maybe something that we did not talk about is important as well. **Can you think of anything?**

Well, just in case you think about anything after I have left or if you feel you want to say anything else about something we talked about, I'll leave this card with you. You can write down anything you think of and just pop it into the post, my address is already on the card and you don't need a stamp. It also has my email address on it, so you can always drop me a line if you think of anything. As I said before, everything we talk about is confidential.

You know we are also talking with your parent. We would like to have a chat with someone in your school as well. Of course we won't tell her/him anything about the things you have said. We just want to hear what they think their role is in helping students in school. **Which teacher or staff member would you say knows you best in this school? Probe:** Who is your form teacher?

Name teacher:

. . . .
. . . .

Subject taught/function: . . . .
. . . .
. . . .

Name school:

. . . .
. . . .

Now there's one more thing I wanted to ask:

May I have a look at the place where you usually do your homework?

Appendix 2 Example of personalized parent interview

Semi-Structured Parent Interviews

Name parent: Ms Peterson
   Student ID: xxxx
   Interview date: 14–1–2009
   Name interviewer: A.Y.M.

Introduction

I'm really happy that we are going to have this interview. I just want to tell you a few things before we get started. First of all, I want you to know that the information you or your child give in these interviews will be reported using different names, so nobody will have to know it was you.

As we discussed before, the reason we are having this interview is because I want to learn more about what parents, such as you, feel is important for their children's school success, or any difficulties, and for their learning opportunities. Therefore I'll be asking you to tell me about things that you personally feel are or have been important for your son's learning experiences. The questions will start with what happened before he started primary school and go up to learning in secondary school and the future. As a reminder I have a paper here with information that I got from the questionnaires that you and your child have filled out since he was 3 years old. It has information about how he was doing in school and names of the schools he went to. We'll keep that in front of us, as it might help you to remember things. Furthermore, as I am not a native speaker I might at times use words and phrases that are unclear to you. Please feel free to ask me to clarify these. Similarly, I might at times ask you to explain a word that I'm not familiar with.

Pre-school

1. Can you tell me what *Steven* was like when he was little? →*very short attention span; hearing difficulties; didn't speak until after 1st birthday, developmentally delayed; grommet and speech therapy.*

2. Can you give me some examples of things you did at home with *Steven* before age 5? How do you think this has helped with later learning? →*HLE=2; no set bedtime; no TV watching; did not play with friends; no family meals; book = every day (no library), looking at books, pointing at letters, play writing, singing abc-songs; counting games during daily grinds; singing songs together.*

3. What made you decide that *Steven* would attend Pre-school? Did you have any particular reasons for choosing *Happy Park EYC*? →*close, older sibling attended.*

4. Were there any staff at *Happy Park EYC* that you feel helped *Steven*'s learning most at that time? Can you give me examples of what they did? →*nursery teacher recognized hearing difficulties, helped to sign and monitor how he played with other children.*

5. In what ways you were involved with *Happy Park EYC*? Why did you feel this was important?

Primary school

6. Was there anything you said to *Steven* about starting Primary school? Why was that?

7. How well did *Steven* settle into *Prior Preston*? Why? →*unhappy going to Prior Preston; Switched to Tutton Primary in last year, why?*

8. Was there any information passed on to *Prior Preston* by the pre-school? How do you think this affected *Steven* settling in to primary school?

9. What do you feel *Steven*'s primary school offered that helped him to learn? *What about at Tutton?* →*reading difficulties?*

10. How did you stay informed about *Steven*'s progress in primary school? *What about at Tutton?* →*newsletters, homework, teacher meetings.*

11. How do you feel about the way *Prior Preston* communicated with you about *Steven*'s progress? *What about at Tutton?* →*very satisfied.*

12. Is there anyway in which *Prior Preston* could have done more for *Steven*'s learning at this time? Why do you think this did not happen? *What about at Tutton?*

13. Can you give me some examples of things you did at home with *Steven* during the primary school years that you feel have been important for his learning? →*often: play computer games, listen to read, read to, shopping; 3–4 hrs TV; occasionally: games, educational*

computer, educational visits outside the home; hardly ever: sports, library.
Plays pretend games and computer games.

14. Did *Steven* have any particular jobs around the house during his primary school years? Why did you believe it was important for him to do/not do such jobs?

15. What rules were important for *Steven* to have at home and how do you think these rules helped with school? ➔*no set bedtime at weekends; shout, tell off and talk to.*

16. Can you tell me how you discussed these rules with *Steven*? Could you give me an example?

17. When *Steven* was in primary school what kind of things did he do in his free time that you feel were important for his school success? Why do you think that is? ➔*dance class & sports.*

Secondary school

18. How did *Steven* adjust to the change from primary to secondary school? ➔*nearest school; Y9: settled in well: 'I like my school and am happy here'.*

19. Can you tell me how you think *Steven* has been doing in Secondary school? Why? What about in English, Maths and Science? ➔*happy; good progress; no worries about his behaviour.*

20. Which of *Steven*'s current teachers do you think is/are helping him most in school? Can you give examples of the way they help?

21. How does *Steven* deal with things that he finds difficult in school or in learning at home? Why do you think he does that?

22. Is there any way in which *Raynes School Language College* could do more for *Steven*'s learning? Why do you think this hasn't happened?

23. How do you feel about the way *Raynes School Language College* communicates with you about *Steven*'s progress? ➔*discussed work 1–3 times with teachers.*

24. Can you tell me about the talks you have with *Steven* about how he is doing in school? Can you give me an example of how this might help his education? ➔*talks about school, friends, GCSEs, school work, behaviour, checked homework.*

25. What can you do as a parent to help *Steven* develop as a person and to do well in school? Why do you feel these things are so important?

26. Are there any other adults, perhaps in your family or in your community or at school who have or have had an important influence on how *Steven* is doing in school? Could you give me an example?

Parent

27. Where do you feel that your own ideas about learning, school and how children develop come from?
28. What was your school and education like? How do you feel your own experience influenced *Steven*'s learning? →*no qualifications*.
29. How has your family's financial and job situation influenced the kind of support you can provide for *Steven*'s learning? Could you give me an example? →*separation*.
30. How have other people (e.g., friends, extended family, community, religious group) supported you with bringing up *Steven*? Has this helped *Steven*'s education and learning now and when he was younger?
31. Do you think there are things that happened in your life that have influenced how well *Steven* has done in school, that we haven't talked about? Can you tell me about some of these things? →*separation*.

Future

32. What kind of qualifications would you like *Steven* to have? Do you think he will achieve that? Why? →*university*.
33. What kind of job would you like *Steven* to have? Do you think he will achieve that? Why?
34. What do you feel that you as a parent can do to help him achieve this future?

Appendix 3   Example of personalized teacher interview

Semi-Structured Teacher Telephone Interview

Name student: Steven
  Name teacher: Ms X
  Class/subject: Science Y10
  Interview date: 26–5–2009 18:30
  Name interviewer: A.Y.M.

ABOUT Steven

1. How is Steven achieving in school? Do you feel that perhaps he is doing better or less well than you'd expect? Why do you think that is?
2. What kind of particular learning strategies does Steven use and how effective do you think these are for him? Can you give me an example?
3. What do you feel that you as a teacher can do for Steven to help him with school and his future? Can you give me an example?
4. How do you feel Steven's learning is influenced by his peers? Can you give me an example?
5. What do you think about the way Steven is supported by his family? Can you give me an example?
6. Could you describe the educational future you see for Steven? Why do you think that is?

Appendix 4 Example of a CFCS retrograph based on longitudinal EPPSE data

Section A: Shown to family
Name student: **Steven P.**
ID number: xxxx

Year	1994	1995	1996	1997	1998	1999	2000	2001	2002	2003	2004	2005	2006	2007	2008	2009
Age	0	1	2	3	4	5	6	7	8	9	10	11	12	13	14	15
School						Reception	Y1	Y2	Y3	Y4	Y5	Y6	Y7	Y8	Y9	Y10

KEY STAGE 1   KEY STAGE 2   KS3 >

Silver Play-group
12.5 hrs/wk

Happy Park EYC
25 hrs/wk

Prior Preston Primary School
- Reading difficulties (dyslexia)
- Hearing difficulties
- Likes English, Maths, Science, Art & PE
- Sports outside of school (swimming?) & tap dance

Tuttons Primary School
- Tap dance

Raynes School Language College
- Excellent at Maths, Science, ICT, Art, Modern Languages

Birth date: 7-7-1994

Family:
Mum
1 Older sister

Section B: Only for researcher, not shown to family

Reading ■
Maths ■

130
120
110
100
90

Y1   Y2   Y5   Y6   Y9

- Birth weight: 3,520 g. (on time & no complication)
- English speaking & white UK
- HLE = 2 (low)
- Parents (married): no qualifications
- Dad part time (postman); mum not working

ECERS-E top 20%

- Glue ear; hospital, hearing difficulties; speech therapist; bereavement
- Mum works part time (12 hrs) as a cleaner
- Flat, owner occupied, feels fairly safe; some contact with neighbours.
- Y5: Likes school and teachers
- School: E= +1sd; Sc+M= within 1sd of mean

- Listen to Steven read
- Physical activities
- Moved house
- Hospital & physiotherapist
- No SEN
- School: E+Sc+M= within 1sd of mean

- Parents separated (conflict & violence); mum works 31 hrs cleaning
- Mum happy with school
- Y9: feels good at school; no mentor; help with homework

Appendix 5   Family demographics during
           pre-school years, primary years
           and secondary years

Group1: low SES, high attainment

| | | | Pre-school period | | | | | |
| | | Qualifications of parents | | Parents' employment | | Family social class | | |
Name	Early HLE[1]	Mother	Father	Mother	Father		Key Stage 1	Key Stage 2
Girls Charley	1	Low	None	None	Part-time	Full-time	Semi-skilled	Semi-skilled	Semi-skilled
Natalie	1	Low	None	–	Not working	–	Never worked	Professional	Professional
Tanya	1	Low	None	–	Part-time	–	Unskilled	Unskilled	Semi-skilled
Sharlene	2	Low	None	None	Full-time	Not employed	Semi-skilled	Unemployed	Semi-skilled
Reanna	2	Low	None	None	Full-time	Full-time	Semi-skilled	Non-manual skilled	Non-manual skilled
Anjali	3	Medium	16 academic[2]	16 academic	Part-time	Full-time	Semi-skilled	Professional	Professional
Ife	3	Medium	Degree	–	Not working	–	Semi-skilled	Non-manual skilled	Professional
Leanna	4	High	Vocational	–	Not working	–	Semi-skilled	Unemployed	Semi-skilled
Brenda	4	High	16 academic	None	Not working	Full-time	Semi-skilled	Semi-skilled	Semi-skilled
Shelly	4	High	None	None	Not working	Not employed	Semi-skilled	Non-manual skilled	Manual skilled
Martha	5	High	Vocational	–	Not working	–	Semi-skilled	Semi-skilled	Semi-skilled
Asya	4	High	None	–	Not working	–	Never worked	Unemployed	Unemployed
Boys Jarell	2	Low	16 academic	None	Full-time	Full-time	Semi-skilled	Non-manual skilled	Professional
Rajnish	2	Low	None	None	Not working	Part-time	Semi-skilled	Unskilled	Semi-skilled
Steven	2	Low	None	None	Not working	Part-time	Semi-skilled	Semi-skilled	Semi-skilled
Abdi	2	Low	18 academic	18 academic	Not working	Not employed	Never worked	Never worked	Never worked
Mark	3	Medium	16 academic	None	Not working	Full-time	Unskilled	Unemployed	Unemployed
Shaquille	4	High	16 academic	–	Part-time	–	Semi-skilled	Professional	Unemployed
Peter	4	High	16 academic	Vocational	Part-time	Full-time	Semi-skilled	Skilled manual	Manual skilled
Robert	4	High	Vocational	–	Full-time	–	Semi-skilled	Semi-skilled	Semi-skilled

[1] The early home learning environment (HLE) scale runs from 0 to 49; the frequency of each of the activities being coded on a scale of 0–7 (0 = *not occurring*, 7 = occurring *very frequently* (Melhuish, Phan, Sylva, Sammons, Siraj-Blatchford & Taggart, 2008); HLE 1=0–13; 2=14–19; 3=20–24; 4=25–32; 5=33–45. We refer to three patterns of early HLE: low early HLE (0–19 points), medium early HLE (20–24 points) and high early HLE (25–45 points).

[2] '16 [18] academic' signifies 'left school at 16 [18] with some academic qualifications'.

Group 2: low SES, predicted attainment

| | | Pre-school period | | | | Family social class | Key Stage 1 | Key Stage 2 |
| | | Qualifications of parents | | Parents' employment | | | | |
Name	Early HLE	Mother	Father	Mother	Father			
Girls								
Amina	1 Low	None	–	Not working	–	Never worked	Never worked	Never worked
Fareeda	4 High	16 academic	16 academic	Not working	Full-time	Semi-skilled	Semi-skilled	Manual skilled
Bunmi	4 High	None	–	Not working	–	Never worked	Never worked	Never worked
Ebun	4 High	None	–	Not working	–	Never worked	Never worked	Never worked
Susan	5 High	16 academic	–	Part-time	–	Semi-skilled	Unemployed	Unemployed
Edward	2 Low	16 academic	16 academic	Full-time	Full-time	Semi-skilled	Non-manual skilled	Professional
Boys								
Christopher	2 Low	None	Vocational	Not working	Full-time	Manual skilled	Manual skilled	Manual skilled
Patrick	2 Low	Vocational	Vocational	Not working	Self-employed	Manual skilled	Unemployed	Non-manual skilled
Ted	2 Low	None	–	Not working	–	Never worked	Never worked	Never worked
Harry	2 Low	None	None	Part-time	Full-time	Semi-skilled	Professional	Professional
Hamid	2 Low	16 academic	16 academic	Not working	Not employed	Never worked	Never worked	Never worked
Jamal	2 Low	16 academic	–	Not working	–	Semi-skilled	Unemployed	Non-manual skilled
Tremaine	2 Low	None	–	Not working	–	Semi-skilled	Unemployed	Professional
Tom	3 Medium	16 academic	None	Not working	Full-time	Semi-skilled	Manual skilled	Manual skilled
Richard	3 Medium	None	–	Not working	–	Never worked	Never worked	Never worked

Group 3: high SES, low attainment

| | Name | Early HLE | Qualifications of parents | | Parents' employment | | Family social class | |
			Mother	Father	Mother	Father	Key Stage 1	Key Stage 2
					Pre-school period			
Girls	Anna	3	Medium	Degree	18 academic	Self-employed	Self-employed	Professional	Professional
	Gimbya	3	Medium	Vocational	Vocational	Part-time	Part-time	Professional	Professional
	Ella	3	Medium	Vocational	18 academic	Part-time	Full-time	Professional	Professional
	Helena	4	High	Degree	Degree	Part-time	Full-time	Professional	Professional
	Laurie	4	High	18 academic	Vocational	Not working	Self-employed	Professional	Professional
	Marcy	5	High	Degree	18 academic	Part-time	Full-time	Professional	Professional
Boys	Sean	2	Low	16 academic	16 academic	Part-time	Full-time	Professional	Professional
	Subash	1	Low	None	16 academic	Full-time	Self-employed	Professional	Professional
	Alex	3	Medium	18 academic	18 academic	Full-time	Full-time	Professional	Professional

271

Group 4: high SES, predicted attainment

	Name	Early HLE	Pre-school period					Key Stage 1	Key Stage 2
			Qualifications of parents		Parents' employment		Family social class		
			Mother	Father	Mother	Father			
Girls	Breona	3	Medium	16 academic	–	Part-time	–	Professional	Professional	Professional
	Abby	5	High	Degree	18 academic	Part-time	Full-time	Professional	Professional	Professional
	Imogene	5	High	Degree	Degree	Self-employed	Full-time	Professional	Professional	Professional
Boys	Lucas	2	Low	Degree	Degree	Part-time	Full-time	Professional	Professional	Professional
	Benjamin	3	Medium	Degree	Degree	Part-time	Full-time	Professional	Professional	Professional
	Jason	3	Medium	Degree	16 academic	Full-time	Full-time	Professional	Professional	Professional

Appendix 6 Overview of child characteristics and pre-school characteristics

Group1: low SES, high attainment

| | Name | Birth weight[1] | Problems | | | Birth term[5] | Pre-school quality[6] | Primary school academic effectiveness[7] | |
			Health[2]	Development[3]	Behaviour[4]			English	Maths
Girls	Charley	–	0	3	3	Spring	Low	Below 1 sd of mean	Below 1 sd of mean
	Natalie	1	0	3	2	Spring	Medium	Within 1 sd of mean	Within 1 sd of mean
	Tanya	2	0	3	3	Summer	Medium	Within 1 sd of mean	Above 1 sd of mean
	Sharlene	–	0	3	3	Spring	High	Above 1 sd of mean	Above 1 sd of mean
	Reanna	2	2	3	3	Summer	Medium	Within 1 sd of mean	Within 1 sd of mean
	Anjali	1	0	3	3	Summer	High	Within 1 sd of mean	Within 1 sd of mean
	Ife	2	0	3	3	Autumn	Medium	Below 1 sd of mean	Below 1 sd of mean
	Leanna	1	0	3	3	Autumn	Medium	Above 1 sd of mean	Above 1 sd of mean
	Brenda	2	0	3	1	Summer	Medium	–	–
	Shelly	2	0	3	3	Spring	Medium	Within 1 sd of mean	Within 1 sd of mean
	Martha	1	1	3	3	Summer	Medium	Within 1 sd of mean	Within 1 sd of mean
	Asya	1	1	3	3	Summer	Home	Within 1 sd of mean	Within 1 sd of mean
Boys	Jarell	2	1	3	3	Summer	High	Within 1 sd of mean	Within 1 sd of mean
	Rajnish	1	0	3	3	Summer	Home	Within 1 sd of mean	Within 1 sd of mean
	Steven	2	1	1	3	Summer	High	Above 1 sd of mean	Within 1 sd of mean
	Abdi	2	0	3	3	Summer	High	Below 2 sd of mean	Below 1 sd of mean
	Mark	2	1	3	1	Summer	High	Within 1 sd of mean	Within 1 sd of mean
	Shaquille	2	1	3	3	Spring	Medium	–	–
	Peter	2	0	3	3	Autumn	Medium	Below 1 sd of mean	Below 1 sd of mean
	Robert	2	0	3	3	Spring	Medium	Within 1 sd of mean	Above 1 sd of mean

[1] Birth weight classification (Scott & Carran, 1989): 0= foetal infant, very low birth weight (<1,500 grams); 1= low birth weight (1,500–2,500 grams); normal birth weight (2,500 and above).

[2] 0 = no health problems; 1= 1 health problem; 2 = 2 health problems; 3= 3 or more health problems.

[3] 1= 1 developmental problem; 2 = 2 or more developmental problems; 3= no developmental problems.

[4] 1= 1 behavioural problem; 2 = 2 or more behavioural problems; 3= no behavioural problems.

[5] In almost all English local authorities the school year runs from September to July, which makes the oldest children in year groups those who were born during the Autumn term. Children who are Autumn born (September, October, November and December) more often attained the highest levels in their Key Stage 2 exams (33.9 per cent compared to 23.3 per cent) than the considerably younger Summer born children (May, June, July and August). The Effective Pre-School and Primary Education study (EPPE 3–11) also found indications that a possible consequence of this difference in cognitive performance was that younger children had a greater chance of being identified as having a special education needs (SEN) (Anders et al., 2010; Sammons et al., 2002b; Taggart et al., 2006; Sharp et al., 2009).

[6] The quality of pre-school settings was measured on the Early Childhood Environment Rating Scales (ECERS-R, see Harms, Clifford & Cryer, 1998; ECERS-E, see Sylva et al., 2003; Sylva et al., 2006).

[7] Using the analysis by Melhuish et al. (2006) that provided indicators of the academic effectiveness of all state primary schools in England from 2002 to 2004, EPPE 3–11 showed that pupils who attended an academically more effective primary school had significantly better outcomes for English and Maths, over and above child and family background (Sammons et al., 2008a, 2008b, 2008d).

Group 2: low SES, predicted attainment

		Problems					Primary school academic effectiveness	
Name	Birth weight	Health	Development	Behaviour	Birth term	Pre-school quality	English	Maths
Girls Amina	–	0	3	3	Autumn	High	Within 1 sd of mean	Within 1 sd of mean
Fareeda	2	0	3	3	Spring	High	Within 1 sd of mean	Within 1 sd of mean
Bunmi	1	0	3	3	Summer	Medium	Within 1 sd of mean	Above 1 sd of mean
Ebun	0	0	3	3	Summer	Medium	Within 1 sd of mean	Above 1 sd of mean
Susan	0	0	3	3	Autumn	Medium	Within 1 sd of mean	Within 1 sd of mean
Boys Edward	2	1	3	3	Autumn	Medium	Above 1 sd of mean	Within 1 sd of mean
Christopher	2	0	3	1	Summer	Medium	Above 1 sd of mean	Above 1 sd of mean
Patrick	2	0	3	3	Summer	Low	Above 1 sd of mean	Within 1 sd of mean
Ted	2	2	3	3	Spring	Low	Within 1 sd of mean	Within 1 sd of mean
Harry	2	3	1	3	Spring	Low	Within 1 sd of mean	Below 1 sd of mean
Hamid	2	3	1	3	Summer	Low	Within 1 sd of mean	Within 1 sd of mean
Jamal	2	0	3	3	Spring	Medium	Within 1 sd of mean	Within 1 sd of mean
Tremaine	2	0	1	3	Autumn	High	Below 1 sd of mean	Below 1 sd of mean
Tom	2	1	3	3	Spring	Low	Within 1 sd of mean	Within 1 sd of mean
Richard	2	0	3	3	Autumn	Medium	Within 1 sd of mean	Above 1 sd of mean

Group 3: high SES, low attainment

Name	Birth weight	Problems			Birth term	Pre-school quality	Primary school academic effectiveness	
		Health	Development	Behaviour			English	Maths
Girls Anna	2	0	3	3	Autumn	Medium	Within 1 sd of mean	Within 1 sd of mean
Gimbya	1	0	3	3	Spring	Medium	Above 1 sd of mean	Within 1 sd of mean
Ella	2	0	3	1	Summer	Medium	Below 2 sd of mean	Within 1 sd of mean
Helena	2	0	3	3	Summer	Medium	Within 1 sd of mean	Within 1 sd of mean
Laurie	2	0	3	3	Summer	Medium	Within 1 sd of mean	Within 1 sd of mean
Marcy	2	0	3	3	Summer	High	Within 1 sd of mean	Above 1 sd of mean
Boys Sean	2	0	3	3	Summer	Medium	Within 1 sd of mean	Within 1 sd of mean
Subash	2	0	3	1	Summer	Medium	Within 1 sd of mean	Below 1 sd of mean
Alex	2	0	3	3	Summer	Medium	Above 1 sd of mean	Above 1 sd of mean

Group 4: high SES, predicted attainment

	Name	Birth weight	Problems			Birth term	Pre-school quality	Primary school academic effectiveness	
			Health	Development	Behaviour			English	Maths
Girls	Breona	0	0	3	3	Spring	Medium	Within 1 sd of mean	Below 1 sd of mean
	Abby	2	0	3	3	Spring	High	–	–
	Imogene	2	0	3	3	Spring	Medium	Above 1 sd of mean	Above 1 sd of mean
Boys	Lucas	2	0	3	3	Autumn	Medium	Within 1 sd of mean	Within 1 sd of mean
	Benjamin	2	0	3	3	Spring	Medium	Within 1 sd of mean	Within 1 sd of mean
	Jason	2	0	3	3	Spring	Medium	Within 1 sd of mean	Above 1 sd of mean

Appendix 7 Individual child trajectories for English and Maths

Group 1: low SES, high attainment

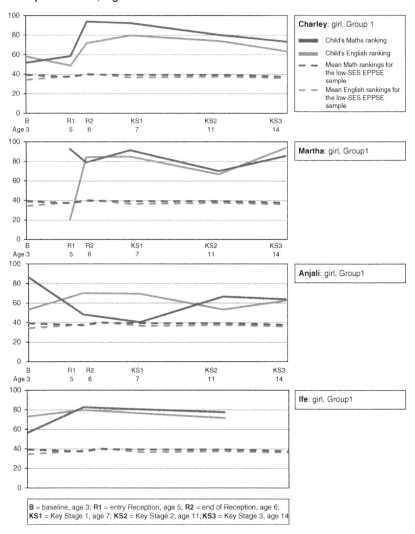

Charley: girl, Group 1

■ Child's Maths ranking

■ Child's English ranking

- - Mean Math rankings for the low-SES EPPSE sample

- - Mean English rankings for the low-SES EPPSE sample

Martha: girl, Group1

Anjali: girl, Group1

Ife: girl, Group1

B = baseline, age 3; **R1** = entry Reception, age 5; **R2** = end of Reception, age 6; **KS1** = Key Stage 1, age 7; **KS2** = Key Stage 2, age 11; **KS3** = Key Stage 3, age 14

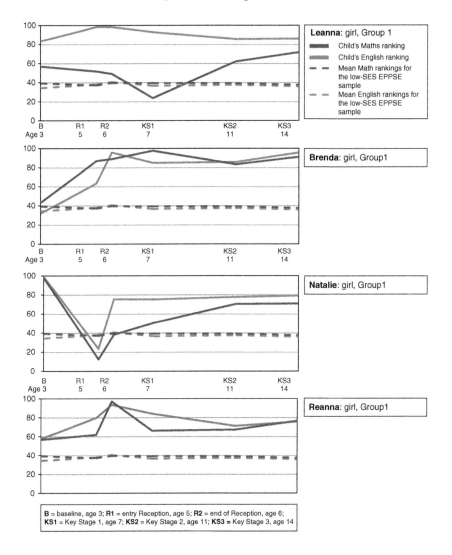

B = baseline, age 3; **R1** = entry Reception, age 5; **R2** = end of Reception, age 6;
KS1 = Key Stage 1, age 7; **KS2** = Key Stage 2, age 11; **KS3** = Key Stage 3, age 14

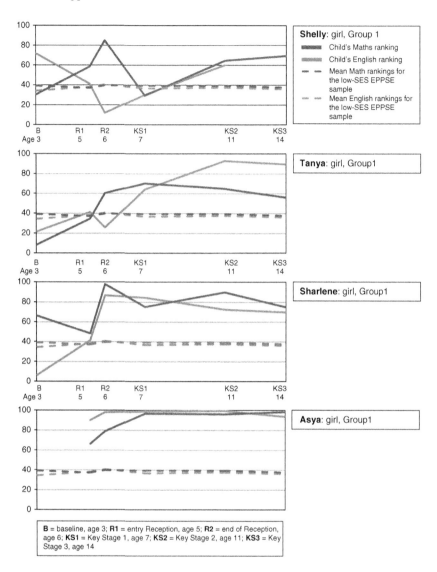

B = baseline, age 3; **R1** = entry Reception, age 5; **R2** = end of Reception, age 6; **KS1** = Key Stage 1, age 7; **KS2** = Key Stage 2, age 11; **KS3** = Key Stage 3, age 14

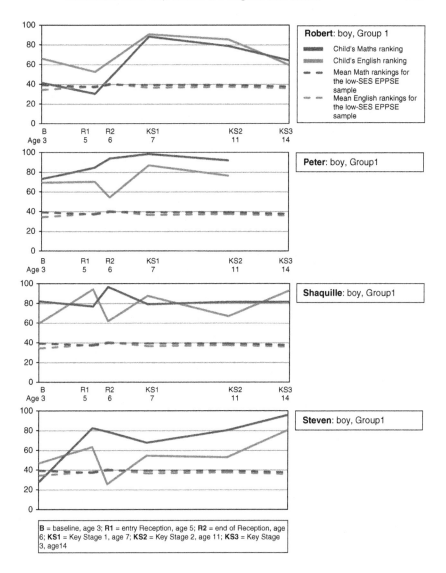

B = baseline, age 3; R1 = entry Reception, age 5; R2 = end of Reception, age 6; KS1 = Key Stage 1, age 7; KS2 = Key Stage 2, age 11; KS3 = Key Stage 3, age14

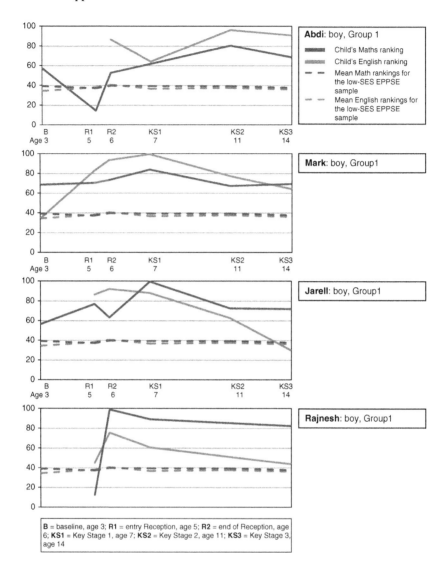

Abdi: boy, Group 1

Child's Maths ranking
Child's English ranking
Mean Math rankings for the low-SES EPPSE sample
Mean English rankings for the low-SES EPPSE sample

Mark: boy, Group1

Jarell: boy, Group1

Rajnesh: boy, Group1

B = baseline, age 3; **R1** = entry Reception, age 5; **R2** = end of Reception, age 6; **KS1** = Key Stage 1, age 7; **KS2** = Key Stage 2, age 11; **KS3** = Key Stage 3, age 14

Group 2: low SES, predicted attainment

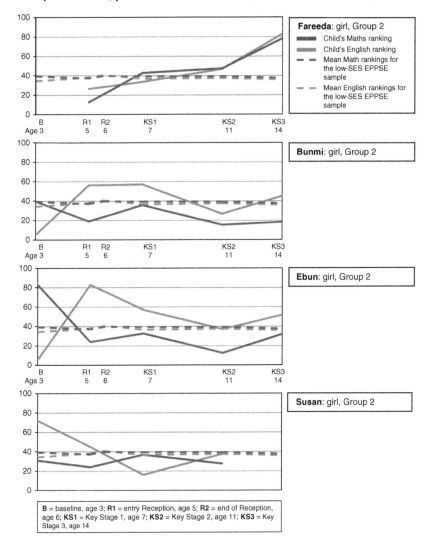

B = baseline, age 3; **R1** = entry Reception, age 5; **R2** = end of Reception, age 6; **KS1** = Key Stage 1, age 7; **KS2** = Key Stage 2, age 11; **KS3** = Key Stage 3, age 14

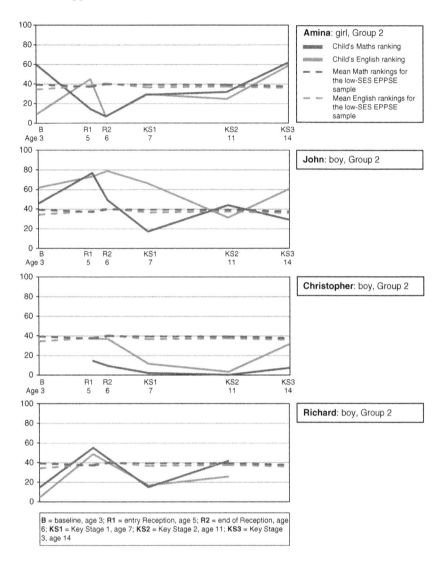

Amina: girl, Group 2

- Child's Maths ranking
- Child's English ranking
- Mean Math rankings for the low-SES EPPSE sample
- Mean English rankings for the low-SES EPPSE sample

John: boy, Group 2

Christopher: boy, Group 2

Richard: boy, Group 2

B = baseline, age 3; **R1** = entry Reception, age 5; **R2** = end of Reception, age 6; **KS1** = Key Stage 1, age 7; **KS2** = Key Stage 2, age 11; **KS3** = Key Stage 3, age 14

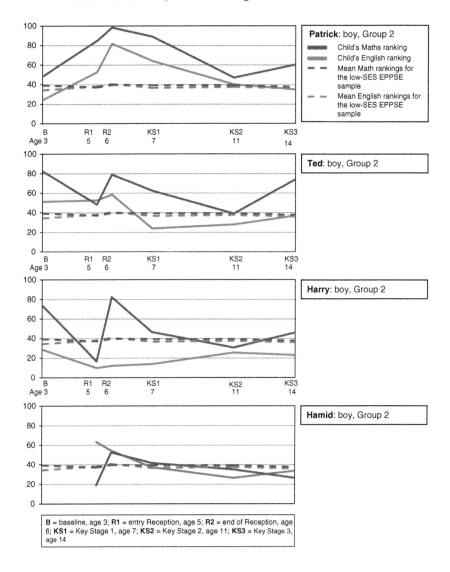

B = baseline, age 3; **R1** = entry Reception, age 5; **R2** = end of Reception, age 6; **KS1** = Key Stage 1, age 7; **KS2** = Key Stage 2, age 11; **KS3** = Key Stage 3, age 14

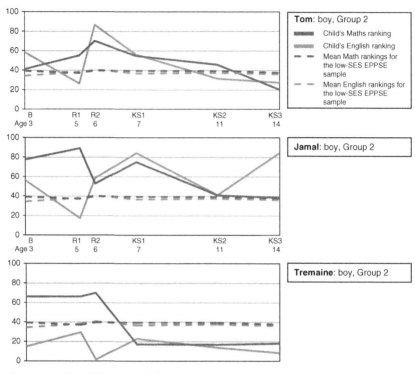

Group 3: high SES, low attainment

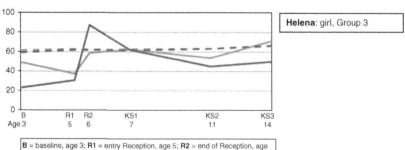

B = baseline, age 3; R1 = entry Reception, age 5; R2 = end of Reception, age 6; KS1 = Key Stage 1, age 7; KS2 = Key Stage 2, age 11; KS3 = Key Stage 3, age 14

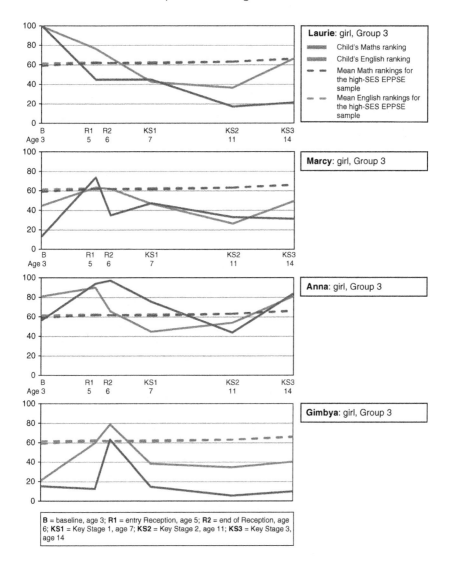

B = baseline, age 3; R1 = entry Reception, age 5; R2 = end of Reception, age 6; KS1 = Key Stage 1, age 7; KS2 = Key Stage 2, age 11; KS3 = Key Stage 3, age 14

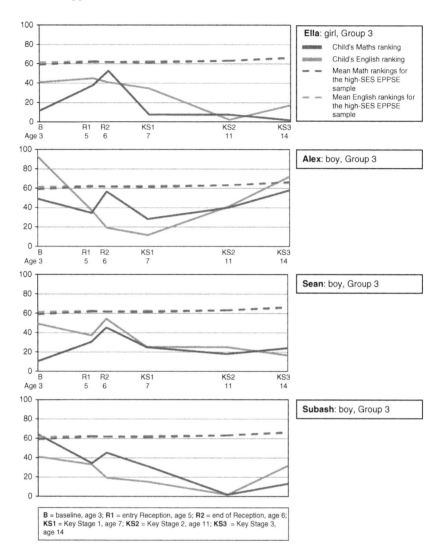

Ella: girl, Group 3

Child's Maths ranking

Child's English ranking

Mean Math rankings for the high-SES EPPSE sample

Mean English rankings for the high-SES EPPSE sample

Alex: boy, Group 3

Sean: boy, Group 3

Subash: boy, Group 3

B = baseline, age 3; **R1** = entry Reception, age 5; **R2** = end of Reception, age 6; **KS1** = Key Stage 1, age 7; **KS2** = Key Stage 2, age 11; **KS3** = Key Stage 3, age 14

Group 4: high SES, predicted attainment

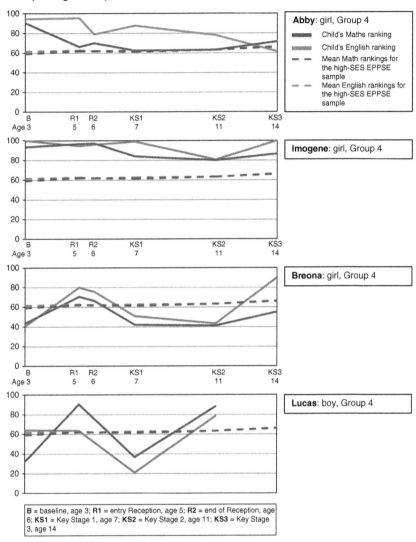

B = baseline, age 3; **R1** = entry Reception, age 5; **R2** = end of Reception, age 6; **KS1** = Key Stage 1, age 7; **KS2** = Key Stage 2, age 11; **KS3** = Key Stage 3, age 14

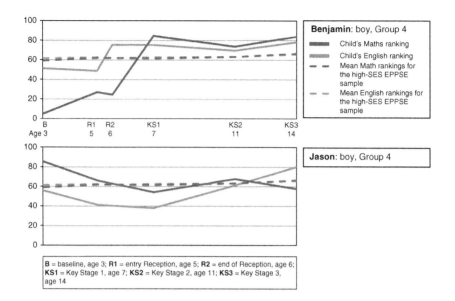

B = baseline, age 3; **R1** = entry Reception, age 5; **R2** = end of Reception, age 6; **KS1** = Key Stage 1, age 7; **KS2** = Key Stage 2, age 11; **KS3** = Key Stage 3, age 14

Appendix 8   Glossary of terms

Age-standardized scores	Assessment scores that have been adjusted to take account of the child's age at testing. This enables a comparison to be made between the performance of an individual student, relative to a representative sample of children in the same age group throughout the country or, in this case, the relative achievement of the EPPE sample.
Baseline measures	Assessments taken by the EPPE child at entry to the study. These assessment scores are subsequently employed as prior attainment measures in a value-added analysis of students' cognitive progress.
Birth weight	Babies born weighing 2,500 grams (5lb 8oz) or less are defined as below normal birth weight, foetal infant classification is 1,000 grams and below, very low birth weight is classified as 1,001–1,500 grams, and low birth weight is classified as 1,501–2,500 grams (Scott and Carran, 1989).
British Ability Scales (BAS)	This is a battery of assessments specially developed by NFER-Nelson to assess very young children's abilities. The assessments used at entry to the EPPE study and entry to Reception were:

> Block building – Visual-perceptual matching, especially in spatial orientation (entry to EPPE study only);
> Naming vocabulary – Expressive language and knowledge of names;

Pattern construction – Non-verbal reasoning and spatial visualization (entry to Reception only);

Picture similarities – Non-verbal reasoning;

Early number concepts – Knowledge of, and problem solving using, pre-numerical and numerical concepts (entry to Reception only);

Copying – Visual–perceptual matching and fine-motor co-ordination. Used specifically for children without English;

Verbal comprehension – Receptive language, understanding of oral instructions involving basic language concepts.

Centre/School level variance — The proportion of variance in a particular child outcome measure (e.g., pre-reading scores at start of primary school) attributable to differences between individual centres/schools rather than differences between individual children.

Child background factors — Child background characteristics such as age, birth weight, gender, ethnicity.

Caregiver Interaction Scale (CIS) — This scale (Arnett, 1989) of adult–child interaction was completed after a sustained period of observation with twenty-six items forming four sub-scales: 'Positive relationships', 'Permissiveness', 'Punitiveness' and 'Detachment'. 'Positive relationships' identifies favourable aspects of adult–child interaction whereas the other three sub-scales represent unfavourable aspects.

Contextualized models — Cross-sectional multilevel models exploring children's cognitive attainment at entry to primary school, controlling for child, parent and home learning environment (HLE) characteristics (but not prior attainment).

Controlling for	Several variables may influence an outcome and these variables may themselves be associated. Multilevel statistical analyses can calculate the influence of one variable upon an outcome having allowed for the effects of other variables. When this is done the net effect of a variable upon an outcome controlling for other variables can be established.
Correlation	A correlation is a measure of statistical association between two measures (e.g., age and attainment) that ranges from $+1$ to -1.
Duration of pre-school	In terms of the value-added models, the duration of pre-school covers the time period between date of BAS assessment at entry to the EPPE study and entry to primary school. Note that the number of months of pre-school attended before the child entered the EPPE study is not included in this duration measure. A separate 'duration' measure of amount of time in pre-school prior to entering the study was tested, but was not found to be significant (note that this 'duration' measure is confounded with prior attainment). In the contextualized models, duration of pre-school refers to the time period between entry to the target pre-school and entry to primary school. These duration measures provide a crude indication of length of pre-school experience.
ECERS-R and ECERS-E	The Early Childhood Environment Rating Scale (ECERS-R) (Harms et al., 1998) is based on child-centred pedagogy, and also assesses resources for indoor and outdoor play. The rating scale developed in England (ECERS-E) (Sylva et al., 2003, 2006) was intended as a supplement to the ECERS-R, and was developed specially for the EPPE study, to reflect the Desirable Learning Outcomes (which have since been replaced by the Early Learning Goals), and more importantly the Curriculum Guidance for the Foundation Stage which at the time was in trial stage.

Educational effectiveness	Research design that seeks to explore the effectiveness of educational institutions in promoting a range of child/student outcomes (often academic measures) while controlling for the influence of intake differences in child/student characteristics (see Teddlie & Reynolds, 2000).
Effect sizes (ES)	Provide a measure of the strength of the relationships between different predictors and the child outcomes under study, usually measured in standard deviation units. For further discussion see Elliot and Sammons (2004).
Family factors	Examples of family factors are mother's qualifications, father's employment and family SES.
Hierarchical nature of the data	Data that clusters into pre-defined sub-groups or levels within a system (e.g., young children within pre-school centres/primary schools, within LAs).
Home learning environment (HLE) characteristics	Measures derived from reports from parents (at interview or using parent questionnaires) about what children do at home, for example playing with numbers and letters, singing songs and nursery rhymes.
Intervention study	A study in which researchers 'intervene' in the sample to control variables, e.g., control by setting the adult : child ratios in order to compare different specific ratios in different settings. EPPE is not an intervention study, in that it investigates naturally occurring variation in pre-school settings.
Intra-centre/school correlation	The intra-centre/school correlation measures the extent to which the scores of children in the same centre/school resemble each other as compared with those from children at different centres/schools. The intra-centre/school correlation provides an indication of the extent to which unexplained variance in children's progress (i.e., that not accounted for by prior attainment) may be attributed to differences between centres/schools. This gives an

	indication of possible variation in pre-school centre/school effectiveness.
Multiple disadvantage	Based on three child variables, six parent variables, and one related to the HLE, which were considered 'risk' indicators when looked at in isolation. A child's 'multiple disadvantage' was calculated by summing the number of indicators the child was at risk on.
Multilevel modelling	A methodology that allows data to be examined simultaneously at different levels within a system (e.g., young children within pre-school centres/ primary schools, within LAs), essentially an extension of multiple regression.
Multiple regression	A method of predicting outcome scores on the basis of the statistical relationship between observed outcome scores and one or more predictor variables.
Net effect	The unique contribution of a particular variable upon an outcome while other variables are controlled.
Pre-reading attainment	Composite formed by adding together the scores for phonological awareness (rhyme and alliteration) and letter recognition.
Prior attainment factors	Measures which describe students' achievement at the beginning of the phase or period under investigation (e.g., taken on entry to primary or secondary school or on entry to the EPPE study).
Quality of pre-school	Measures of pre-school centre quality collected through observational assessments (ECERS-R, ECERS-E and CIS), made by trained researchers.
Quality of teaching	Measures from Year 5 classroom observations using the IEO (Stipek) and COS-5 (Pianta) instruments.
Sampling profile/procedures	The EPPE sample was constructed by:

Five regions (six LAs) randomly selected around the country, but being representative of urban, rural, inner city areas;

	Pre-schools from each of the six types of target provision (nursery classes, nursery schools, local authority day nurseries, private day nurseries, playgroups and integrated centres) randomly selected across the region.
Significance level	Criteria for judging whether differences in scores between groups of children, schools or centres might have arisen by chance. The most common criterion is the 95 per cent level ($p < 0.05$) which can be expected to include the 'true' value in 95 out of 100 samples (i.e., the probability being one in twenty that a difference might have arisen by chance).
Social/behavioural development	A child's ability to 'socialize' with other adults and children, and their general behaviour to others measured by teachers'/pre-school staff ratings.
Socio-economic status (SES)	Parental occupation information was collected by means of a parental interview when children were recruited to the study. The Office of Population Census and Surveys' OPCS (1995) Classification of Occupations was used to classify mothers' and fathers' current employment into one of eight groups: professional (I), other professional non-manual (II), skilled non-manual (III), skilled manual (IV), semi-skilled manual (V), unskilled manual (VI), never worked (VII) and no response (VIII). Family SES was obtained by assigning the SES classification based on the parent with the higher occupational status.
Standard deviation (sd)	A measure of the spread around the mean in a distribution of numerical scores. In a normal distribution, 68 per cent of cases fall within one standard deviation of the mean and 95 per cent of cases fall within two standard deviations.
Total BAS score	By combining four of the BAS sub-scales (two verbal and two non-verbal), a General Cognitive Ability score or Total BAS score at entry to the study can be

	computed. This is a measure of overall cognitive ability.
Value-added models	Longitudinal multilevel models exploring children's cognitive progress, controlling for prior attainment and significant child, parent and HLE characteristics.
Value-added residuals (pre-school effectiveness)	Differences between predicted and actual results for pre-school centres (where predicted results are calculated using value-added models).
Value-added residuals (primary school academic effectiveness)	Differences between predicted and actual results for primary schools, measuring student progress across KS1 and KS2 (see Melhuish et al., 2006a, 2006b).

References

Aarts, R., Demir, S. & Vallen, T. (2011). Characteristics of academic language register occurring in caretaker–child interaction: development and validation of a coding scheme. *Language Learning: Journal of Applied Linguistics* 61 (4), 1173–1221.

Alexander Pan, B., Rowe, M.L., Singer, J.D. & Snow, C.E. (2005). Maternal correlates of growth in toddler vocabulary production in low-income families. *Child Development* 76 (4), 763–782.

Allatt, P. (1993). Becoming privileged: the role of family processes. In I. Bates & G. Riseborough (eds.), *Youth and inequality* (pp.139–159). Buckingham: Open University Press.

Anders, Y., Sammons, P., Taggart, B., Sylva, K., Melhuish, E. & Siraj-Blatchford, I. (2010). The influence of child, family, home factors and pre-school education on the identification of special educational needs at age 10. *British Educational Research Journal* 36 (3), 421–441.

Arnett, J. (1989). Caregivers in day care centres: does training matter? *Journal of Applied Developmental Psychology* 10, 541–552.

Arnold, D.H. & Doctoroff, G.L. (2003). The early education of socio-economically disadvantaged children. *Annual Review of Psychology* 54, 517–545.

Bandura, A. (1995). *Self-efficacy in changing societies.* Cambridge University Press.

Barron, B. (2006). Interest and self-sustained learning as catalysts of development: a learning ecology perspective. *Human Development* 49, 109–244.

Bennett, K.K., Weigel, D.J. & Martin, S.S. (2002). Children's acquisition of early literacy skills: examining family contributions. *Early Childhood Research Quarterly* 17 (3), 295–317.

Bennett, N., Wood, L. & Rogers, S. (1996). *Teaching through play: teachers' theories and classroom practices.* Milton Keynes: Open University Press.

Bernstein, B. (1971). *Class, codes and control.* Volume I. London: Paladin. (1975). *Class, codes and control.* Volume III: *Towards a theory of educational transmissions.* London: Routledge and Kegan Paul.

Bodovski, K. (2011). Parental practices and educational achievement: social class, race, and habitus. *British Journal of Sociology of Education* 31 (2), 139–156.

Bodovski, K. & Farkas, G. (2008). 'Concerted cultivation' and unequal achievement in elementary school. *Social Science Research* 37 (3), 903–919.

Bornstein, M.H., Haynes, M.O. & Painter, K.M. (1998). Sources of child vocabulary competence: a multivariate model. *Journal of Child Language* 25, 367–393.

Bourdieu, P. (1986). The forms of capital. In J.G. Richardson (ed.), *Handbook of theory and research for the sociology of education* (pp. 241–257). New York: Greenwood Press.

 (1987) What makes a social class: on the theoretical and practical existence of groups. *Berkeley Journal of Sociology* 32, 1–17.

Bourdieu, P. & Passeron, J. C., (1977). *Reproduction and education, culture and society*. London: Sage.

Bradley, R. (2002). Environment and parenting. In M.H. Bornstein (ed.), *Handbook of parenting* (2nd edn). Volume II: *Biology and ecology of parenting* (pp. 281–314). Hillsdale, NJ: Lawrence Erlbaum.

Bradley, R.H. & Corwyn, R.F. (2002). Socio-economic status and child development. *Annual Review of Psychology* 53, 371–399.

Bradley, R.H., Corwyn, R.F, Caldwell, B.M., Whiteside-Mansell, L., Wasserman, G.A. & Mink, I.T. (2000). Measuring the home environments of children in early adolescence. *Journal of Research on Adolescence* 10 (3), 247–288.

Bradley, R.H., Corwyn, R.F, Burchinal, M., Pipes McAdoo, H.P. & Garcia Coll, C. (2001). The home environments of children in the United States. Part II: Relations with behavioral development through age thirteen. *Child Development* 72, 1868–1886.

Bredekamp, V.S. & Copple, C. (1997). *Developmentally appropriate practice in early childhood programs*. Washington, DC: NAEYC.

Bronfenbrenner, U. (1979). *The ecology of human development: experiments by nature and design*. Cambridge, MA: Harvard University Press.

 (1993). The ecology of cognitive development: research models and fugitive findings. In R. Wozniak & K. Fisher (eds.), *Development in context: acting and thinking in specific environments* (pp. 3–44). Hillsdale, NJ: Lawrence Erlbaum.

 (1994). Ecological models of human development. In *International encyclopedia of education* (2nd edn, vol. III). Oxford: Elsevier.

 (1995). Developmental ecology through space and time: a future perspective. In P. Moen, G.H. Elder Jr & K. Lüscher (eds.), *Examining lives in context: perspectives on the ecology of human development* (pp. 619–648). Washington, DC: American Psychological Association.

 (1999). Environments of developmental perspective: theoretical and operational models. In S.L. Friedman & T.D. Wachs (eds.), *Measuring environments across the life span: emerging methods and concepts* (pp. 3–28). Washington, DC: American Psychological Association.

 (2005). *Making human beings human*. Thousand Oaks, CA: Sage.

Bronfenbrenner, U. & Ceci S.J. (1994). Nature–nurture reconceptualized in developmental perspective: a bioecological model. *Psychological Review* 101 (4), 568–586.

Bronfenbrenner, U. & Evans, G.W. (2000). Developmental science in the twenty-first century: emerging questions, theoretical models, research designs and empirical findings. *Social Development* 9 (1), 15–25.

Bronfenbrenner, U. & Morris, P.A. (2006). The ecology of developmental processes. In W. Damon & R.M. Lerner (eds.), *Handbook of child psychology* (6th edn). Volume I: *Theoretical models of human development* (pp. 793–828). New York: Wiley.

Brooks-Gunn, J. & Duncan, G.J. (1997). The effects of poverty on children. *Future of Children* 7, 55–71.

Brooks-Gunn, J. & Markman, L.B. (2005). The contribution of parenting to ethnic and racial gaps in school readiness. *Future of Children* 15 (1), 139–168.

Bunge, M. (1993). Realism and antirealism in social science. *Theory and Decision* 35 (3), 207–235.

Burchinal, M.R., Peisner-Feinberg, E., Pianta, R. & Howes, C. (2002). Development of academic skills from pre-school through second grade: family and classroom predictors of developmental trajectories. *Journal of School Psychology* 40 (5), 415–436.

Bursik, K. & Martin, T.A. (2006). Ego development and adolescent academic achievement. *Journal of Research on Adolescence* 16 (1), 1–18.

Bus, A.G.I., Ijzendoorn, M.H. & Pellegrini, A.D. (1995). Joint book reading makes for success in learning to read: a meta-analysis of inter-generational transmission of literacy. *Review of Educational Research* 65, 1–21.

Chen, Z. & Siegler, R.S. (2000). The great divide. *Monographs of the Society for Research in Child Development* 65 (2), 1–95.

Cicchetti, D. & Rogosch, F. A. (1996). Equifinality and multifinality in developmental psychopathology. *Development and Psychopathology* 8, 597–600.

Coleman, P.K. & Hildebrandt Karraker, K. (2000). Parenting self-efficacy among mothers of school-age children: conceptualization, measurement, and correlates. *Family Relations* 49 (1), 13–24.

Cook, T.D., Deng, Y. & Morgano, E. (2007). Friendship influences during early adolescence: the special role of friends' grade point average. *Journal of Research on Adolescence* 17 (2), 325–356.

Crawford, C., Dearden, L. & Meghir, C. (2007). *When you are born matters: the impact of date of birth on child cognitive outcomes in England*. London: The Institute for Fiscal Studies.

Creswell, J. (2003). *Research design: qualitative, quantitative and mixed-methods approaches*. Thousand Oaks, CA: Sage.

Darling, N. & Steinberg, L. (1993). Parenting style as context: an integrative model. *Psychological Bulletin* 113 (3), 487–496.

Dearing, E., McCartney, K., Weiss, H.B., Kreider, H. & Simpkins, S. (2004). The promotive effects of family educational involvement for low-income children's literacy. *Journal of School Psychology* 42, 445–460.

Dearing,E., Kreider, H., Simpkins, S. & Weiss, H.B. (2006). Family involvement in school and low-income children's literacy: longitudinal associations between and within families. *Journal of Educational Psychology* 98 (4), 653–664.

Department for Work and Pensions (2011a). *Households below average income: an analysis of the income distribution 1994/95–2009/10* (22nd edn). London: Department for Work and Pensions.

(2011b). *National statistics on households below average income (HBAI)*. Produced by the Department for Work and Pensions; released on 12 May 2011. http://research.dwp.gov.uk/asd/index.php?page=hbai

Desforges, C. & Abouchaar, A. (2003). *The impact of parental involvement, parental support and family education on pupil achievement and adjustment: a literature review*. Research Report 433. London: Department for Education and Skills.

Driessen, G. & Valkenberg, P. (2000). Islamic schools in the Netherlands: compromising between identity and quality? *British Journal of Religious Education* 23, 15–26.

Duursma, E., Romero-Contreras, S., Szuber, A., Proctor, P. & Snow, C.E. (2007). The role of home literacy and language environment on bilinguals' English and Spanish vocabulary development. *Applied Psycholinguistics* 28, 171–190.

Dweck, C.S. (1999). *Self-theories: their role in motivation, personality, and development*. Philadelphia, PA: The Psychology Press.

Eccles, J.S. & Harold, R.D. (1996). Family involvement in children's and adolescents' schooling. In A. Booth & J.F. Dunn (eds.) *Family-school links: how do they affect educational outcomes?* (pp. 3–34). Mahwah, NJ: Lawrence Erlbaum.

Elder, G.H., Jr (1974). *Children of the great depression*. University of Chicago Press.

(1998a). The life-course as developmental theory. *Child Development* 69 (1), 1–12.

(1998b). Life course and development. In W. Damon & R.M. Lerner (eds.), *Handbook of child psychology* (5th edn). Volume I: *Theoretical models of human development* (pp. 1–24). New York: Wiley.

Elliot, C., Smith, P. & McCulloch, K. (1996). *British Ability Scales, Second Edition (BAS II)*. Windsor: NFER-Nelson Publishing.

Elliot, K. & Sammons, P. (2004). Exploring the use of effect sizes to evaluate the impact of different influences on child outcomes. In K. Elliot & I. Schlagens (eds.), *What does it mean? The use of effect sizes in educational research*. Slough: NfER.

Epstein, J. L. (1992). School and family partnerships. In M. Aikin (ed.) *Encyclopedia of educational research* (6th edn) (pp. 1139–1151). New York: MacMillan.

Evans, G.W. & Rosenbaum, J. (2008). Self-regulation and the income-achievement gap. *Early Childhood Research Quarterly* 23 (4), 505–514.

Fan, X. & Chen, M. (2001). Parental involvement and students' academic achievement: a meta-analysis. *Educational Psychology Review* 13 (1), 1–22.

Fantuzzo, J., Tighe, E. & Childs, S. (2000). Family involvement questionnaire: a multivariate assessment of family involvement in early childhood education. *Journal of Educational Psychology* 92 (2), 367–376.

Fantuzzo, J., McWayne, C., Perry, M.A. & Childs, S. (2004). Multiple dimensions of family involvement and their relations to behavioural and learning competencies for urban, low-income children. *School Psychology Review* 33 (4), 467–480.

Feinstein, L., Duckworth, K. & Sabates, R. (2008). *Education and the family: passing success across the generations*. London: Routledge.

Fischer, K.W. & Bidell, T.R. (1998). Dynamic development of psychological structures in action and thought. In W. Damon & R.M. Lerner (eds.), *Handbook of child psychology* (5th edn). Volume I: *Theoretical models of human development* (pp. 467–561). New York: Wiley.

Forget-Dubois, N., Dionne,G., Lemelin, P., Perusse, D., Tremblay, R.E. & Boivin, M. (2009). Early child language mediates the relationship between home environment and school readiness. *Child Development* 80 (3), 736–749.

Foster, M.A., Lambert, R., Abbott-Shim, M., McCarty F. & Franze, S. (2005). A model of home learning environment and social risk factors in relation to children's emergent literacy and social outcomes. *Early Childhood Research Quarterly* 20 (1), 13–36.

Fuchs, S. (2001). *Against essentialism*. University of Chicago Press.

Furlong, J. (2003). *BERA at 30: have we come of age?* Presidential address to the annual conference of the British Educational Research Association, Heriot Watt University, Edinburgh, UK.

Gauvain, M. (1998). Cognitive development in social and cultural context. *Current Directions in Psychological Science* 7 (6), 188–192.

(2001). *The social context of cognitive development*. New York: Guilford.

Geertz, C. (1979). From the native's point of view: on the nature of anthropological understanding. In P. Rabinow & W. Sullivan (eds.), *Interpretative social science* (pp. 225–241). Berkeley: University of California Press.

Goodman, R. (1997). The Strengths and Difficulties Questionnaire: a research note. *Journal of Child Psychology & Psychiatry* 38, 581–586.

Gorard, S. & Taylor, C. (2004). *Combining methods in educational and social research*. London: Open University Press.

Gottlieb, G. (2001). The relevance of developmental-psychobiological metatheory to developmental neuropsychology. *Developmental Neuropsychology* 19 (1), 1–9.

(2002). Developmental-behavioral initiation of evolutionary change. *Psychological Review* 109 (2), 211–218.

Green, C.L., Walker, J.M.T., Hoover-Dempsey, K.V. & Sandler, H.M. (2007). Parents' motivations for involvement in children's education: an empirical test of a theoretical model of parental involvement. *Journal of Educational Psychology* 99 (3), 532–544.

Greene, J. (2005). The generative potential of mixed-methods enquiry. *International Journal of Research and Method in Education* 28 (2), 207–211.

Greene, J. & Caracelli, V. (eds.) (1997). *Advances in mixed-method evaluation: the challenges and benefits of integrating diverse paradigms*. New directions for evaluation, 74. San Francisco: Jossey-Bass.

(2003). Making paradigmatic sense of mixed-methods inquiry. In A. Tashakkori & C. Teddlie (eds.), *Handbook of mixed methods in social and behavioral research*. Thousand Oaks, CA: Sage.

Greene, M.L. & Way, N. (2005). Self-esteem trajectories among ethnic minority adolescents: a growth curve analysis of the patterns and predictors of change. *Journal of Research on Adolescence* 15 (2), 151–178.

Greenfield, P.M. (2002). The mutual definition of culture and biology in development. In H. Keller, Y.H. Poortinga & A. Schoelmerich (eds.), *Between culture and biology*. Cambridge University Press.

Greenfield, P.M., Keller, H., Fuligni, A. & Maynard, A. (2003). Cultural pathways through universal development. *Annual Review of Psychology* 54, 461–490.

Griswold, W., McDonnell, T. & Wright, N. (2005). Reading and the reading class in the twenty-first century. *Annual Review of Sociology* 31, 127–141.

Gunnar, M.R. & Cheatham, C.L. (2003). Brain and behavior interface: stress and the developing brain. *Infant Mental Health Journal* 24 (3), 195–211.

Hall, J., Sylva, K., Melhuish, E., Sammons, P., Siraj-Blatchford, I. & Taggart, B. (2009). The role of pre-school quality in promoting resilience in the cognitive development of young children. *Oxford Review of Education* 35 (3), 331–352.

Harkness, S. & Super, C.M. (1992). Parental ethnotheories in action. In I.E. Sigel, A.V. McGillicuddy-DeLisi & J.J. Goodnow (eds.), *Parental belief systems: the psychological consequences for children* (2nd edn) (pp. 393–414). Hillsdale, NJ: Lawrence Erlbaum.

   (1999). From parents' cultural belief systems to behavior. In L. Eldering & P.P.M. Leseman (eds.), *Effective early education: cross-cultural perspectives* (pp. 67–90). New York: Palmer Press.

Harkness, S., Super, C.M. & Van Tijen, N. (2000). Individualism and the "Western mind" reconsidered: American and Dutch parents' ethnotheories of the child. *New Directions of Child and Adolescent Development* 87, 23–40.

Harms, T., Clifford, M. & Cryer, D. (1998). *Early childhood environment rating scale, revised edition (ECERS-R)*. Vermont: Teachers College Press.

Harris, A., Clarke, P., James, S., Harris, B. & Gunraj, J. (2006). *Improving schools in difficulty*. London: Continuum Press.

Hart, B. & Risley, T.R. (1995). *Meaningful differences in everyday experiences of young American children*. Baltimore, MD: Paul H. Brooks Publishing.

Hatano, G. & Wertsch, J.V. (2001). Sociocultural approaches to cognitive development: the constitutions of culture in mind. *Human Development* 44 (2–3), 77–83.

Heckman, J.J. (2006). Skill formation and the economics of investing in disadvantaged children. *Science* 312 (5782), 1900–1902.

Henrichs, L.F. (2010). *Academic language in early childhood interactions: a longitudinal study of 3- to 6-year-old Dutch monolingual children*. Amsterdam, The Netherlands: Amsterdam Centre for Language and Communication.

Hill, N.E. & Tyson, D.F. (2009). Parental involvement in middle school: a meta-analytic assessment of the strategies that promote achievement. *Developmental Psychology* 45 (3), 740–763.

HMRC (2008). *Survey of personal income 2007–08*; www.hmrc.gov.uk/stats/income_distribution/3-1table-jan2010.pdf (accessed 10 December 2011).

Hoff, E. (2003). The specificity of environmental influence: socioeconomic status affects early vocabulary development via maternal speech. *Child Development* 74 (5), 1368–1378.

   (2006). How social contexts support and shape language development. *Developmental Review* 26, 55–88.

Hoff, E. & Tian, C. (2005). Socioeconomic status and cultural influences on language. *Journal of Communication Disorders* 38, 271–278.

Hoff, E., Laursen, B. & Tardif, T. (2002). Socioeconomic status and parenting. In M.H. Bornstein (ed.), *Handbook of parenting* (2nd edn). Volume II: *Ecology and biology of parenting* (pp. 161–188). Mahwah, NJ: Lawrence Erlbaum.

Hohmann, M. & Weikart, D.P. (1995). *Educating young children*. Michigan: High/Scope Educational Research Foundation.

Hoover-Dempsey, K.V. & Sandler, H.M. (1995). Parental involvement in children's education: why does it make a difference? *Teachers College Record* 95, 310–331.

   (1997). Why do parents become involved in their children's education? *Review of Educational Research* 67 (1), 3–42.

Hoover-Dempsey, K.V., Battiato, A.C., Walker, J.M.T., Reed, R.P., DeJong, J.M. & Jones, K.P. (2001). Parental involvement in homework. *Educational Psychologist* 36 (3), 195–209.

Jeynes, W.H. (2005). A meta-analysis of the relation of parental involvement to urban elementary school student academic achievement. *Urban Education* 40 (3), 237–269.

Ko, J. & Sammons, P. (2011). *Effective teaching: a review of research*. CfBT Education Trust.

Kohn, M.L. (1995). Social structure and personality through time and space. In P. Moen, G.H. Elder Jr & K. Lüscher (eds.), *Examining lives in context: perspectives on the ecology of human development* (pp. 141–169). Washington, DC: American Psychological Association.

Kohn, M.L. & Schooler, C. (1983). *Work and personality: an enquiry into the impact of social stratification*. Norwood, NJ: Ablex.

Kumpulainen, K. & Kaartinen, S. (2003). The interpersonal dynamics of collaborative reasoning in peer interactive dyads. *The Journal of Experimental Education* 21 (4), 333–370.

Laland, K.N., Odling-Smee, J. & Feldman, M.W. (2000). Niche construction, biological evolution, and cultural change. *Behavioral and Brain Sciences* 23, 131–175.

Landry, S.H., Smith, K.E. & Swank, P.R. (2003). The importance of parenting during early childhood for school-age development. *Developmental Neuropsychology* 24 (2–3), 559–591.

Lareau, A. (2003). *Unequal childhoods. Class, race, and family life*. London: University of California Press.

Lee, V.E., Loeb, S. & Lubeck, S. (1998). Contextual effects of pre-kindergarten classrooms for disadvantaged children on cognitive development: the case of chapter 1. *Child Development* 69 (2), 479–494.

Leseman, P.P.M. & van den Boom, D.C. (1999). Effects of quantity and quality of home proximal processes on Dutch, Surinamese-Dutch and Turkish-Dutch pre-schoolers' cognitive development. *Infant and Child Development* 8, 19–38.

Leseman, P.P.M., Scheele, A.F., Mayo, A.Y. & Messer, M.H. (2007). Home literacy as special language environment to prepare children for school. *Zeitschrift für Erziehungswissenschaft* 10 (3), 334–355.

Luthar, S.S., Cicchetti, D. & Becker, B. (2000). The construct of resilience: a critical evaluation and guidelines for future work. *Child Development* 71 (3), 543–562.

Marsh, H.W. (2006). *Self-concept theory, measurement and research into practice: the role of self-concept in educational psychology.* Leicester: The British Psychological Society.

Marsh, H.W., Smith, I.D. & Barnes, J. (1985). Multidimensional self-concepts: relations with sex and academic achievement. *Journal of Educational Psychology* 77, 581–596.

Matthews, P. & Sammons, P. (2004). *Improvement through inspection: an evaluation of the impact of Ofsted's work.* (HMI 2244). London: Ofsted. (2005). Survival of the weakest: the differential improvement of schools causing concern in England. *London Review of Education* 3 (2), 159–176.

Mayo, A.Y. & Leseman, P.P.M. (2008). Off to a good start? Vocabulary development and differences in early family and classroom experiences of children from native-Dutch and immigrant families in the Netherlands. *Educational and Child Psychology* 25 (3), 70–82.

McNeal, R.B. (2001). Differential effects of parental involvement on cognitive and behavioural outcomes by socioeconomic status. *Journal of Socio-Economics* 30, 171–179.

Melhuish, E. (2010). Why children, parents and home learning are important. In K. Sylva, E. Melhuish, P. Sammons, I. Siraj-Blatchford & B. Taggart (eds.), *Early childhood matters: evidence from the Effective Pre-school and Primary Education Project* (pp. 44–69). London: Routledge.

Melhuish, E., Sylva, K., Sammons, P., Siraj-Blatchford, I. & Taggart, B. (2001). *The Effective Provision of Pre-School Education (EPPE) project.* Technical paper 7: *Social/behavioural and cognitive development at 3–4 years in relation to family background.* London: DfES/Institute of Education, University of London.

Melhuish, E., Romaniuk, H., Sammons, P., Sylva, K., Siraj-Blatchford, I. & Taggart, B. (2006). *Effective Pre-school and Primary Education 3–11 project (EPPE 3–11): the effectiveness of primary schools in England in Key Stage 2 for 2002, 2003 and 2004. Full report.* Institute of Education, University of London.

Melhuish, E.C., Phan, M.B., Sylva, K., Sammons, P., Siraj-Blatchford, I. & Taggart B. (2008). Effects of the home learning environment and pre-school centre experience upon literacy and numeracy development in early primary school. *Journal of Social Issues* 64 (1), 95–114.

Melhuish, E., Sylva, K., Sammons, P., Siraj-Blatchford, I., Taggart, B. & Toth, K. (2011). *EPPSE Report on trajectories for literacy and numeracy – cohorts 1 to 4.* London: DfES/Institute of Education, University of London.

Mertens, D. (1999). Inclusive evaluation: implications of transformative theory for evaluation. *American Journal of Evaluation* 20 (1), 1–14.

Moen, P. & Erickson, M.A. (1995). Linked lives: a transgenerational approach to resilience. In P. Moen, G.H. Elder Jr & K. Lüscher (eds.), *Examining lives in context: perspectives on the ecology of human development* (pp. 169–210). Washington, DC: American Psychological Association.

Molfese, V.J., Modglin, A. & Molfese, D.L. (2003). The role of environment in the development of reading skills: a longitudinal study of pre-school and school-age measures. *Journal of Learning Disabilities* 36 (1), 59–67.

Moriarty, V. & Siraj-Blatchford, I. (1998). *An introduction to curriculum for 3 to 5 year olds.* Nottingham: Education Now Books.

Mortimore, P., Sammons, P., Stoll, L., Lewis, D. & Ecob, R. (1988). *School matters: the junior years*. Wells: Open Books.

Mounts, N. S. (2000). Parental management of adolescent peer relationships: what are its effects on friend selection? In K.A. Kerns, J.M. Contreras & A.M. Neal-Barnett (eds.), *Family and peers: linking two social worlds* (pp. 169–94). Westport, CT: Praeger.

Muijs, D., Harris, A., Chapman, C., Stoll, L. & Russ, J. (2004). Improving schools in socio-economically disadvantaged areas: a review of research. *School Effectiveness and School Improvement* 15 (2), 149–175.

NICHD/ECCRN (National Institute of Child Health and Human Development/ Early Child Care Research Network) (2002). The relation of global first-grade classroom environment to structural classroom features and teacher and student behaviors. *The Elementary School Journal* 102 (5), 367–387.

Niglas, K. (2001a). *Combining quantitative and qualitative inquiry in educational Research*. Dissertation submitted for the degree of Doctor of Philosophy. Tallinn Pedagogical University.

(2001b). *Paradigms and methodology in educational research*. Paper presented at the European Conference on Educational Research, Lille, 5–8 September 2001. www.leeds.ac.uk/educol/documents/00001840.htm

Oakley, A. (2004). The researcher's agenda for evidence. *Evaluation and Research in Education* 18 (1–2), 12–27.

Ofsted (2000). *Improving city schools*. London: Ofsted.

(2009). *Twelve outstanding secondary schools excelling against the odds*. London: Ofsted.

Okagaki, L. & French, P.A. (1998). Parenting and children's school achievement: a perspective. *American Educational Research Journal* 35 (1), 123–144.

Okagaki, L. & Sternberg, R.J. (1993). Parental beliefs and children's school performance. *Child Development* 64, 36–56.

Palacios, J., Gonzales, M. & Moreno, M. (1992). Stimulating the child in the zone of proximal development: the role of parents' ideas. In I.E. Sigel, A.V. McGillicuddy-DeLisi & J.J. Goodnow (eds.), *Parental belief systems: the psychological consequences for children* (2nd edn) (pp. 71–94). Hillsdale, NJ: Lawrence Erlbaum.

Parke, R.D. (2004). Development in the family. *Annual Review of Psychology* 55, 365–399.

Pianta, R.C., La Paro, K.M., Payne, C., Cox, M.J. & Bradley, R. (2002). The relation of kindergarten classroom environment to teacher, family, and school characteristics and child outcomes. *The Elementary School Journal* 102 (3), 226–238.

Raviv, T., Kessenich, M. & Morisson, F.J. (2004). A mediational model of the association between socioeconomic status and 3-year-old language abilities: the role of parenting factors. *Early Childhood Research Quarterly* 19, 528–547.

Reynolds, T. (2006a). Caribbean young people, family relationships and social capital. *Journal of Ethnic and Racial Studies* 29 (6) (Special issue: Social capital, migration and transnational families), 1087–1103.

(2006b). Family and community networks in the (re)making of ethnic identity of Caribbean young people in Britain. *Community, Work and Family* 9 (3), 273–290.

Rogoff, B. (1993). Children's guided participation and participatory appropriation in sociocultural activity. In R.H. Wozniak & K.W. Fischer (eds.), *Development in context: acting and thinking in specific environments* (pp.121–153). Hillsdale, NJ: Lawrence Erlbaum.

(1998). *Cognition as a collaborative process*. In B. Damon, D. Kuhn & R.S. Siegler (eds.), *Handbook of child psychology* (5th edn). Volume 2: *Cognition, perception and language* (pp. 679–744). New York: Wiley.

(2003). *The cultural nature of human development*. New York: Oxford University Press.

Rogoff, B. & Toma, C. (1997). Shared thinking: community and institutional variations. *Discourse Processes* 23 (3), 965–980.

Rogoff, B., Baker-Smith, J., Lacasa, P. & Goldsmith, D. (1995). Development through participation in sociocultural activity. *New Directions for Child Development* 67, 45–65.

Rogoff, B., Paradise, R., Mejía Arauz, R., Correa- Chávez, M. & Angelillo, C. (2003). Firsthand learning through intent participation. *Annual Review of Psychology* 54, 175–203.

Rutter, M. (1987). Psychosocial resilience and protective mechanisms. *American Journal of Orthopsychiatry* 57, 316–331.

(2007). Resilience, competence, and coping. *Child Abuse & Neglect* 31, 205–209.

Sammons, P. (2007). *School effectiveness and equity: making connections*. Reading: CfBT Education Trust.

(2010a). Does pre-school make a difference? Identifying the impact of pre-school on children's cognitive and social behavioural development. In K. Sylva, E. Melhuish, P. Sammons, I. Siraj-Blatchford & B. Taggart (eds.), *Early childhood matters: evidence from the Effective Pre-school and Primary Education project* (pp. 92–113). London: Routledge, Taylor and Francis Group.

(2010b). Do the benefits of pre-school last? Investigating pupil outcomes to the end of Key Stage 2 (aged 11). In K Sylva, E. Melhuish, P. Sammons, I. Siraj-Blatchford & B. Taggart (eds.), *Early childhood matters: evidence from the Effective Pre-school and Primary Education project*. London: Routledge, Taylor and Francis Group.

Sammons, P., Sylva, K., Melhuish, E., Siraj-Blatchford, I., Taggart, B. & Elliot, K. (2002a). *The Effective Provision of Pre-School Education (EPPE) project*. Technical paper 8a: *Measuring the impact of pre-school on children's cognitive progress over the pre-school period*. London: DfES/Institute of Education, University of London.

Sammons, P., Smees, R., Taggart, B., Sylva, K., Melhuish, E. C., Siraj-Blatchford, I. & Elliot, K. (2002b). *The Early Years Transition and Special Educational Needs (EYTSEN) project*. Technical paper 1: *Special needs across the pre-school period*. London: DfES/Institute of Education, University of London.

Sammons, P., Taggart, B., Smees, R., Sylva, K., Melhuish, E., Siraj-Blatchford, I. & Elliot, K. (2003). *The Early Years Transition and Special Educational Needs (EYTSEN) project*. DfES research report 431. Nottingham: DfES Publications.

Sammons, P., Elliot, K., Sylva, K., Melhuish, E., Siraj-Blatchford, I. & Taggart, B. (2004). The impact of pre-school on young children's cognitive attainments at entry to reception. *British Education Research Journal* 30 (5), 691–712.

Sammons, P., Siraj-Blatchford, I., Sylva, K., Melhuish, E., Taggart, B. & Elliot, K. (2005). Investigating the effects of pre-school provision: using mixed methods in the EPPE research. *International Journal of Social Research Methodology* 8 (3) (special issue on mixed methods in educational research), 207–224.

Sammons, P., Sylva, K., Melhuish, E., Siraj-Blatchford, I., Taggart, B. & Hunt, S. (2008a). *The Effective Pre-School and Primary Education 3–11 project (EPPE 3–11): influences on children's attainment and progress in Key Stage 2: cognitive outcomes in Year 6.* London: DCSF/Institute of Education, University of London.

Sammons, P., Sylva, K., Melhuish, E., Siraj-Blatchford, I., Taggart, B. & Jelicic, H. (2008b). *The Effective Pre-School and Primary Education 3–11 project (EPPE 3–11): influences on children's attainment and progress in Key Stage 2: social/behavioural outcomes in Year 6.* London: DCSF/Institute of Education, University of London.

Sammons, P., Sylva, K., Melhuish, E., Siraj-Blatchford, I., Taggart, B., Barreau, S. & Grabbe, Y. (2008c). *The Effective Pre-School and Primary Education 3–11 project (EPPE 3–11): the influence of school and teaching quality on children's progress in primary school.* London: DCSF/Institute of Education, University of London.

Sammons, P., Anders, Y., Sylva, K., Melhuish, E., Siraj-Blatchford, I., Taggart, B. & Barreau, S. (2008d). Children's cognitive attainment and progress in English primary schools during Key Stage 2: investigating the potential continuing influences of pre-school education. *Zeitschrift für Erziehungswissenschaften* 10 (11), 179–198.

Sammons, P., Sylva, K., Melhuish, E., Siraj-Blatchford, I., Taggart, B., Toth, K., Draghici, D. & Smees, R. (2012a). *Effective Pre-School, Primary and Secondary Education project (EPPSE 3–14): influences on students' attainment and progress in Key Stage 3: academic outcomes in English, Maths and science in Year 9.* DfE RB 184a. London: Department for Education.

Sammons, P., Sylva, K., Melhuish, E., Siraj-Blatchford, I., Taggart, B., Draghici, D., Smees, R. & Toth, K. (2012b). *Effective Pre-School, Primary and Secondary Education project (EPPSE 3–14): influences on students' development in Key Stage 3: social–behavioural outcomes in Year 9.* DfE RB 184b. London: Department for Education.

Sampson, W.A. (2007). *Race, class, and family intervention. Engaging parents and families for academic success.* Maryland: Rowman & Littlefield Education.

Sanders, W.L. (1998). Value-added assessment. *The School Administrator* 55 (11), 30–32.

Savage, M. (2007). Changing social class identities in post-war Britain: perspectives from mass-observation. *Sociological Research Online* 12 (3); www.socresonline.org.uk/12/3/6.html (Accessed December 2011).

Scheerens, J. & Bosker, R. (1997). *The foundations of educational effectiveness.* Oxford: Pergamon.

Schoon, I. (2001). Teenage job aspirations and career attainment in adulthood: a 17-year follow-up study of teenagers who aspired to become scientists, health professionals, or engineers. *International Journal of Behavioural Development* 25 (2), 124–132.

(2006). *Risk and Resilience: adaptations in changing times.* Cambridge University Press.

Schweinhart, L.J. & Weikart, D.P. (1997). The High/Scope pre-school curriculum comparison through age 23. *Early Childhood Research Quarterly* 12, 117–143.

Scott, D. (2007). Resolving the quantitative-qualitative dilemma: a critical realist approach. *International Journal of Research & Method in Education* 30 (1), 3–17.

Scott, K. & Carran, D. (1989). Identification and referral of handicapped infants. In M.C. Wang, M.C. Reynolds & H.J. Walberg (eds.), *Handbook of special education research and practice.* Volume III: *Low incidence conditions* (pp. 227–241). Oxford: Pergamon Press.

Sharp, C., George, N., Sargent, C., O'Donnell, S. & Heron, M. (2009). *International thematic probe: the influence of relative age on learner attainment and development.* Slough: National Foundation for Educational Research.

Sheldon, S.B. & Epstein, J.L. (2005). Involvement counts: family and community partnerships and mathematics achievement. *The Journal of Educational Research* 98 (4), 196–206.

Sigel, I.E. (1992). The belief-behavior connection: a resolvable dilemma? In I.E. Sigel, A.V. McGillicuddy-DeLisi & J.J. Goodnow (eds.), *Parental belief systems: the psychological consequences for children* (2nd edition) (pp. 433–455). Hillsdale, NJ: Lawrence Erlbaum.

Siraj-Blatchford, I. (2010a). Learning in the home and at school: how working-class children 'succeed against the odds'. *British Educational Research Journal* 36 (3), 463–428.

(2010b). Mixing methods in early childhood research: moving beyond the quantitative, qualitative divide. In G. MacNaughton, S. Rolfe and I. Siraj-Blatchford (eds.), *Doing early childhood research: international perspectives on theory and practice* (2nd edn) (pp. 193–208). Sydney: Allen & Unwin; Buckingham and Philadelphia: Open University Press.

Siraj-Blatchford, I. & Mayo, A.Y. (eds.) (2012). *Early childhood education.* Sage library of educational thought and practice. London: Sage.

Siraj-Blatchford, I. & Siraj-Blatchford, J. (2009). *Improving children's attainment through a better quality of family-based support for early learning.* Early Years Knowledge Review 2. London: Centre for Excellence and Outcomes in Children and Young People's Services (C4EO).

Siraj-Blatchford, I. & Sylva, K. (2004). Researching pedagogy in English pre-schools. *British Educational Research Journal* 30 (5), 713–730.

Siraj-Blatchford, I., Sylva, K., Muttock, S., Gilden, R. & Bell, D. (2002). *Researching Effective Pedagogy in the Early Years (REPEY).* London: Department for Education and Skills/Institute of Education, University of London.

Siraj-Blatchford, I., Sylva, K., Taggart, B., Sammons, P., Melhuish, E.C. & Elliot, K. (2003). *The Effective Provision of Pre-School Education (EPPE)* project. *Technical paper 10: Intensive case studies of practice across the foundation stage*. London: DfES/Institute of Education, University of London.

Siraj-Blatchford, I., Sammons, P., Taggart, B., Sylva, K. & Melhuish, E. (2006). Educational research and evidence-based policy: the mixed-method approach of the EPPE project. *Evaluation of Research in Education* 19 (2), 63–82.

Siraj-Blatchford, I., Siraj-Blatchford, J., Taggart, B., Sylva, K., Melhuish, E., Sammons, P. & Hunt., S. (2007). *How low-SES families support children's learning at home: promoting equality in the early years (part 3)*. The EPPE 3–11 research team report to the Equalities Review. London: The Cabinet Office.

Siraj-Blatchford, I., Mayo, A.Y., Melhuish, E.C., Taggart, B., Sammons, P. & Sylva, K. (2011a). *Performing against the odds: developmental trajectories of children in the EPPSE 3–16 study*. London: Department for Education/ Institute of Education, University of London.

Siraj-Blatchford, I., Shepherd, D.L., Sylva, K., Melhuish, E., Sammons, P. & Taggart, B. (2011b). *The Effective Pre-School, Primary and Secondary Education project (EPPSE): Effective Primary Pedagogical Strategies in English and Maths (EPPSEM) in Key Stage 2 study*. London: DCSF/Institute of Education, University of London.

Siraj-Blatchford, I., Mayo, A., Melhuish, E.,Taggart, B., Sammons, P. & Sylva, K. (2013). The learning life-course of 'at risk' children aged 3–16: perceptions of students and parents about 'succeeding against the odds'. *Scottish Educational Review* 45 (2), 5–17.

Siraj-Blatchford, I., Taggart, B., Sammons, P., Melhuish, E. & Sylva, K. (2014). *Effective teachers in primary schools: key research on pedagogy and children's learning*. Stoke on Trent: Trentham Books.

Smith, J. & Heshusius, L. (1986). Closing down the conversation: the end of the quantitative–qualitative debate among educational researchers. *Educational Researcher* 15 (4), 4–12.

Smith, M.W. & Dickinson, D.K. (1994). Describing oral language opportunities and environments in Head Start and other pre-school classrooms. *Early Childhood Research Quarterly* 9, 345–366.

Sonnenschein, A. & Munsterman, K. (2002). The influence of home-based reading interactions on 5-year-olds' reading motivations and early literacy development. *Early Childhood Research Quarterly* 17 (3), 318–337.

Soucacou, E. P. & Sylva, K. (2010). Developing observation instruments and arriving at inter-rater reliability for a range of contexts and raters: the Early Childhood Environment Rating Scales. In G. Walford, E. Tucker & M. Viswanathan (eds.), *The Sage handbook of measurement: how social scientists generate, modify, and validate indicators and scales* (pp. 61–86). London: Sage Publications.

Steinberg, L. (2001). We know some things: parent-adolescent relationships in retrospect and prospect. *Journal of Research on Adolescence* 11 (1), 1–19.

Steinberg, L. & Morris, A.S. (2001). Adolescent development. *Annual Review of Psychology* 52, 83–110.

Steinberg, L., Mounts, N.S., Lamborn, S.D. & Dornbusch, S.M. (1991). Authoritative parenting and adolescent adjustment across varied ecological niches. *Journal of Research on Adolescence* 1 (1), 19–36.

Stipek, D.J. (2001). Pathways to constructive lives: the importance of early school success. In A. Bohart & D. Stipek (eds.), *Constructive and destructive behavior: implications for family, school, and society* (pp. 291–316). Washington, DC: American Psychological Association.

Stoolmiller, M., Patterson, G.R. & Snyder, J. (2000). Parental discipline and child antisocial behaviour: a contingency-based theory and some methodological refinements. *Psychological Inquiry* 8, 223–229.

Stryker, S. (2008). From mead to a structural symbolic interactionism and beyond. *Annual Review of Sociology* 34, 15–31.

Sylva, K., Siraj-Blatchford, I. & Taggart, B. (2003). *Assessing quality in the early years: Early Childhood Environment Rating Scale Extension (ECERS-E): four curricular subscales*. Stoke-on Trent: Trentham Books.

Sylva, K., Melhuish, E., Sammons, P., Siraj-Blatchford, I. & Taggart, B. (2004). *The Effective Provision of Pre-school Education (EPPE) project: final report*. London: DfES/Institute of Education, University of London.

Sylva, K., Siraj-Blatchford, I., Taggart, B., Sammons, P., Melhuish, E., Elliot, K. & Totsika, V. (2006). Capturing quality in early childhood through environmental rating scales. *Early Childhood Research Quarterly* 21, 76–92.

(2007). *The EPPE 3–11 research team promoting equality in the early years: report to the Equalities Review*. London: The Cabinet Office.

(2008). *Final Report from the primary phase: pre-school, school and family influences on children's development during Key Stage 2 (7–11)*. DCSF RR 061. Nottingham: DCSF.

(2010). *Early childhood matters: evidence from the Effective Pre-school and Primary Education project*. London: Routledge.

Sylva, K., Melhuish, E.C., Sammons, P., Siraj-Blatchford, I. & Taggart, B. (2012). *Effective Pre-school, Primary and Secondary Education 3–14 project (EPPSE 3–14) – final report from the Key Stage 3 phase: influences on students' development from age 11–14*. DfE RR 202. London: Department for Education.

Taggart, B., Sammons, P., Smees, R., Sylva, K., Melhuish, E., Siraj-Blatchford, I. et al. (2006). Early identification of special needs and the definition of 'at risk': the Early Years Transition and Special Education Needs (EYTSEN) project. *British Journal of Special Education* 33 (1), 40–45.

Tashakkori, A. & Teddlie, C. (eds.) (2003). *Handbook of mixed methods in social and behavioural research*. Thousand Oaks, CA: Sage.

Teddlie, C. & Reynolds, D. (2000). *The international handbook of school effectiveness research*. London: Falmer Press.

Teddlie, C. & Stringfield, S. (1993). *Schools make a difference: lessons learned from a 10-year study of school effects*. New York: Teachers College Press.

Thomas, A. & Chess, S. (1977). *Temperament and development*. New York: Brunner/Mazel.

Tizard, B. & Hughes, M. (1984). *Children learning at home and in school*. London: Fontana.

Tomasello, M. (1999). *The cultural origins of human cognition*. Cambridge, MA: Harvard University Press.

(2001). Cultural transmission: a view from chimpanzees and human infants. *Journal of Cross-Cultural Psychology* 32 (2), 135–146.

Trevarthen, C. & Aitken, K.J. (2001). Infant intersubjectivity: research, theory, and clinical applications. *Journal of Child Psychology and Psychiatry* 42 (1), 3–48.

Tudge, J.R.H. (2008). *The everyday lives of young children: culture, class, and childrearing in diverse societies.* New York: Cambridge University Press.

Tudge, J.R.H., Gray, J. & Hogan, D. (1997). Ecological perspectives in human development: a comparison of Gibson and Bronfenbrenner. In J. Tudge, M. Shanahan & J. Valsiner (eds.), *Comparisons in human development: understanding time and context* (pp. 72–105). New York: Cambridge University Press.

Tudge, J.R.H., Odero, D.A., Hogan, D.M. & Etz, K.E. (2003). Relations between the everyday activities of pre-schoolers and their teachers' perceptions of their competence in the first year of school. *Early Childhood Research Quarterly* 18, 42–64.

Tudge, J.R.H., Doucet, F., Odero, D.A., Sperb, T.M., Piccinini, C.A. & Lopes, R.S. (2006). A window into different cultural worlds: young children's everyday activities in the United States, Brazil, and Kenya. *Child Development* 77 (5), 1446–1469.

Tudge, J.R.H., Mokrove, I., Hatfield, B.E. & Karnik, R.B. (2009). Uses and misuses of Bronfenbrenner's bioecological theory of human development. *Journal of Family Theory & Review* 1, 198–210.

Turkheimer, E., Haley, A., D'Onofrio, B., Waldron, M. & Gottesman, I.I. (2003). Socioeconomic status modifies heritability of IQ in young children. *Psychological Science* 14 (6), 623–628.

UNDP Human development report 2010. *The real wealth of nations: pathways to human development. 20th anniversary edition.* New York: United Nations Development Programme.

Ungar, M. (2004). A constructionist discourse on resilience: multiple contexts, multiple realities among at-risk children and youth. *Youth Society* 35, 341–365.

Van der Werf, G. (2006). *General and differential effects of constructivist teaching.* Keynote presentation at the annual meeting of the International Congress for School Effectiveness and Improvement, Florida, 3–6 January 2006.

Vincent, C. & Ball, S.J. (2006). *Childcare, choice and class practices: middle-class parents and their children.* London: Routledge.

Wa Wong, S. & Hughes, J.N. (2006). Ethnicity and language contributions to dimensions of parent involvement. *School Psychology Review* 35 (4), 645–662.

Weizman, Z.O. & Snow, C.E. (2001). Lexical input as related to children's vocabulary acquisition: effects of sophisticated exposure and support for meaning. *Developmental Psychology* 37 (2), 265–279.

Willis, P.E. (1977). *Learning to labour: how working-class kids get working-class jobs.* Farnborough: Saxon House.

Wood, D. (1986). Aspects of teaching and learning. In M. Richards & P. Light (eds.), *Children of social worlds.* Cambridge: Polity Press.

Index